PLANNING IN CRIMINAL JUSTICE ORGANIZATIONS AND SYSTEMS

PLANNING IN CRIMINAL JUSTICE ORGANIZATIONS AND SYSTEMS

JOHN K. HUDZIK
Michigan State University

GARY W. CORDNER
University of Baltimore

MACMILLAN PUBLISHING CO., INC.
New York

COLLIER MACMILLAN PUBLISHERS
London

Macmillan Publishing Co., Inc.
866 Third Avenue, New York, New York 10022

Collier Macmillan Canada, Inc.

Library of Congress Cataloging in Publication Data

Hudzik, John K.
Planning in criminal justice organizations and systems.

Includes index.
1. Criminal justice, Administration of–Planning.
I. Cordner, Gary W. II. Title.
HV6025.H8 364'.068 82-15313
ISBN 0-02-475170-7 AACR2

Printing: 2 3 4 5 6 7 8 Year: 6 7 8 9 0

ISBN 0-02-475170-7

For Anne, Julie, and our parents

·ACKNOWLEDGMENTS·

Our interest in writing a book on criminal justice planning was stimulated by colleagues and students. In particular, our experience with teaching the course in criminal justice planning at Michigan State University provided much of the grist for what subsequently developed into a manuscript. We are grateful to colleagues for encouraging our efforts and to students for giving us the opportunity to test various ideas and approaches.

Our associate Steven M. Edwards deserves special mention. He provided much information and valuable assistance as we developed the prospectus and chapter outline for the manuscript. Several of the chapters also substantially reflect his thinking and research. Two other colleagues, Tim S. Bynum and Jack R. Greene, made significant personal and professional contributions over the last few years to the effort that produced this book. We gratefully acknowledge their friendship and scholarship.

Katherine McCracken, of the Social Science Research Bureau at Michigan State University, lent expert editorial assistance. Her reading of several draft chapters and her suggestions for changes markedly improved the manuscript. Betsy McGuire provided much appreciated help in checking citations and in typing portions of the manuscript. Maryellen Geyer gave her usual high-quality typing and administrative assistance.

Part of the credit for finishing this book (nearly on time!) must go to the facilities, personnel, and ambience of Michigan State University, Washington State University, and the University of Baltimore. These are three fine institutions, and we are proud to have been associated with them.

We were greatly aided by the manuscript reviews provided by Thomas A. Johnson and John Ortiz Smykla. Their insights and guidance have made this a better book than it otherwise would have been.

We have also received first-class cooperation and direction from everyone with whom we have dealt at Macmillan Publishing Company. First Judy Ziajka, and then John J. Beck, got us going and kept us on track. Later in the process, Jack Snyder oversaw the editorial work and Dave Novack the production end of things. Each was very helpful, fully professional, and indulgent of our ignorance about the book business.

To these individuals, and to the many others not specifically named, we offer our gratitude. Although we remain finally responsible for what appears in this book, their contributions have been most valuable.

·CONTENTS·

· *Chapter 12* ·
Methods of Data Collection for Criminal Justice Planning 221

· *PART V* ·
CRIMINAL JUSTICE PLANNING APPLICATIONS 243

· *Chapter 13* ·
Fiscal Planning 245

· *Chapter 14* ·
Manpower Planning 269

· *Chapter 15* ·
Strategic Policy Planning 289

Index 303

· LIST OF FIGURES ·

· LIST OF TABLES ·

PLANNING IN CRIMINAL JUSTICE ORGANIZATIONS AND SYSTEMS

OVERVIEW

Since the Omnibus Crime Control and Safe Streets Act of 1968, *planning* has become a common word in the vocabulary of criminal justice. What seems largely missing is a thorough examination of what *planning* means or can mean in the operation of a criminal justice organization. With the withdrawal of Law Enforcement Assistance Administration (LEAA) planning funds, it is especially important that a fresh look be taken at criminal justice, that its essential features and its utility be analyzed.

Planning may be simply defined as thinking about the future, thinking about what we want that future to be, and thinking about what we need to do now to achieve it. Put another way, *planning* concerns linking present actions to future conditions. Implicit in this is the understanding that there is a conscious process of gathering information in support of assumptions or assertions about cause and effect—about linking the present and the future. There is also an assumption that planning is oriented to action: that is, the purpose of planning is not just thinking, but rather first determining what we should do and then doing it. Finally, planning is associated with empirical rationalism: planners supposedly gather and analyze objective data and reach objective conclusions. As will be seen, this last proposition is the subject of substantial debate, but the commonly held belief is that planning is at least intended to be a scientific endeavor.

This book is an introduction to planning methods and their application to managing both the criminal justice system and its individual operational agencies. It includes consideration of both theory and practice, although ultimately it focuses on what a manager does when planning and what can be accomplished by planning. Its objective is to examine planning from the vantage point of theory, and of application as well.

The literature of planning theory is abundant and rich, but a perusal of that literature indicates that most of the conceptual development of planning originated in fields and disciplines other than criminal justice. Furthermore, the literature of criminal justice planning itself is at best only partially developed and hardly systematic. Although a fair amount has already been written about criminal justice planning, as evidenced by many LEAA-sponsored monographs and technical guides, the literature is largely piece-meal, and its impact on criminal justice agencies has been uneven.

The idea of criminal justice planning is relatively new and not without its critics. Some argue that meaningful planning is impossible in criminal justice owing to the fragmentation of organizations, an inability to formulate goals clearly, and an inability to agree on the causes of crime or on how to deal with it. In support of this criticism, antagonists of criminal justice planning point to several evaluations made of the twelve-year LEAA-funded program to introduce planning into criminal justice—evaluations that conclude that this multimillion-dollar effort produced little meaningful or helpful planning. Others argue that these evaluations are neither accurate nor fair; they note a rapid increase in the use of planning-oriented scientific inquiry (data collection and analysis) by criminal justice agencies. They also note that twelve years is hardly enough time to take an entire system from near ground zero to a fully operational and systematic planning orientation.

The debate reflects confusion about the purposes and the limitations of rational planning. It might be argued, for example, that the critics are evaluating the potential for criminal justice planning against a set of goals and criteria that no sane planner would ever suggest were possible. Indeed, the underlying philosophy adopted in this book is that rational planning can only supplement, not substitute for, professional judgment and intuition. Similar limitations are clearly delineated in much of the planning theory from other fields, and this is one reason why a consideration of that literature is important to understanding the potential for, and limitations of, rational criminal justice planning. One encouraging development of the last few years is the increasing recognition that planning will not solve, or even identify, all the problems confronting criminal justice. Perhaps we are learning from experience what the literature of planning theory noted earlier—that practical and manageable objectives must be set for planning. Thus, we appear to be moving from simple, all-or-nothing expectations about planning toward more realistic, bounded expectations.

We cannot ignore the critics who assert that the criminal justice system is fragmented, that its goals are unclear, and that opinions about the causes of crime and about the proper response to it seem to change almost daily. Certainly, these conditions pose real constraints on a fully rational approach to planning and policy-making. The question, however, is whether such constraints render worthless any attempt at rational planning. What kind of planning is possible within these constraints? The exploration of this question is the subject of this book.

DEBATES ABOUT PLANNING'S ULTIMATE PURPOSE

Those who agree that planning does have a meaningful role in criminal justice have argued among themselves about its ultimate purpose. One aspect of the discussion in the past decade has focused on whether planning should be aimed at having an impact on crime or on improving the system. The distinction between the two kinds of planning is not totally clear. Nonetheless, the obvious ultimate purpose of planning designed to have an impact on crime is to reduce crime. This seems reasonable enough, but some maintain that such planning is illusory, given our inability to identify and to deal with the causes of crime. The ultimate purpose of planning designed to improve the system is to increase the efficiency and effectiveness of the system in dealing with crime and criminals. This type of planning comes very close to common understandings of managerial planning and treats an increase in the efficiency and effectiveness of the system as a primary and realistic goal. The two approaches merge if effectiveness is designed as goal attainment and if crime control is assumed to be the system's goal. An important point may be that crime control is only *one* of several goals of the system.

Another subject of debate among planning's proponents is the amount and kind of coordination planning can foster. Specifically, there is disagreement about whether planning should be focused on individual agencies or on aggregates of criminal justice agencies (as, for example, in comprehensive criminal justice systems planning). A commonly accepted precept of the last decade has been that the fragmentation of the system is one of the chief causes of its inefficiency and ineffectiveness. The 1968

Safe Streets Act and its block-grant program adopted "comprehensive systems planning" as the best means of dealing with the problems of fragmentation. Comprehensive systems planning was not defined in the legislation, nor very well subsequently, but it appeared to mean that agencies and components of the system should *coordinate* their programming and activities. Coordination would seem to imply cooperation toward achieving shared goals, resulting in joint planning and policy-making among the various agencies and components of the system. Critics of comprehensive planning praise its goals but argue that the criminal justice system is composed of semi-independent agencies, most of which seem more interested in maintaining their own power and independence than in cooperating in a comprehensive response to crime. The only reasonable alternative, as these critics see it, is to foster planning within individual agencies and thus preserve the essentially local character of American criminal justice.

Critics of comprehensive planning view themselves as pragmatists, noting that the decade-long LEAA effort to fund comprehensive planning at state and regional levels was largely a dismal failure. Supporters of comprehensive planning disagree, countering that important progress has been made and that more progress can and must be made.

More recently, these discussions about planning have come under attack from those who believe that all present approaches ignore the "justice" aspects of criminal justice, that planning focused exclusively on reducing crime or on increasing the efficiency of the system may lead us conveniently to forget that the ultimate purpose of the system is justice. Their criticism is based on the view that rational planning designed either to reduce crime or to increase the efficiency of the system cannot adequately take into account the value-laden aspects of justice, for justice is not easily defined nor can it be measured through empirical rationalism and quantification.

Though these arguments and counterarguments seem complicated and confusing, this may be one case in which confusion serves a useful purpose. The 1968 Safe Streets Act seems to assume that planning can be easily and simply established in the criminal justice system. We have found that assumption rather naïve, probably because the debates and arguments have increased the system's awareness of planning as a complicated subject. With that awareness, the level of sophistication in dealing with the concept of planning and its application to criminal justice promises to increase.

It is essential to a full consideration of criminal-justice planning that these various positions on the objectives of planning be discussed. Thus, the book is organized to consider planning for the system and planning for the individual organization. It also considers planning designed to have an impact on crime, and planning designed to improve the system, as well as the qualifying views of those concerned with facilitating justice planning. There are current examples of planning at the level of the system and at the level of the individual agency, of planning to increase system efficiency, to have an impact on crime, and to promote justice. An examination of the state of the art will help to provide a basis for discussing the various possible futures for criminal-justice planning.

ORGANIZATION OF THE BOOK

This book is divided into five parts. Part I explores the various concepts, theories, definitions, meanings, and processes of planning, acknowledging that most of our conceptual and theoretical understanding of planning derives from a literature that comes largely from outside the field of criminal justice.

Chapter 1 describes the basic features of planning in general and of managerial planning in particular, distinguishing both from concepts of social planning; it also examines "economic rationalism" and "political rationalism" as contexts for planning in general and for criminal justice planning. Chapter 2 examines alternative theories, definitions, and varieties of planning. Chapter 3 discusses specific approaches to planning as a process. Both chapters rely heavily on the general planning literature from other fields. Thus, Part I lays a basis for understanding the theorist's conception of planning, its purposes, and its process, and it provides the reader with some common understanding of the terms and purposes associated with planning.

Part II focuses on criminal justice, examining the degree to which and the ways in which the concepts, theories, definitions, purposes and processes of planning, as discussed in Part I, have found their way into criminal justice. Chapter 4 presents the most salient, planning-related aspects of the current structure and organization of criminal justice. Chapters 5 and 6 review the brief history and current condition of criminal justice planning both at the level of the system and at the level of individual agencies. These chapters also examine current efforts to have an impact on crime and to improve the system through planning. Chapter 7 discusses staffing and organization for criminal justice planning units and agencies, with particular attention to the roles of planners, their placement, their attributes, and their work in planning units and in planning agencies. Parts I and II together provide the foundation of theory and history, the understanding of the current state of the art, on which subsequent sections are based.

Parts III, IV, and V deal with the specific problems and possibilities of applying planning theories and techniques to the field of criminal justice. Part III focuses attention on the key processes of planning: setting goals and identifying problems (Chapter 8), forecasting (Chapter 9), and generating and testing alternatives (Chapter 10). These processes are the principal conceptual elements of planning; they are, however, presented within the context of the constraints we find when attempting to utilize them in criminal justice. Some aspects of planning theory do not apply neatly to the criminal justice setting, where, for example, there is great difficulty in specifying or setting goals for a system or for an organization. Compromises must be struck between theory and the reality criminal justice. Finally, we examine possible future alternatives for these key processes in criminal justice.

Part IV focuses on the elements of rational planning and on its principal ingredients: criminal justice data, their collection, and their analysis. The context for discussion is roughly the same as that in Part III: the difference between the ideal, and the constraints reality imposes. More specifically, Part IV discusses alternative sources of criminal justice data, modes of data collection, and types of analytical models, with their attendant prerequisites, costs, and payoffs. It is at this point that the conflict between theory and practice becomes most evident, because planning without collection and analysis of data seems a contradiction in terms. Yet the process of collecting and analyzing data is costly, time-consuming, and sometimes beyond technical capability.

Part V addresses in detail several important species of planning, its "subfields" and specific substantive foci. Separate chapters in Part V deal with some of the particularly important subfields of planning: fiscal planning, manpower planning, and strategic-policy planning. These have been selected for special attention because they reflect the critical substantive aspects of organizational management.

Thus the book, as a whole, explores planning concepts and the ways in which they can be applied to the actual settings and environments of criminal justice. But it would be misleading to suggest that it will tell the reader all that it is necessary to know in order to become a planner or in order to plan. As will be seen, the environments of criminal justice planning are far too diverse and complicated for this to be possible. Furthermore, many have argued, as do we, that the "cookbook" approach is misleading and fosters simplistic approaches to planning.

We maintain that planning is both a science and an art. One consequence of this is that planning can be seen both as a set of procedures to be followed and as a frame of mind that allows innovation and flexibility in applying those procedures. A master chef does not simply adhere to a cookbook and its set recipes; culinary sophistication results from a sound understanding of the principles that underlie taste, appeal, and nutrition. By the same token, planning involves more than simply learning and following a specific set of procedures: it is the concepts and principles of planning that offer the best guide. Examples of specific procedures are just that—examples of some of the ways in which the principles can be put into action.

· Part I ·

BASIC PLANNING CONCEPTS

Chapters 1, 2, and 3 provide a conceptual basis for understanding planning as an analytical process. Chapter 1 discusses the general activities associated with planning (prediction and control of the future, determining and discovering goals, defining problems, identifying alternative solutions and their consequences, making choices), examines the concept of managerial planning in organizations and the levels and types of planning within organizations, and discusses the relationships of planning to implementation of programs and to evaluation of organizations and programs. The chapter ends with an examination of economic cost-benefit analyses as means for developing plans, and of the constraints imposed on "economic rationalism" by political considerations and realities.

Chapters 2 and 3 move the focus of discussion to alternative theories, definitions, and varieties of planning. We explore how these alternative views of planning can be put together into something that is manageable and coherent. Chapter 3 focuses on the process of planning and on what planners do. A discussion of rational planning is followed by an ideal model for rational planning, an examination of the factors that limit our ability to realize an ideal model, and a revision of the ideal model that is more applicable to the real world and the constraints it imposes.

• *Chapter I* •

INTRODUCTION TO PLANNING

We are all planners, by nature if not by job title. Philosophers and scientists agree that the ability to think about the future and to consider how present actions may affect that future is chiefly what separates man from lower animals. This human trait is central to the activity of planning.

Planning means deliberately linking present actions to future conditions. For example, a decision to spend money can be made with or without considering whether sufficient funds will be left for other purposes. In either case, the decision to spend money will have at least one consequence: less cash in the future. Thus present actions do affect the future, whether or not we choose to consider that future. Thinking about the future, the essential aspect of planning, is not easy, because there is always the likelihood that however we imagine the future, we will be dead wrong.

The difficulties inherent in thinking about the future sometimes appear so insurmountable that conscious planning is replaced with less burdensome philosophies: "Live for today and tomorrow will take care of itself," or, "What will be, will be." Such notions have a superficial logic, because it is true that tomorrow *will* come and what will be *will* indeed be. But this shallow fatalism is the antithesis of planning, because planning assumes some possibility of affecting the future, or at least of consciously preparing for that future. Ernest Dale refers to planning as "bridging the gap" between today and tomorrow.[1]

Crime, and our response to crime, is one of the most complex issues facing our society, and thinking it through in any deliberate and rational way often appears impossible. Fatalistic notions, such as, "Crime will always be with us," even if true, may lead us to ignore important questions about the best ways of both anticipating and responding to crime. It is these latter questions that are important, not the fact that crime will always be with us; and it is conscious thinking about crime that permits determination rather than determinism to govern our response to it.

Criminal justice planning has a less than enviable history. Predictions about crime patterns have often been erroneous, and expectations that certain expenditures would have some ameliorating effect on crime have also often proven to be wrong. So cynicism abounds in criminal justice, contributing to the attitude that planning with regard to such a complex issue is a waste of time. And if this were not enough, criminal justice planning has also suffered from simplistic reasoning: "A crime is committed; you catch the perpetrator, adjudicate, and punish—so what's to plan?"

In Fiscal Year 1977, some $22 billion were spent in the United States to combat crime.[2] This represented an increase of over 100 per cent in such expenditures since 1971—much more than could be accounted for by simple inflation.[3] The size of the expenditure, rate of its growth, and the complex programs and agencies supported by it hardly indicate that society's response to crime can be as straightforward as simple logic suggests. Furthermore, although the history of planning is spotty, neither is there evidence or proof that planning is a waste of time. Planning is a formally recognized activity in criminal justice. A recent survey of the 250 largest law-enforcement agencies in the United States revealed that over 90 per cent of those responding had a personnel position or a departmental unit specifically responsible for planning.[4] Over 75 per cent of the state corrections agencies surveyed reported having such personnel or units. For the past ten years, all fifty states have cooperated with the Federal government in jointly funding state criminal justice planning agencies. And well over 400 substate regional-planning units have been established in criminal justice.[5]

Formal recognition of planning in criminal justice is a relatively new phenomenon, probably having received its major impetus and funding support from the 1968 Omnibus Crime Control and Safe Streets Act. The Act itself was a response to the frustrating rise in crime rates in the 1960s as well as to society's apparent inability to cope adequately with crime. The Act, following the recommendations of the 1967 *Report of the President's Commission on Law Enforcement and Administration of Justice*, offered planning as one of the chief means for enhancing the effectiveness of the increasingly complex response to crime required of a postindustrial society. Inherent in the Act was the belief that increasing complexity required more conscious planning. Both the Act and the report are a denial of the cynic's view that planning is a waste of time when things become complex. Indeed, it seems a matter of common sense that as matters become more complex, the need for a conscious plan of action increases. This point is reflected in the writings of Sun Tzu, a Chinese military strategist, dating from 500 B.C.:

> Now the general who wins a battle makes many calculations in his temple ere the battle is fought. The general who loses a battle makes few calculations before hand [sic]. It is by attention to this point that I can see who is likely to win or lose.[6]

CRIMINAL JUSTICE PLANNING: ELEMENTS AND PROBLEMS

The most important aspect of planning is that it takes place in advance of action. This may appear so evident as to be trivial, yet the need to act is often so compelling that we act before sufficient information and thought have been brought to bear on the issue. When a course of action and its consequences seem patently clear, a grand planning exercise may be unnecessary and inefficient. When consequences are not clear, however, or when there may be better or undiscovered alternative courses of action, the value of planning increases greatly.

This view of planning suggests a number of points. It suggests there are times at which planning would seem to be more beneficial than at others. It also suggests the potential benefits of planning: the identification of consequences, the consideration of alternatives, and the selection of a course or courses of action. Less obvious, but nonetheless true, is the idea that planning assumes the *prediction* of the future and the *control* of the future. These and other aspects of planning will be considered.

Prediction and Control

Prediction and control of the future are separable aims associated with planning, and it seems a matter of human nature that preference be given to controlling and shaping the future instead of merely predicting it (assuming that we have some choice in the matter). Neither prediction nor control are easy to accomplish, however, particularly when human behavior and social institutions are involved. It seems infinitely easier today to predict and control the course of a rocket to the moon or the other planets than, say, to predict and control the effects of a juvenile-delinquency treatment program.

Difficult or not, prediction and control lie at the heart of the planning enterprise. As Russell Ackoff suggests, they are the very cornerstone of wise action:

> Wisdom is the ability to see the long-run consequences of current actions, the willingness to sacrifice short-run gains for larger long-run benefits, and the ability to control what is controllable and not to fret over what is not. Therefore the essence of wisdom is concern with the future. It is not the type of concern with the future that the fortune teller has; he only tries to predict it. The wise man tries to *control* it.[7]

An important part of Ackoff's view is the realization that some things are predictable and controllable and others are not. The role of planning is first to determine such constraints, then to proceed to determine ways of predicting and controlling what can be influenced. Unless the constraints inherent in, say, criminal justice planning are clearly understood, unrealistic expectations may arise. When these expectations are not realized, planning is unfairly judged a failure. At least part of the reason for the demise of LEAA and its planning funds in 1980 can be traced to such ill-considered expectations—expectations generated by relatively unexamined notions (beginning with the 1968 Safe Streets Act) about what planning could accomplish in criminal justice and, more important, how soon it could be accomplished.

Finding a manageable area for planning is sometimes a matter of whittling to reasonable size the scope and number of issues. But more often, the environment itself discourages any reasonable consideration of the future and how to meet it. Crisis environments are particularly generative of such discouragement, and it is the view of many that criminal justice is inherently crisis-prone, so that the opportunity for planning is severely diminished. Some attribute a good share of the crisis to the "sheer input and uncoordinated processing of offenders"[8] that keeps the system constantly off balance, lacking the time to take a good look at itself. Herman Goldstein's views about the police apply to the criminal-justice system as a whole:

> In an atmosphere of tension and crises, both in the community and within the agency, planning for the future is extremely difficult and, at times even seems irrelevant. The need for change may be readily recognized, but as a somewhat idealistic notion to which the agency might hopefully turn its attention at some future time when the current pressures abate. Since the problems do not diminish, but actually grow both in number and severity, what is characterized as a temporary attitude toward change tends to become the permanent posture of the agency.[9]

There is also the problem that criminal justice is highly visible to the public, especially insofar as the media seek to monitor the administration of justice. The job-related death of an employee, or the death of a prison inmate or of an accused person, reports of a heinous crime or a riot raise public and political cries for "action." The action taken may be hurried, ill-conceived, and ill-planned, but it is nonetheless important symbolically in meeting the public demand.

Goals: Determination versus Discovery

Predicting the future is one thing; determining whether that future is acceptable or whether we want to change and control it is quite another. "To adopt policies or plans without having given thought as to why they are being adopted, to what is expected to happen as a result, is plainly to be discouraged."[10] Clearly part of the planning process is developing an understanding of the goals of the plan: what it is we want to achieve and why. Goals involve human preferences or values; the "goodness" or "badness" of a goal is not determined by scientific test but by personal or societal ethics.

There is little, if any, disagreement among planning theorists that *discovering* goals is a prime function of the planning process. Discovery implies that the planner has an objective role—discovering what the goals are and then devising the best courses of action to achieve them. Goal *determination*, on the other hand, is assumed to be quite another matter and one that few, especially in this country, seem willing to consign to the planner or the policy-maker alone. There is a presumption here that the discovery of goals is value-free while the determination of goals is value-laden. But the distinction is hardly so clear:

> The notion that policy-makers [and planners] can have grasp and understanding of the overall public interest is untenable. The problems the policy-making machine chooses to focus on, those it ignores or those it remains ignorant of altogether, are a reflection of its values and preferences. So too are the solutions and priorities it chooses to adopt relative to those problems. . . . There are several examples which illustrate the dangers either of goals and objectives being the goals and objectives of those professionally involved in the planning process perhaps in a rather paternalistic way or for the stating of goals and objectives to become a ritual with little later connection with the planning process.[11]

Defining the overall public interest by some objective means is very much a problem in criminal justice. Of course, even if there is total agreement of certain goals and objectives, the goals remain subjective as there is no way to validate them empirically. But the problem of setting goals in the public sector revolves around discovering the common good. If a truly common good cannot be discovered, inevitably somebody's good is advanced by a certain goal and somebody else's is not.

The fact is that there is little collective agreement about crime, its causes, or how to deal with it. We may agree, for example, that the goal is "to reduce crime through a just application of the law," but there is little agreement about what specifically is to be done.[12] If there is lack of agreement on specific goals and courses of action, planning cannot be value-neutral; it comes to reflect the values of those who plan and those who make policy.

Although planning probably cannot be value-neutral in any strict sense, it is not necessarily a worthless endeavor. We must recognize that planning can never be wholly objective. So, too, we must recognize that those who plan and those who make policy represent the values of some and not those of others. This view is most strongly criticized by Marxist criminologists, who contend that criminal justice policy is a tool of the capitalist elite.[13] Another, less ideological, criticism is expressed in a parodic version of the golden rule: He who has the gold makes the rules.

Aaron Wildavsky and Charles Lindblom argue from similar premises and reach slightly different conclusions.[14] From their perspective, the making and planning of policy are not value-neutral; rather, they represent mutual partisan (political) adjustments, and often some parties wield more influence than others. That is, individual preferences or values are brought into the political arena and adjusted to attract the interest and support of the majority. Still, the compromising of individual preferences is not a value-neutral exercise: it simply defines the common good as the majority interest. Minority interests may take exception to this view.

These and related issues are discussed more fully in Chapter 8. It is sufficient here to stress that though there may be little point in merely discovering goals, this does not obviate the need for planning but rather casts it more appropriately in a subjective mode.

Defining Problems

Often the need for planning arises from the discovery that a problem exists or is anticipated. The problem may arise from an intricate and unsettled question, or from the difference between what we prefer and what we have. Both meanings of the word *problem* apply: planning necessarily entails discovering answers to questions as well as defining and offering means for resolving the differences between what we want and what we have. However, it is probably in the latter sense that the term *problem* has the most relevance for the planning that takes place in organizations.

Thinking about planning's role in discovering goals is rather abstract; more often than not goal discovery is given practical meaning in organizational planning when a problem is defined as a resolution of that difference. This may be particularly true in criminal justice, and an LEAA publication entitled, *Criminal Justice Planning for Local Governments*, states as much:

> A problem-oriented approach to planning, which relies heavily on the problem identification and analysis phase of the planning cycle, can help policy-makers to formulate goals and priorities in terms that are focused on specific problems and solutions. Criminal justice planners have found it easier to galvanize cooperative efforts around problem-oriented goals and priorities rather than around more abstract notions. It is easier to mobilize efforts toward the goals of reducing the number of commerical burglaries in the central city than around the more amorphous goal of "reducing crime and delinquency."[15]

Therefore, one way of defining the nature of criminal justice planning is to understand it as problem-solving. Certainly this is a limited perspective, but it may the more accurately reflect the current reality of criminal justice planning, in which the crisis environment focuses attention on existing problems. As the following passage from *Criminal Justice Planning for Local Governments* suggests, the ordering of problem-identification and goal-setting steps should not be confused:

> Competent planning produces the data needed by local officials and agency executives to improve their understanding of criminal justice problems. A constant flow of timely and relevant information helps decision-makers to define criminal-justice problems, set goals and priorities, and implement and evaluate strategies for accomplishing goals.[16]

The role of planning includes discovering problems, defining the nature of problems, and proposing means for resolving them. These are related but distinct aspects of the planning process. One part of the planning apparatus may consist of an ongoing monitoring system designed to anticipate or to detect problems, particularly those that do not readily manifest themselves. Another aspect of the planning process concerns itself with defining the nature of these problems—their magnitude, cause, duration and so on. A third aspect of the planning process involves developing and recommending means for dealing with the problem. Chapter 8 will more fully address this issue of planning's problem-solving role as well as its relationship to the setting of goals.

Alternatives and Consequences

Rarely is there only one course of future action for achieving a goal or resolving a problem. Usually, several courses present themselves, each with different consequences and, thus, with different potential for reaching the goal or solving the problem. This greatly increases the burden of calculation that is part of the planning process, but it is the prime function of planning to identify and to weigh alternative courses of action, and perhaps to select what seems the best course of action. That selection raises at least two serious questions: By what criteria is *best* defined? Do we ever have the time, the resources, and the technical capability to determine the "best"? The first problem is particularly acute in criminal justice, where "simple" notions of cost and benefit are confused by not-so-simple notions of "justice." Consider, for example, Robert Reich's view on this subject:

> [The] symbols of managerial expertise and the ideology of control and comprehension which they represent enable us to perceive that the problems of controlling crime are soluble and that our seemingly conflicting desires with regard to such problems are in fact reconcilable in an *optimal solution*. . . . The problem of controlling crime is thereby rendered comprehensible; by juggling resources and inputs, one can be dominate [sic] and manipulate crime with a facility similar to that with which small children master their dollhouses and model cars. . . . [But] an allocation of police resources that minimizes the monetary cost of crime, for example, with the consequence that police response time will vary depending upon neighborhood wealth, may fundamentally alter the community's understanding of the meaning of crime and its assumptions about the role of the police in controlling it.[17]

"Best" is an issue of value perspective, because the central question seems to be: "Whose best?" Also, finding a "best" solution may raise problems of cost and technical capability. Consideration of planning's role in defining alternative courses of action and in determining the consequences of those alternatives leads directly to problems of values.

Perhaps the most serious effort in recent years to devise analytical systems for finding the best or optimal alternatives has been in budget planning. Planning, programming, and budgeting (PPB) and zero-base budgeting (ZBB) embody, in spirit at least, the attempt to develop objective optimal solutions. Chapter 13 will more fully examine these and other budget-planning options; they are mentioned here because they explicitly require the consideration of consequences and the weighing of alternatives. Fiscal planning under these two formats includes the necessity of rationally calculating the cost and the benefit of *each* alternative. Aaron Wildavsky, commenting on the negative consequences of attempting to be too analytical under these budget formats, suggests that

> ZBB insists on making all possible vertical calculations, from zero to base, as it were, until the most efficient ways of achieving objectives are chosen. PPB covers at least all major horizontal relationships between related programs so the most cost-effective combination for achieving objectives is chosen. Ergo, the lesson is that budgeting should not be comprehensive. Since knowledge, time, and manpower are usually in short supply, most policy analysis is concerned with reducing rather than increasing the cost of calculations.[18]

Wildavsky's point is that the effort to be too rational is irrational: it costs more and takes more time than it is worth. Certainly the purpose of considering alternatives and consequences is not to end in an analytical maze. But, ignoring the possibility of more feasible and effective alternatives for future actions seems myopic. Perhaps what is needed is a compromise—a reasonable approach to the rational consideration of alternatives and their consequences. One reasonable approach to planning would include analysis of the most promising alternatives and their most likely consequences, which would limit the degree of calculation required but allow comparison of old or existing approaches with new ones.

Actually, the seeds for such a compromise were sown in 1955, when Herbert Simon defined the concept of "satisficing,"[19] which involves finding a satisfactory solution to a problem rather than looking for an optimal solution. Charles Lindblom, in 1968, developed Simon's usage:

> In the conventional ideal of a rational decision, a decision-maker maximizes something—utility or want satisfaction, income, national security. the general welfare, or some other such value. But, as we have already noted, an exhaustive search for the maximum, for the best of all possible policies, is not usually worth what it costs, and may in fact be impossible of accomplishment. An alternative strategy, therefore is not to try too hard—to decide instead on some acceptable level of goal accomplishment short of maximization, and then to pursue the search until a policy is found that attains that level. One "satisfices" instead of maximizes.[20]

Such an approach limits not only the search for alternatives and the resulting calculations involved, but the goals themselves. Movement toward a goal is conceived as "incremental"—a series of short, manageable steps.[21] This is appealing in a field such as criminal justice, where basic problems appear to be numerous, complicated, and little understood.

It is also clear, however, that the search for alternative goals, programs, and operational methods is already a well-developed activity in criminal justice. In the corrections field there is seemingly endless debate about institutionalization and its alternatives: community treatment, probation, parole, or diversion. Operational alternatives in the time-honored and fundamental activities of law enforcement—foot patrol, motorized patrol, team policing—are also debated. In the courts, alternative models for selecting and utilizing juries, and alternatives in scheduling cases and managing case-flow are elementary examples.

The question of alternatives in criminal justice has focused on the distribution of resources among the components of the system: e.g., among police, courts, and corrections. In the middle and late 1970s, it seemed popular to hold the view that LEAA funding had done its job in upgrading the capacity of the police to catch the criminal perpetrator but that this "success" had placed unendurable burdens on the judiciary and on corrections in dealing with the increased caseloads. It then seemed time to look at alternative funding levels among the components and at the effect such alternative levels would have on crime. In one such study, Eli Noam, who used logical modeling and some empirical data, concluded:

> The crime-reducing effects of additional budget allocations for court and prosecution are very high. They are, respectively ten and twenty times larger than for police. The crime-reducing effectiveness of additional budget allocation to the prison system is fairly low for both its deterrence and insulation components.[22]

Although the assumptions underlying Noam's mode are questionable, as are the conclusions, the effort is itself noteworthy, for it reflects an increased interest within criminal justice in analyzing alternatives and their consequences. It is not clear, and probably not important, whether or not this concern for analyzing alternatives results from the growth of, and interest in, planning. What is important is that the system is apparently interested in considering alternatives as an important aspect of planning.

Choices

Davidoff and Reiner, in their classic 1962 article, "A Choice Theory of Planning," define the most important aspect of planning as the making of choices about goals and about means of achieving those goals.[23] Unless the process of identifying problems, setting goals, predicting the future, and generating and testing alternatives ends with a choice about a specific goal and a specific course of action, planning is no more than empty intellectualizing.

Several kinds of choices must be made. First, choices must be made about preferred states or goals. An important and sometimes ignored aspect of this choice involves the choice of tne criteria for measuring goal attainment.[24] This is often hard, much harder than setting the goal itself. For example, the goal of a juvenile-treatment program may be to reduce recidivism among those treated. Yet, in measuring goal attainment several questions arise. First, what constitutes recidivism? Technical or status violations? Arrest for criminal violations? Conviction on a criminal violation, and only for those crimes against which the juvenile program may have been directed? Also, over how long a period will recidivism be monitored? A year? Two years? Five years? Ten years? It is not that these questions cannot be answered, but securing agreement on the appropriate criteria becomes a major difficulty.

The second kind of choice involves linking general ends or goals to specific means, choosing among alternative ways of working toward goals. A plan of action is the outcome of these choices, the principal step in making planning something other than just thinking. The connection between choosing goals and choosing means is important, because both sets of choices virtually determine what actually happens. Duffee and O'Leary, writing about correctional management, emphasize these connections in their presentation of four correctional policies models: rehabilitation, restraint, reintegration, and reform. Consider, for example, their comments on the restraint and reintegration models:

> [The restraint model] is characterized by minimal concern for both the community and the offender. In this model it is believed that people change only if they want to. Therefore, no member of the staff is actively responsible for trying to change anyone. This mode merely accepts the people the court sends and tries to make supervision of offenders as routine and trouble-free as possible for both offenders and staff. Punishment is not prescribed to change the offender but only to control the offender or calm him or her down. The appearance of efficiency is important in helping the organization to survive and perhaps to prosper. . . . [The] philosophy is that the only possible achievements are "keeping the lid on" and "maintaining a good front." Both staff and inmates are "serving their own time." Higher education for staff is not required, except in technical skills necessary for maintenance.
>
> [The reintegration model] stresses both the community and the offender. Correctional internalization is the predominant influence style. Unlike the reform model, the reintegration model does not superimpose rules and regulations unilaterally on offenders. Instead, offenders work with a range of alternatives. . . . This model attempts to reduce the stigma attached to criminality that acts as a blockage to reintegration in the community. . . . In this model, confinement has specific objectives and is used as infrequently as possible. The preferred program is community supervision. . . . There is no "ideal" staff member in this model. All staff members are valued for the change-producing skills that they can bring to the team effort. Custodial staff are expected to participate as actively in the task of change as are the professional staff.[25]

These and other models represent differing and conflicting expectations about what can and should be done in corrections. The ultimate outcome desired may not differ, as all models imply the hope that after release there will be no further criminal behavior. But the models present different ways of achieving this goal and different assumptions about whether anything can be done to achieve such an objective. The model chosen, with its goals and assumptions, naturally leads toward some course of action and away from others. The differences between "correctional" activity under the restraint model and that under the reintegration model illustrate this point.

The problems of choice and the linkage between goals and means apply at all levels of organizational behavior and are not, of course, limited to corrections. Similar kinds of problems prevail in law enforcement. For example, traditional goals for the police are crime prevention and law enforcement. In a sense, these two goals are contradictory: an increase in arrests and convictions reflects more law enforcement, but the same statistic also seems to reflect less crime prevention. Such goals affect the actions the organization takes—swift apprehension, associated with law enforcement, may take precedence over crime-prevention activities for example—and the action deemed to have priority may well lead to very different decisions about assignment of organizational resources and personnel.

Choices among potentially competing goals and about assignments of resources are obviously not made easily, and sometimes organizational and personal survival dictate that choices be flexible and allowed to change as conditions do. The ultimate "flexibility"—to make no clear choices at all—is dangerous, but, as John Heaphy suggests, it may be seen by some as the only ploy in the game of survival:

> The objectives of most police departments today are set very haphazardly or are in fact never stated. A variety of forces influence determinations within the department concerning where resources are going to be expended, and what objectives are going to be pursued.

Indeed, one major city's police chief, speaking before an audience of his peers recently, went so far as to say that the primary objective of most police chiefs today is simply to stay politically alive.[26]

A principal cause of this situation, as pointed out by Heaphy, is the broadness of the mandate given to the police: it becomes impossible to plan or to make clear choices because expectations are so vast and so muddled. Nonetheless, few can escape the necessity of making choices about goals and means. And one of the primary functions of planning is to decide what is manageable and what is not, and then to focus on a manageable set of choices.

MANAGERIAL PLANNING

Management theorists generally see planning as the first step in the management process.[27] The role of management has been variously defined but generally includes coordination, integration, and the creation of an orderly environment in which results can be accomplished. The administrative theorist Luther Gulick, writing in the 1930s, formulated the now-classic acronym "POSDCORB" to identify the chief managerial functions: planning, organizing, staffing, directing, coordinating, reporting, and budgeting.[28] Similar lists generated by other management theorists usually include planning, and usually list it first.

Claude George summarizes the total function of a manager as "determining the collective objectives of an undertaking and generating an environment for their achievement."[29] George's environment includes a physical aspect and a conceptual aspect: the physical aspect containing "the materials, the tools, the methods, and the sequencing [of] these and like items"; the conceptual aspect of the environment includes the perspective of the individual workers, who (ideally) perceive it as advantageous to their personal goals that the goals of the organization be advanced.[30]

Given these definitions of management, it is inevitable that planning should so often be designated the first step in the managerial process. Indeed, the terms *management* and *planning* may be so intertwined that it makes little sense to consider one without the other, and certainly there is more than a casual connection between the manager's style and how he views the future. Le Breton and Henning extend the connection between planning and management to its fullest, suggesting that all other managerial tasks are dependent on planning.[31]

Approaches and Purposes

Dale McConkey, followed by Burt Scanlan, has identified three types of organizations (and management systems) according to their respective views on the future: the "pussycats," the "fat cats," and the "tigers."[32] The pussycats loll in the past; and the fat cats, in the present; but the tigers confront the future, believing "the future is what you make it."[33]

> The pussycat organization operates under the mistaken assumption that today and tomorrow are reflections of the past. This organization is content to ride the waves and follows others only after success is assured. . . . Management is thoroughly convinced that it can meet tomorrow's challenges with yesterday's talent and resources. . . . The fat cats, to some extent have shed the complacency of the pussycats. The realization that the future is not just a projection of the past leads to some positive initiative. . . . The fat cat organization is [however] still content to follow the leader and engages in little innovative management. . . . [The tiger] organization continually monitors the environment for new ideas and developments. Its primary concern is with bridging the nebulous gap between the present and the future. . . .
>
> Although there are many factors which distinguish a tiger from the other two managements, one of the most critical is the amount of planning involvement. Results don't just happen, they are planned. In its simplest form, planning involves establishing objectives and organizing all efforts to meet them.[34]

Scanlan's underlying premise is that management style and its orientation toward the future are tightly interrelated. Such a view applies not only to the management of organizations but to the management of our private lives and our political system as well. Certainly, parallels can be observed between Scanlon's three types of felines and, for example, how people manage their personal finances. And political conservatives and liberals differ, in part, in their view of whether the good life is to be found in the past or in the future, in a cautious or in a daring approach to change.

It would be a mistake, however, to assume that planning is synonymous with headlong change, with liberalism, or with discarding the past. Planning may be directed toward maintaining the status quo, toward cautious change, or toward high-level risk-taking. Contrary to the implications of Scanlon's views, the real distinction among managers may be not the *amount* of planning they do, but the *purposes* for which they plan.

Ronald Lynch, writing about the police manager, has recognized this distinction and suggests that there may be four management-planning models among police managers: purposeful planning, traditional planning, crisis planning, and entrepreneurial planning.[35] These four models differ principally in two ways: the degree to which the police manager has a concern for the "system" and is aware that individual facts or events are interrelated, and the degree to which the police manager views risk as threat or as opportunity:

1. Planning under the *purposeful* model weighs both risk and opportunity within the context of effect on the entire organization.
2. Planning under the *traditional* model seeks to maintain the status quo by minimizing risk and "eliminating" threats to the stability of the system.
3. Planning under the *crisis* model is directed toward a specific event or issue, outside the context of the system; risk is controlled by constant and close monitoring of subordinates, and management moves from one crisis to another.
4. Planning under the *entrepreneurial* model is highly risk-oriented, and does not weigh the potential effects of risk-taking ventures on the system as a whole; management may be seen as moving from one roll of the dice to another.

As Lynch points out, under both the crisis and entrepreneurial models planning is suspect and incomplete. Crisis planning tends to wait for problems rather than anticipating them, and handles problems on a day-to-day basis. Entrepreneurial planning tends to be random and disconnected, with little regard for integration, coordination, or maintenance of acceptable levels of organizational stability.

There is ample opportunity in criminal justice for the crisis approach to planning and management. On the other hand, entrepreneurial planning and management may be discouraged by political sensitivities and by the potential political costs associated with criminal justice. Indeed, as one state corrections commissioner recently remarked, "My political future depends on keeping the department off the front page."[36] Entrepreneurial planning, successful or not, hardly assures anonymity.

Purposeful and traditional planning perhaps most clearly point out the two chief alternative aims associated with planning: control and change. Both approaches allow long-range consideration of the future, extensive collection and analysis of data about alternatives and consequences, consideration of potential effect on the system as a whole, and a clear understanding of organizational goals and objectives. The difference between the two, in Lynch's view, seems to be that traditional planning gives top priority to organizational stability and to maintenance of the status quo while purposeful planning gives top priority to achieving organizational missions and objectives. Lynch's views are discussed, in the context of organizing and staffing planning units, in Chapter 7.

Modern systems theory recognizes that organizations constantly pursue two prime goals: maintaining the organization and meeting its service missions.[37] These two goals may, and often do, conflict, but both must be pursued, and the purpose of managerial planning can at least theoretically be seen as encompassing both. The implications of this for criminal justice seem clear: so complex is crime and the response to it, and sometimes so hostile is the environment for criminal justice agencies, that criminal justice managers often seek at least to secure the relative peace and benefits of a stable organization; on the other hand, the service missions of criminal justice agencies are highly visible and cannot be subordinated to the maintenance of organizational stability.

One purpose of criminal justice planning is to maintain a stable organizational response to crime; another is to change the organization so as to improve its response to crime and to changes in crime. Both purposes are valid. Which of them receives priority at any given time largely depends on the environment faced by the organization. As modern systems theory recognizes, in some periods change is required for survival. Thus, the two prime systemic goals of organizations, survival and goal attainment, are not necessarily in conflict.

Resources, Activities, and Objectives

In fulfilling its mission to coordinate, to integrate, and to create a productive environment, management principally works with three factors: resources, activities, and objectives. These factors may be conceptually defined:

Objectives are the goals or missions of an organization, or, in other words, the purposes for which the organization was formed.

Activities are the work or tasks the organization undertakes to achieve its missions or goals.

Resources are the material commodities the organization expends in undertaking work or tasks. These materials may be measured in terms of dollar costs and, for the most part, are the costs involved in purchasing things and hiring people.

There is a logical connection among resources, activities, and objectives in managerial planning: first, objectives are set; then, the activities necessary to achieve the objectives are determined; and finally the resources necessary to undertake the work are identified. This is essentially a conditional process: work programs and expenditures are conditioned and justified by the stated or assumed objectives. At a purely conceptual level, this formulation makes sense, but, as will be seen, applying it to the real world of criminal justice agencies sometimes raises problems.

An example of such a "logical" approach is given in Figure 1-1. The process begins with the statement of an objective: determining who should have custody of a child so as to assure the child's safety and well-being. (In this simple example *safety* and *well-being* are not defined.) Several kinds of activity might conceivably be necessary to achieve this objective, including the gathering of information about likely parenting environments. The process of gathering information (investigating) will require manpower and other resources.

Logically, the selection of the objective "dictates" the activity to be undertaken, and the activity selected "dictates" the resources required. Resources are justified by the activity; the activity, by the objective.

The origins of the "logical" approach to managerial planning (0 → A → R) cannot be precisely determined, but it seems most clearly described in the management-science literature known as results management.[38] It has also appeared under the general label of "management by objectives" (MBO).[39] In either case, the importance of first setting objectives is emphasized. There is also a frequent connection made between MBO and motivation, the rationale being that results and an understanding of the connection between work and results link individual motivations to the achievement of organizational objectives. The pertinent aspect of results management for our purposes, however, is its concern with setting objectives and planning how to achieve them.

Figure 1-1. Relating Resources, Activities, and Objectives

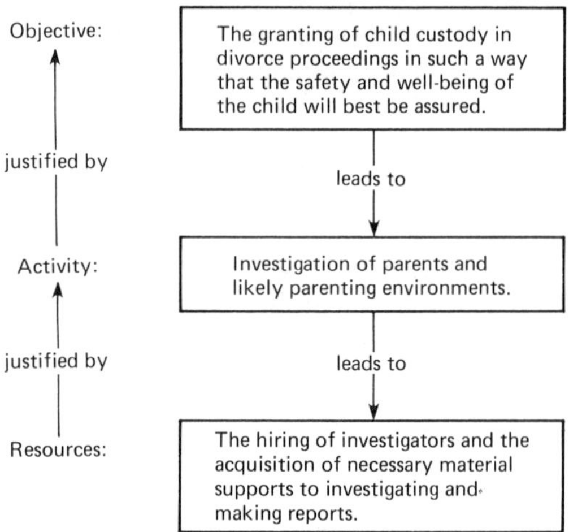

Moving from theory to action results in great difficulties. Stating objectives does not guarantee that means of achieving them can be found, or agreed upon, or afforded. These difficulties raise a question: Can objectives be meaningfully stated first, or can they be set only in reference to what is possible and affordable?

Consider, for example, a crime-prevention objective related to breaking and entering (B&E). Conceivably an objective could be set to prevent all B&Es within a given jurisdiction. But this would be unrealistic, for usually there are neither acceptable means nor sufficient resources to achieve such an objective. A more limited objective—say, a 10 per cent reduction in B&Es—would be more possible and affordable, because a certain set of crime-prevention activities would be known to be both feasible and affordable, and the activities and expenditures would be justified by the objective.

The reality of managerial planning in criminal justice may require reciprocal consideration of resources, activities, and objectives. And reciprocal consideration may well be part of the process of making plans and planning manageable. Yet, such an approach is not without its dangers and its critics. Defining objectives only in terms of available means or resources may stifle innovation and change or displace the organization's goals.

Merton, Selznick, and many others have commented on the tendency of organizations to displace intangible goals with more tangible or down-to-earth ones.[40] Also, goal displacement can be viewed as the process whereby the means available dictate what the goals will be. McFarland has commented on this problem in business organizations, and his views seem equally applicable to the public sector and to criminal justice:

> Goal displacement in a business organization occurs when decision-makers substitute tangible goals for broader, riskier, more uncertain, long-range goals. . . . Risky but creative activity may be avoided in favor of following rules and sticking to past experience. Managers may "play for the record" and be numbers-oriented, rather than focus on the actual goals.[41]

Setting manageable goals can be interpreted as a process whereby risk is minimized, and minimization of risk may become an organizational goal in itself with priority given to maintaining the organization rather than achieving its missions. On the other hand, as McFarland notes, concentrating on intangible mission-oriented goals also carries negative consequences: the generation of expectations that cannot be met (e.g., preventing most crime or halting most recidivism) may cause the organization's staff to become disillusioned, pessimistic, and cynical.

There is no simple solution to the problem of setting objectives that are simultaneously realistic and idealistic. One attempt at a solution in the public sector involves the program approach to budgeting and the design of goal-oriented program structures. The program structure is a top-down design process, with, at the top, basic government or agency missions and, at the bottom, more specific statements of action to be undertaken. Between are the intermediate steps that become more detailed and concrete as one moves from top to bottom. Each level is logically related to the next: lower levels of the program structure are the means for achieving all or a part of the higher level.

> The purpose is to go from a statement of values that something is deemed good to a statement of fact that activities are contributing to the attainment of that good, to go from non-quantifiable value statements or goals to quantifiable facts relevant to objectives.[42]

Program structures have been used extensively in the Federal LEAA grant program as a means of encouraging criminal justice agencies to think about the relationship between realistic (manageable) program goals and idealistic (intangible) goals of the system. The success of this approach is highly questionable. Yet, the logic of the program structure offers some guidance for the planner who needs to think about both idealistic and realistic goals. Two sample program structures relating to criminal justice are found in Figures 1-2 and 1-3. The first comes from a 1973 LEAA publication entitled, "Evaluation in Criminal Justice Programs: Guidelines and Examples."[43] The second comes from a report on the implementation of the planning, programming, budgeting system in the state of Pennsylvania.[44]

The LEAA program structure (Figure 1-2) for reducing stranger-to-stranger crime is indicative of the basic logic inherent in the program-structure approach. Specificity increases as one moves from top to bottom, and abstract goals become concrete. A connection is drawn between objectives and the specific activities that will comprise the work program. The program structure thus becomes a plan of operation, or at least a proposed plan of operation, that defines the connection perceived by management between the work of the agency and its ultimate missions.

Another aspect of the program structure is its implicit treatment of short-, mid-, and long-range objectives. The problem of organizational cynicism and pessimism is at times traceable to an inadequate distinction between short-range goals and mid- or long-range goals. Short-range manageable objectives move us toward the achievement of broader or long-range objectives that at present do not seem manageable. Short-range planning, then, is a "bit-and-chunk" movement toward larger objectives. A point discussed more fully in Chapter 8 must be stressed

Figure 1-2. National Impact Goal: Reduce Stranger-to-Stranger Crime and Burglary

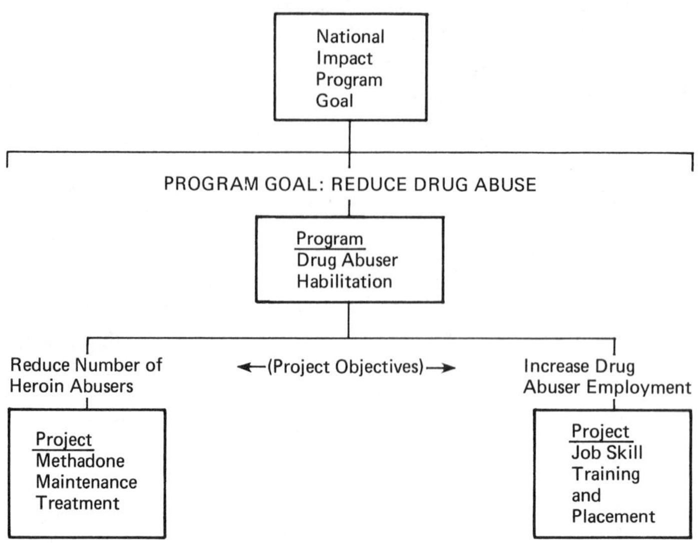

Figure 1-3. Sample Program Structure Number 1

Program Objective = Protection of Persons and Property

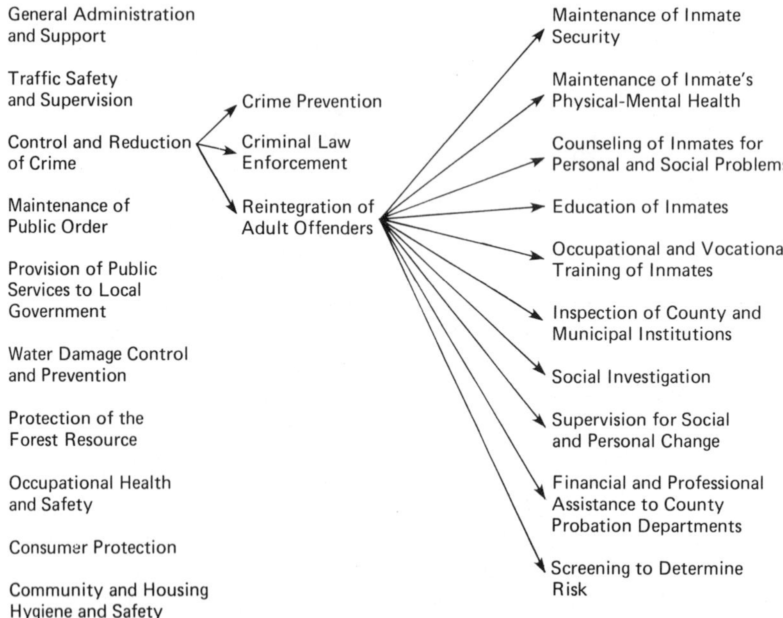

Adapted from and used with permission of Robert J. Mowitz, "The Design and Implementation of Pennsylvania's Planning Programming, Budgeting System", University Park, Pennsylvania State University, Institute of Public Administration, first printing 1970, second printing 1973.

here: designing manageable plans is not necessarily counterproductive to the achievement of broader long-range organizational missions.

This section opened with the suggestion that managerial planning manipulates three factors: resources, activities, and objectives. Agencies do not formulate objectives and plan activities without recognizing the constraints posed by availability of resources. The theory that objectives must be set first, and required activities and resources determined subsequently does not accord with the reality of organizational decision-making. Managerial planning should be seen as a continuous and reiterative examination of resources, activities, and objectives. Preferred objectives must be evaluated in light of those actions and expenditures that are possible and feasible. Thus, whether planning begins with a consideration of what is available (resources), with a consideration of what can be done (activities), or with a consideration of the results desired (objectives), it is important to recognize that managerial planning is a product of all three. Goals are not determined by preference alone; they are influenced also by an understanding of what is possible.

Suboptimization

Goal displacement, in giving organizational survival precedence over organizational missions, can be one consequence of focusing on manageable objectives. Another related consequence is suboptimization, in which activities become more important than objectives. This problem is generated by the failure to recognize that resources, activities, and objectives are very different things.

The confusion of these terms has typically blurred the difference between activities and objectives. Police departments provide traffic patrol, but traffic patrol is not an objective of a police agency, only one of its activities. The objective is to prevent accidents. By the same token, fire departments conduct programs to educate the public about fire hazards, but this is only an activity that serves the broader objective of keeping people safe from fire. Corrections institutions provide counseling to inmates not as an objective, but as an activity.

Activities produce *outputs*, such as road miles patrolled or number of inmates counselled. The achievement of objectives, on the other hand, produces *outcomes*, such as a decline in the death-rate associated with automobile accidents. Unfortunately, some managerial planning efforts concentrate on achieving and measuring outputs while largely ignoring the achievement of outcomes. This is managerial suboptimization: the misplacing of emphasis on lower-level concerns, such as activities, while ignoring higher-level purposes or ends.

Implicit in this understanding of the difference between activities and objectives is the difference in kinds of managerial planning. (See also Chapters 2, 3, and 6.) Concentration on certain kinds of planning to the neglect of others, will encourage suboptimization. For example, no one denies the importance of planning how certain activities will actually be carried out as well as planning for the necessary resources and the use of those resources. This has been called "operational planning," and, though effective in combination with other kinds of planning, by itself may lead to suboptimization.

Operational planning, the coordination and integration of agency resources in undertaking work or activities, has very much been a focus of planning efforts in criminal justice during the past decade. The most obvious examples are the various operational planning models related to developing more efficient police-patrol resource allocation and beat design. A large proportion of these models concentrate on producing a more effective and efficient patrol activity. Success tends to be measured in terms of the performance of the activity, and seldom are questions raised about the contribution the activity makes to the achievement of organizational missions.

Results planning could affect views about the ultimate worth of any given operational plan. For example, the Kansas City Preventive Patrol Experiment called attention to the potential suboptimizing effects of police-patrol operational planning: the distribution of police-patrol resources, efficient or not, did not appear to affect crime prevention.[45] Managerial planning must not concentrate exclusively on lower-level, or suboptimizing, concerns.

Levels of Managerial Planning

The dangers of goal displacement and suboptimization lead to a consideration of what McFarland has called the "hierarchy of plans" in an organization.[46] The issues facing any but the smallest criminal justice agency are so complex that no single individual or single level in the organization is capable of planning fully for organizational needs.

Planning may be subdivided not only according to what takes place at different levels in the organization, but also according to "conceptual" levels or hierarchies of plans. It is generally recognized that the highest form of planning—that having the widest scope and time span—is strategic planning. ***Strategic planning*** is concerned with "anticipating events, making diagnoses, and shaping appropriate courses of action" in connection with long-range policies.[47] In a sense, the purpose of strategic planning is to enable the organization consistently to pursue basic missions, and to respond effectively to new contingencies.

Strategic planning is distinguished from *tactical planning*, which usually involves management control or allocative planning. Friedmann describes tactical planning as concerned with the "distribution of existing resources among competing users."[48] Others have noted that tactical planning is akin to operational planning.[49] According to Glaser, strategic planning is the major innovating force in an organization—the planning that identifies the basic missions, any needed organizational change, and the constraints within which the organization will operate, while tactical planning is more concerned with identifying the means by which the organization operates within the constraints imposed by strategic planning.[50] Tactical planning without strategic planning may well lead to a form of suboptimization that ignores both basic mission and needed innovation.

Another distinction may be that strategic planning is concerned with organizational change while tactical planning assumes a more stable organization with which to confront the environment. At any rate, strategic planning provides a framework for all other levels of organizational planning. Tactical planning itself would appear to have differing scopes and time-spans. Certainly the tactical or operational planning done by top and middle management differs in scope from that done by, say, first-line supervision. For example, top and middle management of a state department of corrections will be concerned with overall questions of resource allocation and expenditure during a given fiscal year. First-line supervisors will of course be affected by such questions, but their tactical planning responsibilities will be personnel scheduling, fixed-post assignments, and the like.

There is no single best way of presenting these levels of planning graphically. Figure 1-4, one of a number of possible formulations, shows the distinction between strategic and tactical planning. The subdivisions of strategic planning do not necessarily represent distinctions of scope or time-span, but those of tactical planning do.

Criminal justice managerial planning includes wide scope as well as operational detail, long-range as well as short-range thinking, and it concerns all levels of the agency. The problem of relating resources, activities, and objectives is too complex to be solved by a few people sitting down once a year "to write next year's plan."

The volatility of crime and of the public's reaction to it does not allow criminal justice managerial planning to be equated with writing a plan. Yet, LEAA-generated planning efforts seem to have cast the process into just such a mold. Their encouragement of goals and standards commissions, for example, led to one-shot goal-planning exercises that formulated long-range goals, but ignored operational or tactical planning; and the long-range goals and the standards were infrequently, if ever, updated. The planning required of agencies by LEAA in awarding grants often encouraged treatment of suboptimal concerns but neglected consideration of results and strategic agency missions.

Of course, LEAA cannot bear all the blame. Most of the agencies in the system have lacked the skill and experience to undertake the full range of planning activities implied by Figure 1-4. Nonetheless, agencies in the criminal justice system can hardly be expected to mitigate their present crisis environments unless strategic analysis of crime trends, demographic trends, legislation and court rulings, and scores of other environmental factors is undertaken. Nor can these agencies expect significant improvement in productivity and performance without constructing operational plans designed to attain and to measure basic agency goals and missions.

Planning, Implementation, and Evaluation

Designing a plan is one thing; putting it into operation and measuring its results is quite an-

Figure 1-4. Levels of Planning: Strategic versus Tactical

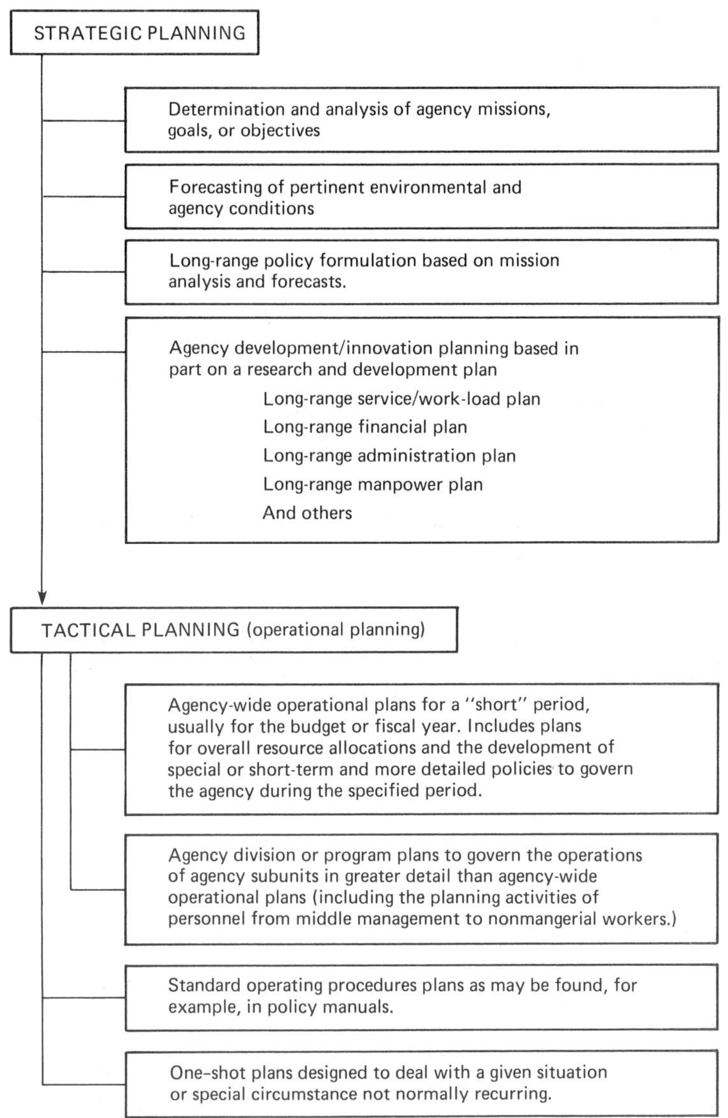

other. Indeed, managerial planning has very little meaning unless plans lead to action that achieves results of some kind. Although planning is the first step in the managerial process, implementation and evaluation are essential both to test the plan and to measure its results. The management process may be viewed as a four-step sequence that starts with planning and, as Figure 1-5 shows, this sequence applies not only to management in general but to its various component aspects (e.g., fiscal planning).

Planning is anticipatory in that we say, "When and if we do X, this or that condition will result." Implementation involves doing X and also collecting information for later appraisals of the result. Evaluation is retrospective: Did the plan accomplish what was intended? Evaluation, properly conceived, supplies data for future planning efforts. This sequence of events roughly parallels the process of empirical research. The researcher begins by preparing a research design (a plan), tests the design either through experiment or through collection of data (implementation), analyzes the data (evaluation) and uses that information for subsequent research designs and tests.

Figure 1-5. Managerial Processes

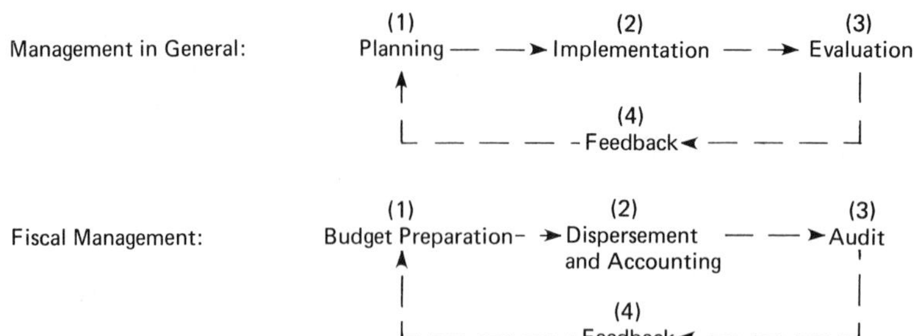

There are, of course, important differences between basic empirical research and the research associated with managerial planning, implementation, and evaluation. Some of the more important differences suggested by Carol Weiss, whose comments are focused on the differences between basic research and evaluation research but are applicable to planning and implementation research, are paraphrased below:[51]

1. Basic research emphasizes gaining new knowledge, leaving the use of the knowledge to others and to the future. Evaluation research "starts out with use in mind"; the objective is to aid decision-makers and the decisions they seek to reach.
2. Basic research is predicated on the interests of the researcher; evaluation research seeks to answer questions generated by management decision-makers or by organization concerns.
3. "Evaluation [research] compares 'what is' with 'what should be.'" Basic research is much less fundamentally concerned with making judgments about the degree to which stated goals have been achieved.

Planning is not merely the first step in the sequence of managerial events; it is the primary organizing force for implementation and evaluation as well. Planning involves the design of a detailed work plan that specifies (1) what events and actions are necessary, (2) when they must take place, (3) who is to be involved in each action and for how long, and (4) how the various actions will interlock with one another. A classic work-plan diagram was developed over seventy years ago by Henry L. Gantt.[52] The "Gantt chart" lists activities or outputs along one dimension, and time across another; in this way the sequence of events and their timing can be viewed in summary fashion. Other more recent developments in devising convenient work-plan diagrams include critical-path analysis and network analysis (also known as PERT) that organize essentially the same kinds of information found in the Gantt chart, but in different ways.[53]

Planning extends into implementation; it monitors implementation, noting departures from the plan and determines the need for mid-course corrections. Mid-course corrections may include putting the organization back on track with regard to the plan, but may also include changes in the plan itself. The role of the planner does not end with the designing of the plan: there must be a relationship between the planner and the implementer as planning staff and line personnel work together to put the plan into effect.

Although planning and implementation are distinct concepts, their interrelationship is critical. As Stuart Nagel pointed out, a plan may fail to produce the intended results either because it was a bad plan or because the plan was never really put into effect.[54] Monitoring the implementation of a plan in criminal justice is particularly important because crime policy is administered by a tangled web of semi-independent agencies at the Federal, state, and local levels. Thus, local agency plans may be countered by those of a state agency, those of a local police department may, in effect, be altered by countervailing actions of the local prosecutor, or through shifts in basic political values.

Certainly, a well-conceived plan would take into account the possible countervailing influences of other agencies. But not everything can be anticipated; thus, monitoring for plan compliance and making mid-course corrections is essential. So too, the subsequent evaluation of a plan must distinguish between failure generated by poor implementation and failure generated by a poor plan.

Although evaluation is retrospective (did we accomplish what was intended?) initial as well as subsequent stages of the planning process must include planning for evaluation. Too often—because of simple omission, or ignorance, or the unexamined assumption that the plan will work—evaluation is neglected or treated as an afterthought.

The failure adequately to plan for evaluation has often plagued criminal justice. The consequence has usually been that evaluation in any objective sense becomes impossible. Part of the problem stems from poorly conceived evaluation plans—plans that lack clear or clearly expressed objectives, that do not operationally define objectives, that do not specify requisite data collection for evaluation purposes. But there are other, special problems in criminal justice associated with attempts to evaluate.

First, base-line data are often unavailable in criminal justice: data collection has become a serious concern of the system only in the last decade. For example, the absence of information from prior years on juvenile recidivism or the characteristics of juvenile recidivists makes it difficult to determine trends in juvenile recidivism or to determine whether a given plan to deal with juvenile recidivism has had any real effect.

Second, data are often inaccurate or a poor measure of a phenomenon.[55] The use of Uniform Crime Reports (UCR) data is a case in point: UCR data are often an inaccurate reflection of true crime levels because of inaccurate record keeping. In criminal justice, inaccurate data may not simply be a matter of poor record-keeping but may also evolve out of political sensitivities associated with crime:

> When official [crime] statistics do become available, they are at times tainted with such pronounced political overtones that they are virtually worthless as means of evaluation. To take a single example, consider the compilation of statistics on volume of crime. . . . Total volume of crime, it appears, is a highly sensitive issue. A city or a region could look very bad if it were to appear at the top of an index of crime. Tourism, industry, and economic growth could decline. Pressure is often brought to bear by city fathers to "dampen" these statistics. Then too, police departments themselves look bad if there is a high proportion of unsolved crime. Some cities have been notorious for "wiping the blotter clear" at the end of the year.[56]

Third, data must often be collected from a number of different criminal-justice agencies; yet, because the agencies are semi-independent, there is no centralized control over the collection or retrieval of data.

Fourth, criminal justice goals and objectives are highly complex and often contradictory. For example, traditional correctional goals are punishment, rehabilitation, and incapacitation. A given correctional plan may emphasize one of these and structure evaluation criteria around it. But the lack of public or political agreement on such goals means that the evaluation criteria selected by the agency may not necessarily be those subsequently applied by the public or by political decision makers.

These and other problems are not unique to criminal justice and they can be dealt with. The past decade has seen numerous advances in, for example, the kinds of base-line data regularly collected in the system. The Expenditure and Employment Data of the Criminal Justice System, published by LEAA annually, is a good case in point.[57] Also, strides have been taken in increasing the accuracy of data, as, for example, by the use of victimization survey data as a supplement to UCR data. And cross-agency data have burgeoned in the last few years, as have models for collecting it. For example, Offender Based Transaction Statistics (OBTS) and its variants are collections and collations of data from numerous criminal justice agencies.

These types of problems and their solutions notwithstanding, evaluations must be planned, and must be part of the planning process. The overall planning process includes the following:

1. Development of operational and quantifiable measures of goals and objectives.
2. Development of operational and quantifiable measures of work or activities.
3. Identification of evaluation measures.
4. Identification and planning of the evaluation techniques.
5. Identification of data needs, data-collection points, data collectors, and records-keeping systems.
6. Identification of methods of analysis to be used and of points at which analysis is to take place.

It is important to plan the evaluation because generally it is difficult to secure agreement on the goals and objectives of criminal justice. Unless goals and objectives are clearly defined beforehand, the criteria for evaluating a plan and its programs may be manipulated along the way, thereby distorting the meaning of the results.

IS RATIONAL CRIMINAL JUSTICE PLANNING POSSIBLE?

This discussion of the planning process and its application to criminal justice no doubt reflects some mixed feelings about the degree to which rational, objective planning is possible in the criminal justice system. The problems associated with planning, and with planning in criminal justice, suggest that there are constraints on rationality and objectivity. Are these constraints such as to preclude any meaningful form of rational or objective planning? Chapter 3 considers this question in detail, but some general comments are warranted here.

Tony Eddison, of the Institute of Local Government Studies at the University of Birmingham, England, identifies six alternative models of the planning process.[58] His views may be paraphrased:

1. *The Pure-Rationality Model.* Establish a complete set of goals; inventory all values and relative weights of values on which the goals are based; examine all alternative policies available to the decision-maker and all the consequences of each; calculate the net benefit for each alternative; select the alternative with the highest net benefit.
2. *The Economically Rational Model.* Follow as closely as possible the pure-rationality model, but when the costs of trying to be rational exceed the benefits, limit or stop any further rational analysis.
3. *The Sequential-Decision Model.* "If some of the information needed to succeed in an activity can be learned only during the early stages of carrying out that activity, the more promising alternative ways to carry it out should be undertaken simultaneously, and the decision as to which is the best alternative should be delayed until the information has been learned."[59]
4. *The Incremental Change Model.* Reject any of the rational approaches because decisions are not made in such ways in practice. Rather, planning and decisions are incremental, remedial, serial, exploratory, fragmented, and disjointed. The planning process can only be "disjointed incrementalism."
5. *The Satisfying Model.* "Policy-makers identify obvious alternatives based on recent policy-making experience, and evaluate their expected payoffs in terms of the satisfactory quality." If the expected payoff from a given alternative appears satisfactory, conclude analysis. Only when the obvious alternatives do not appear to produce satisfactory payoffs do we search for more alternatives.
6. *The Extrarational Model.* Intuition and judgment are essential processes, if not the major processes in planning and policy-making. Information use and analysis is not made explicit; impressions and "feelings" about what should be done are the real bases for making policy.

The limitations of the pure-rationality model are obvious: the model seems to have little, if any, application to criminal justice. At the other extreme, the extrarational model no doubt is representative of much of the "planning" in criminal justice. The remaining four models all seem applicable because they acknowledge limits on the extent to which pure rationality and objectivity are either possible or beneficial.

The proposition can be ventured that all but the pure-rationality planning model apply to criminal justice. But the application of any one or more models depends on the situation.[60] Certainly, some planning issues appear to defy any but a judgmental or intuitional approach. A good example involves current efforts to examine the comparative payoffs of adopting correctional policy models of reform, rehabilitation, reintegration, or restraint. Research efforts (and they have been numerous) to measure the comparative payoffs of these four approaches have really demonstrated only that we do not know how analytically to determine such payoffs. Exercising judgment and intuition, perhaps with some incremental tinkering, may be the only alternative.

On other issues facing criminal justice, the economically rational model, the sequential-decision model, or the satisfying model clearly apply. For example, it is entirely possible to compare the costs of incarceration in institutions and in halfway houses; and it is possible to determine which of these is associated with greater subsequent criminal behavior. This analysis, though by no means complete, would nonetheless feed some objective information into the planning process.

A bounded rationality in criminal justice planning, then, seems possible and fruitful. The important question has been posed by J. Yehezkel Dror: "What is the best possible mix of rationality, extrarationality, and their various subtypes?"[61]

Rationalism, most simply defined, is the reliance on reason to establish truth or knowledge. Reasoning may be abstract and deductive, as for example in Descarte's classic "Cogito ergo sum"—"I think; therefore I am." Reasoning may also be based on experience: our plans for the future are grounded on our experience that certain things have worked in the past and others have not.

Anglo-Saxon legal traditions are steeped in deductive reasoning, which have resulted in the development of case law and the judicial doctrine of *stare decisis.* Case law results from applying to new situations the legal principles recorded in precedent cases. The attempt is to develop a logical, coherent, and historically consistent set of legal principles. The Anglo-Saxon legal tradition is experientially based as well, for case law is a recording of past experiences and decisions as a guide for the present and the future.

Experiential reasoning is best represented by the British empirical tradition. Blackstone's legal reasoning, Adam Smith's economic reasoning, and certainly Jeremy Bentham's theory of utilitarianism, with its calculation of pleasure and pain, suggest an attempt to develop a rational public policy based on the collection and analysis of empirical data.[62] The underlying assumption of Bentham's theory, for example, is that man seeks to maximize his self-interest, to maximize pleasure and minimize pain. Bentham suggested that we identify what causes pleasure and what causes pain, and then devise a criminal justice system that makes the pain of a criminal act greater than its pleasure for the perpetrator.

Bentham's nineteenth-century calculation of pleasure and pain has its twentieth-century parallel in analyses of cost-benefit, and cost-effectiveness. The underlying premise of these forms of analysis is that public policy should maximize the ratio of benefit to cost. Cost-benefit analysis, applied to planning, means that alternative goals and programs are evaluated on the degree to which each maximizes benefit and minimizes cost. Few people would argue that this is a bad idea; the problem is to devise means of objectively measuring cost and benefit.

Economic rationalism is one alternative: calculations are made "scientifically" and "objectively" through the collection of "hard" data. An example of method is the attempt to compare the costs in dollars of a new traffic-enforcement program with the benefits (diminished property loss and injury), in dollars, accruing from the program. Another example, already cited, is the comparison of the dollar costs of institutional incarceration with the dollar cost of halfway houses. Or benefits might be calculated in nondollar terms, by a comparison of the recidivism rates associated with each of the alternatives.

The necessity of drawing a relationship between costs and benefits lies at the heart of making public agencies accountable. Yet, an assumption that such relationships can be objectively determined as in calculating dollar costs and dollar benefits, is questionable. Not all benefits can be measured in dollars. What is the dollar value of a human life saved through a traffic-control program? How do we measure the dollar value of a methadone-treatment program? The value of a human life saved or rehabilitated would appear to be beyond expression in mere dollars. One alternative is to measure benefits by the amount and kind of goods and services produced (e.g., the number of lives saved, the decrease in Part I crimes, the number of complaints cleared, the number of offenders successfully reintegrated, the decline in juvenile recidivism).

But another very large problem makes purely objective economic rationalism difficult if not impossible: even if we know all the costs of an undertaking, and exactly how many goods and services it will provide, what standard shall we apply in deciding whether the costs are acceptable in relation to the returns? For example, we may indeed be able to determine that Alternative A costs less than Alternative B and will produce less juvenile recidivism, but how shall we determine whether there should be any juvenile-recidivism program at all, or whether the return justifies the expenditure?

The fact is that decisions about public policy often have little or no justification in terms of economic rationality. Many public programs are undertaken in the expectation of economic loss, and this is nowhere more evident than in the field of criminal justice. For example, the imprisonment of an incorrigible offender for life can be viewed as a relative waste of public funds; capital punishment for such offenders would be much more economically efficient. Yet the society seems to have judged the "economically rational" solution to be morally reprehensible.

The alternative to calculating economic costs and benefits in the public sector is to calculate political costs and benefits. The decision not to use capital punishment as the means of dealing with habitual offenders is a moral or ethical decision translated into a political decision. Political questions concern power, and any form of government must calculate the political advantages and disadvantages of alternatives.

Economic calculations often lead to different policy conclusions than political calculations. For example, comparison of the economic costs of institutionalization with those of halfway houses might yield a decision to shift resources to halfway houses because they are less expensive, but comparison of the respective political costs and benefits may point to the opposite decision, because the public, for reasons other than economics, prefers to incarcerate convicted offenders. A question arises: Are such political calculations irrational?

During a recent research project, for example, several top command personnel in police departments around the country were interviewed about their manpower-planning practices.[63] One police chief related that his department had undertaken an intensive review of its workloads and personnel requirements and had concluded that the department could fulfill its basic missions more efficiently with several hundred fewer sworn officers. The mayor, however, assigned several hundred additional positions to the department, on the grounds that the department had not met its affirmative-action goals and that the new positions would allow significant new hiring of minority-group members and women. On purely economic grounds the mayor's decision would appear irrational, but political considerations—the values of the community and the distribution of political power in the city—were such that the mayor's decision could be seen as highly rational.

Decisions based on political considerations are not necessarily irrational, even if such decisions contradict rational analysis of purely economic costs and benefits. "Reason" and "rationality" are tempered by values. The "best" solution is not always the one that is cost-effective in economic terms. Planning, therefore, is not based solely on the mechanical production of quantitative ratios. Indeed some have argued, as has Aaron Wildavsky, that planning in the public sector can really be nothing more than political maneuvering:

> Power is the probability of changing the behavior of others against opposition. As soon as the prevalence of disagreement over social goals or policies is admitted into the discussion, it becomes clear that there can be no planning without the ability to cause other people to act differently than they otherwise would. Planning assumes power. Planning is politics.[64]

Wildavsky's views seem to question any attempt to calculate anything other than political sentiments. If all decisions in the public sector are based on political considerations, rational economic calculation may be a waste of time. But it is doubtful that Wildavsky would really choose such an extreme position. What is clear, is that political considerations are a large element in criminal justice policy-making; thus, rational economic analysis and objective planning can be only one of many components in the creation and formulation of policy. And planning grounded in objective and verifiable descriptions and analyses can itself, properly understood and managed, forcefully affect the political process.

The remaining chapters of this book will trace the various applications of rational planning in criminal justice and explore its contexts, constraints, and problems. Abstract theories of planning will be compared with the realities of a politically volatile and changing area of public policy.

SUMMARY

This chapter has presented planning as a future-oriented activity that links present actions to future conditions. Planning is not a passive intellectual exercise, but an attempt to control the future.

Planning is goal-oriented, and the role of

planners is more appropriately to discover goals than to determine them. Planners identify possible goals and means; decision-makers make the choice. Yet the work of planners is not value-neutral: because goals are often unclear or contradictory, and must be sifted by planners, subjectivity naturally enters into the process, and planners participate in discovering the choices about both goals and means.

Planning is also directed toward the resolution of problems, the attempt to find ways of redressing differences between what we have and what we want. Rarely does only one way exist by which problems can be solved or goals attained. The planner must weigh alternative courses of action, identify and measure the consequences of each, and (ideally) choose the one that seems best. But picking the "best" is not easy because values differ, and also because not all consequences can be identified or measured objectively. This has led some to conclude that the work of planners and decision-makers is more appropriately described as finding a satisfactory set of goals and a satisfactory set of means for achieving them, rather than as looking for the best.

Planning is a key managerial function, central to the effective functioning of organizations. The scope, structure, and purpose of planning is greatly influenced by whether the managerial style is purposeful, traditional, crisis-oriented, or entrepreneurial. The goal of all organizations is to survive and to achieve objectives. In pursuing this goal, both managers and planners strategically and tactically manipulate resources, activites, and objectives. Strategic planning sets long-range goals and basic organizational missions; tactical planning sets shorter-range goals and directs more concrete aspects of agency operations. Ignoring strategic-level concerns in order to concentrate on details is one form of managerial suboptimization. Another form of suboptimization results from emphasizing the production of outputs (work) while ignoring or neglecting the achievement of outcomes (objectives). Both forms of suboptimization decrease the effectiveness of organizational management and limit the organizational utility of planning.

One of the questions explored in this chapter concerns rational criminal justice planning and whether it is possible. Criminal justice agencies confront political considerations and realities that are hard to resolve solely in terms of economically based cost-benefit analyses. "Scientific" and objective analysis must be supplemented by political astuteness, value judgments, and intuition. The degree to which economic rationalism can be applied to planning in criminal justice varies. We have, therefore, adopted a model of bounded rationality for planning in criminal justice, and this model serves as the basis for the chapters that follow.

· *Chapter 1* ·
NOTES

1. Earnest Dale, *Management Theory and Practice* (New York: McGraw-Hill Book Company, 1965), p. 383.

2. Timothy J. Flanagan, Michael J. Hindelang, and Michael R. Gottfredson, eds., *Sourcebook of Criminal Justice Statistics–1979* (Washington, D.C.: U.S. Law Enforcement Assistance Administration, National Criminal Justice Information and Statistics Service, U.S. Government Printing Office, 1980), p. 5.

3. Ibid., p. 7

4. Gary W. Cordner, *Law Enforcement Survey Results* (East Lansing, Mich.: School of Criminal Justice, Michigan State University, 1980). Also see Tim Bynum, *Corrections Survey Results* (East Lansing, Mich.: School of Criminal Justice, Michigan State University, 1980), Question A-6.

5. This figure was taken from the unpublished and internal LEAA mailing list. The actual figure tabulated was approximately 480, but several of the entries appeared to be something other than substate regional planning units.

6. Chen Huan-Chang, as quoted by Claude S. George, Jr., in *The History of Management Thought* (Englewood Cliffs, N.J.: Prentice-Hall, Inc., 1968), p. 13.

7. Russell L. Ackoff, *A Concept of Corporate Planning* (New York: Wiley-Interscience, 1970), p. 1.

8. Herbert R. Sigurdson, Robert M. Carter, and A. W. McEachern, "Methodological Impediments to Comprehensive Criminal Justice Planning," *Criminology*, 9(August-November 1971), 248–67.

9. Herman Goldstein, *Policing a Free Society* (Cambridge, Mass.: Ballinger Publishing Co., 1977), p. 329.

10. Tony Eddison, *Local Government: Management and Corporate Planning* (New York: Harper & Row, Publishers, Barnes and Noble Import Division, 1973), p. 27.

11. Ibid., pp. 27–28.

12. A similar point is made by David Duffee in *Correctional Management: Change and Control in Correctional Organizations* (Englewood Cliffs, N.J.: Prentice-Hall, Inc., 1980), p. 65.

13. Richard Quinney, *Critique of Legal Order: Crime Control in Capitalist Society* (Boston: Little, Brown and Company, 1974). See Chap. 3.

14. Aaron Wildavsky, *Politics of the Budgetary Process*, 3rd ed. (Boston: Little, Brown and Company, 1979); Charles E. Lindblom, *The Policy-Making Process* (Englewood Cliffs, N.J., Prentice-Hall, Inc., 1968).

15. Robert C. Cushman, *Criminal Justice Planning for Local Governments* (Washington, D.C.: U.S. Department of Justice, Law Enforcement Assistance Administration, National Institute of Law Enforcement and Criminal Justice, 1980), p. 41. For further discussion, see Leonard Oberlander, ed., *Quantitative Tools for Criminal Justice Planning* (Washington, D.C.: LEAA, U.S. Department of Justice, 1975).

16. Ibid., p. 31.

17. Robert Reich, "Can Justice Be Optimized," in Stuart S. Nagel, ed., *Modeling the Criminal Justice System* (Beverly Hills, Calif.: Sage Publications, 1977), pp. 59–60.

18. Wildavsky, op. cit., p. 219.

19. Herbert A. Simon, "A Behavioral Model of Rational Choice," *The Quarterly Journal of Economics*, 69:1 (February 1955), 99–118.

20. Lindblom, op. cit., p. 24.

21. Ibid., pp. 26–27.

22. Eli Noam, "The Criminal Justice System: An Economic Model." in Nagel, op. cit., p. 42.

23. Paul Davidoff and Thomas A. Reiner, "A Choice Theory of Planning," *Journal of the American Institute of Planners* (May 1962), 103–115.

24. James P. Levine, Michael C. Musheno, and Dennis J. Palumbo, *Criminal Justice: A Public Policy Approach* (New York: Harcourt Brace Jovanovich, Inc., 1980), p. 539.

25. David Duffee and Vincent O'Leary, "Formulating Correctional Goals: The Interaction of Environment, Belief, and Organizational Structure," in Duffee, op. cit., pp. 92–95.

26. John F. Heaphy, "The Future of Police Improvement" in Alvin W. Cohn, ed., *The Future of Policing* (Beverly Hills, Calif.: Sage Publications, 1978), pp. 277–78. Heaphy is quoting Robert diGrazia.

27. See, for example, Luther Gulick and Lydoll Urwick, eds., *Papers on the Science of Administration* (New York: Institute of Public Administration, 1937).; Earnest Dale, op. cit.; Harold Koontz and Cyril O'Donnell, *Principles of Management: An Analysis of Managerial Functions* (New York: McGraw-Hill Book Company, 1968); Dalton E. McFarland, *Management: Principles and Practices*, 3rd ed. (New York: Macmillan Publishing Co., Inc., 1970), Chap 6.

28. Gulick and Urwick, op. cit., p. 13.

29. George, Jr., op. cit., p. 162.

30. Ibid., p. 162.

31. Preston P. LeBreton and Dale A. Henning, *Planning Theory* (Englewood Cliffs, N.J.: Prentice-Hall, Inc., 1961), Chap 1, esp. p. 4.

32. Dale D. McConkey, *Planning Next Year's Profit* (American Management Association, 1968), pp. 151–155.

33. Burt K. Scanlan, *Principles of Management and Organizational Behavior* (New York: John Wiley & Sons, Inc., 1973), p. 40.

34. Ibid.

35. Ronald G. Lynch, *The Police Manager: Professional Leadership Skills*, 2nd ed. (Boston Allyn & Bacon, Inc., 1978), p. 122.

36. John K. Hudzik, et al., *Summary Information from the Manpower Planning Project Interviews* (East Lansing, Mich: School of Criminal Justice, Michigan State University, 1980). Confidential report.

37. Walter Buckley, *Sociology and Modern Systems Theory* (Englewood Cliffs, N.J.,: Prentice-Hall, 1967).

38. See for example, Edward C. Schleh, *Management By Results* (New York: McGraw-Hill Book Company, 1961).

39. See for example, George S. Odiorne, *Management by Objectives: A System of Managerial Leadership* (New York: Pitman Publishing Corporation, 1965). Also see, Walter S. Wikstrom, "Management by Objectives, or Appraisal by Results," *Conference Board Record*, 3:7 (July 1966), 27–31.

40. Robert K. Merton, *Social Theory and Social Structure* (New York: The Free Press, 1957); Philip Selznick, *Leadership in Administration* (Evanston, Ill.: Row, Peterson and Company, 1957), Chap 3.

41. McFarland, op. cit., p. 190.

42. Robert D. Lee, Jr., and Ronald W. Johnson, *Public Budgeting Systems* (Baltimore: University Park Press, 1973), pp. 161–64.

43. Ellen Albright, et al., *Criminal Justice Research: Evaluation in Criminal Justice Pro-*

grams–Guidelines and Examples (Washington, D.C.: U.S. Department of Justice, LEAA, National Institute of Law Enforcement and Criminal Justice, U.S. Government Printing Office, 1973), p. 7.

44. Robert J. Mowitz, *The Design and Implementation of Pennsylvania's Planning, Programming, Budgeting System.* (Institute of Public Administration Pennsylvania State University Park, Pa., 1970), p. 52.

45. George L. Kelling, et al., *The Kansas City Preventive Patrol Experiment: A Summary Report* (Washington, D. C.,: Police Foundation, 1974).

46. McFarland, op. cit., p. 146.

47. Charles M. Mottley, "Strategic Planning," in Fremont J. Lyden and Ernest G. Miller, eds., *Planning-Programming-Budgeting: A Systems Approach to Management*, 2nd ed. (Chicago: Rand McNally & Company, 1973), p. 125.

48. Gibbons, et al., op. cit., p. 75 fn.

49. Burt Nanus, "A General Model for Criminal Justice Planning," in Jim Munro, *Classes, Conflict, and Control: Studies in Criminal Justice Management*, (Cincinnati: Anderson Publishing, 1976). This also appeared in *The Journal of Criminal Justice*, 2 (1974), 345–56.

50. Daniel Glaser, *Strategic Criminal Justice Planning* (Rockville, Md.: National Institute of Mental Health, 1975).

51. Carol H. Weiss, *Evaluation Research: Methods of Assessing Program Effectiveness* (Englewood Cliffs, N.J.: Prentice-Hall, Inc., 1972), pp. 6–7.

52. See Claude S. George, Jr., op. cit., pp. 100–102 for a short description of Gantt's major contributions to management science.

53. For a discussion of this and related techniques, see Daniel D. Roman, "The PERT System: An Appraisal of Program Evaluation Review Technique," *The Journal of the Academy of Management*, 5 (April 1962), 57–65.

54. Stuart S. Nagel, "Series Editor's Introduction," in Helen M. Ingram and Dean E. Mann, eds., *Why Policies Succeed or Fail, Sage Yearbooks in Politics and Public Policy:* Vol. 8 (Beverly Hills, Calif.: Sage Publications, 1980), p.7.

55. See Wesley G. Skogan, "Measurement Problems in Official and Survey Crime Rates," in Susette M. Talarico, ed., *Criminal Justice Research: Approaches, Problems, and Policy* (Cincinnati: Anderson Publishing, 1980), pp. 45–61.

56. Richard Henshel, "Political and Ethical Considerations of Evaluation Research," in Susette M. Talarico, op. cit., pp. 232–33.

57. For example, U.S. Department of Justice, Law Enforcement Assistance Administration and U.S. Bureau of the Census, *Expenditure and Employment Data for the Criminal Justice System: 1976* (Washington, D.C.: U.S. Government Printing Office, 1978).

58. Tony Eddison, op, cit., pp. 19–23.

59. Ibid., p. 20, quoting J. Yehezkel Dror, *Public Policymaking Re-examined* (Novato, Calif.: Chandler Publishing Company, 1968), p. 142.

60. A similar argument that form of decision-making depends on the situation is made in Lawrence B. Mohr, "Organizations, Decisions, and Courts," *Law and Society Review*, 10:4 (1976) 621–42.

61. Eddison, op, cit., p. 23, quoting Dror.

62. Werner A. Hirsch, "Policy Analysis of Legal Policies," in Stuart S. Nagel, ed., *Improving Policy Analysis* (Beverly Hills, Calif.: Sage Publications, 1980), pp. 59–71.

63. John K. Hudzik, op. cit.

64. Aaron Wildavsky, "If Planning is Everything, Maybe It's Nothing," *Policy Sciences* 4(1973), 132.

• Chapter 2 •

DEFINITIONS, VARIETIES, AND THEORIES OF PLANNING

Planning is an often loosely defined, much maligned, poorly understood multipurpose social activity. Broad conceptions of planning include much of politics and administration, the entire programming cycle (including implementation and evaluation) and such technical fields as architecture and engineering. A detailed analysis of planning behavior could incorporate most of psychology, and such matters as perception, design, decision-making, problem-solving, goal and value systems, and learning. From the literature, one could easily get the impression that planning is everything.[1]

In fact, planning isn't quite everything, despite its breadth and the occasional claims of its proponents. This chapter will discuss what planning is and how it differs from some other approaches to rational social action, and examine some of the varieties of planning that are to be found, the justifications for engaging in planning, and some theories of planning.

DEFINITIONS OF PLANNING

The popular misconception that planning is synonymous with control is probably the cause of much of the distrust of planning, particularly in this country, where "social planning" or proposals for a "planned economy" engender fear and hostility. Of course, a capitalist system places a great deal of faith in the "unseen hand" that presumably directs and controls the market. The concept of the "unseen hand" is in many ways the very opposite of the concept of planning. Thus the market is controlled through the vigorous pursuit of self-interest by all involved, rather than through planning by a central authority.

Americans tend to chafe at the idea of social planning, because it suggests that the government would make decisions for us, and thus limit our freedom. We like to perceive our society as one in which rugged individualists make their own way, through their personal skills and energy. Many hold that social planning thwarts individual initiative and leads to government control of individual lives. Many people once perceived control through planning as a key characteristic of socialism, and thus strongly opposed all forms of planning. But it has become evident that planning is an element of all forms of government and most forms of human behavior, and that planning, in and of itself, is not evil. Noting the association of planning with social control, Robert Dahl concluded many years ago that "this perverse and narrow meaning has not proved useful."[2]

What observers like Dahl have noted is that in all societies—democratic, socialist, capitalist, autocratic—the need for efficiency and effectiveness creates pressure to plan. Under diverse forms of government the distribution of authority, responsibility, and ownership of property may differ widely, but all are interested in wisely using resources to attain goals. This realization leads to the view that planning is rational social action—not a threat to liberty but a means toward individual and social fulfillment. Planning has been defined as "a social process for reaching a rational decision, . . . any deliberate effort to increase the proportion of goals attained by increasing awareness and understanding of the factors involved."[3]

This concept of planning has given rise to the more recent criticism that planning proponents claim it to be everything. Noted scholars have argued that planning is the very essence of rational activity. John Friedmann, for example, has described planning as "an activity by which man in society endeavors to gain mastery over himself and to shape his collective future consciously by power of his reason,"[4] and as "the guidance of change within a social system."[5] David Ewing defined planning as essentially "the job of making things happen that would not otherwise occur."[6] A bit more expansively, Andreas Faludi identifies planning as "a continuous process of carefully devising future courses of action within the framework of overall appreciation of the social system, and with a view of their net contribution to human fulfillment."[7] Friedmann and Hudson have perhaps described planning most broadly: as "an activity centrally concerned with the linkage between knowledge and organized action."[8]

There can scarcely be a broader topic in all the arts and sciences than the link between knowledge and action. It doesn't leave out much, and so tells us little about planning. Though planning is not a narrow concept or activity, it can still legitimately be defined.

Planning can best be understood as what is done before making a decision or taking action. It is a process of preparation: information is gathered, alternatives are considered, and the likely effects of alternatives are estimated. Two additional characteristics set planning apart from other analytic strategies: in planning, the future is given explicit consideration, and comprehensiveness, or at least coordination, is sought among sets of interrelated decisions or actions. Without the kind of preparation provided through planning, decisions and actions are taken without regard to their long-term effects or to their effect on related decisions or actions.

A simple example may help to illustrate some of these characteristics of planning. Many states have overcrowded prisons and must decide whether or not to build additional facilities for the imprisonment of convicted offenders. Some states may make their decisions without bothering to plan, or for purely political reasons: they may decide to build more prisons in order to satisfy public demands for law and order, or they may decide not to build prisons because of public opposition to higher taxes. Vote-getting politics aside, the decisions about prison construction may be made in some states on the basis of tradition ("This has always been a law-and-order state") or on the basis of unexamined assumptions ("Putting people in prison never rehabilitated anybody," or, "We need more prisons because without the deterrent effect of doing hard time the streets would turn into jungles").

By contrast, some states use planning as an aid to making decisions. These states will collect information about the degree of overcrowding in the prisons, the number of state prisoners being held in county jails, the present capacity of the prison system, the patterns of sentencing and parole over the last few years, and applicable court rulings and accreditation standards. These states will also attempt to identify all the possible solutions to the problem of overcrowding—not only the construction of new prisons, but also including such strategies as increased use of probation, quicker parole, establishment of community treatment centers, and so on. Having identified these alternatives, they will estimate the probable consequences of each. Estimates of costs and benefits at least provide the best available information to aid in identifying the most desirable alternative.

As part of this planning process, the future would be carefully considered. One important issue would be the long-term costs and benefits of the various alternatives. For example, building a new prison might seem rather costly, but the long-term benefits might be substantial, and construction is unlikely to get cheaper in the future. Possible future changes in the problems or situations must also be considered. Some observers feel, for example, that present overcrowding in prisons is the result of the "age bubble" phenomenon, so that there are inordinate numbers of citizens in the crime-prone fifteen- to twenty-four-year-old age bracket. These observers argue that as the members of this demographic bubble outgrow their offensive tendencies, the size of prison populations will decrease. This expectation, if correct, would influence the decision, for if new prisons were built now, they might soon be unnecessary, and thus represent wasted investments. Others, however, argue that available prison space, as history shows, is almost always filled.

Besides considering the future, planning also involves considering related decisions or actions that might be affected, as part of the process of estimating the effects or consequences of different alternatives. The planner must go beyond simple, direct consequences and estimate side or indirect effects. For example, the availability of more prison space might encourage judges to sentence more harshly. Even more indirectly, increases in the rate or length of incarceration might eventually lead to heavier parole workloads, and might also lead to increased demands for welfare payments from dependents of prisoners. A decision not to build more prisons, on the other hand, might increase overcrowding in local and county jails, and could also cause court congestion as judges delayed sentencing in the hope that prison space would become available.

The planning process also presents the opportunity to coordinate decisions or actions that are to be undertaken in the same period. For example, a state may be facing simultaneously problems of prison overcrowding, court congestion, overburdened probation and parole agents, and escalating public fear of crime. The planning process might devise a comprehensive or at least coordinated approach to these related problems. Without planning, it is highly likely that the problems would be addressed singly and in fact disjointedly, as if each existed in a vacuum. Planning certainly does not guarantee a magical solution to all problems, and sometimes the problems and their interrelationships are too complex to be dealt with as one. But the planning process quite often provides the only opportunity for comprehensiveness and coordination in public policy-making.

A rough picture of planning now emerges. We intend to sharpen the picture throughout the rest of this chapter, first by distinguishing planning from some other similar activities, and then by discussing varieties, justifications, and theories of planning.

PROCESSES RELATED TO PLANNING

The discussion of definitions noted that a major concern of planning is decision-making. Many authors have discussed the similarities and differences between the two activities. John Dyckman sees planning as "filling a gap" within other forms of decision-making by "dealing with the future and the extensive repercussions of limited goals."[9] Churchman sees planning as concerned with "multistage decision-making,"[10] and Kaplan views it as a means of "facilitating and rationalizing" decisions.[11] According to Dror, the specific characteristic of planning is that it deals with "a set of decisions[:] i.e., a matrix of interdependent and sequential series of systematically related decisions."[12] Dahl notes that decisions, or choices, are accompanied by uncertainty, and describes planning as the effort to increase understanding, or to reduce uncertainty.[13] Finally, Herbert Simon has suggested that, beyond reducing uncertainty, planning is aimed at providing "images," or ideas and increased choices, for consideration by decision-makers.[14]

Taken together, these views provide several distinctions between planning and decision-making: planning ordinarily precedes decision-making (although it is certainly true that one must decide to plan, just as one must plan to plan); planning specifically considers the future; planning attempts to be systematic and comprehensive by dealing with a set or series of decisions; and planning supports decision-making through the provision of information and ideas. Planning, then, is an effort to widen the range of available information and choices to be considered by the decision-maker, while decision-making narrows the range through choosing among alternatives.

Another process closely related to both planning and decision-making is policy analysis. Like planning, policy analysis seems to be an activity undertaken in support of decision-making, particularly in support of decisions about policies. One observer has defined policy analysis as "the systematic investigation of alternative policy options and the assembly and integration of the evidence for and against each option."[15] In his landmark article urging a wide role for policy analysts in government, Yehezkel Dror indicated that "the aim of policy analysis is to permit improvements in decision-making and policy-making by permitting fuller consideration of a broader set of alternatives, within a wider context, with the help of more systematic tools."[16] Both descriptions are quite similar to descriptions of planning. However, to one highly regarded and close observer, Allen Schick, "in practice, policy analysis tends to be social science opportunistically applied to the issues of the day."[17]

On the whole, there seem to be three primary differences between policy analysis and planning. First, policy analysis is generally more concerned with a single policy or decision than with comprehensiveness.[18] Also, although policy analysis is concerned with decreasing uncertainty through the provision of valid information, it is not greatly concerned with the development of new ideas and choices: it is focused on determining the effects of present or proposed policies. Finally, policy analysis is not as emphatically concerned with future considerations as is planning. Like planning, policy analysis is essentially aimed at supporting and improving decisions, but the scope and promise of its efforts are more limited. Whereas planning has analysis as but one of its components, policy analysis is more "analycentric."[19]

Perhaps the most general form of analytic activity is problem-solving, another process related to planning. Simon has described problem-solving as "basically a form of means-end analysis that aims at discovering a process description of the path that leads to a desired goal."[20] Viewed thus, problem-solving is an organizing concept for a cluster of analytic and inventive behaviors such as policy analysis, systems analysis, applied research and development, and design. Like policy analysis, problem-solving is only a component of planning. Again, planning's orientation toward the future and its concern for comprehensiveness distinguish it from narrower analytic strategies, including problem-solving.

Another set of analytic strategies related to planning includes cost-benefit analysis, systems analysis, operations research, and management science. These are largely techniques that might be used in the course of policy analysis, problem-solving, or planning. The techniques strive to identify the alternative that will maximize efficiency, provide the optimal solution for a problem, or otherwise yield the most desirable benefits in relation to costs. Cost-benefit analysis is distinguished by its emphasis on economic welfare and utility and its reliance on the competitive market; systems analysis focuses on the functioning of whole systems rather than on alternatives and their relationships to particular objectives.[21] Operations research and management science are mathematically sophisticated approaches to determining which alternatives would maximize the attainment of clearly specified objectives. All these analytic techniques might well be undertaken as part of the planning process, but planning includes much more, including the generation of alternatives, an explicit orientation to the future, and coordination of related decisions.

Two processes intertwined with planning in the governmental and organizational setting are programming and budgeting. Programming involves the implementation of the ideas, designs, and decisions generated through the planning process. Budgeting is the allocation and timely consumption of resources throughout the organization. Programming and budgeting are intended to assist in the realization of plans. One indication of the connections among these three processes is that program planning and budget planning are among the major types of planning. Also, these three administrative processes have been formally united in the celebrated and controversial planning-programming-budgeting system (PPBS). Many practical and technical problems have confronted PPBS, but the three processes are obviously interdependent in any systematic and concerted approach to making things happen as we want.

Some of the distinctions between planning and related processes are more easily drawn than others, and many of the labels given to the processes are loosely used. The prison-overcrowding example may provide some clarification. As has been suggested, planning with respect to such a problem might include an analysis of the problem, a search for alternative solutions, an estimate of the effects of the alternatives, an explicit consideration of the future, and a concern for related problems and decisions. All these activities help to increase the information and available choices when the time for decision-making arrives.

Policy anlaysis in such a situation would have a more limited scope. The primary focus of the policy analyst would be to determine what would result from various policy options or, retrospectively, what did result. For example, if a state chose to alter its basic penal policy from incapacitation to reintegration by emphasizing probation, parole, and other forms of community corrections, what would be the result? The policy analyst would also be less interested in the state's description of its penal policy than in its actual practice. The principal end sought through policy analysis is valid knowledge of the relationships among policy, practice, and outcome.

Problem-solving in this situation would involve searching for the best solution to the problem of prison overcrowding. The kind of information gained through policy analysis would be needed to evaluate alternatives, but problem-solving would include searching for, designing, or inventing alternative solutions. This approach usually focuses one problem at a time, however, with an immediacy that obscures long-range considerations. The problem-solving approach to prison overcrowding would be likely to ignore related problems in probation, parole, and the courts, and also would tend to produce a solution favorable for the present but perhaps soon outmoded.

A cost-benefit analysis would produce estimates of the costs and benefits, most likely monetary, of the various alternatives suggested for reducing prison overcrowding. A systems analysis would produce a model that attempts to explain how the criminal-justice system works. The model then could be used to predict the consequences of different alternatives. If the objective were, say, to minimize delays between sentencing and incarceration, an operations-research or management-science approach would provide the most efficient solution. (It should be noted that the application of any of these analytic techniques, particularly to complex social problems, involves numerous assumptions that often go unrecognized. This discussion is designed to describe the techniques rather than to evaluate them.[22])

Planning a solution to the problem of prison overcrowding would involve a wide range of activities; the other processes just described, though they aid in the decision-making process, are much narrower in scope. Because of these differences, and on the basis of the definitions and descriptions discussed earlier, it seems reasonable to regard planning as a separate and identifiable activity.

VARIETIES OF PLANNING

There are probably endless varieties of planning, or at least one for every organized form of human activity. Just looking at different major policy areas, we can quickly identify energy planning, economic planning, defense planning, health planning, education planning, welfare planning, criminal justice planning, and on and on. There are, however, some basic divisions among types of planning.

One major division is that between *normative* planning and functional, or *instrumental*, planning.[23] The aim of both varieties is to identify the means that will lead to desired ends, but they differ in other respects. Functional or instrumental planning accepts the ends (goals, values) as given, and submits only the means, or alternatives, to rational analysis. The ends being sought may be defined by higher administrators, by politicians, or by "the people." In any event, the role of the functional planner is to determine how to achieve those goals. The normative planner, however, focuses on ends as well as means. Ends or goals developed outside the planning system are not assumed to be suitable and desirable, but are analyzed and evaluated in much the same way as means. Because the planner is concerned with values as well as with facts, this variety of planning is termed normative.

For several reasons, the distinction between instrumental and normative planning is not, in practice, so clear. First, planning is never value-free, despite the claims sometimes made for instrumental or functional planning. The acceptance of ends from another source or authority is a value-laden act in itself, and choices among means are also based on values. Second, functional planners do not claim to be divorced from the consideration of ends: they would certainly balk at developing means toward heinous or unthinkable ends. Because they do reserve the right to scrutinize the ends of planning, they differ from normative planners only in degree. Third, normative planning is very susceptible to the charge of pursuing its own preferences instead of some notion of social good or public interest; but its focus on ends may take the form of rational analysis, which can then be defended as a traditional scientific process.[24] Inasmuch as the ends of most policies and programs are themselves means toward some larger end,[25] rational analysis and defense of goals may be possible. For example, rational analysis of the consequences of a crime-control program might show that they do not contribute to, or that they may even inhibit, the larger end of justice. Normative planning might expose this situation, whereas instrumental planning probably would not, for it would accept the ends of the crime-control program as given.

This consideration of normative planning, with its concern for values, raises the question of the difference between planning and politics. The means and ends that are the substance of planning are directly involved with the distribution of wealth, status, and influence in society, with who gets what. So planning is inescapably a political endeavor. This does not necessarily imply that planners and politicians do exactly the same things, or that they are similarly motivated. One important difference is that planning attempts to reduce the personal and partisan normativeness that pervades politics. Planning explicitly utilizes reason and analysis in gathering information and developing choices, whereas politics is more concerned with individual and collective preferences as bases for decisions. In addition, "the activity of planning has its center of gravity in the future whereas politics must be concerned with the present."[26] Also, political decisions tend to be disjointed, whereas planning aims to be systematic and comprehensive. In several respects, then, planning behavior and political behavior are distinguishable.

Another important division among varieties of planning is that of *blueprint* and *process* planning.[27] Blueprint planning has as its end-product a *plan*; in process planning the end-product is *planning*. Blueprint planning involves choosing a goal or identifying a problem and developing a plan; then presumably the task is completed. This approach, closely allied with the engineering and architectural perspectives on planning, tends to be frustrated by the failure of people to behave as they should. Blueprint planners are often driven by a desire to produce the perfect design, one that would lead irresistably to the elimination of the problem or the achievement of the goal. Process planning, on the other hand, may never produce a plan at all: it is seen as a continuous learning endeavor, in which feedback is sought and used to adapt means to ever-changing and perhaps unattainable ends or to lessen the severity of problems that cannot be entirely eliminated. Process planning is allied with management and the social sciences, and process planners tend to be very aware of the gap between plan and actual practice.

The domain or jurisdiction of planning activity produces a very significant division among varieties of planning. *Government jurisdictions* include international planning, national planning, state planning, regional planning, county planning, city planning, and neighborhood planning. City planning, in particular, is a very common and distinct variety, and a good deal of the planning literature is focused on it. Three other basic planning domains are the economy, the industry, and the firm. Planning for a firm focuses on a single company; planning for an industry focuses on all those involved in making the same product or providing the same service; planning for the economy focuses on all entities involved in production of goods or services.

A division related to jurisdiction or *scope* particularly crucial to criminal justice is that between system planning and organizational planning. System planning involves collecting information, developing alternatives, forecasting, and otherwise planning for the entire process of criminal justice. This obviously presents difficulties, as the system includes numerous separate agencies, some of which are designed to have adversarial relations with each other, and over all of which there is no single authority. Also, in the typical criminal justice system some agencies are funded through local governments—city and county—while others are funded through the state. Organizational planning, the effort of an individual agency to plan for itself, presents fewer difficulties. The organization is a single entity with a central authority, and it has a clearer purpose and a stronger sense of cooperation than the whole system can have. Of course, the plans of an individual criminal justice agency may conflict with the plans of other agencies, which gives rise to the need for system-wide planning. (System planning and organizational planning will be more fully discussed in Chapters 5 and 6, respectively.)

Yet another important distinction among types of planning stems from the difference in kinds of influence used to translate plans into action. John Friedmann has used this difference to distinguish among *command* planning, *inducement* planning, and *indicative* planning.[28] Command planning utilizes sanctions to compel adherence to specified activities or objectives, and is obviously most appropriate in situations of clear authority. Inducement planning makes use of rewards to encourage adherence to a plan. Inducement planning is often used by the Federal government and state governments in order to encourage localities to follow plans developed in state capitals or in Washington. The third variety, indicative planning, focuses more on process than on plan, and encourages the participation of interested parties in formulating the plan as a means of enlisting their later support and compliance. In place of sanctions or rewards as modes of influence, indicative planning uses participation, persuasion, and negotiation, and the authority behind the planning is essentially advisory.[29] Indicative planning at the national level is particularly associated with France and Japan.

In criminal justice, counterparts of command planning, inducement planning, and indicative planning exist. The Federal LEAA effort, with its carrot-and-stick approach to block grants, was inducement-oriented. The LEAA-funded effort to establish standards and goals was indicative-oriented. Most of the planning undertaken within individual operating agencies and under fairly firm chains of authority is command-oriented.

A final set of planning types derives from the management concerns of objectives, resources, and activities. Although the objectives of a public agency are sometimes mandated by law or higher authority, frequently they are not, or they may be so vague as to yield little direction. In all these instances, planning activity may be undertaken in order to collect information, to develop alternatives, to forecast, and so on. An organization also must determine what resources it will need, and must provide for their acquisition and use. The principal varieties of resource planning include *fiscal planning*, *physical planning* (facilities, equipment, and so on), and *manpower planning*. Lastly, an organization must plan how to utilize its resources in order to attain its objectives. These kinds of planning go by such names as *operational planning*, *tactical planning*, *program planning*, *policy planning*, and *procedural planning*.

LEVEL AND RANGE OF PLANNING

Distinctions are usually drawn among levels of planning, and between long-range and short-range planning. Basically, distinctions based on level reflect the extent to which planning focuses on the purpose and mission of the organization rather than on the implementation of actions mandated by others. The distinction between short-range and long-range planning reflects the degree to which planning is oriented toward the future—and how distant that future is.

The level and range of planning within an organization varies according to the level in the organization at which the planning is undertaken. A planner's level within the organization is probably the major determinant of the type of planning he will do.

The relationship between the organizational level of the planner and types of planning, as described by McFarland for business planning, is presented in Table 2-1. The classification scheme in Table 2-1 is based on a number of variables or dimensions. The first is detail, concreteness, or specificity: planning that takes place at the top levels of the organization is more general in focus than that which takes place at the bottom levels. Another variable is scope: top-level planning deals with the broad missions and general strategies of the organization; lower-level planning deals with segments or aspects of those missions and strategies. A third variable is time-span: top management is most concerned with long-range planning; lower-level management deals with shorter-range planning.

Higher-level long-range planning, concerned with utilizing resources and designing activities in order to achieve objectives, is usually termed strategic planning (as discussed in Chapter 1). It includes efforts to determine what objectives are to be pursued, and how best to pursue them. Strategic planning is thus "concerned with anticipating events, making diagnoses, and shaping appropriate courses of action."[30] In a sense, the purpose of strategic planning is to place the organization in a position consistently to attain basic missions and to respond effectively to contingencies as they develop.

Strategic planning is usually distinguished from tactical or operational planning, which is shorter-range, narrower in scope, and focused mainly on activities and their implementation.[31] Tactical or operational planning essentially takes place within the context and constraints established by strategic planning. Strategic planning sets the stage, whereas tactical or operational planning is concerned with performing, as it were, the roles and script.[32]

This discussion has examined several varieties of planning. Some of the more important distinctions among them are summarized in Table 2-2.

In this discussion of varieties of planning and of related processes, several themes have emerged. Each variety of planning is aimed at developing images and information designed to improve decision-making, and planning is distinguished from similar activities by its concern

Table 2-1. Types of Planning Undertaken at Different Levels in Organizations

Level of Organization	Types of Planning
Top Management	Goals, policies, long-range plans, company-wide sphere
Middle Management	Quotas, programs, supplementary goals, policies
Supervisory Management	Projects, schedules, short-range goals, supplementary policies, operational planning
Nonmanagerial Employees	Limited to work routines and minor procedures

From Dalton E. McFarland, *Management: Principles and Practices*, 3rd ed. (New York: Macmillan Publishing Co., 1970), p. 149.

Table 2-2. Summary of Varieties of Planning

Varieties	Key Differences
Normative vs. Functional	In normative planning, both ends and means are subjected to analysis; in functional planning, ends are accepted as given.
Blueprint vs. Process	"The plan" is the end-product of blueprint planning; the planning process itself is the end-product of process planning.
System vs. Organization	System planning is concerned with a set of organizations over which there may be no single authority; organizational planning involves one entity usually with central authority.
Command vs. Inducement vs. Indicative	Command planning relies on sanctions; inducement planning relies on rewards; indicative planning relies on persuasion and participation.
Objectives vs. Resources vs. Activities	These correspond to the three basic commodities management deals with and must plan for.
Long-Range vs. Short-Range	These refer to how far into the future forecasts are made and how long-term the effects of a plan or decision will be.
Strategic vs. Tactical	Strategic planning is longer-range, general, and concerned with what objectives should be and how they can be attained; tactical planning focuses on detail and the implementation of activities.

for comprehensiveness and for the future. One important question, however, has not yet been directly addressed: Why plan?

JUSTIFICATIONS OF PLANNING

The justification of planning rests upon several assumptions, the most basic of which have been identified by John Seeley, who notes that the orientation of planning toward the future "presupposes that it is in some sense 'open'—that is, that actions, in some sense free, in 'this now' affect 'that then.' "[33] Planning assumes that man has some freedom to choose, that the future is not completely determined. These assumptions may seem obvious, but in some cultures they are not, and there planning is seriously hindered.[34]

Planning also presupposes that the future can be influenced in intended ways, and it assumes some agreement on ends, and some knowledge and skill in the manipulation of means. Seeley has argued, however, that agreement on ends is not actually a prerequisite for planning.

> It must also be believed—if planning is to be justified—that acts now are able to affect acts, conditions, or situations then, in the respects men care about; that is, that we are capable by action now of affecting the net amount of good in the world then. . . . I wish to leave open here an alternative: that, although we do not

know what is good (even with sufficient clarity for this purpose), we do know what is evil, and might aim at a sensible net diminution of evils then by our acts of planning now.[35]

This justification of planning is important, because conflicts and dissension and the inability to articulate a common or public interest are sometimes cited as proving the folly of planning.[36] Seeley's argument that we can at least agree on what we don't like is pleasing to many planners, whose experience often has been that goal-oriented planning bogs down in acrimonious debate over goals, whereas problem-oriented planning is more likely to proceed to fruition—for which reason, perhaps, a recent LEAA publication explicitly recommended the problem-oriented approach.[37] For such controversial topics as crime and criminal justice, agreement is more likely on evils to be avoided than on an ideal good to be achieved.

Once the basic assumptions are accepted, the justification of planning rests primarily on the value of the information it produces—information on where we are, where we want to be (or at least what we want to eliminate or avoid), and how we can get there. Skjei has described information as "the lever by which the likelihood of a gap between goals and achievements is reduced."[38] Information can reduce uncertainty and lead to improved decisions.

For information to have these effects, though, it must be good, and it must be used. Our best information has to do with where we are, but often we have difficulty defining and locating problems.[39] Information about where we want to go is usually rendered vague, by dissension and conflicting goals, and by our ineptness at "imagining the future."[40] And information about how goals might be achieved or problems eliminated is probably least developed. Four observations presented several years ago by Alice Rivlin summarize this situation:

1. Considerable progress has been made in identifying and measuring social problems in our society.
2. Systematic analysis has improved our knowledge of the distribution of the initial costs and benefits of social-action programs.
3. Little progress has been made in comparing the benefits of different social-action programs.
4. Little is known about how to produce more effective health, education, and other social services.[41]

For planning to be justified, it must produce information of value to decision-making, and it is also necessary that the information produced be put to some use. Certainly a common complaint is that planning has no effect on decisions.[42] Of course, most decisions, particularly in the public sector, involve important questions of values and thus cannot be determined solely by planning or with objective information. It is important to realize, too, that information produced by planning is sometimes used indirectly, affecting the decision-maker's view and understanding of the world, and the kinds of solutions he considers.[43]

An important consideration in the justification of planning is the cost involved. For planning to be justified, the improvement in decision-making must exceed in value the costs of the planning endeavor. Such a determination must take into consideration the opportunity costs of planning. These costs represent what could have been accomplished if the resources invested in planning had been invested in some other activity. This economic perspective is a helpful one but, as Moore notes, its application is somewhat difficult:

> Information should be processed until the marginal benefits of the information are just equal to the marginal costs of collecting and managing the information;. . . however, the decision about the proper level of information collection is a difficult one because, without a knowledge of what the information will reveal, its value is uncertain.[44]

The basic justification of planning, however, rests on the belief that the future can be affected in intended ways, and that agreement on goals to be achieved, or at least evils to be avoided, is possible. It is very difficult to know in advance of planning how much planning would be economically optimal. A retrospective evaluation of a planning effort would include questions about the validity of the information produced and the uses to which that information was put. It would be short-sighted to recognize only direct, instrumental uses of information as indicators of success or utilization. The consequences of planning are often much more diffuse and indirect, and any evaluation of planning, or inquiry into its justification, would necessarily have to consider these indirect effects.

PLANNING THEORY

Probably no topic in the literature of planning has generated as much attention and controversy, or as little clarification or agreement, as planning theory. One recent series of articles in the principal planning journal was introduced in the following way:

> We have always been unsure about planning theory. We have argued whether there could be a theory of planning, what form it would take, and how it would relate to practice. We have never resolved these issues to the satisfaction of our professional community or even to the satisfaction of those, mainly in planning education, who worry about the state of theory in planning.[45]

Basically, a planning theory would answer unambiguously a few simple (or seemingly simple) questions about planning: What is it? What do planners do? How do they do it?[46] Planners and planning educators want this kind of straightforward explanation so that they can better understand their roles and how to perform them, and also so that they can explain to others what they do. In his article, "If Planning is Everything, Maybe It's Nothing,"[47] Aaron Wildavsky illustrated with an anecdote the kind of skepticism with which many people regard planning:

> Once I was asked to head up a new long-range planning effort. My wife listened to my glowing description of my new job. Next evening she blew the whole schmeer out of the water by asking: "What did you plan today, dear?"[48]

One difficulty in making sense of planning theory is that several different kinds of investigations have been so labelled. Friedmann and Hudson identified four major traditions, or categories, in planning thought and theory.[49] One they labelled *philosophical synthesis*, which included the development of definitions and varieties of planning. This approach to planning theory is most concerned with a basic question: What is planning? A second tradition was *rationalism*, which has its basis in economic and decision theory. It addresses a primary question: How do we figure out the most efficient thing to do? A third tradition is *organization development*, which deals with planning "not as an intellectual process of efficiently adapting means to given ends, but as primarily a method for inducing organizational change."[50] The final tradition identified is *empiricism*, or the study of how planning is practiced in the real world. This approach addresses several questions: How is planning done? What do planners do?

These, then, are the central themes of planning theory, and the directions it has taken. In an attempt to impose coherence and structure on this diversity, Richard Bolan has described what he terms the "planning theory terrain."[51] He suggests that planning be viewed from two basic perspectives: as a thinking process, and as a social process. The thinking, or cognitive, perspective is composed of ways of understanding the past and present, ways of imagining the future, and ways of achieving the future. The social perspective is composed of a substantive framework of things and relations, a cultural framework of ideas and norms, an institutional framework of control and order, and a psychological framework of behavior and stimuli. Using these two perspectives as perpendicular axes, Bolan creates a twelve-cell matrix that "maps the planning theory terrain" (see Figure 2-1).

Bolan's mapping exercise is not itself a planning theory, but Bolan goes beyond simply designating the terrain of planning theory by evaluating the state of knowledge and skill with respect to the cognitive and social perspectives on planning:

> From a cognitive perspective, we have developed the strongest understanding of the past and present, although much of that understanding still must be viewed as surface knowledge rather than knowledge in depth. While we have been inventive in ways to imagine the future, our efforts to give it a technical or rigorous cast have boomeranged to some extent. Our understanding of ways to achieve the future is the least developed and is marked largely by normative views about what we think ought to take place when we implement plans.
>
> From a social perspective, we seem to have learned to most understand the objective world of things and the institutional framework of control and order. In the areas of understanding behavior and value systems we are most defi-

Figure 2-1. Outline of Mapping Categories for Planning Theory Terrain (From Richard S. Bolan, "Mapping the Planning Theory Terrain," *Urban and Social Change Review*, 8 [1975], 37.)

Social Perspective / Time Cognitive Perspective	Substantive Framework of Things and Relations	Cultural Frameowrk of Ideas and Norms	Institutional Framework of Control and Order	Psycholgical Framework of Behavior and Behavioral Stimuli
Ways of understanding the past and present	Basic physical and social sciences Architecture Engineering Economics Demography Geography Sociology	History Ethics Jurisprudence Theology Culture Fashion	Political theory Administrative theory Institutional structure Judicial precedent Administrative rules and regulations	Personality development Conditioning Transactional analysis Small group behavior Political behavior Environmental psychology
Ways of imagining the future	Straight-line extrapolation Incremental-marginal analysis Predictive modeling Systems theory Game theory Decision theory	Utopian constructs Master planning Futuristics	Organizational development Allocative planning Innovative planning Scientific management Temporary society	Behavior modification Market research Political voting research Behavioral technology
Ways of achieving the future	Persuasion by force of reason and rationality	Ideological indoctrination Ideological revolution	Coercion Regulation and rule-making Power elite strategies Institutional change strategies Conflict strategies	Communication and diffusion strategies Education and learning strategies Participation and exchange strategies

cient. We can create buildings, corporations, and bureaucracies, but we have little understanding of how these creations take their toll on culture and values or on the private world of man's mind.[52]

Bolan signals, as do Friedmann and Hudson, an awakening recognition that planning is more than just an intellectual or thinking process. Bolan's social perspective on planning introduces several action- and value-oriented considerations. The planning tradition of organizational change discussed by Friedmann and Hudson is oriented toward inducing change. These perspectives certainly go well beyond the more traditional view of planning as cognitive activity aimed at producing valid and objective information for the improvement of decisions.

A good representative of the traditional approach to planning is the choice theory proposed in 1962 by Davidoff and Reiner.[53] It is based on the proposition that planning is a process or set of procedures that can be divorced from any particular substantive issue under consideration. The common element in transportation planning, health planning, criminal justice planning, and economic planning is the planning process. Three levels of choices constitute that process: the selection of ends or goals; the identification and selection of means for achieving those goals; and the effectuation, or the guidance, of action. The theory also includes a set of postulates about the environment, the purposes, and the characteristics of planning. Because they comprise one of the most complete yet brief descriptions of the traditional approach to planning, these postulates are presented in their entirety:

Planning Environment

1. Individuals have preferences and behave in accordance with them. Actors are to some extent able to order their preferences.

2. Actors vary in their preferences.

3. Goods are produced and services, including labor, are performed subject to the constraint that diminishing returns set in at a given level.

4. Resources are scarce and consequently output is limited.

5. The entity for which planning is undertaken will typically consist of interrelated parts generally in flux.

6. Man operates with imperfect knowledge. He also is often illogical (by formal canons), as where his preferences are not transitive, or where his several values, at least at the levels at which he perceives them, are in conflict with each other.

Planning Purposes

1. Efficiency and rational action: in a world of scarcity there is a need to conserve resources and also to allocate them in an efficient manner.

2. Market aid or replacement: planning would be of little, if any, use for an environment where an open, fully competitive market (either political or economic) operated perfectly.

3. Change or widening of choice: given scarcities, social and individual choices must be made about the manner in which resources are to be allocated; how, when, to whom, to what purpose, and in what combination.

Planning Characteristics

1. The achievement of ends: planning incorporates a concept of a purposive process keyed to preferred, ordered ends.

2. Exercise of choice: as the characteristic intellectual act of planning.

3. Orientation to the future: time is a valued and depletable resource consumed in effecting any end.

4. Action: planning is employed to bring about results.

5. Comprehensiveness: in order to allow decision-makers to choose rationally among alternative programs, the planner must detail fully the ramifications of proposals.[54]

In this traditional approach to planning, the roles of the planner and the decision-maker are clearly separated. Among the varieties of planning discussed earlier, the choice theory and other traditional approaches describe functional or instrumental planning, in which planners search for means to attain goals already determined. In contrast, the organizational-change tradition in planning theory is frankly normative. The roles of the planner and the decision-maker are less distinct, and planning is more a social act than a cognitive one. Aids and obstacles to change are the principal components of the planning environment for this approach.

A view of planning now emerges that is, in some respects, between these traditional and change approaches and between functional and narrowly normative planning. This emerging view of planning mirrors more general recent developments in the social sciences, and draws upon critical theory and phenomenology for theoretical support.[55] The philosophical debate is much too complex to cover here satisfactorily,[56] but some of its implications for planning theory can be suggested.[57]

In this emerging view, planning is more than a technical fitting of means to consensual goals or ends. In fact, one of the primary functions of the planner is to attempt to develop agreement on the ends to be pursued. How does the planner do this? What planners actually do is to interact and communicate with other people, through various media. By talking, listening, negotiating, and explaining, planners "help people bring together the objective facts of a situation and their subjective feelings about themselves in the situation."[58] The planners work with people to reach shared understandings of where they are, how they got there, where they would like to be, and what alternative means are available for getting there.

One of the key ideas underlying this approach is that the traditional, empirical approach yields only superficial information about human behavior. Empirical social science has sought to describe and to explain by focusing purely on behavior. Behavior is visible and, by focusing on it, social science could emulate the supposed objectivity of the natural and physical sciences. In empiricism, "when we explain an action we describe it; we say what it is."[59] More recently, however, the view has developed in the social sciences that behavior can have many meanings that are missed or incorrectly interpreted by pure empiricists or be-

Table 2-3. Three Views of Planning

	Instrumental Model	Social Change Model	Critical or Phenomenological Model
What is planning?	Technical activity	Social activity	Moral activity
What do planners do?	Act as analysts	Act as change agents	Act as communicators
How do they do it?	Use the scientific method to explain human behavior	Use strategies designed to induce change	Use language to understand human behavior

Adapted in part from George C. Hemmens, "New Directions in Planning Theory: Introduction," *Journal of the American Planning Association* (July 1980), 250-60.

haviorists. It has become increasingly clear that the intentions underlying behavior are important, and that these intentions can be learned only through communication. Rather than merely explaining or describing behavior, this approach seeks to understand it. The difference, according to Hemmens, is that "when we understand an action we know why it was done; we say what it is for."[60]

Traditional planning is based on traditional, empirical social science. The traditional planner is one who conducts empirical analysis in support of decision-making. The phenomenological and critical approaches to planning, however, emphasize communication and interaction. In this approach, the principal tool of the planner is language, rather than research or design techniques. And, "in the final analysis, the professional can be seen as a *moral* agent—not a purely instrumental problem-solver."[61]

The various views of planning are summarized in Table 2-3. Whether these three views can be encompassed by any one planning theory remains to be seen, but it is more important to realize that these different and competing conceptions of planning exist than it is to design some grand theory incorporating them. There are several different ways of describing, explaining, and understanding what is known as planning. Those who have worked as planners, or who have had planning as a major responsibility in a job, would probably argue that each view of planning has some merit, and that some combination of them will be needed to elaborate a definitive planning theory. Implicit in the rest of the discussion of planning will be a combination of these views.

SUMMARY

Planning precedes decision and action and is a preparation for them. It involves explicit consideration of the future and of related decisions and actions. These characteristics distinguish planning from policy analysis, decision-making, problem-solving, and other processes, although these various activities are all interrelated.

The varieties of planning discussed included normative and instrumental; blueprint and process; system and organizational; and command, inducement, and indicative. Distinctions were drawn between long-range and short-range planning, between strategic and tactical planning. Attention was also given to the justification of planning, and to the difficult questions of whether to plan, when to plan, and how much to invest in planning.

The chapter concluded with a discussion of planning theory, which provides the framework for answers to such questions as what is planning? what do planners do? how do they do it? Several major traditions in planning theory were presented, as well as the "terrain" that planning theory must cover. The debate over planning theory demonstrates the lack of consensus on such fundamental issues as the nature and functions of planning.

· *Chapter 2* ·
NOTES

1. Aaron Wildavsky, "If Planning is Everything, Maybe It's Nothing," *Policy Sciences*, 4 (1973), 127–53.

2. Robert A. Dahl, "The Politics of Planning," *International Social Science Journal*, 11 (1959), 340.

3. Ibid.

4. John Friedmann, "The Study and Practice of Planning," *International Social Science Journal*, 11 (1959), 327–28.

5. John Friedmann, "A Conceptual Model for the Analysis of Planning Behavior," *Administrative Science Quarterly* (1967), 227.

6. David W. Ewing, *Long-Range Planning for Management* (New York: Harper & Row, Publishers, 1964).

7. Andreas Faludi, "The Planning Environment and the Meaning of Planning," *Regional Studies*, 4 (1970), 8.

8. John Friedmann and Barclay Hudson, "Knowledge and Action: A Guide to Planning Theory," *Journal of the American Institute of Planners*, 42 (January 1974), 2.

9. John W. Dyckman, "Planning and Decision Theory," *Journal of the American Institute of Planners*, 29 (1961), 335–45.

10. C. West Churchman, *The Systems Approach* (New York: Dell Publishing Company, 1968), p. 150.

11. Abraham Kaplan, "On the Strategy of Social Planning," *Policy Sciences*, 4 (1973), 44–45.

12. Yehezkel Dror, "The Planning Process: A Facet Design," *International Review of Administrative Sciences*, 29 (1963), 51.

13. Dahl, op. cit., p. 340.

14. Herbert A. Simon, "Decision-Making and Planning," in Harvey Perloff, ed., *Planning and the Urban Community* (Pittsburgh: University of Pittsburgh, 1961), p. 192.

15. Jacob B. Ukeles, "Policy Analysis: Myth or Reality?" *Public Administration Review* (May/June 1977), 223.

16. Yehezkel Dror, "Policy Analysts: A New Professional Role in Government Service," *Public Administration Review* (September 1967), 202.

17. Allen Schick, "Beyond Analysis," *Public Administration Review* (May/June 1977), 261.

18. John W. Dyckman, "New Normative Styles in Urban Studies," *Public Administration Review*, 31 (May/June 1971), 327–34.

19. Schick, op. cit, p. 259.

20. Herbert A. Simon, *The Sciences of the Artificial* (Cambridge, Ma.: Massachusetts Institute of Technology, 1969), p. 112.

21. Aaron Wildavsky, "The Political Economy of Efficiency: Cost-Benefit Analysis, Systems Analysis, and Program Budgeting," *Public Administration Review* (December 1966), 292–310.

22. For evaluative views of these techniques, see Alice M. Rivlin, *Systematic Thinking for Social Action* (Washington, D.C.: The Brookings Institution, 1971); Ida R. Hoos, "Systems Techniques for Managing Society: A Critique," *Public Administration Review* (March/April 1973), 157–64; Robert B. Reich. "Operations Research and Criminal Justice," *Journal of Public Law* (1974), 357–87; and Wildavsky, 1966, op. cit.,

23. Faludi, op. cit.; and Richard E. Klosterman, "Foundations for Normative Planning," *Journal of the American Institute of Planners*, (January 1978), 37–46.

24. See Martin Rein, *Social Science and Public Policy* (Middlesex, England: Penguin Books, 1976), for a discussion of the analysis of goals and values.

25. Herbert A. Simon, *Administrative Behavior*, 3rd ed. (New York: The Free Press, 1976), pp. 61–66.

26. Basil Dimitriou, "The Interpenetration of Politics and Planning," *Socio-Economic Planning Sciences*, 7 (1973), 64.

27. Faludi, op. cit.

28. Friedmann, 1967, op. cit.

29. Otis L. Graham, Jr., "Planning the Soiety," *The Center Magazine*, 10 (May/June 1977), 8–14.

30. Charles M. Mottley, "Strategic Planning," in Fremont J. Lyden and Ernest G. Miller, eds., *Planning-Programming-Budgeting: A Systems Approach to Management*, 2nd ed. (Chicago: Rand McNally & Company, 1973), p. 125.

31. See Burt Nanus, "A General Model for Criminal Justice Planning," *Journal of Criminal Justice*, 2 (1974), 345–56; Daniel Glaser, *Strategic Criminal Justice Planning* (Rockville, Md: National Institute of Mental Health, 1975); and Don C. Gibbons, *et al.*, *Criminal Justice Planning: An Introduction* (Englewood Cliffs, N.J.: Prentice-Hall, Inc., 1977), pp. 73–74.

32. Glaser, op. cit.

33. John R. Seeley, "What is Planning? Definition and Strategy," *Journal of the American Institute of Planners*, 28 (May 1962), 93.

34. Friedmann, 1959, op. cit.; Faludi, op. cit.

35. Seeley, op. cit., p. 94.

36. See Richard E. Klosterman, "A Public Interest Criterion," *Journal of the American*

Planning Association (July 1980), 323-33, for a recent review of these arguments and a rebuttal.

37. Robert C. Cushman, *Criminal Justice Planning for Local Governments* (Washington, D.C.: U.S. Department of Justice, Law Enforcement Assistance Administration, National Institute of Law Enforcement and Criminal Justice, 1980).

38. Stephen S. Skjei, "Urban Problems and the Theoretical Justification of Urban Planning," *Urban Affairs Quarterly*, 11 (1976), 333.

39. Horst W. J. Rittel and Melvin M. Webber, "Dilemmas in a General Theory of Planning," *Policy Sciences*, 4 (1973), 155–69.

40. Richard S. Bolan, "Mapping the Planning Theory Terrain," *Urban and Social Change Review*, 8 (1975), 35–43.

41. Rivlin, op. cit., p. 7.

42. See Ewing, op. cit.; Murray L. Weidenbaum and A. Bruce Rozet, *Potential Industrial Adjustments to Shifts in Defense Spending* (Menlo Park, Calif.: Stanford Research Institute, 1963); and Robert J. Mockler, *Business Planning and Policy Formulation* (New York: Appleton-Century-Crofts, 1972).

43. David K. Cohen and Michael S. Garet, "Reforming Educational Policy with Applied Social Research," *Harvard Educational Review*, 45 (February 1975), 17–43.

44. Terry Moore, "Why Allow Planners to Do What They Do? A Justification from Economic Theory," *Journal of the American Institute of Planners*, 44 (October 1978), 396.

45. George C. Hemmens, "New Directions in Planning Theory: Introduction," *Journal of the American Planning Association* (July 1980), 259.

46. Ibid.

47. Wildavsky, 1973, op. cit.

48. Robert Townsend, *Up the Organization* (New York: Alfred A. Knopf, Inc., 1970), p. 146.

49. Friedmann and Hudson, op. cit.

50. Ibid., p. 10.

51. Bolan, op. cit.

52. Ibid., p. 41.

53. Paul Davidoff and Thomas A. Reiner, "A Choice Theory of Planning," *Journal of the American Institute of Planners*, 30 (May 1962), 103–15.

54. Ibid. Reprinted by permission of the *Journal of the American Institute of Planners.*

55. See Richard S. Bolan, "The Practitioner as Theorist: The Phenomenology of the Professional Episode," *Journal of the American Planning Association* (July 1980), 264–74; and John Forester, "Critical Theory and Planning Practice," *Journal of the American Planning Association* (July 1980), 275–86.

56. See Richard J. Bernstein, *The Restructuring of Social and Policital Theory* (New York: Harcourt Brace Jovanovich, Inc., 1976).

57. Much of the following discussion is based on Hemmens, op. cit.

58. Ibid., p. 259.

59. Ibid., p. 260.

60. Ibid., p. 260.

61. Bolan, 1980, op. cit., p. 273.

• Chapter 3 •

THE PLANNING PROCESS

The focus of this chapter is on the *process of planning,* or the steps that are undertaken when one plans. We will first examine the idealized rational planning process, which is a model of how we "ought" to plan if we were solely interested in achieving our goals, and had no significant constraints on our planning activity. Then we will examine a variety of factors that limit rational planning in the "real world." After that, we will examine more closely how the context of planning influences the planning process. Finally, we will examine a revised model of planning that incorporates the rational ideal, the real-world limitations, and the contextual determinants. This chapter is an introduction to the process of planning; the key stages in that process will be discussed more thoroughly in Part III.

RATIONAL PLANNING

Few people would argue that rationality is undesirable in human behavior, but there is confusion over the meaning of the term. If a student goes to college for the purpose of having a good time, for example, and succeeds but at the expense of not graduating, was his behavior rational? If a judge who gives priority to reintegration grants probation to a convicted armed robber who then commits further felonies while on probation, was the judge's behavior rational? If a police officer thinks he sees a life-threatening situation and shoots a burglary suspect, only to discover that the burglar was twelve years old and his "weapon" a battery-operated drill, was the officer's behavior rational?

In an important sense, the behavior in each of these three examples may have been rational. Generally speaking, rational behavior is that most likely to attain the purposes or objectives of the act. Thus the question of rationality must always be considered in relation to intended achievements, and to the system of values pertinent to the behavior. The rationality of the student, the judge, and the police officer would have to be evaluated according to how far their chosen behaviors led to, or could reasonably have been expected to lead to, desired consequences.

The three examples also illustrate some situational variants of rational behavior. The judge and the police officer intended to act rationally, although the results their behavior achieved were not those they desired. The student achieved his goal and thus had acted rationally, although his behavior might be regarded as short-sighted and his choice of goals unwise. Writing specifically about rationality in decision-making, Herbert Simon argued that the term *rational* should probably always be preceded or accompanied by an appropriate adverb. He identified several varieties of rationality in decision-making.

> [A] decision may be called "objectively" rational if *in fact* it is the correct behavior for maximizing given values in a given situation. It is "subjectively" rational if it maximizes attainment relative to the actual knowledge of the subject. It is "consciously" rational to the degree that the adjustment of means to ends is a conscious process. It is "deliberately" rational to the degree that the adjustment of means to ends has been deliberately brought about (by the individual or by the organization). A decision is "organizationally" rational if it is oriented to the organization's goals; it is "personally" rational if it is oriented to the individual's goals.[1]

Idealized versions of purely rational planning (see the discussion of Eddison's views in Chapter 1), set a standard of objective rationality. They purport to describe how the planner can assure optimal achievement of desired goals. At the least, they can deliver subjective rationality, or maximum achievement given less than perfect knowledge. Some other observers are not quite so optimistic, however, and suggest limitations beyond subjective rationality.

A Simple Method

Rational decision-making or planning primarily involves the manipulation of means and ends. Ends are goals, objectives, or purposes; means are alternatives, plans, or strategies. Objective rationality requires the implementation of those means that most completely accomplish or attain a chosen end.

For example, one "end" mandated by the U.S. Supreme Court for state and local judicial systems is effective legal representation for indigent criminal defendants. In order to achieve this end, any of several means might be adopted. A lawyer from the rolls of the local bar association might be assigned to such defendants; the services of a legal-aid society might be purchased with public funds; or a government agency might be established to represent impoverished defendants. Objective rationality would require the implementation of that alternative which would most completely attain the goal of effective representation of the indigent.

An Expanded Model

Although the manipulation of means and ends is at the heart of rational action, things are a bit more complicated than this simple model suggests. This is particularly the case with rational *planning* and its special concern for the future and for coordination. The eight-stage planning process termed the modern-classical model by Rittel and Webber provides a more detailed look at the requirements of rationality:

1. Continuously searching out goals
2. Identifying problems
3. Forecasting uncontrollable contextual changes
4. Inventing alternative strategies, tactics, actions
5. Simulating alternative and plausible actions and consequences
6. Evaluating alternatively forecasted outcomes
7. Statistically monitoring germane conditions
8. Feeding back information to simulation and decision channels[2]

The first step in this planning process, continuously searching our goals, recognizes that ends are not obvious, and that they change. For example, when the Supreme Court first made the right to free counsel widely applicable in the state courts, it said only that legal assistance was a necessity for those charged with serious crimes.[3] Until further cases came along, local and state officials had to interpret whether the goal actually was legal counsel for all felony defendants or only for serious felony defendants, legal counsel for all criminal defendants or only for those facing incarceration. Also, the goal changed over time. Free legal counsel, once not required at all, was then required in capital cases, later required for a confusing class of special circumstances, still later required in all serious cases, and finally required in all criminal trials.

Although this example shows that ends are neither static nor always obvious, it still greatly understates the complexity of goal-related planning. In this situation, the Supreme Court provided the goal, although state and local planners had to interpret it and to monitor its changes. Often, planners must actively *search* for goals, as is the case for city planners, who must seek out the goals that are to guide their plans and decisions about transportation, economic development, housing, recreation, and similar matters. Because the goals to be sought are not automatically defined for the planner, the modern-classical model refers to "searching out goals," and because these ends may change, the search is described as continuous.

The second step in the planning process, identifying problems, serves to measure the present against the desired future. When goals have been discovered or determined, it does not follow that painstaking planning is required. Until goals have been compared with present conditions, the planner does not know whether there is a "problem." If the present conditions are such that the goal is completely attained, then means for attaining it are not required.

When the U.S. Supreme Court established the goal of free legal counsel for the indigent, the states had to compare this goal with prevailing conditions. Many states were already providing counsel to indigent defendants who faced serious charges, and so these states had no "problem" that needed to be solved. Other states were confronted with a discrepancy between prevailing conditions and the new Supreme Court mandate, and thus clearly had a problem to resolve.

After the identification of problems, the planning process moves to the forecasting stage, which represents part of planning's explicit orientation toward the future. Described as "the forecasting of uncontrollable contextual changes," this stage calls for an effort to predict what the world outside of the control of the planner or the decision-maker will look like at some point in the future. Decisions and plans are always (by definition) implemented in the future. The aim of the forecast is to identify the characteristics of the future situation or context within which the decisions or plans will be expected to work. This forecast is especially concerned with those characteristics of the future situation that are uncontrollable and that therefore must be adapted to, rather than manipulated.

For example, the states that found discrepancies between current practice and the new right-to-counsel mandate had to develop means for resolving those discrepancies, for attaining the new ends that had been established. Searching for means, they needed to think about the future: a solution that was affordable then might be too costly for public financing two years later; an immediately satisfactory solution—as one that provided counsel only for felony defendants—might be clearly insufficient for even the near future, given the expanding scope of due process and of the concept of the right to counsel. (This latter example suggests that "uncontrollable contextual changes" can include changes in goals, and that forecasting of goals is an important component of future-oriented planning.)

The next stage in the planning process is the inventing of alternative strategies, tactics, actions. Having searched out goals, compared them to present conditions, and forecast contextual changes, the planner needs to devise different ways of solving the identified problems or of attaining the desired ends. In some instances alternatives may be readily available or obvious; in others, the planner may have to search for them; and in some cases he may actually have to design or invent them. If the planning is to be objectively rational, the alternatives developed must include that alternative that will optimally attain the desired ends.

Among the alternatives that states might have considered to attain the ends mandated by the Supreme Court, for example, were legal-aid societies, a public-defender system, and assignments of lawyers from the local bar association. None of these alternatives had to be invented in 1963 when the Supreme Court issued its landmark decision. States might have found these alternatives in use in some of their own local governments, or in other states. In the quest for rationality, states might also have developed other alternatives, perhaps inventing them or searching for them in out-of-the-way places (among the practices of other countries, for example).

Once alternatives have been found and/or invented, the planner must envision the consequences of implementing each of the alternatives. This stage of the planning process is the simulation of alternative and plausible actions and consequences. With relevant information about the world, and forecasts of uncontrollable contextual changes, the planner has a model (formal or informal) of the situation within which the alternative will be implemented. This model, which may be only in the planner's head, includes hypotheses and theories about important variables, relationships, and, most important, causation. By testing or "simulating" each alternative within the model, the planner learns the probable consequences of each.

At this stage in the planning process, the states faced with the Supreme Court mandate, for example, would have had to test the likely consequences of a legal-aid society, a public-defender office, and appointed counsel from the bar association. If a mathematical model of the judicial system were available, each alternative might be simulated and information about its results collected. Or, as is more likely, information might be sought from other states that had tried the alternatives, and used by knowledgeable people to "think through" the probable effects of the three alternatives.

Once the likely outcomes of the proposed alternatives have been established, the planning process moves to the task of evaluation, a comparison of the probable consequences of each alternative with the specified goals in order to determine which alternative most completely attains the desired ends. That alternative is the preferred or "best" one, and the objectively rational planner or decision-maker will naturally choose that one.

The states, for example, would compare the probable consequences of each alternative—legal aid, a public defender, assigned counsel—to the mandated end of free legal assistance for indigent defendants. If the assumption was made that the quality of legal assistance under each alternative either did not vary or did not matter, then the comparison would primarily focus on the costs of each, and the alternative chosen would be the one that cost least. If the quality of the legal assistance provided under the different alternatives were deemed to be important and variable, then that factor would have to be considered, along with cost, in determining the best alternative.

The modern-classical planning model includes two steps beyond the evaluation of alternatives and choice. The stage of "statistically monitoring germane conditions" is designed to update descriptions of the present state so that forecasting can proceed from accurate information about the present, and so that alternatives can be simulated in as valid as possible a model of the world. The monitoring is also designed to provide specific information about the actual consequences of alternatives chosen and implemented, information valuable not only for later forecasting and simulating but also for immediate mid-course corrections during implementation of the alternative itself. The final stage of the planning process simply provides that the information derived from monitoring be fed back to the appropriate planning and decision-making channels.

For the right-to-counsel planning problem, the monitoring of germane conditions should probably include such things as costs, pretrial delays, conviction and plea rates for indigent and nonindigent defendants, expressed satisfaction or dissatisfaction with the alternative implemented, experiences of other states with the same and other alternatives, new court rulings that impinge on the mandated standard, and similar matters. This kind of information would be helpful both for a general understanding of the judicial system (the context for which the planner needs a model), and for assessment of the effects of the alternative chosen and applied. Also, such monitoring might reveal that the implemented alternative needs immediate alteration. For example, rapidly increasing pretrial delays might indicate inadequate resources in the public defender offices, necessitating more personnel or perhaps the use of assigned counsel from the bar association to supplement the efforts of the public defender.

This modern-classical planning model seems to be a logical and orderly way of attaining rationality. In presenting it, however, we have deliberately played down many of the severe difficulties that one would encounter in trying to carry out such a planning process. It may be the way we *should* plan in order to be objectively, or even subjectively, rational; whether or not we actually *can* plan that way is quite another question.

LIMITATIONS ON THE PLANNING PROCESS

The modern-classical planning model may seem logical and systematic, but for a number of reasons real-world planning behavior does not follow its dictates. For example, the task of continuously searching out goals is extremely difficult: it imposes a very heavy burden of time, energy, and cost, and the assumption that goals are there to be found may not be accurate.

A large part of the problem arises from the difficulty of identifying the "public" whose goal or "interest" is to be served by a plan or a decision. The public is, in fact, a collection of individuals, each of whom has specific interests. Kenneth Arrow demonstrated years ago the impossibility of deriving a community-welfare function or public-interest function from the aggregate of individual preferences.[4] Essentially, he showed that there is no simple or straightforward way of creating a consensual solution out of the competing interests found in any community. Thus, the planner faced with the technical task of finding a hidden common goal in reality confronts the political problem of devising a position that will satisfy a whole host of conflicting individual and group preferences.

Another part of the problem is that the goals of an individual or a group may be internally inconsistent, making conflict even more inevitable. Also, Banfield has argued that the goal-states of public organizations are commonly unclear and complex, and that focusing attention on them is more likely to produce conflict than consensus.[5] Because it is difficult for the planner to identify the goals to be achieved or maximized, it has been suggested that planning and decision-making should be directed toward avoiding specified evils[6] or satisfying a set of constraints[7] rather than toward attaining desired ends.

Goal-related difficulties are very evident in planning in the field of corrections. As noted in Chapter 1, the goals of corrections can be described in several ways, but one common set includes restraint, reform, rehabilitation, and reintegration.[8] The planner is immediately faced with the problem of figuring out how to combine, rank, or otherwise deal with such a complex set of desired ends. Why is this important? Suppose that farther along in the planning process, at the evaluation stage, the planner finds that two competing alternatives have the following probable goal attainment:

	Restraint	Reform	Rehabilitation	Reintegration
Alternative A	90%	10%	10%	10%
Alternative B	60%	20%	20%	20%

The planner will need some basis for choosing between the two alternatives, and the basis will be the relative importance of the four goals. It is not obvious, however, by what method the planner is supposed to determine their relative importance. Such information is not likely to be stated in formal legislative or executive pronouncements, nor is the "public" likely to be of one mind about the goals. The problem is further complicated by the changeableness of public opinion, especially regarding such emotion-charged topics.

Another difficulty is that these goals are, at least in part, contradictory, and progress toward one may preclude progress toward others. The clearest conflict is between restraint, on the one hand, and rehabilitation and reintegration on the other. The achievement of restraint requires emphasis on control, discipline, rule observance and enforcement, bureaucratic staff behavior, and other forms of custodial severity. To achieve rehabilitation or reintegration, however, emphasis must be placed on freedom, dignity, treatment, personal responsibility, professional staff behavior, and generally on minimizing the difference between prison and the outside world.[9] Each of the four goals is associated with a different set of staff roles, change strategies, and punishments.[10] The planner presented with these four goals is not in a very good position to know what ends are actually desired.

The correctional situation provides good examples of planning oriented toward avoiding evils and satisfying constraints rather than toward attaining goals. Two predominant evils that planning and decision-making in this field seek to avoid are escapes and riots. Success is often defined as surviving and avoiding these evils, rather than as achieving any positive goal.[11] The kinds of constraints that must be satisfied include those imposed by budgets, by court-requirements, and by what is really the single dominant goal: restraint or custody. The problem faced by the planner might be formulated as a question: Within the constraints of the budget and of court-required services and amenities, how can escapes and riots be minimized, restraint maximized, and some measure of reform, rehabilitation, and/or reintegration attained?

So far, we have considered only the limitations on the continuous search for goals. Because of the difficulties encountered in specifying goals, the stage of problem identification is also fundamentally altered. With clear goals, identifying problems merely involves comparing desired ends with present states, and noting discrepancies. Without clear goals as a yardstick, however, the process becomes complex and more subjective. Instead of precisely quantified problems such as "Our rockets are providing 10 percent less power than is needed to propel the capsule into orbit," criminal justice planners are more likely to work with hazy problems, such as, "There is too much crime," or, "The police are wasting their time dealing with minor victimless offenses." Although vague notions such as these may reflect public sentiment and point toward problems that need attention, they do not set the stage for systematic rational planning in the same way that very precisely defined problems do.

Rendered difficult by confused or conflicting goals, the identification of problems is also hampered by uncertainty about present conditions. In the ideal planning process, problems are found in the form of discrepancies between desired ends and the present state. In actual practice, we have some vague notions of how we would like things to be, some information—incomplete and of untested validity, about the present state, and the sense that *some*thing isn't just right. Rittel and Webber describe this difficulty: "One of the most intractable problems is that of defining problems (of knowing what distinguishes an observed condition from a desired condition) and of locating problems (finding where in the complex causal networks the trouble really lies)."[12]

The third stage in the modern-classical planning process is the forecasting of uncontrollable contextual changes. Yet our knowledge of the future is even less complete and less sure than our knowledge of the present. As Bolan has pointed out, rigorous prediction of future states has not yet proved very successful.[13] Earlier, Banfield showed that planners are unable to predict the future very far.[14] He noted another consideration with implications for the future-orientation of planning: it is often imprudent, especially for public organizations, to make decisions very far in advance of necessity.

It is at the stage of inventing alternative strategies that the limitations on rational planning usually become most clear. In practice, the search for alternatives is less than completely exhaustive, partly because there are rarely clear goals to guide the search, and partly because there are limitations on time, cost, and human understanding. As Simon originally suggested, although objective rationality requires examination of all possible alternatives, "in actual behavior, only a very few of all these possible alternatives ever come to mind."[15] Also, because the invention of alternatives is costly and time-consuming, only a partial subset of all alternatives will be developed.[16]

These are very important limitations. Ideally, the rational planner would have to consider *every* possible alternative means of resolving a problem or attaining a goal. Because the possible alternatives for any situation are many, if not infinite in number, objective rationality would seem to be rendered impractical.

How does the planning stage of inventing alternatives actually proceed? March and Simon prefer to describe it as a process of search rather than of invention, and describe three principles that guide the identification of alternatives:

1. Those variables that are largely within the control of the problem-solving individual or organizational unit will be considered first. There will be a serious attempt to elaborate a program of activity based on the control of these variables.
2. If a satisfactory program is not discovered by these means, attention will be directed to changing other variables that are not under the direct control of the problem-solvers.
3. If a satisfactory program is still not evolved, attention will be turned to the criteria that the program must satisfy, and an effort will be made to relax these criteria so that a satisfactory program can be found.[17]

These principles indicate that, at some point in the search for alternatives, if a satisfactory one has not been found, the desired goal may be modified so that an alternative can be chosen and implemented. This search process is certainly a far cry from the exhaustive search for optimal attainment required in objective rational planning.

There are also major limitations on the task of simulating the consequences of alternatives. First, only a limited set of possible alternatives will have been identified. Simulating the implementation of these alternatives, in order to predict the probable effects of each, is further and severely constrained by incomplete knowledge. The process of simulation depends on information about present conditions, future states, and, most important, causation. Simulations are based on models or theories about the world and how it changes. But our understanding of the world, and particularly of how and why it changes, is far from complete; thus, unpredictable errors are introduced into the simulation and, without perfect predictions of the consequences of alternatives, the planner cannot be sure of choosing the optimal alternative.

Next in the modern-classical planning model

is the evaluation of the simulated outcomes of each alternative. The evaluation is supposed to involve comparison of likely consequences to desired ends. But the absence of clear goals renders difficult the determination of "best" outcomes—as, for example, in the projected attainment of the correctional aims of restraint, reform, rehabilitation, and reintegration. With so complex a set of goals, each partially attained by the alternatives, the choice of the "best" alternative is very difficult. Rittel and Webber describe the basic dilemma faced by the planner;

> Our point . . . is that diverse values are held by different groups of individuals—that what satisfies one may be abhorrent to another, that what comprises problem-solution for one is problem-generation for another. Under such circumstances, and in the absence of an overriding social theory or an overriding social ethic, there is no gainsaying which group is right and which should have its ends served.[18]

A related implication for evaluation is that alternatives tend to be compared to one another, rather than to desired ends, in the process of identifying the preferred one. In addition, the criterion for comparison and choice, as March and Simon noted earlier, is not the attainment of optimal goals, but satisfaction. Thus, the evaluation stage involves the comparison of a limited number of alternatives to one another and to a notion of what would be a satisfactory goal attainment or a satisfactory resolution of the problem. If no alternatives that promise satisfactory results are readily found, the criterion, or definition of a satisfactory outcome, may be lowered.

None of the individual limitations on rational planning may be fatal, but collectively they present some very serious problems. In considering, for example, whether lawyers should be provided for indigent criminal defendants, here are some of the questions and issues that would have to be resolved:

Goals

1. How is indigency to be defined? If a defendant can pay for legal services, but only by using all his savings or going into debt, is the defendant indigent?

2. Who is a defendant? At what stage of the criminal justice process—trial, preliminary hearing, arraignment, booking, arrest, or custodial interrogation—does a person become eligible for legal assistance? Does the right to counsel extend beyond trial, to sentencing, appeals, parole, or revocation?

3. Is the defendant to have a lawyer or "effective legal representation"? If the latter, how is it to be defined?

4. Most important, where is the planner to get the answers to these questions? If there is disagreement or vagueness, how is the planner supposed to resolve and to clarify the goals? Whose interests are to be served?

Problems

1. How is the planner to know whether present practices will attain the goal? How is the planner even to know what present conditions are? How can the planner measure the present level of "effective legal representation" and then determine whether it meets desired ends?

2. Given a notion that "something isn't just right" in the provision of counsel for indigent defendants, how does the planner determine what is wrong and what is causing the problem?

Alternatives

1. Where does the planner go, or what does the planner do, in order to come up with alternative plans or strategies for dealing with the problem or attaining the goals?

2. How would the planner know when *all* possible alternatives have been identified? How does the planner know when all reasonable, plausible alternatives have been identified?

3. Having identified the alternatives of legal aid, public defenders, and assigned counsel, how does the planner decide whether it is worth the time and cost involved to search for, or to design, additional alternatives?

Simulation

1. How is the planner to determine the likely consequences of the alternative means of providing counsel for indigent defendants? Given competing theories of plea-bargaining, judicial decision-making, and the practice of law, how does the planner choose the theories on which to base predictions?

2. Given information from other jurisdictions about their experiences with different alternatives, how does the planner assess the extent to which those experiences are applicable to his state?

Evaluation

1. Given some guesses about the likely consequences of alternatives, how does the planner decide which consequences, and thus which alternative, comes closest to attaining the goal or solving the problem? If a public defender would provide moderately good representation at a cost of $10 million, legal aid would provide moderately good representation at a cost of $8 million but would increase pretrial delays, and assigned counsel would provide good representation at a cost of $12 million but would also increase pretrial delays, how does the planner decide which alternative is best?

Some of the questions posed are merely hard to answer; others are nearly or actually unanswerable. Nor do the questions address problems related to forecasting, monitoring, or feeding back information.

This discussion of the limitations on rational planning was designed to stress the difficulties involved in objectively rational planning. But, as later portions of this discussion will indicate, it is possible to pursue rationality through planning. Objective rationality may not be attainable, but planning can help to point us in desired directions.

THE PLANNING CONTEXT

Comparison of the ideal form of rational planning with the limitations posed by the real world naturally raises questions about the forms that planning takes in actual practice. Is actual planning nearly rational, altogether irrational, or somewhere in between?

These questions cannot be authoritatively answered, because planning practices vary. Planning is sometimes done very well, and sometimes very poorly. What determines the quality, or relative rationality, of planning in any particular situation? One important factor is certainly the resources available.[19] Resources are not always available; when they are, the decision-maker may not always be willing to invest those resources in planning. Another important factor in determining the quality of planning is the extent to which the decision-maker perceives relevant parts of the situation as fixed, and therefore not susceptible to manipulation. The initiation of extensive planning, the kinds of alternatives considered and chosen, depend largely on "what is taken as given and what is treated as subject to manipulation."[20]

If the decision-makers in a given situation have some interest in acting rationally, and if they are willing and able to devote some reasonable level of resources to the task of planning, the process undertaken will primarily depend on the characteristics of the means and ends involved in the situation. Planning basically involves the manipulation of means and ends, and the characteristics of these means and ends are important elements of the planning context. Four kinds of situations resulting from different combinations of means and ends are presented in Figure 3-1.[21]

A distinction is made in Figure 3-1 between situations with clear and well-known goals, and situations in which the goals are vague or conflicting. The other important dimension is the relationships between means and ends. A distinction is drawn between situations in which the relationships between means and ends are

Figure 3-1. Planning Contexts Determined by Characteristics of Means and Ends

		GOALS	
		Clear, Known, or Knowable	Vague or in Conflict
MEANS/ENDS RELATIONSHIPS	Fairly Well Known	Rational Planning	Problem Solving
	Unknown, or Very Uncertain	Research	Disjointed Incrementalism

reasonably well understood and situations in which such relationships are unknown or very uncertain. The four kinds of situations identified lead to different forms of planning behavior: rational planning, research, problem-solving, and disjointed incrementalism.

Rational Planning

When goals are clearly identified and the relationships between means and ends are fairly well known, rational forms of planning are possible. This does not mean that objective rationality will be attained, for goals may not be precise or congruent, alternative consequences may not be perfectly known, forecasting may be inaccurate, information about present conditions may not be complete, and it may not be possible to identify and to consider all possible alternatives. But subjective rationality (maximum attainment relative to knowledge actually available) may be achievable: different alternatives can be considered in relation to clear goals; thought can be given to the future; and the alternative promising the most desired outcomes can be selected.

The problem of providing free legal representation for indigent criminal defendants is susceptible to rational planning. The U.S. Supreme Court has now mandated fairly clear goals that are now widely known and accepted. (The fact that most states had systems for providing counsel for impoverished defendants *before* the Supreme Court issued its mandate suggests that wide acceptance of the goals did not merely reflect obedience to higher authority.) Several different alternatives have been tested around the country and their consequences are reasonably well known. There may not be complete agreement about the costs and benefits of each alternative, and not all possible alternatives may have been considered, but a good bit of information is available, upon which planners and decision-makers may at least attempt to act rationally.

Research

In situations characterized by clear, known goals but unknown or very uncertain relationships between means and ends, the need is for research. When the planner knows what he would like to achieve, but does not know how to achieve it, and/or when he has thought of several alternatives but simply cannot estimate their likely consequences, he needs instrumental knowledge, and efforts to develop such knowledge are usually termed research.

These are the situations in which technologically-oriented approaches, such as operations research and systems analysis, are most successful. The finest recent example is the space program. After his election in 1960, President Kennedy essentially said to the scientific community, "We must put a man on the moon in ten years, and your job is to figure out how." The goal was clear, but a tremendous amount of knowledge about how to achieve it was initially lacking. There began a concerted (and expensive) research and development effort, and in a relatively short time the knowledge had been found or discovered that was required to achieve the goal.

A comparable situation in criminal justice involves the issue of allocation and deployment of police patrols. A common goal is the minimization of the time required for patrols to respond to some class of serious calls (say, crimes in progress, alarms, personal-injury accidents, and officers in need of assistance). The problem is to determine which configuration of patrol beats, manpower allocation, patrol strategies, and dispatching policies will achieve that goal. Some police departments have already made this determination, and need only periodically to revise that configuration as workload patterns change. But for most police departments, the array of possible alternatives is bewildering, and the likely outcomes of known alternatives are not well understood. These departments need, therefore, the kind of knowledge available through research. They need to know the effect on response time to serious calls of flexible beats, split-force patrol, beat reassignment by dispatchers, different allocations of personnel around the clock, and many other alternatives. This kind of knowledge can be, and has been, sought through field research[22] and through computer simulation.[23]

Research is also necessary in situations in which goals are less clearly defined or less widely agreed upon. In the 1960s and early 1970s, for example, within substantial budgetary and custody constraints, at least some states espoused fairly clear correctional goals for rehabilitation and reintegration. Having adopted those goals, however, the states were not at all clear about how to attain them. A wide variety of practices, ranging from unsupervised probation to frontal lobotomies, were available, but the consequences of each were not (and still are not) very accurately known. The need was for research designed to determine the effects of known alternatives or to discover new alternatives that could attain the stated goals of rehabilitation and reintegration. A great deal of research was conducted, yielding a tremendous amount of information, although often not the knowledge that was needed.[24]

Problem Solving

Problem-solving situations are those in which the relationships between means and ends are reasonably well known, but in which goals are vague or conflicting. In a sense, any planning context might involve behavior oriented toward the solving of problems, but the term is particularly applicable to situations in which purposive activity is undertaken despite the absence of clear goals. When there is a sense that something is wrong, that there is a problem, but the goals are vague or lacking in consensus, planning can be directed toward solving the generally perceived problem. This kind of problem-oriented planning seems to be very common in many fields of public and private planning.

In his description of the "science of muddling through," Charles Lindblom discussed a frequent occurrence in policy-making that fits this category of problem-solving. He noted that analysts or decision-makers can often agree on a particular policy (alternative), "without their agreeing that it is the most appropriate means to an agreed objective."[25] That this is common and possible is important, because it indicates that the absence of clear goals need not lead to an abandonment of the planning effort.

Problem-solving situations frequently present themselves in criminal justice. There is, for example, considerable controversy over judicial sentencing. Should the primary purpose of sentencing be to punish the convicted offender? to rehabilitate him? to deter potential offenders? to satisfy some notion of justice? There is great disagreement among legislators, judges, and the general public about the relative importance of these goals. Also, there is some conflict among the goals themselves, so that all cannot be maximally attained. But despite these multiple, vague, and conflicting goals, agreement can often be reached about particular problems, such as disparities in sentences. Though we might not agree on what sentencing is supposed to achieve, we might agree that when one armed robber is put on probation while another with a virtually identical criminal history and case is sentenced to twenty years, we have a problem.

Agreement on desired alternatives without agreement on goals can also be found in criminal justice. For example, police chiefs and defense attorneys might agree that additional legal training for police officers is desirable. The goals of the police chiefs might include higher conviction rates and fewer civil suits, both of which might be attained if officers had a better understanding of the law. The goals of the defense attorneys, on the other hand, might include fewer nuisance arrests and closer adherence to the rule of law by police officers. In general, the police chiefs might be proponents of a crime-control model of criminal justice, and the defense lawyers might prefer a due-process model.[26] These goals might appear to be opposed yet both groups could support a policy of increased legal training for police officers.

Disjointed Incrementalism

In some situations there may be uncertainty both about goals and about the relationships between means and ends, about the ends desired, and about the consequences of different alternatives. Even though there may be agreement that problems exist, there may be no certainty about how to address them or about the effects of proposed solutions.

Many managers, including those in criminal justice agencies, have experienced this uncertainty. A manager may sense that productivity, commitment, or morale is not what it should be, but not be able to pinpoint or articulate the problem, or think of any actions to take. A teacher, for example, may be aware that a class is not going as well as it should, but be unable to specify the goals that are to be achieved, to identify the problem that has developed, or to predict the consequences of different alternatives that might be implemented.

In this kind of situation, planning often takes the form of "disjointed incrementalism" or "successive limited comparisons."[27] A promising alternative is tried, probably in a limited application, and if the results are not displeasing, the application may be continued or expanded.

If side effects or negative consequences are encountered, small or incremental changes are made. The generation of alternatives generally results from tinkering or local search, rather than from extended search, design, or invention. The consequences of alternatives are compared to one another, rather than to any sort of goal or desired end. Because of the trial-and-error methodology and the commitment to incremental changes, little in the way of formal simulation or forecasting is undertaken.

This kind of planning, if it can be called that, is quite common in criminal justice as well as in many other fields. It may be particularly dominant in public agencies. Indeed, James Q. Wilson has argued that "we turn to government in part precisely *because* we wish to attain vague, complex, controversial, hard-to-produce objectives (clear, easily attained, noncontroversial goals are more often than not left to the market or to private arrangements)."[28] He also points to the importance of a proven technology for achieving goals, and points out that "the Bureau of Public Roads knows how to build highways, but the Bureau of Prisons does not know how to rehabilitate a criminal, nor does the National Institute of Drug Abuse know how to cure a heroin addict."[29] In the absence both of clear goals and of a proven technology, rational action is greatly constrained.

The general approach to police patrol at present is one of disjointed incrementalism. Patrol, and the police presence generally, are associated with vague notions of controlling crime and maintaining order rather than with clear goals. Minimizing response time to serious calls may be a clear goal of patrol-allocation methodologies, but this would not be an important terminal goal of the entire patrol operation. (Moreover, recent research has cast considerable doubt upon the presumed relationship between rapid response and the likelihood of arrests.[30]) Knowledge about the relationships between means and ends is very uncertain: important recent studies have suggested that traditional, routine patrol contributes rather little to crime control and public tranquility.[31] As a result, there is a prevailing uneasiness about conventional patrol practices, but no one is really sure what should be done instead of routine patrol. A number of incrementally different strategies, such as community-oriented patrol, team policing, saturation patrol, split-force patrol, and directed patrol have been implemented around the country.[32] As results of evaluation studies become available, minor tinkering with these strategies is undertaken in the hope of marginally improving their effectiveness. But real planning is difficult because clear goals are lacking and the relationships between means and ends are not well understood.

A REVISED PLANNING MODEL

This discussion of a rational or "modern-classical" planning model, the host of real-life constraints that limit rationality in planning, and the characteristics of the planning context that influence how much rationality is possible in any given situation, makes clear that objective rationality may be impossible to attain in actual planning practice. Nevertheless, rationality plays a role in planning and decision-making: planning often is, and should be, "intendedly rational". Some kinds of situations permit closer adherence than others to a rational planning process, but that does not alter the intention to be rational. In situations favoring disjointed incrementalism, the behavior undertaken may not seem much like planning, but it may be optimally rational behavior under those circumstances.

To say that behavior is intendedly rational is not merely to legitimate the status quo. Planning that is intended to be rational may not be as rational as it could be. But, other things being equal, planning should be as rational as possible: one should adhere as closely as possible to a rational planning process.

Most of the rest of this book is about the effort to be rational. The rational planning model presented earlier in this chapter, slightly reorganized and revised, can still serve as a useful standard and guide. That revised model is briefly described in the sections that follow, and later elaborated in Chapters 8, 9, and 10.

Identifying Goals and Problems

One of the principal tasks involved in planning is the identification of purpose. Except perhaps in the most extreme forms of disjointed incrementalism, some idea of a goal to be attained or a problem to be solved guides the planning process. Even in extreme situations, a system of values is important for identifying the class of legitimate means with which one will try to achieve incremental changes in trial-and-error fashion. Very frequently, consideration of goals and values may be only implicit, and founded on numerous unspoken assumptions. Though implicit, these goals and values nevertheless guide the definition of problems and the selection of means for solving them.

Rationality in planning is aided by clarity of goals, problems, and values. Thus, the planner is well advised to take advantage of opportunities to clarify these matters. On the other hand, goals, problems, and values are often vague and/or in conflict. In the pursuit of rationality, the planner may need to direct attention away from goals and toward problems, or away from problems and toward mutually valued alternatives. In addition to very situational factors such as the distribution of power and authority or the availability of resources, the planner can be guided as well by the planning context typology presented in the last section.

The identification of problems depends on information about present conditions. Although constant or continuous monitoring of the state of the world, like continuous searching for goals, would be too exhausting realistically to expect, the attempt to be rational must involve the collection of some information. Perhaps a more reasonable expectation would be the periodic monitoring of relevant conditions. In addition to facilitating the identification of problems, this collecting of information will also aid later steps in the planning process.

Forecasting

Forecasting explicitly sets planning apart from decision-making. Having identified the subjects the planning will be about, and before turning to alternative ways of approaching the problems or goals, the rationally oriented planner makes sure that thought is given to the future. Thinking about the future focuses on goals, problems, values, and relevant conditions, and in particular on the future context in which a chosen alternative will be applied and expected to work.

Like consideration of goals and values, forecasting is frequently only implicit. The most common implicit assumption is that the future context will be exactly like the present. Because planning takes time, though, it is always the future in which alternatives are applied, and not the present. It is for this reason that the modern-classical model of planning explicitly incorporates a forecasting stage, and planning's orientation to the future is a major characteristic distinguishing it from other approaches to rationality such as policy analysis, systems analysis, and decision-making. How closely the forecast resembles what actually comes about is an important determinant of the success of the chosen alternative. Subsequent stages in the planning process are dependent on forecasting for simulating and evaluating alternatives and for making choices.

The extent to which forecasting should be formally undertaken, the resources that should be invested in it, and the validity of its predictions vary. In the extreme case of disjointed incrementalism, in which only small changes are made and regular readjustments are intended, forecasting may not be terribly crucial. But, an organization that does not foresee a dramatic change in its environment might endanger its own survival, and might be unable to adapt to changes rapidly enough, both because of its orientation to the present and because of its incremental strategy. In less extreme cases of incrementalism, the need for forecasting becomes even more apparent. Alternatives under consideration may have long-range consequences, and may require the commitment of even future generations to particular courses of action. The clearest examples of such long-range commitment are in the realm of energy policy. Some practices may seriously deplete scarce resources, while others may have long-term environmental effects or create toxic wastes with seemingly infinite life-spans. Examples from criminal justice are less dramatic but equally significant. Decisions about prison construction, for instance, have important long-range consequences because of their capital costs, the constraints they place on correctional policy, and the effects they have on the locales chosen for the facilities.

Generating and Testing Alternatives

Once a view of the future has been developed, even if only implicitly, the search for alternatives or solutions can be conducted. The generation of alternatives usually begins in familiar territory, with consideration of variables already under control and strategies utilized earlier. If none of the responses already implemented is deemed likely to produce a satisfactory result, other alternatives are sought. If no satisfactory alternatives are found through this search, an effort may then be made to design or to invent new alternatives that will operate satisfactorily. Thus the process proceeds through review, search, and design stages.

To describe the process as aimed at generating "satisfactory" alternatives is not to imply that standards or criteria of success in planning are necessarily mediocre, but to acknowledge—once again—that the ideal of optimal goal attainment or problem resolution is not achieved in the real world. Typically, we conceive a goal to pursue or recognize a problem to lessen, we think of several ways of proceeding, and we try to figure out the likely consequences of each alternative in order to choose the one with the most desirable consequences. Sometimes we may not be satisfied with any of the sets of likely consequences, in which case we may go in search of other alternatives. Sometimes, however, we may lower our expectations, so that one of the alternatives under consideration comes to be seen as satisfactory. The context of the planning decision and the perceived importance of the matter, may influence levels of acceptability. Those levels are always less than optimal, however, because we cannot think of all possible alternatives, or perfectly estimate consequences, and because our resources are always limited. The definition of a "satisfactory" alternative will vary with the situation.

Alternatives, once generated, must be tested. This simply means that somehow the likely consequences of each alternative, were it to be adopted, must be estimated. The testing of alternatives may range from simple guessing to formal simulation to actual pilot-testing in the field. Except in pilot-testing, the estimation of consequences completely depends on the validity of theories and assumptions about how things work. Even in pilot-testing, the conclusions drawn about the probable effects once the tested alternative is generally applied are based on theoretical notions (often implicit) that may or may not be valid.

Like the identification of goals and problems and forecasting, the generating and testing of alternatives will and must vary in actual practice. Resource constraints will limit the exhaustiveness of search and design efforts. In some situations, well-developed alternatives with well-understood consequences may be readily available; in others, means may be few and the relationships between means and ends uncertain. Emergency conditions may require immediate choice and implementation of the first reasonable alternative generated; in other situations, one may have the time to consider many alternatives.

Identifying goals and problems, forecasting, and generating and testing alternatives are the three basic components of the planning process. But these three basic steps include a wide range of activities, some of which are incredibly complex and taxing, especially when one tries to be rational in less-than-hospitable circumstances. We will continue to explore these stages and components of planning, and the forms that planning can take, in later chapters.

SUMMARY

This chapter discussed how planning is and should be done. The rational model of the planning process specifies how planning *ought* to be carried out, and provides an ideal that can never be matched in practice, owing to a variety of real-world constraints. The actual practice of planning, though limited by numerous constraints, ranges from not rational to nearly rational. The form taken by planning may depend to some extent on the situation, including the certainty of relationships between means and ends, and the clarity and consensus of goals.

The revised and simplified planning model presented at the end of the chapter includes three stages: identifying goals and problems, forecasting, and generating and testing alternatives. These stages will be explored in detail in Chapters 8, 9, and 10.

· *Chapter 3* ·
NOTES

1. Herbert A. Simon, *Administrative Behavior*, 3rd ed. (New York: The Free Press, 1976), pp. 76–77.

2. Horst W. J. Rittel and Melvin M. Webber, "Dilemmas in a General Theory of Planning," *Policy Sciences*, 4 (1973), 159.

3. *Gideon* v. *Wainwright*, 372 U.S. 335, 1963. See also Anthony Lewis, *Gideon's Trumpet* (New York: Random House, 1964).

4. Kenneth J. Arrow, *Social Choice and Individual Values* (New York: John Wiley & Sons, Inc., 1951).

5. Edward C. Banfield, "Ends and Means in Planning," *International Social Science Journal*, 11 (1959), 361–68.

6. John R. Seeley, "What is Planning? Definition and Strategy," *Journal of the American Institute of Planners*, 28 (May 1962), 91–97.

7. Herbert A. Simon, "On the Concept of Organizational Goal," *Administrative Science Quarterly*, 9 (1964), 1–22.

8. Vincent O'Leary and David Duffee, "Managerial Behavior and Correctional Policy," *Public Administration Review* (November/December 1971), 603–16.

9. Donald R. Cressey, "Prison Organizations," in James G. March, ed., *Handbook of Organizations* (Chicago: Rand McNally & Company, 1965).

10. O'Leary and Duffee, op. cit.

11. Alvin W. Cohn, "The Failure of Correctional Management—Revisited," *Federal Probation* (March 1979), 10–15.

12. Rittel and Webber, op. cit., p. 159.

13. Richard S. Bolan, "Mapping the Planning Theory Terrain," *Urban and Social Change Review*, 8 (1975), 35–43.

14. Banfield, op. cit.

15. Simon, *Administrative Behavior*, p. 81.

16. David Braybrooke and Charles E. Lindblom, *A Strategy of Decision* (New York: The Free Press, 1963).

17. James G. March and Herbert A. Simon, *Organizations* (New York: John Wiley & Sons, Inc., 1958), 179–80.

18. Rittel and Webber, op. cit., p. 169.

19. Lawrence B. Mohr, "Organizations, Decisions, and Courts," *Law & Society* (Summer 1976), 621–42. See also C. Wiseman, "Selection of Major Planning Issues," *Policy Sciences*, 9 (1978), 71–86.

20. Richard M. Cyert and James G. March, *A Behavioral Theory of the Firm* (Englewood Cliffs, N.J.: Prentice-Hall, Inc., 1963), p. 20.

21. The figure is adapted from James D. Thompson and Arthur Tuden, "Strategies, Structures and Processes of Organizational Decision," in James D. Thompson, et al., eds., *Comparative Studies in Administration* (Pittsburgh: University of Pittsburgh Press, 1959); and Ph. Lasserre, "Planning through Incrementalism," *Socio-Economic Planning Sciences*, 8 (1974), 129–34.

22. See, for example, George L. Kelling, et al., *The Kansas City Preventive Patrol Experiment: A Summary Report* (Washington, D.C.: Police Foundation, 1974); James M. Tien, et al., *An Alternative Approach in Police Patrol: The Wilmington Split-Force Experiment* (Cambridge, MA.:Public Systems Evaluation, 1977); and Gilbert C. Larson and James W. Simon, *Evaluation of a Police Automatic Vehicle Monitoring (AVM) System* (Washington, D.C.: U.S. Government Printing Office, 1979).

23. See, for example, Operations Research Task Force, *Allocations of Resources in the Chicago Police Department* (Washington, D.C.: U.S. Government Printing Office, 1972); Jerry L. Carlin and Colin L. Moodie, "A Comparison of Some Patrol Methods," *Police*, 16 (August 1972), 27–31; and Richard C. Larson, symposium editor, "Police Deployment," *Management Science*, 24 (August 1978), 1278–1327.

24. See, for example, Robert Martinson, "What Works—Questions and Answers about Prison Reform," *The Public Interest* (Spring 1974), 22–54; and Douglas Lipton, et al., *The Effectiveness of Correctional Treatment* (New York: Praeger Publishers, Inc., 1975).

25. Charles E. Lindblom, "The Science of 'Muddling Through'," *Public Administration Review*, 19 (Spring 1959), 81.

26. Herbert Packer, *The Limits of the Criminal Sanction* (Stanford, Calif.: Stanford University Press, 1968).

27. Lindblom, op. cit.; Braybrooke and Lindblom, op. cit.; and Lasserre, op. cit. See Susan S. Fainstein and Norman I. Fainstein, "City Planning and Political Values," *Urban Affairs Quarterly*, 6 (March 1971), 341–62, for an argument that incrementalism is not planning.

28. James Q. Wilson, *The Investigators: Managing FBI and Narcotics Agents* (New York: Basic Books, 1978), p. 204.

29. Ibid., p. 203.

30. See Tony Pate, et al., *Police Response Time: Its Determinants and Effects* (Washington, D.C.: Police Foundation, 1976); and Kansas City, Missouri, Police Department, *Response Time Analysis: Executive Summary*

(Washington, D.C.: U.S. Government Printing Office, 1978).

31. The Kansas City Preventive Patrol Experiment remains the landmark study. Kelling, et al., op. cit.

32. See Gary W. Cordner, "Police Patrol Research and Its Utilization," *Police Studies*, 2 (Winter 1980), 12-21, for a discussion of these strategies and their relationship to research and knowledge.

· Part II ·

THE CONTEXT OF CRIMINAL JUSTICE PLANNING

Part II examines the context or setting for criminal justice planning. Chapter 4 provides an introduction to criminal justice for those who may not be familiar with the organizations, decisions, policies, and underlying principles that constitute society's response to the problems of crime and disorder. Chapter 5 examines criminal justice *system* planning; Chapter 6, *organizational* planning. Fundamental characteristics of systems and of organizations, and their applicability to criminal justice, are discussed, and the role of planning in systems and organizations is considered. Chapter 7 focuses on the administrative concerns of organizing and staffing the criminal justice planning function: who plans? how many planners are needed? where should the planners be located in the organization? how should planning be tied to other functions? what authority and tasks should be assigned to planners? This section helps set the stage for later discussions of the planning process and its applications to criminal justice.

·Chapter 4·

CRIMINAL JUSTICE SYSTEMS AND ORGANIZATIONS

This chapter provides a short overview of the criminal justice system and its components.

A review of such basic considerations as federalism and separation of powers is followed by a description of criminal justice as a series of decisions about the processing of cases. Then the component organizations and personnel of the criminal justice system, and some other organizations peripherally related to criminal justice, are discussed. Finally, the major crime-control policies that guide decision-making in criminal justice are examined.

UNDERLYING PHILOSOPHIES AND PRINCIPLES

The system for the administration of justice in the United States, compared with that of some other nations, is noteworthy for its fragmentation and restraint of government authority. The founding fathers had some experience with unbridled government power and their own mercantile interests to protect; they were wary of centralization of authority and concentration of power. So they devised a political system characterized by all kinds of checks and balances.

Our system of government and of criminal justice is based upon our Constitution, a document nearing its two hundredth birthday. Although many amendments have been added to the Constitution since its adoption in 1787, it remains very much the document hammered out following the Revolutionary War. Of course, the precise meaning of words and phrases is often in dispute, and the Supreme Court is the final arbiter of such disputes. But the principles outlined in the Constitution endure.

Separation of Powers

One important way in which government authority is fragmented by the Constitution is through the creation of separate legislative, executive, and judicial branches. The power to make laws and establish taxes is given to the legislative branch of government; the responsibility for implementing laws, to the executive branch; the responsibility for adjudicating alleged infringements of the law and for reviewing the constitutionality of laws and of government actions to the judicial branch. The courts cannot convict unless laws exist and the executive branch enforces existing laws. Laws made by legislators would have little effect without the cooperation of the executive and judicial branches. And the executive branch, the enforcers of the laws, cannot make the laws or sit in judment of those accused of breaking laws. The net effect of the separation of powers, or at least the intention that led to that separation, is to make it relatively difficult for the government to assert its authority against any particular individual.

Federalism

Another basic feature of the governmental system in the United States is the separation of powers among the Federal, state, and local levels of jurisdiction. The powers of the national government are enumerated, as well as specifically restricted, in the Constitution, which also places some specific restrictions on state authority and provides that "the United States shall guarantee to every State in this Union a republican form of government" and that "the powers not delegated to the United States by the Constitution, nor probibited by it to the States, are reserved to the States respectively, or to the people." Furthermore, each state has its own constitution, which further fragments authority among branches of government, levels of jurisdiction, and individuals.

Local and state governments generally have more responsibility than the national government for making, enforcing, and adjudicating criminal laws. Each state has its own set of criminal laws applicable throughout its jurisdiction. The national government also has a criminal code, but with a more limited jurisdiction. In general, the Federal criminal code applies only to certain specified offenses (e.g., bank robbery), and to offenses committed on Federal property (e.g., the burglarizing of a post office). It is under the authority of the states that the vast majority of criminal matters, from disorderly conduct through murder, are handled.

Responsibility for the administration of state criminal law is shared by local and state government. Usually, the police are under the jurisdiction of local government; prosecutors and judges, sometimes under that of local government, sometimes under that of the state. Jails are usually maintained by the local government, while prisons are operated by the state. Probation departments may come under the jurisdiction of local or state government, but parole programs are ordinarily administered by the state. These components of the criminal justice system will be examined later in this discussion.

Bill of Rights

The first ten amendments to the Constitution, known collectively as the Bill of Rights, were proposed the same year that the Constitution went into effect (1789), and were ratified two years later. These amendments further restrict the powers of the government, and some of their provisions are directly pertinent to the administration of criminal justice:

–Congress shall make no law respecting an establishment of religion, or prohibiting the free exercise thereof; or abridging the freedom of speech, or of the press; or the right of the people peaceably to assemble, and to petition the Government for a redress of grievances. (First Amendment)

–The right of the people to be secure in their persons, houses, papers, and effects, against unreasonable searches and seizures, shall not be violated, and no warrants shall issue, but upon probable cause, supported by oath or affirmation, and particularly describing the place to be searched, and the persons or things to be seized. (Fourth Amendment)

–No person shall be held to answer for a capital, or otherwise infamous crime, unless on a presentment or indictment of a grand jury[;] . . . nor shall any person be subject for the same offense to be twice put in jeopardy of life or limb; nor shall be compelled in any criminal case to be a witness against himself, nor be deprived of life, liberty, or property, without due process of law. (Fifth Amendment)

–In all criminal prosecutions, the accused shall enjoy the right to a speedy and public trial, by an impartial jury[;] . . . and to be informed of the nature and cause of the accusation; to be confronted with the witnesses against him; to have compulsory process for obtaining witnesses in his favor, and to have the assistance of counsel for his defense. (Sixth Amendment)

–Excessive bail shall not be required, nor excessive fines imposed, nor cruel and unusual punishments inflicted. (Eighth Amendment)

–The enumeration in the Constitution, of certain rights, shall not be construed to deny or disparage others retained by the people. (Ninth Amendment)

Legal Principles

The administration of criminal justice is based upon a variety of legal principles; some derive directly from the Constitution, and others have evolved through the process of interpreting the Constitution. One basic principle is due process, which requires the government to follow prescribed rules when exercising its authority; another is that all people are entitled to equal protection under the laws; and yet another is an accused person is presumed innocent until proven guilty—beyond a reasonable doubt—in a court of law. This last principle poses an exacting standard, and reflects the belief that it is better for a guilty person to go free than for an innocent person to be punished. As a further protection for the accused, self-incrimination is not required, and in fact the accused need say nothing at all; thus the entire burden for proving beyond a reasonable doubt that the accused is guilty as charged is placed upon the state. The protection against self-incrimination was extended in the controversial *Miranda* v. *Arizona* decision of the U.S. Supreme Court, which required the police to advise suspects of their right to remain silent, prior to questioning them.[1] Just as controversial is the exclusionary rule, enunciated in *Mapp* v. *Ohio*, which prohibits the courts from recognizing evidence –however relevant and decisive–obtained unlawfully by the police.[2]

Another important characteristic of the justice system, and especially of the courts, is that it is an adversarial system. The prosecutor and the police endeavor to prove that the accused acted as the charge alleges. The accused and his counsel try to prevent the state from proving the allegation by remaining silent, attacking the state's witnesses and evidence, and/or presenting an alternative version of events. The judge and/or jury play a relatively neutral, detached role, weighing each side's case and deciding whether proof of guilt beyond a reasonable doubt was established. The system is not designed as a concerted inquiry into the truth; rather, it is a formal contest between advocates, from whose efforts and arguments the truth is expected to emerge. The goal is a "fair" trial, in which the accused receives due process of law, and the emphasis is on procedural justice rather than substantive justice.

Rule of Law and Discretion

The discussion so far has presented some "civics textbook" ideas about criminal justice in America, and to a considerable degree they are valid. The separation of powers *has* created a complex set of checks and balances; the Bill of Rights *does* protect the individual from arbitrary and unreasonable exercise of government authority; the courts *do* exclude evidence that was improperly obtained; the legal system *is* (sometimes) adversarial.

On the basis of these kinds of ideas, gradeschool children are taught that the United States is governed by laws, not by men–that is, that we are governed by the rule of law, not by the whims of those in power at any particular moment. But if this is true, why do we also suspect that "It isn't *what* you know, but *who* you know, that counts"? And we all know that a defendant's chances of being acquitted depend on whether he can afford to hire a good enough lawyer.

There is obviously some truth to both the cynical and the "textbook" views. Constitutional and legal principles establish the broad outlines of the system, some of its rules, and some of the values held by the people who administer it. But there remains a great deal of room for individuals to exercise discretion in making decisions. Judges or juries decide whether the evidence presented proves the charge beyond a reasonable doubt; more important, judges decide what sentence to give to the convicted. Prosecutors decide whether to file charges against those arrested or otherwise complained about, and what charges to file. The police decide which violators of the law will be arrested or will receive tickets. The parole board decides whether and when to release convicts from prison. None of these decisions is wholly discretionary–but none is completely prescribed by law.

The discretionary nature of decision-making in criminal justice creates the potential both for compassion and for abuse, and makes the subject much more interesting to study. The next two sections will examine how criminal justice actually is dispensed, as well as how the system is "supposed" to work.

THE CRIMINAL JUSTICE PROCESS

Criminal justice may be viewed as a series of decisions. The first decision is actually legislative: elected politicians decide which human behaviors will be defined as criminal. Once such definitions are established, each individual decides whether or not to engage in criminal behavior. The extent to which people truly "decide" to commit criminal acts is, of course, a psychological and sociological question. Fortunately, the issue need not be resolved here, as our interest really commences with those decisions that follow the commission of criminal acts.

Detection

Most criminal behavior never gets processed through the criminal justice system because it is not formally detected. A murder, for example, may be mistakenly classified as an accidental or natural death. An intoxicated driver may avoid collision and escape the attention of the police. A few dollars stolen from a wallet might never be missed by the victim. In such instances, only the perpetrators know a criminal act has been committed, and few of them report their own behavior to the authorities.

A large portion of the crimes discovered, by victims or bystanders, also are not reported to the police, and thus evade formal detection. Victims sometimes fail to report "trivial" offenses because they doubt that the police would do anything, because they do not want to go through all the trouble, because they know the offender and choose to deal with the problem informally, or because they fear retaliation from the offender if the police are notified.

How much crime goes unreported is not precisely known, but informed estimates place the real volume of serious crime at two or three times the level reported to the police.[3] The serious crimes generally included in such estimates are murder, rape, robbery, aggravated assault, burglary, auto theft, and larceny. "True" levels of such crimes as drug possession, gambling, and illegal sexual acts presumably exceed reported levels by an even larger margin. Thus an inescapable feature of the criminal justice process is that it never gets the chance to deal with most criminal behavior.

Apprehension

Reported crimes become the responsibility of the police. Unless the police make an arrest, the case proceeds no further. Generally, "probable cause" is needed to justify the issuance of an arrest warrant or the execution of a warrantless arrest. In many cases, the police never develop sufficient evidence against a suspect, and so no arrest is made. In many other crimes, especially those involving less serious crimes, the police establish probable cause but still do not make an arrest. Police exercise their discretion *not* to arrest for any of several reasons: limitations of manpower; lack of cooperation from witnesses or victim; the minor nature of the offense; a sincere effort to do what is just; and the realization that full enforcement of some laws was never intended.[4]

The police make arrests for only about 20-25 percent of all *reported* serious crimes.[5] This "clearance-by-arrest" rate varies according to the type of crime: the rates for murder, rape, and aggravated assault are relatively higher; those for burglary and theft, relatively low. Average clearance-by-arrest rates for twenty-five major U.S. cities are presented in the middle column of Table 4.1.[6] The first column shows the reporting rates for those cities, as

Table 4-1. Average Detection and Arrest Rates by Crime Type for Twenty-Five Major United States Cities (all figures shown are percentages)

Crime	Detection Rate[1]	Clearance by Arrest Rate[2]	"True" Clearance by Arrest Rate[3]
Rape	42.3	54.6	23.3
Robbery	37.2	30.3	10.3
Aggravated Assault	62.7	64.0	40.4
Burglary	33.2	21.9	6.8
Larceny	37.4	18.8	6.0
Auto Theft	95.7	16.0	14.5
Property Crime	39.2	18.5	6.7
Violent Crime	41.9	43.7	17.7
Total Serious Crime	37.5	22.4	8.3

[1]Detection Rate = Reported Crime ÷ Victimization

[2]Clearance-by-Arrest Rate = Arrests ÷ Reported Crime

[3]"True" Clearance-by-Arrest Rate = Arrests ÷ Victimization

Adapted from Scott H. Decker, "Alternate Measures of Police Output," *American Journal of Police*, 1 (1981), 30.

estimated by surveys of crime victims; the third column lists "true" clearance rates, or the portion of all crimes (reported or not) that are cleared by arrest. Actually these figures overestimate arrest effectiveness, because undiscovered crimes are not included in the computations. Even by this optimistic measure, the police are shown to make arrests for only about one in twelve serious crimes (8.3 percent).

Prosecution

When the police do make arrests, a decision is made whether or not to prosecute. This decision is initially made by the police: they choose whether or not to seek formal charges against the arrested suspect. The police may release a suspect without charge if they consider their evidence insufficient or inadmissable, if the suspect has established an alibi, if the suspect has agreed to become an informant, if the victim or key witnesses show reluctance to follow through on prosecution, or for other reasons. Quite often police arrests are made in order to quell a disturbance or conflict, with no intention to prosecute ever entertained by the arresting officers.

When the police do seek formal charges, the prosecutor must decide whether to issue an information or seek a bill of indictment from a grand jury. The exact procedure varies among jurisdictions, but the discretion of the prosecutor is everywhere broad and nearly unregulated. The portion of police arrests "dropped" by the prosecutor varies, but is generally considerable. No national averages are available, but one comprehensive study in Washington, D.C., found that about one-half of all police arrests for *serious* crimes were not prosecuted, sometimes because admissible evidence was lacking and sometimes owing to the scarce resources and the priorities of the prosecutor's office.[7] At best, one in twelve serious crimes gets to the prosecution stage; if the Washington, D.C., figure is representative, only one in twenty-four serious crimes gets prosecuted (about 4 per cent).

Adjudication

When a case is prosecuted, the guilt or innocence of the defendant must be determined. A preliminary hearing of some sort is usually held first, at which the probable cause supporting the charges is reviewed and defense motions concerning the admissability of the prosecution's evidence are considered. In some jurisdictions, many cases are dismissed at this stage (probably to compensate for minimal screening by prosecutors). It has been reported, for example, that 85 per cent of felony cases that receive preliminary hearing in Chicago are dismissed at that stage.[8]

Cases that are not dismissed at the preliminary hearing are "bound over" for trial. Most of the cases, however, are not contested in an adversary trial: "plea-bargaining" results in the defendant agreeing to plead guilty to a lesser charge, or to fewer charges, than the prosecution had threatened to file. National averages do not reflect variations among jurisdictions, but about 80-90 per cent of all convictions result from guilty pleas, almost all of which are negotiated.[9] In New York City, 98 per cent of felony convictions in 1971 resulted from guilty pleas,[10] and 80 percent of homicide prosecutions in 1973 led to negotiated guilty pleas to lesser charges.[11]

What portion of defendants are found guilty of something? It is difficult to compare adjudication figures among jurisdictions because differences in prosecution and preliminary-hearing practices lead to widely varying pools of defendants at the trial stage (as illustrated by the Chicago example). More revealing is a comparison of the number of convictions with the number of police arrests passed on for further processing that result in convictions. Cases are dropped as a result of prosecutorial screening, dismissal at preliminary hearing, or acquittal at trial. No national averages are available, but the proportions of police-forwarded felony arrests resulting in conviction on some charge have been found to be 29 per cent in Washington, D.C.,[12] 51 per cent in Baltimore, 43 per cent in Detroit, and 23 per cent in Chicago.[13] It would appear from these figures that only one quarter to one half of police-forwarded felony arrests result in convictions. Thus only 2-4 per cent of all serious crimes lead to convictions, and most of these convictions result from guilty pleas to reduced charges.

Sentencing

Most convictions result from plea-bargaining, and plea-bargaining largely involves negotiation over the appropriate penalty for the defendant.

In other words, the prosecutor and the defense attorney (often the public defender) agree upon a sentence, and then determine the charge to which the defendant should plead guilty in order to justify that sentence.[14] The judge is not bound by the plea-bargaining sentence but usually, in practice, accedes to it. Of course, when the prosecutor and the defense attorney are negotiating, they are aware of what the judge will probably regard as reasonable and appropriate. Thus the judge is not without influence, though the prosecutor and the defense attorney may be more directly involved in determining the sentence.

Some cases, including the most sensational and complex ones, do go to trial, as a result of which most defendants are found guilty (the weaker cases having been screened out long before this stage). For these cases judges (or occasionally juries, especially for capital crimes) are called upon to render sentences. The nature of judicial sentencing varies dramatically. When penalties are mandatory and fixed, sentencing involves little more than "looking up" the penalty for the offense for which the defendant was convicted. When penalties are completely indeterminate, the judge exercises his discretion, choosing a sentence that ranges anywhere from unsupervised probation to life in prison. (With indeterminate sentencing, corrections and parole authorities may also have complete discretion in deciding when to release the persons imprisoned.)

In most states and for most crimes, statutory penalties are partially determined. Burglary, for example, may be punishable by a term of up to five years in the state prison. A judge sentencing under this statute could ordinarily give a defendant up to five years of probation (supervised or unsupervised), up to five years in prison (though incarceration of six months or less would probably be served in a county jail), or some combination of the two (for example, a sentence of three years in prison, suspension of which is contingent upon satisfactory completion of three years of supervised probation). The statute might also permit a monetary fine up to a certain amount to be imposed. The judge might also have the authority to require restitution or community service of the convicted defendant, perhaps as a condition of probation.[15]

Generally speaking, the trend over the last decade has been toward determinate sentencing. Mandatory penalties have become especially common for weapons offenses, narcotics violations, and intoxicated driving. It has also become common for judges to establish (or have forced upon them) sentencing guidelines. These guidelines, which vary in specificity, establish norms for types of offenses and offenders. For example, the norm for a first-time offender convicted of a daytime residential burglary in which no one was home and property loss was minimal might be a sentence of three years of supervised probation. All judges would be expected, though not required, to follow these norms. When deviating substantially from a guideline, a judge would be required to present in writing the reaons for rendering a sentence much lighter or much harsher than the established norm.[16]

So what is the result of sentencing? As usual, valid generalizations for the entire nation are difficult to draw, but data from several jurisdictions may help to indicate the range of sentencing practices. For the 1972–73 period, the portions of defendants convicted of a felony sent to prison in Baltimore, Chicago, and Detroit were 63.1 per cent, 60 per cent, and 34.8 per cent, respectively.[17] In Washington, D.C., in 1974 about 32 percent of all defendants arrested for felonies and convicted (though not necessarily of felonies) received sentences that included incarceration.[18] For the year ending June 30, 1979, approximately 56 percent of defendants convicted of felonies in the U.S. District Courts were imprisoned.[19] Overall, then, a reasonable estimate might be that about one half of the defendants initially arrested for serious crimes who are found guilty receive sentences that include a period of incarceration. This incarceration rate leads to the conclusion that 1–2 per cent of all serious crimes result in somebody being sentenced to jail or prison.

How long do these defendants remain incarcerated? National figures are elusive, and variation by type of crime is substantial. Average sentences of incarceration in 1972–73 for those convicted of armed robbery, as an example, were 105 months in Baltimore, 57 months in Chicago, and 46 months in Detroit.[20] For those convicted of felonious assault, the averages for the same cities were 78 months, 25 months, and 24 months, respectively. For all of the U.S. District Courts for the year ending June 30, 1979, the average sentence length for those convicted of robbery was 147 months (almost all convictions were for bank robberies); for those convicted of assault, 38 months.[21] The average incarceration sentence in these federal courts for all felonies was 52 months. Of course, sentence length and time actually served differ, as most prisoners in most states are released sometime before the end of their sentences.

Conditions of Sentence

When a person is sentenced additional decisions determine whether that sentence will be served in an institution or in the community. Decisions are also made about what kinds of treatment (if any) the convicted person should undergo. These and other decisions are usually based on some sort of a diagnosis of the person's problems. If the person has been sentenced to prison, his first stop will ordinarily be a diagnostic and reception center, where he will be subjected to a variety of tests and interviews. If the person has been put on probation, there may already have been a presentence diagnosis; in any event the probation officer assigned the case will make some diagnostic judgments about the client.

In the case of a person sentenced to prison, an important initial decision concerns the kind of institution to which he will be sent. The principal distinction is among minimum- medium- and maximum-security correctional facilities. Generally, the higher degree of security, the less comfortable the accomodations and the more limited the freedom enjoyed by inmates. Except in the cases of persons convicted of a first or a minor offense, it is common in many states to send offenders first to maximum-security facilities, allowing them the opportunity to "earn their way" into less secure institutions by exhibiting good behavior. In 1971, 56 per cent of all state prisoners were in maximum-security prisons; 30 percent, in medium-security prisons; the rest, in minimum-security custody.[22]

The conditions of imprisonment today are strongly affected by two factors operating at crosspurposes. Most prisons, which tend to be very old structures in poor condition, are severely overcrowded. Overcrowding makes prisons dirty and dangerous and renders available services and programs inadequate. Pressure to rectify these conditions has come in recent years from the courts. The Federal courts in particular have mandated all sorts of improvements and changes in prison facilities and administration. Overcrowding, however, often overwhelms these improvements. The courts have addressed the problem of overcrowding, requiring reductions in prison populations by specified dates, but progress has been slow. In the meantime, state criminal courts continue to sentence defendants to prison at current or higher rates. In Maryland, the result has been an increase in overcrowding in spite of an ambitious prison-construction program.[23] In 1980 a consultant predicted that the state's prison population would peak in 1987 at about 9800 inmates; before the end of 1981, the system already held 9876 prisoners.

Release and Revocation

Of those offenders sent to jail or prison, only a very small number (less than one per cent) die there.[24] The rest are released (at the completion of their sentence or before the completion of their sentence as a reward for accumulated "good time") or are paroled. Jail inmates, serving relatively short sentences, usually are not released until the end of their sentences. Prison inmates, including those serving life sentences, usually get out before they have completed their sentences.

In most states prisoners become eligible for parole after having served one third to one half of their sentences. The decision, a discretionary one, is usually made by a parole board, which may be independent of, or part of, the Department of Corrections. The parole board reviews the inmate's institutional record and reports from treatment and custodial staff, and may interview the inmate. If the board decides not to release the inmate, it will ordinarily review and reconsider his case periodically until the sentence is completed.

Paroled offenders are dealt with in much the same way as probationers are, but probably are somewhat more closely supervised, as their offenses and previous records are usually more serious. They are assigned to a parole officer, just as a probationer is assigned to a probation officer. Quite likely, the paroled offender will be enrolled in an educational or vocational program, a drug- or alcohol-treatment program, and/or a halfway house, and will be required to locate lawful employment–all as conditions of parole. Close supervision and support is especially crucial for parolees who have been in prison for extended periods and for those who have previously failed on parole.

Both probationers and parolees face the threat of revocation if they violate their conditions of release. A probationer who violates a condition might be brought back before the court, at which time the probation could be revoked and the person could be incarcerated. In the case of a parolee, a violation could lead the parole board to reconsider and revoke the release, and return the offender to prison. In the United States in 1977, about 16 per cent of parolees failed in their first year of release, by violating a condition of their parole, committing another crime and being convicted, or absconding.[25] A longer follow-up period would indicate a somewhat higher failure rate, but most parolees manage to avoid revocation. Revocation of probation is even more unusual, requiring as it does action by the courts to change an already rendered sentence.

CRIMINAL JUSTICE ORGANIZATIONS

Chapter 6 will examine different types of criminal justice organizations, focusing especially on their goals, structure, technology, decision-making and control processes, and environments. What follows here is a brief overview of the organizations and personnel engaged in dispensing criminal justice.

Police

More than any other aspect of crimal justice, policing in the United States is a local function. As of 1977, about 95 per cent of the roughly 20,000 law-enforcement agencies in the country represented local jurisdictions. These included 13,414 "general-purpose" police departments, 3,077 sheriff's offices, and several thousand other assorted agencies (campus security forces, coroners' offices, and so on) providing some kind of police protection. Most of these law-enforcement agencies are very small: more than half have nine or few "sworn" officers; more than a third have four or fewer.[26] State and Federal policing agencies tend to be larger than local ones, as might be expected, although the largest of all is the New York Police Department, with nearly 30,000 employees.

As of October 1978, the number of full-time equivalent police-protection employees in the United States was approximately 650,000, with about three quarters employed at the local level.[27] Roughly 80 per cent of these police employees are sworn, which means that they have the authority to exercise police powers.[28] It has recently been estimated that for large-city police agencies, about 5 per cent of sworn employees are female, 16 per cent are black, and 7.7 per cent have Spanish surnames.[29] These proportions have generally been increasing in recent years, but these figures probably overestimate minority representation in police employment in the nation as a whole. Also increasing has been the proportion of police employees with at least some college education. The best available figures indicate that "the proportion of sworn personnel with some college attainment went from 20 per cent in 1960 to 32 per cent in 1970 and to 46 per cent in 1974."[30] It seems very likely that the proportion is considerably higher today.

The work of the police primarily involves responding to citizens' calls for assistance, investigating crimes, patrolling assigned areas, looking for suspicious activity, monitoring traffic, and seeking to deter crime by giving the impression of police omnipresence. About one third of the time of patrol officers is spent handling calls and assigned details; most of the rest of the time is spent patrolling. Of patrol encounters with citizens, about 60 per cent involve crime or disorder, and 40 per cent involve traffic problems and the delivery of other kinds of services.[31] Detectives spend more of their time on clearly crime-related matters, but they spend most of their time in the office, processing papers and making phone calls.[32] Recent studies have provided strong evidence that police patrols in marked cars have little or not effect on crime or on citizens feelings of safety[33]; that foot patrols have little effect on crime but do make many citizens feel safer[34]; that rapid police response to citizen crime reports makes little difference in most cases because of citizen delays in discovering and reporting crimes[35]; and that most detective follow-up investigations produce little in the way of new information.[36] The cases that are "solved" by the police owe their solution primarily to the observations of victims and witnesses, with very few cases made as a result of "detective work" as popularly conceived. The effectiveness of just about all traditional police practices has been thrown into doubt, but few truly innovative alternatives have been identified or tested.[37]

Prosecution

Next to policing, prosecution is the most local of the criminal justice functions. As of 1977, 91 per cent of the roughly 8,000 state and local prosecution and civil-attorney agencies in the United States were to be found at the local (municipal, township, or county) level of government. If agencies handling only civil matters (corporation counsel, city solicitor, and so on) are excluded, the proportion of prosecutorial agencies attached to local governments is about 80 per cent. Most of these prosecution agencies are very small. Approximately 61 per cent of all such agencies employ but one attorney, and 65 per cent of local prosecution offices have only one attorney. Only about 5 per cent of all prosecution agencies have ten or more attorneys.[38] As of October 1978, the number of full-time equivalent legal-services (civil attorney) and prosecution employees in the United States was approximately 69,000, of whom about 63 per cent were employed at the local level.[39]

Prosecutors get most of their workload from the police, although occasionally victims will bring allegations directly to the prosecutor. As has already been noted, prosecutors have wide discretion in deciding whether or not to issue formal charges, what charges to issue, and whether or not to engage in plea-bargaining. In a large office, assistant prosecutors may operate under some direction from their elected superior, but they are also influenced by the judges and defense attorneys with whom they regularly work.[40] Public opinion is usually another consideration in decision- and policy-making, for in most jurisdictions the prosecutor is an elected official. The position of prosecutor has traditionally been a stepping stone to higher office, so that ambitious incumbents are often very eager to please their constituencies.

Defense

It is difficult to describe the defense function in organizational terms because a major portion of defense services are provided by private attorneys. Some of these private attorneys are paid by their clients; others (on a case-by-case basis), by the government. The latter are not truly government employees, however. Reliable figures are available only for public-defender agencies, which represent the vast majority of defendants in some jurisdictions, but do not even exist in others.

Of 490 public-defender agencies identified in the United States in 1977, almost 80 per cent were at the local level of government. Their distribution differs from that of police and prosecution agencies, however: nearly three quarters of all public-defender agencies are found at the county level, compared to 35 per cent of prosecution agencies and 23 per cent of law-enforcement agencies. Police and prosecutors are found mainly at the municipal level of government, whereas public defenders are by far more likely to be found at the county level. And over 20 per cent of public-defender agencies are part of state governments.[41]

Though generally small, public-defender agencies tend to be larger than prosecutors' offices. Although 61 per cent of prosecutors' offices had only one attorney, about 74 per cent of public-defender agencies have at least two attorneys. And whereas only 5 per cent of prosecutors' offices had ten or more attorneys, about 23 per cent of public-defender agencies have at least ten lawyers. Because of the small number of such agencies, though, public defense is easily the smallest sector of the criminal justice system. As of October 1978, the number of full-time equivalent public-defense employees in the United States was about 8,300, with 59 per cent employed at the local level. This represents fewer than one per cent of all criminal justice employees. When criminal justice expenditures are considered, however, which includes government payments to private counsel, the public-defense sector "swells" to 2.2 per cent of the total for the entire system.[42] Still, about three times as many tax dollars are spent on prosecution as are spent on defense.

Public defenders generally get the least "defendable" clients, of course, and their caseloads are usually overwhelming. It is not uncommon for public defenders to meet their clients only moments before trial or just before approaching the prosecutor to negotiate a plea. Extensive case preparation is rarely possible and, as most cases are plea-bargained anyway, would frequently be fruitless. Though it has become part of the conventional wisdom that the better lawyers go into private practice, and that defendants who can afford these better lawyers fare better in court, one careful study in three cities concluded that "public defenders are not less effective than retained counsel."[43]

Courts

Courts too are difficult to characterize organizationally. Many courts have both criminal and civil, as well as perhaps juvenile, jurisdiction. Some states have unified court systems, in which all courts are state agencies and all judges are state employees; other states have decentralized court systems, with courts and their employees attached to local governments; and some states have systems that are partially unified, partially local. There are also levels of courts: supreme courts, appeals courts, special-appeals courts, circuit courts, district courts, traffic courts, municipal courts, and magistrates' courts.

If each court is counted as a separate agency, regardless of whether it is part of a larger system or independent, there are approximately 14,000 courts in the United States that have at least some criminal jurisdiction. In addition, there are about 1,200 courts with solely juvenile jurisdiction. About three quarters of the courts with criminal jurisdiction are limited or special-jurisdiction courts, and the vast majority of these, as well as of courts with solely juvenile jurisdiction, are found at the local level. About 90 per cent of the courts with general and appellate jurisdiction, however, are attached to state governments.[44] It is probably accurate to infer that most traffic and misdemeanor cases are tried in local courts, while most felony cases are tried in state courts.

As of October 1978, there were about 150,000 full-time equivalent judicial employees in the United States, two thirds of whom were employed at the local level of government. This total represents approximately 13 per cent of all criminal justice employees, and the courts account for roughly the same proportion of criminal justice expenditures.[45] The major figures among judicial employees are judges, of course, but the majority of the employees are clerks, bailiffs, stenographers, and other support personnel. A trend in recent years has been the appointment of court administrators, whose purpose ostensibly is to manage the workflow, the budget, and the personnel of the court, but in practice these administrators often find it difficult to wrest sufficient authority from judges to do more than traditional "court clerk" duties.[46]

Probation and Parole

Probation and parole agencies are described together because over half such agencies have multiple functions–juvenile and adult jurisdiction, parole and probation functions, or some combination thereof. In 1976, there were about 3,600 state and local probation and/or parole agencies in the United States. Of these, almost 1,700 handled just probation, 1,500 performed both probation and parole, 340 handled just parole supervision, and 60 were "parole authorities," which are the decision-making bodies that decide when prisoners get released. The vast majority of the parole authorities, parole agencies, and combined probation and parole agencies were located in state governments, whereas most of the agencies handling only probation were at the local level (predominantly county).[47]

In October 1978 there were 51,000 full-time equivalent state and local probation and parole employees in the United States, with about 60 per cent employed by local governments.[48] With the exception of parole authorities, these agencies and their employees are primarily concerned with the supervision of caseloads of clients (probationers and parolees). In September 1976, probation and parole agencies had over 1.4 million adults and juveniles under supervision, with an average caseload per counselor of about fifty clients. The median agency caseload was about 150, with 17 per cent of probation and parole agencies supervising in excess of 500 clients.[49]

Jails and Prisons

The general distribution of jails, prisons, and juvenile institutions is presented in Table 4.2. As would be expected, almost all prisons are operated by the states (the exceptions are all in Washington, D.C., which in many respects could be considered a state). Jails, on the other hand, are under local (usually county) supervision. Juvenile institutions are somewhat more evenly distributed among levels of government. Long-term juvenile institutions, though, tend to be state agencies, whereas short-term juvenile institutions are found predominantly

Table 4-2. State and Local Jails, Prisons, and Juvenile Institutions in the United States (figures from 1977, 1978, and 1979 studies)

Type of Facilities	Total	State	County	Municipal
Adult Facilities	4,056	558	2,905	593
Prisons	563	558	0	5
Jails	3,493	0	2,905	588
Juvenile Institutions	596	228	336	32
Long-term	197	152	39	6
Short-term	399	76	297	26
TOTAL	4,652	786	3,241	625

Adapted from *Justice Agencies in the United States: Summary Report 1980* (Washington, D.C.: U.S. Department of Justice, 1980), p. 20.

at the county level. Overall, more than two thirds of adult and juvenile institutions are county agencies, and the vast majority of these are local jails.[50]

These institutions vary widely in size. Prisons tend to be the largest, with an average of nearly 500 inmates per institution. On any given day there are over 250,000 people in prison in the United States. The number of people in jail on any day is closer to 150,000, so that the average jail population is about fifty, and actually 80 per cent of all jails can accommodate fewer than fifty inmates. Of these jail inmates, roughly 60 per cent are serving sentences and 40 per cent are awaiting trial.[51] Juvenile institutions tend to be smaller yet, except for some state-operated long-term facilities. It is estimated that the daily population of juvenile-detention (secure, closed) facilities is 10,000–12,000. Juveniles are sometimes also detained in adult jails, however, as well as in "open" facilities, so that the number of juveniles in custody on any day is probably closer to 50,000.[52] These figures represent only public agencies, and at any time there are another 30,000 "residents" of privately operated juvenile-custody facilities.

Except for the police, the institutional-corrections sector has the largest employment and expenditures of any sector of the criminal justice system. Approximately 75 per cent of all correctional expenditures are in the institutional sector. As of October 1978, there were almost 190,000 full-time equivalent employees in institutional correctional facilities, about 120,000 of whom worked for state-level agencies. About three quarters of these state employees worked in adult institutions.[53] A comparable statistic for local institutions could not be found, but the preponderance of county jails among the local agencies suggests that even higher proportions of employees work in adult, rather than juvenile, institutions.

Community Corrections

In addition to jails, prisons, and juvenile institutions, there are other kinds of correctional agencies, such as halfway houses, group homes, prerelease and work-release facilities, ranches, shelters, and drug/alcohol-treatment facilities. It is particularly difficult to get an accurate census of these agencies and their clients, because they tend to be small, grant-funded, privately operated, and short-lived. Also, the clients of these agencies may be on probation or parole, and thus already "counted."

There an estimated 400 halfway houses in the United States, serving an average daily population of 10,000 adults.[54] No estimates of the numbers of other kinds of noninstitutional adult correctional facilities are available. There were about 1,400 open juvenile correctional facilities (group homes, ranches, and so on) in 1977.[55] A total of 60,000 or so juveniles "in custody" who were not detained in a secure institution were served by such public and private agencies.[56] The distribution of these youngsters among the different kinds of noninstitutional facilities is not precisely known. Reliable employment and expenditure information for community corrections agencies is also unavailable, particularly as so many of these agencies are tenuously funded through grants and special allocations. Resource commitments to community corrections clearly increased through most of the 1970s, though, but the status of such programs is far less secure in the "get tough" atmosphere of the early 1980s. Still, the costs per client for community corrections programs are generally far less than comparable costs for institutionalization, and if there is one other dominant theme these days besides law and order, it is fiscal austerity.

OTHER ORGANIZATIONS INVOLVED IN CRIMINAL JUSTICE

In addition to the criminal justice agencies already discussed, there are other kinds of organizations that play important roles in criminal justice.

LEAA and Its Successors

In response to increases in crime, urban riots, and public concern for law and order, the Federal government decided in the mid-1960s to aid state and local efforts to reduce crime and improve criminal justice. An Office of Law Enforcement Assistance (OLEA), and then the Law Enforcement Assistance Administration (LEAA), were formed. These were primarily grant-letting agencies, although they also performed some planning and research activities. Most of the grants were allocated to the states, each of which determined its priorities and further allocated the money to specific agencies and localities. Some discretionary grants were also made by LEAA directly to criminal justice agencies and to local governments.

Despite spending several billion dollars, LEAA could not point to any crime decreases for which it deserved credit, and in the late 1970s it came under heated attack for its presumed lack of accomplishments. The agency's funding level was greatly reduced, and LEAA was made a unit within the new Office of Justice Assistance, Research and Statistics (OJARS). The emphasis at the Federal level was changed from distributing grants to collecting and disseminating information, conducting research, and providing technical assistance. Finally, on April 15, 1982, LEAA officially went out of existence.

State and Regional Planning Agencies

During the LEAA era, each state had a criminal justice planning agency that allocated the LEAA block grants among local governments and agencies. Part of the LEAA appropriation helped to underwrite the state planning agencies (SPAs). Each state prepared an annual "comprehensive plan" that identified problems and priorities and specified how LEAA funds would be spent. Most SPA activity, however, was not devoted to planning but to managing and administering the grants.

Also during the LEAA era many Regional Planning Units (RPUs) were established. These varied in function and power. The more significant RPUs had either funds to disburse or some voice in the allocation of SPA funds within their region. In some states, for example, local criminal justice agencies had first to get RPU approval of their applications for grants before these could be forwarded to the SPA.

With the tremendous reduction in Federal criminal justice grants in the last few years, SPAs and RPUs have fallen on hard times. Many of these agencies have so far survived, however, albeit with fewer personnel. Those that have survived have emphasized their roles as coordinators of the components of the criminal justice system and as advisors on criminal justice fiscal responsibilities, such as reviewing the annual budget requests of criminal justice agencies and making recommendations to executive and legislative decision-makers.[57]

Standards and Training Commissions

As of 1981, forty-six of the fifty states had agencies with some responsibility for establishing and/or enforcing police employment and/or training standards.[58] Some of these agencies or commissions also have similar responsibilities with respect to correctional personnel. Most of the agencies deal primarily with training standards, certifying acceptable training programs, offering or sponsoring training (especially for personnel from small departments that cannot afford to maintain their own academies), and monitoring compliance with the standards. Some of the commissions also enforce employment standards, and a few actually "license" police officers. Without such a license, in these states, one is prohibited from working as a police officer. The license, like that for any other regulated occupation, can be revoked for sufficiently improper behavior.

State Court Administrators

Even as individual courts increasingly are employing administrators to assist judges with their managerial duties, so many states have administrative offices of the courts or state court administrators with limited managerial authority over the entire court system. These administrative offices are often attached to the state supreme courts. Their authority is generally limited to coordinating state judicial activity, identifying problems and recommending solutions, and advising on the allocation of judicial resources. Moreover, even the administrative authority of their superiors, the state supreme courts, is often quite limited. Consequently, state court administrative offices usually have to rely heavily on reasoned argument and persuasion to get their way.

Departments of Justice

In emulation of the Federal government, many states have created departments of justice or of public safety and corrections as cabinet-level umbrella agencies for police, correctional, and other criminal justice organizations. The potential significance of this mode of organization is that criminal justice fiscal and policy decisions might be coordinated to a degree not usually otherwise achieved. Merely establishing such an agency, however, does not guarantee such coordination. Also, the many criminal justice agencies found at the local level are not under the direct authority of a state department of justice, and the judiciary remains an independent branch. Still, some coordination, at least at the state level, might reasonably be expected.

Crime Victim-Compensation Commissions

Twenty-nine states offer some form of compensation, usually administered by a commission, to victims of crime.[59] These commissions usually have very limited budgets and small staffs, and are unable to aid more than a tiny fraction of all crime victims. Emphasis is ordinarily placed on victims of serious crimes who have suffered major injury or loss, whose attackers can provide no restitution, and who are clearly in need of compensation. Most of the compensation commissions are located in the executive branch of state government, although a few are attached to the courts. Some states offer a limited maximum compensation ($1,000-5,000), while others offer far larger sums or even unlimited reimbursement of medical expenses.

Juvenile Services Agencies

Juvenile courts are, of course, judicial agencies. They are sometimes actually separate courts, but more often are merely special sessions of courts of general jurisdiction. Juvenile correctional agencies sometimes are organizationally attached to adult agencies, sometimes are completely independent agencies in the executive branch, and sometimes are located within social service or health and hygiene agencies. These juvenile agencies counsel and supervise youths referred to them by the courts, the police, and the schools.

A kind of juvenile agency that gained some popularity in the 1970s is the youth service bureau (YSB).[60] YSBs were intended to be separate from juvenile criminal justice agencies, although such independence has not always been maintained. The YSBs were to serve as alternatives to traditional processing of delinquent and dependent juveniles, so that formal labels and records would not be unnecessarily created. The YSBs were also to function as advocates for individual youths and for children as a class, based on the proposition that juveniles need an advocate. In practice, YSBs have tended to emphasize their diversion (alternative processing) function rather than advocacy, and are often difficult to distinguish from regular juvenile justice agencies.

Social Service Agencies

A whole host of noncriminal justice agencies provide social services that directly affect victims, offenders, and the justice agencies themselves. These include medical and psychological services, family counselors, battered-spouse shelters, drug- and alcohol-abuse programs, big-brother and big-sister programs, and a multitude of other services. The police commonly refer victims and troubled persons, and divert minor offenders, to such programs. The prosecutor and the courts similarly refer and divert. Probation and parole officers, as part of the supervision process, may require their clients to take advantage of such social services. The availability of these social services, though, has diminished since the 1960s and 1970s. Exactly how this will affect crime and criminal justice is not yet known, but the prognosis is not good.

Private Security

In addition to the 650,000 or so public police personnel in this country are another 300,000 privately employed detectives and security guards.[61] The jurisdiction of these security personnel is generally limited to the private property of their employers, but this may include giant amusement parks, shopping malls, or huge industrial plants, all with large numbers of visitors, customers, or employees. On this private property security personnel have extensive authority, often including arrest powers. Private detectives and guards may also be armed. It has been estimated that about 500,000 arrests each year are made by private security personnel.

On the one hand, private security clearly augments the protection offered by the police. Offenders are apprehended and crimes are no doubt prevented through the efforts of guards and private detectives. Also, the public presumably should not have to bear the costs of policing private property. There are some dangers, however, that need to be recognized. Employment and training standards for private detectives and guards are minimal or nonexistent. Yet these personnel have considerable legal authority and often carry firearms. The public police have such powers but they are better trained and generally more accountable to the public, to the elected representatives of the people, and to the courts. Private police are less easily held accountable.

MAJOR CRIMINAL JUSTICE POLICIES

The basic policies that guide criminal justice decisions and practices are based on varying theories of crime causation and on varying views of proper government conduct in crime control. The policies are carried out, well or poorly, by the criminal justice agencies and process just described. They are formulated and implemented within the context of the philosophies and principles discussed at the beginning of this chapter.

Deterrence

The policy of deterrence is the attempt to reduce criminal behavior through the use or threat of punishment, and to make the risks of committing a crime greater than the benefits. A policy of deterrence is implemented by deploying police and having them respond immediately to calls for assistance, by prosecuting offenders who are arrested, by punishing offenders who are convicted, and generally by specifying penalties for those who break the law. Punishment presumably encourages the offender not to commit a crime again (specific deterrence) and deters others from criminal behavior (general deterrence). The ultimate implementation of deterrence is, of course, the utilization of capital punishment.

There are several prerequisites for effective deterrence. One is that the offender must actually calculate risks, but in cases of passion or other impulsive crimes, the threat of punishment may never be considered. Another condition is that the threat must be communicated—stiff penalties will not deter if potential offenders are not aware of them. Also, the risk must be reasonably certain—harsh penalties rarely applied may not deter. Finally, the threatened punishment must be sufficiently severe to outweigh the probable benefits to be gained from the crime.

These conditions for the effective implementation of deterrence are very demanding. Some crimes, perhaps many, are committed impulsively, so that deterrence has little effect on them. For all crimes the likelihood of detection, reporting, arrest, prosecution, and conviction is very slight. Though the possible penalties upon conviction are harsh in the United States, the probability of getting to the point of sentencing is negligible. In short, the risk is not very great. Consequently, deterrence, probably our fundamental criminal justice policy, does not work well.

Incapacitation

A policy that works better, when we are willing to pay the moral and financial costs, is incapacitation. This policy seeks to reduce crime by imprisoning for long periods those who habitually commit crimes, or who commit especially heinous crimes. Although few criminal acts result in convictions, almost all habitual offenders eventually get caught and convicted for some of their acts. If these habitual offenders can be identified and incarcerated for lengthy periods, crime will have been reduced by at least the number of offenses they would have committed if they had been on the streets. Some argue that this policy could significantly reduce crime.[62]

Implementation of such a policy would undoubtedly require more prisons, however, which would cost many millions to build and more millions to run. The policy of incapacitation is not only costly, it also implies that society has, in effect, given up on a large segment of the population. These are harsh moral judgments, with ramifications for our whole way of life.

Crime Prevention

The policy of crime prevention essentially aims to make it harder to commit crimes. The assumption is that some crimes can be prevented, or at least displaced, by making them harder to commit. This policy is implemented through such measures as improved lighting, better locks and alarms, exact-change requirements for public transportation, physical obstructions, and improved architectural design of residences, businesses, and entire communities. Citizen patrols such as the Guardian Angels and block-watch groups, and the marking of valuable possessions are other crime-prevention methods. This policy has become very popular in recent years, but its effects have yet to be fully evaluated.

Rehabilitation

The policy of rehabilitation seeks to reduce the future criminality of someone who has offended against the law. This policy is based on the assumption that the offender has a problem and that it can and must be cured. First the offender's problem must be diagnosed, after which a suitable treatment can be identified. A variety of treatment modes are possible, including psychiatric care, psychological therapy, medical intervention, education, or vocational training. When and if the person is cured, he can be permitted to return to the community.

Rehabilitation has been an important policy for the last one hundred years. Custody (for deterrence and incapacitation) has probably always been dominant, however. Rehabilitation peaked with indeterminate sentencing in the 1960s, but since then has fallen out of favor. One reason is that few of its methods were found to reduce future criminal behavior.[63] Nor does it any longer seem reasonable to locate the "problem" solely within the offender. Unfortunately, rehabilitation has come to be associated with the "coddling" of criminals, which is rarely popular, especially when fear of crime is high and the public is inclined to "get tough."

Reintegration

The reintegration policy includes rehabilitation of the offender but also admits that there may be problems in the community that also need to be solved. The key idea behind reintegration is that it is in the community that the offender will succeed or fail upon release, so that the offender must be prepared for life in the community, *and* the community must be prepared to accept the offender. To "cure" the offender requires not just providing him with therapy in prison, but also providing him with a decent job and a support system in the community after his release. The policy of reintegration relies generally on community correctional agencies, including work-release centers and halfway houses, as well as on parole, for its implementation.

On the whole, the reintegration policy seems neither more nor less effective than traditional custody and rehabilitation.[64] The fact that community corrections programs are cheaper than imprisonment should then be a strong argument in favor of reintegration. The general public doubts that the reintegration policy provides adequate protection, however, and perceives it as even more "permissive" than rehabilitation. As a result, it tends not to be a popular policy, although financial exigencies promise to sustain its use for the time being.

Diversion

Diversion is a traditional informal criminal justice practice that has recently become a formal policy. It involves diverting some offenders, usually misdemeanants and juveniles, from the official criminal justice process. The police, and to a lesser extent the prosecutors and the courts, have always diverted some cases—those which involved minor offenses, or those in which the victim did not wish to press charges, or those in which justice seemed to warrant diversion. Diversion now has two additional purposes: to avoid stigmatizing offenders who seem likely to refrain from future criminality, and to free the criminal justice system for the processing of serious cases.

Several complaints are heard about the diversion policy. Some critics fear that serious offenders get diverted, so that deterrence and incapacitation policies are thwarted. Horror stories are often told, for example, of juveniles finally charged with serious crimes who had been diverted several times for burglaries and robberies. Not only does this seem to show the ineffectiveness of diversion, but it also may result in the treatment of such juveniles as first offenders, because their earlier offenses did not result in convictions.[65] Other critics charge that the offer of diversion is often used to coerce defendants out of exercising their right to force the prosecution to prove its case. Innocent defendants may agree to diversion rather than risk the possibility of being found guilty, remote as that possibility might be. Another criticism is that formal diversion results in "widening the net." According to this argument, the police now arrest, and prosecutors now charge, offenders who in the past would have been let go, because the police and prosecutors know that the offenders will be diverted anyway, so that "nothing really serious will happen to them." On the whole, diversion seems a promising policy with vocal adherents and detractors.

Decriminalization

Decriminalization is a policy that aims to reduce crime by reducing the amount of criminal law. It is a reaction against what is often termed the "overreach" of criminal law—the possibility that many more human acts are defined as crimes than is necessary. The kinds of offenses that are usually seen as candidates for decriminalization are public drunkenness, sexual activity among consenting adults, possession of marijuana for personal use, and other so-called victimless crimes. Decriminalization or legalization of these acts could reduce the overall amount of crime, and also perhaps relieve some of the burden on the criminal justice system.

A number of states have decriminalized such offenses, and there is no evidence that the behaviors increased as a result.[66] Implementation problems vary, however: in some situations decriminalization would require no new criminal justice system activity, but the decriminalization of public drunkenness, for example, might require a new response (police transportation of drunks to detoxification centers instead of jail). Practical considerations aside, though, some groups in the community remain morally opposed to certain kinds of behavior and lobby strongly to keep such behavior illegal. The police also generally favor keeping the laws, not necessarily out of moral concern but because the laws are handy tools for solving problems and dealing with difficult people. These debates are probably endless, and it is worth keeping in mind that the crimes of major concern—burglaries, robberies, aggravated assaults, and rapes—are not likely candidates for decriminalization.

Social Reform

Until recently it was widely believed that crime was caused by poor social and economic conditions, and that crime could be reduced by improving such conditions.[67] Now it is considered naïve to suggest social reform as a principal approach to reducing crime in America.[68] There is widespread agreement today that we cannot afford social reform on the scale necessary to substantially reduce crime, and that even if we could, we would need to protect ourselves through deterrence and incapacitation while waiting for the more basic reforms to be accomplished. Some also feel strongly that social reform in the 1960s, with the War on Poverty and the Great Society, failed as a crime-control policy.

Whether these views are unduly pessimistic, the result of fear and unmet expectations in the 1960s, or accurate in their rejection of social reform as the basis of crime reduction efforts, only time will tell. But as Herbert Wechsler noted many years ago, "one can say for social reform as a means to the end of improved crime control what . . . cannot be said for drastic tightening of the process of the criminal law—that even if the end should not be achieved, the means is desirable for its own sake."[69]

SUMMARY

This chapter has provided an introduction to some of the philosophies and principles that underly the administration of justice in the United States, such as federalism, separation of power, the Bill of Rights, and due process of law, and a description of the criminal justice process as a series of decisions, from detection through release and revocation. The institutions that carry out the criminal justice process include "mainstream" criminal justice agencies, such as the police, prosecution, defense, courts, probation, parole, prisons, jails, and community corrections, as well as other organizations such as state planning agencies, training commissions, youth service bureaus, and private security. Some of the major policies that guide criminal justice decision-making and practice are deterrence, incapacitation, crime prevention, rehabilitation, reintegration, diversion, decriminalization, and social reform. These policies vary in their costs, in the values on which they are based, and in the types of crimes against which they are likely to be effective.

· *Chapter 4* · NOTES

1. *Miranda* v. *Arizona*, 384 U.S. 436 (1966).
2. *Mapp* v. *Ohio*, 367 U.S. 643 (1961).
3. *Criminal Victimization in the United States, 1979* (Washington, D.C.: U.S. Department of Justice, 1981).
4. Herman Goldstein, "Police Discretion: The Ideal versus the Real," *Public Administration Review*, 23 (September 1963), 148–56.
5. *Crime in the United States, 1979* (Washington, D.C.: U.S. Department of Justice, 1981).
6. Scott H. Decker, "Alternate Measures of Police Output," *American Journal of Police*, 1 (1981), 23–25.
7. Brian Forst, et al., *What Happens After Arrest?* (Washington, D.C.: Institute for Law and Social Research, 1977), p. 16.
8. James Eisenstein and Herbert Jacob, *Felony Justice* (Boston, Ma.: Little, Brown and Company, 1977), p. 232.
9. President's Commission on Law Enforcement and Administration of Justice, *Task Force Report: The Courts* (Washington, D.C.: U.S. Government Printing Office, 1967), p. 9.
10. Vera Institute of Justice, *Felony Arrests* (New York: Vera Institute of Justice, 1977), p. 134.
11. Selwyn Rabb, "Plea Bargains Resolve 8 of 10 Homicide Cases," *The New York Times* (January 27, 1975), p. 1, as cited in James P. Levine, et al., *Criminal Justice: A Public Policy Approach* (New York: Harcourt Brace Jovanovich, Inc., 1980), p. 214.
12. Forst, et al., op. cit., p. 17.
13. Eisenstein and Jacob, op. cit., p. 259, fn. 3.
14. Arthur Rosett and Donald R. Cressey, *Justice by Consent: Plea Bargains in the American Courthouse* (New York: J. B. Lippincott Company, 1976).
15. John Ortiz Smykla, *Community-Based Corrections: Principles and Practices* (New York: Macmillan Publishing Co., Inc., 1981), pp. 219–53.
16. J. S. Bainbridge, Jr., and Karen E. Warmkessel, "Sentencing Guidelines Draw Mixed Reaction," *Baltimore Sun*, November 9, 1981.
17. Eisenstein and Jacob, op. cit., p. 275.
18. Forst, et al., op. cit., p. 18.
19. Michael J. Hindelang, et al., eds., *Sourcebook of Criminal Justice Statistics–1980* (Washington, D.C.: U.S. Department of Justice, 1981), p. 434.
20. Eisenstein and Jacob, op. cit., p. 280.
21. Hindelang, et al., op. cit., p. 434.
22. American Correctional Association, *1971 Directory of Correctional Institutions and Agencies of America, Canada, and Great Britain* (College Park, Md.: American Correctional Association, 1971), as cited in Donald J. Newman, *Introduction to Criminal Justice*, 2nd ed. (New York: J. B. Lippincott Company, 1978), p. 328.
23. Doug Struck, "Inmate Increase Overtakes Prison Building Plans," *Baltimore Sun*, December 8, 1981.
24. Newman, op. cit., p. 351.
25. Hindelang, et al., op. cit., p. 519.

26. *Justice Agencies in the United States: Summary Report 1980* (Washington, D.C.: U.S. Department of Justice, 1980), pp. 2–7.

27. *Summary Report–Expenditure and Employment Data for the Criminal Justice System: 1978* (Washington, D.C.: U.S. Department of Justice, 1980), p. 12.

28. John F. Heaphy, ed., *Police Practices: The General Administrative Survey* (Washington, D.C.: Police Foundation, 1978), and *The National Manpower Survey of the Criminal Justice System: Volume Two* (Washington, D.C.: U.S. Department of Justice, 1978), p. 2.

29. Heaphy, op. cit.

30. *The National Manpower Survey*, op. cit., p. 3.

31. Gordon P. Whitaker, "What is Patrol Work?" *Police Studies*, 4 (Winter 1982), 19.

32. Peter W. Greenwood and Joan Petersilia, *The Criminal Investigation Process Volume I: Summary and Policy Implications* (Santa Monica, Calif.: Rand Corporation, 1975).

33. George L. Kelling, et al., *The Kansas City Preventive Patrol Experiment: A Summary Report* (Washington, D.C.: Police Foundation, 1974).

34. *The Newark Foot Patrol Experiment* (Washington, D.C.: Police Foundation, 1981).

35. Tony Pate, et al., *Police Response Time: Its Determinants and Effects* (Washington, D.C.: Police Foundation, 1976), and *Response Time Analysis: Executive Summary*, (Washington, D.C.: U.S. Department of Justice, 1978).

36. Greenwood and Petersilia, op. cit.

37. James Q. Wilson, "Police Research and Experimentation," in Richard A. Staufenberger, ed., *Progress in Policing: Essays on Change* (Cambridge, Ma.: Ballinger Publishing Co., 1980), pp. 129–52.

38. *Justice Agencies in the United States*, op. cit., pp. 9–10.

39. *Summary Report–Expenditure and Employment Data*, p. 12.

40. Rosett and Cressey, op. cit.

41. *Justice Agencies in the United States*, p. 11.

42. *Summary Report–Expenditure and Employment Data*, pp. 11–12.

43. Eisenstein and Jacob, op. cit., p. v.

44. *Justice Agencies in the United States*, p. 14.

45. *Summary Report–Expenditure and Employment Data*, p. 11.

46. Ernest C. Friesen, "Constraints and Conflicts in Court Administration," *Public Administration Review*, 31 (March–April 1971), 121–24, and Steven W. Hays and Larry C. Berkson, "The New Managers: Court Administrators," in Larry C. Berkson, et al., *Managing the State Courts* (St. Paul, Minn.: West Publishing Co., 1977), pp. 188–98.

47. *Justice Agencies in the United States*, p. 16.

48. *Expenditure and Employment Data for the Criminal Justice System, 1978* (Washington, D.C.: U.S. Department of Justice, 1981), p. 321.

49. *Justice Agencies in the United States*, pp. 15–17.

50. Ibid., p. 20.

51. Ibid., pp. 18–20.

52. *Children in Custody: A Report on the Juvenile Detention and Correctional Facility Census of 1975* (Washington, D.C: U.S. Department of Justice, 1979), p. 5.

53. *Employment and Expenditure Data for the Criminal Justice System, 1978*, pp. 320, 337–39.

54. Smykla, op. cit., p. 158.

55. Ibid., p. 205, citing undated reports of 1977 census of public and private juvenile detention facilities.

56. Hindelang, et al., op. cit., p. 481.

57. John K. Hudzik, et al., *Criminal Justice Manpower Planning: An Overview* (Washington, D.C.: U.S. Department of Justice, 1981), pp. 132–63.

58. Ibid., pp. 164–79.

59. Deborah M. Carrow, *Crime Victim Compensation: Program Model* (Washington, D.C.: U.S. Department of Justice, 1980).

60. Smykla, op. cit., pp. 175–93.

61. Levine, et al., op. cit., pp. 173–75.

62. James Q. Wilson, *Thinking About Crime* (New York: Basic Books, 1975).

63. Robert Martinson, "What Works? Questions and Answers About Prison Reform," *The Public Interest* (Spring 1974), 22–65.

64. Smykla, op. cit., pp. 157–73.

65. Patrick A. McGuire, "Curb Repeat Offenders, Study Asks," *Baltimore Sun*, February 2, 1982.

66. Levine, et al., op. cit., pp. 430–61.

67. Ramsey Clark, *Crime in America* (New York: Simon & Schuster, Inc., 1970).

68. Wilson, *Thinking About Crime*, op. cit.

69. As quoted in Charles E. Silberman, *Criminal Violence, Criminal Justice* (New York: Vintage Books, 1978), p. 224.

• Chapter 5 •

COMPREHENSIVE SYSTEM PLANNING

This chapter examines criminal justice as a system and discusses the role of comprehensive planning as a tool and a process in systems analysis. The idea of comprehensive planning has nearly as long a history as the criminal justice system itself, and this discussion will consider some of these historical origins.

Comprehensive planning, though largely an ill-defined concept, nonetheless is understood to have as its basic concern the notion that planning in criminal justice includes coordinating the activities and objectives of the agencies that constitute the criminal justice system. It is also understood to be concerned with uncovering and resolving duplication and crosspurposes among those agencies, and with advancing the overall efficiency and effectiveness of the system. These and related ideas will be discussed, along with the criticism that comprehensive planning is too complex to be practical under our fragmented justice system.

The 1968 Omnibus Crime Control and Safe Streets Act has probably been the single most important factor in American criminal justice in fostering and advancing the notion of comprehensive planning. The Act undertook to create and to finance comprehensive criminal justice planning agencies at state and local levels. The history of that endeavor reveals both the potential for, and the problems associated with, such planning.

HISTORICAL ANTECEDENTS

A prime feature of the American justice system is its decentralized structure. Several positive effects may be attributed to decentralization: justice is administered with reference to local community standards; there is relative freedom from the control of a centralized national bureaucracy; and, perhaps most important, *enforcement* of the law is in the hands of the community. Since the Revolution, it has been held that national police forces, as well as standing armies, are repugnant to democratic values, and the Constitution itself reserves substantial justice administration to the individual states.

Although the local administration of justice is a national value, countervailing influences have had their effect: dramatic population and economic growth; massive population migrations; industrialization; the actions of the Supreme Court in interpreting a *national* Constitution. Crime is an inter-community phenomenon to such an extent that local justice systems have become increasingly incapable of dealing independently with it. Indeed decentralization itself, with all of its attendant ideological and political values, has increasingly come to be viewed pejoratively, as fragmentation, dysfunction, inefficiency, ineffectiveness, and lack of coordination.

The American criminal justice system is not just politically fragmented but also composed of functionally semi-independent agencies. The courts are constitutionally a separate branch of government; many law-enforcement agency heads (sheriffs) are independently elected officials, and so are most prosecutors; corrections fall under a variety of administrative and bureaucratic arrangements but are most commonly found within the executive branch. This separation of powers engenders fragmentation in decision-making and difficulties in coordinating various criminal justice processes, and threatens thereby the overall efficiency and effectiveness of the criminal justice apparatus.

The conflict between fragmentation and efficient and effective justice has been a matter of concern for some time. The concern may at least be traced back to the Progressive and Populist movements of the last half of the nineteenth century and the early part of this century. The criminal justice historian, Samuel Walker, traces it back even further:

> Between 1815 and 1900 the United States created its modern criminal justice system. In 1815 key institutions—the police, the prison, probation, parole, did not yet exist in their modern form. By 1900 they were parts of a new apparatus of social control. . . . The people who created the new agencies [did not] think in terms of a system at first. Instead, they created separate agencies in a halting and uncertain attempt to deal with immediate problems. Not until late in the nineteenth century did a few individuals begin to understand the interrelationships and to think in terms of a systematic approach to social control.[1]

It is probably safe to say the most twentieth-century reforms of the criminal justice system have been aimed toward increasing the effectiveness and sophistication of local police, courts, and jails in dealing with the scope and pattern of contemporary crime. These reforms have taken several directions, including attempts to "professionalize" the police and the legal system, to establish citizen "watchdog" commissions, and, most important, to view the administration of justice within a "systemic" context—that is, to think about an interrelated set of processes and agencies involved in crime control and to develop a common aim of overall efficiency and effectiveness.

Partly under leadership provided by Theodore Roosevelt and Woodrow Wilson, significant developments in professionalizing the police and in developing rehabilitation programs in corrections were initiated. Intellectuals, as well as practitioners, began to think through some of the common purposes underlying the administration of justice, noting that several interrelated agencies, each with specialized tasks, comprised the effort directed toward controlling crime, deviance, and disorder. The experts were divided, however, on the common purpose: one group stressed efficiency; the other, social justice. This division endures: even now some define improvement in the administration of justice as the enhancement of the means of apprehending, convicting, and punishing offenders, while others define it as increased effectiveness in dealing with the causes of crime at its core.[2]

During the 1920s important forces in criminal justice reform included numerous local, state, and Federal crime commissions. One of these commissions, the Cleveland Survey of Criminal Justice, proved to be a forerunner for contemporary thinking about the criminal justice complex. Other commissions of the period focused on the discrete components of the criminal justice process, but the Cleveland Survey conceptualized criminal justice as a "system," emphasizing the flow and processing of criminal cases from beginning to end, and raising for the first time some idea of inputs and outputs being processed by a series of interrelated "crime-fighting" agencies.[3]

Employing the Cleveland Survey as a model, Missouri and Illinois shortly became the first states during the 1920s to establish state crime commissions. The mandates of the statewide commissions, much broader than those of the Cleveland Survey, included statewide rural law enforcement and the operations of state correctional programs.

At the Federal level, similar concerns over the coordination and the professionalism of the justice system were being registered. In 1929, President Hoover appointed the Wickersham Commission to examine the problems of law enforcement and criminal administration, as well as to examine the problems growing out of Prohibition. Hoover, an engineer by training, was of the opinion that solving social problems required application of a multidisciplinary approach. The Wickersham Commission made use of diverse expert consultants who emphasized the need for coordination and efficiency within the justice complex. The efficiency-oriented crime-control model gained ascendancy and became the guiding force for the newly formed Federal Bureau of Investigation under the leadership of J. Edgar Hoover. Also established was the first national crime-records systems, the Uniform Crime Report, which had as its purpose the provision of the data necessary to "measure" progress made toward dealing with crime.

Thus, the idea that the justice system was—or should be—something more than a loose amalgamation of independent agencies can be traced back to the beginning of the present century, as can the idea that criminal justice processes should be viewed comprehensively and in an integrated fashion. Not until the late 1960s, however, was there explicit concentration on the need for systemwide coordination through comprehensive criminal justice planning.

THE IDEA OF COMPREHENSIVE SYSTEM PLANNING

The aim of comprehensive system planning is to increase the coordination of activities among the various parts of the criminal justice apparatus in anticipating as well as responding to crime, and to increase the efficiency and effectiveness of crime control within some overall concept of constitutionally guaranteed justice. Achieving this aim has proven difficult: not only is the justice system fragmented, but there is also confusion and disagreement over the terms *system* and *comprehensive*, and uncertainty as to whether criminal justice *is* a system and whether *comprehensive* planning is possible. The term *comprehensive planning* has given rise to grave concerns: it has normative implications such that notions of local control seem directly challenged by the common view that the most fully developed examples of comprehensive planning are to be found in totalitarian states (e.g., Nazi Germany and the Soviet Union).

The conceptual difficulty associated with comprehensive planning is partly rooted in the lack of an acceptable definition of the term. The definition of comprehensive planning as "a complete consideration of all factors or variables that have an impact on the functioning of the criminal justice system as a whole" does little to resolve questions about what role the planner has in transforming comprehensive plans into implemented policy decisions. This last difficulty has most directly impaired efforts to achieve consensus on the meaning of comprehensive planning.

Thus there are organizational, conceptual, and ideological impediments to understanding and implementing notions of comprehensive planning in criminal justice. The idea that comprehensive planning can provide coordination of efforts to deal with crime—and thereby increase their effectiveness—is appealing and deserves consideration but not necessarily blind acceptance. Because many present-day conceptions of comprehensive planning are intimately associated with the concept of systems, an understanding of some of the key features of systems theory is essential if the idea of comprehensive criminal justice planning is to be explored at all.

The Idea of a Criminal Justice System

During the 1960s and 1970s, the term *system* achieved considerable vogue. As millions of Americans tuned in to the lastest space launch, frequent attention was focused on life-support systems, guidance systems, power systems, and a host of other systems. This served to popularize the term, if not to clarify the concept. Then, the same period marked the widespread introduction of the concept of a criminal justice system.[4] The idea had its first wide exposure in the report of the President's Crime Commission *The Challenge of Crime in a Free Society*. Included in the report was a diagram of the movement of cases through the criminal justice system," showing the types of agencies involved in each step of the process.[5] (This may be the single diagram in criminal justice most often reproduced and referred to—it has caught the fancy of a great number of people.) Then the 1969 Law Enforcement Assistance Administration guidelines stated that the newly created criminal justice state planning agencies were to consider "all facets and elements of law enforcement activity, including police, court and correctional programs, and *systems* as well as general crime prevention and control."[6]

Adoption of the concept of system was not simply a fad but an attempt to communicate the essential aspects of earlier reform movements:

1. Increased coordination among criminal justice agencies, incorporating fuller appreciation of citizen-oriented service delivery;
2. Greater focus on the end products of the entire process of criminal justice rather than the intermediate products of police, corrections, or courts individually.[7]

The concept of system, initially developed in the natural sciences[8] and later adopted in the social sciences,[9] now found at least a conceptual application in criminal justice.

The idea of a system is rather straightforward.[10] A system is composed of *elements* or components that are in relatively constant *interaction* with one another, having both impact or effect and mutual dependence on one another. The human body, for example, is a system composed of heart, hands, brain, kidneys, and so on. In criminal justice, police, corrections, courts, probation and parole, juvenile programs, prosecution, and public defenders are some of the elements or components that form the system. The elements of a system are usually held to have *specialized functions*; each contributes to the whole, and each depends for survival and accomplishment on the contributions made by each part.

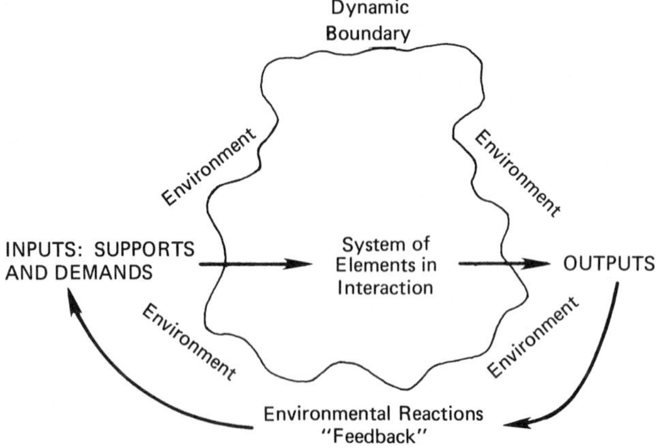

In a simple system, the objective is to maintain an *equilibrium*, as a thermostat, in conjunction with a furnace and an air-conditioner, maintains a relatively constant temperature. A more complex system, however, is *morphogenic*[11]; that is, the system may change its own structure, adapting in response to outside influences, or in order to survive or to achieve some internally determined goal. Social systems, such as the criminal justice system, are commonly held to be complex and morphogenic.

Another key aspect of systems theory is that systems do not exist in a vacuum; rather, they function within an *environment*. There is assumed to be an ongoing interaction between the system and its environment: supports, demands, and pressures emanate from the environment and require the system to respond or to act. The supports and demands coming from the environment are *inputs*; the responses of the system are *outputs*. The environment of criminal justice includes—but is not limited to—public opinion, public expectations, and economic conditions. The system's responses affect the environment, producing further environmental reaction or *feedback*. This interaction can be represented by a simple block diagram:[12]

A system that ignores changes in environmental supports and demands risks extinction. Analysis of systems without regard to environmental factors is a *closed-system* approach; analysis that includes environmental factors is called an *open-system* approach. In complex social systems, interactions with the environment often will lead to morphogenesis, or changes in the system itself, as a means of better responding to these environmental exigencies. For example, rapid expansion of such options as halfway houses and various pretrial diversion programs represent significant alterations in the nature of the traditional criminal justice system, and may have in part been responses to environmental pressures to find both more efficient and effective ways of dealing with crime. So too, changes in the definitions of crime itself may be seen as morphogenic processes. Samuel Walker implicitly notes such a morphogenic process in describing changes between 1815 and 1900:

> The development of a criminal justice system in the United States was a response to the extraordinary disorder wrought by social change. . . . Americans launched what historian Robert

Wiebe called a "search for order." The search led to the creation of a network of specialized bureaucratic agencies, each designed to deal with a particular social problem. The criminal-justice system was only one part of this new network.[13]

Unfortunately, the boundary between a social system and its environment is hardly ever clear because it is often impossible to distinguish aspects of the system from aspects of the environment. For example, should welfare agencies providing probation-related services be considered part of the criminal justice system? A truly open-system approach may easily lead to the conclusion that *every*thing has to be considered, which is virtually impossible. And simple systems or biological systems do not provide accurate analogies for complex social systems.

Most important, however, is that the systems concept, evolving out of the physical sciences and mechanistic notions of cause and effect, does not easily recognize or take into account the independent behavior characteristic of human and social systems. Human and social systems do not simply react to environmental influences; rather, they pursue independent goals in a fashion not easily explained through simple cause-and-effect mechanisms. Nonetheless, in the writings of authors from the mechanistic school of sociology,[14] in the applications of systems approaches to war production during World War II, and in their applications to the space program, systems concepts are treated in simple mechanical terms, and simplicity appeals.

Perhaps the most serious challenge to the application of systems concepts to social entities comes from such writers as Aaron Wildavsky,[15] Robert Chin,[16] and Ida Hoos.[17] All have concluded that the extension of the system approach from the natural sciences and engineering to the social sciences is an attempt to simplify very complex and value-laden processes. They accuse "system-concept importers" of hiding important questions of value behind the thin veil of objectivity, promising that systematic thinking leads to objective answers. Systems analysis must confront important and difficult value questions, with or without systematically derived cost/benefit analyses.

Opponents of systems analysis also point out that systems analysis cannot deal "systematically" with all relevant policy variables when social systems are under scrutiny. James Webb, former head of NASA, has commented, for example, that the engineering and human systems required to put a man on the moon were far easier to handle and manipulate than have been attempts systematically to manage just the court subsystem. The goals of social systems are far more complex than those of the aerospace program, which are determined in a highly structured environment with a specific end.[18] In criminal justice, goals are determined in a highly unstructured political environment—anathema for a systems approach with its objective of stating clear, unconflicting, and uncluttered goals.

Another problem that plagues attempts to apply systems analysis to social areas is that of securing information and a full understanding of pertinent factors. Ida Hoos, in "Systems Analysis in Public Policy: A Critique," describes an attempt to develop an information system linking criminal justice agencies in California to serve in evaluating system effectiveness:

> The engineers who won the [design] contract based their calculations on statistics of convicted offenders and in so doing disclosed the simple-minded belief that crime is that which gets punished. . . . Really identifed in their study was the shared haplessness that renders certain groups, under certain conditions, more susceptible to the embrace of law than others. . . . Crime in the ghetto areas is underreported, much that occurs going unrecorded. Certain classes of "crime" in upper-class white neighborhoods is dismissed as "reprimand and release," while other types, such as burglary and rape, barely noted in the slums, are meticulously recorded because of the insurance aspects.[19]

Yet the idea of systems captured the imagination of the criminal justice community during the late 1960s and early 1970s. Scores of articles appeared in various professional journals purporting to explain the system concept or applying it to various aspects of criminal justice.[20] Attempts to introduce the concept did not escape criticism. One writer, for example, took the view that criminal justice was not a true system because law enforcement and corrections do not "understand" each other and they act as separate entities.[21] Somehow the writer seemed to have missed the point that police and corrections do interact with, and influence and affect, one another. That elements do not "understand" one another may mean the system is *pathological*; it does not mean the system does not *exist*.

Many attempted to deal with the complexity posed by the new formulation by thinking of criminal justice as a set of interrelated processes. The resulting *systems modelling*, produced input-output flow models like the ones described in the 1976 LEAA publication entitled, *Criminal Justice Models: An Overview,*[22] which contains police, corrections, and court models, all having systemic-process orientations; some of the police models included, for example, beat-design models, patrol-allocation models, and manpower-scheduling models. Each of these and other models systematically takes into account a range of pertinent variables in an integrated fashion to aid in decision-making. The entire third chapter of this LEAA publication concerned overall models of the criminal justice system and included JUSSIM, a flow model intended "to address policy issues that propose changes in the flow and processing of crimes, offenders, and prisoners in the overall criminal justice system."[23] The basic idea of JUSSIM was that an understanding of how cases flow through the criminal justice system and how decisions reached at each step affect subsequent steps and agencies, could lead to more effective and systematic evaluation of policies. To facilitate this, JUSSIM permitted analyses of workload and system rates for each stage of the process, identifying imbalances and bottlenecks.

These and similar attempts to look at criminal justice as a system also focused on a variety of new research endeavors, including the creation of standards and goals commissions. Such commissions develop system objectives and aim to coordinate the goals and objectives of police, courts, and corrections with those of the entire system. The idea began to emerge that simply maximizing efficiency in one sector, such as law enforcement, was hardly synonymous with increasing the efficiency of the whole system. For example, more "efficient," less costly programs for apprehension might later increase the costs of prosecution and trial because of declines in the quality of arrests (e.g., arrests made without sufficient evidence or regard to due process). Criminal justice goals are such that maximizing efficiency and productivity for one goal (e.g., apprehension and confinement) can be counterproductive for other goals (e.g., crime prevention and rehabilitation).

System Planning

Adoption of the system concept involved new efforts at system-level planning. From the notion that systems are composed of elements in constant interaction, that systems interact with constantly changing environments, and that social systems are complex and adaptive structures that must change in order not only to survive but to pursue goals, emerges a distinctive role for system planning.

Adapting to changing conditions and anticipating changes in the system's environment seem to be minimum necessities in such planning, as do coordinating diverse parts of the system and controlling dysfunction (self-serving action by one part that is counterproductive to the system's goals as a whole). Planning as coordination, as guidance for adaptation of the system and its parts, as a tool for controlling dysfunction and eliminating crosspurposes among parts, was intended as the keystone in the Federally led "safe-street" initiative to improve the criminal justice system.

SAFE STREETS THROUGH COMPREHENSIVE PLANNING

In 1968, Congress passed the Omnibus Crime Control and Safe Streets Act and created the Law Enforcement Assistance Administration. LEAA was assigned the prime task of increasing the efficiency and effectiveness of the criminal justice system through the administration of Federal anticrime block grants.[24] The Act encouraged development and innovation in the system's response to crime through the development of systematic planning processes within the system and the development of criminal justice planning as a profession.[25] Federal block grants were offered to encourage state and local governments to institutionalize comprehensive criminal justice planning. The prerequisite to receiving these funds was that a "professional" planning apparatus be established in each state, giving planners important and formal recognition in the criminal justice decision-making process. This raised the question of whether planners in a political system should rightly become involved in a normative process of setting goals and selecting alternatives. The idea that normative planning might be linked to the concept of comprehensive system planning made for grave concern in the criminal justice community, where a layered and fractionated grouping of semi-independent agencies all seemed more interested in increasing their relative independence than in achieving "comprehensiveness."

Concerns also arise over the association of planning with control. Hayek and Popper (in reaction to the excesses of fascist state planning) linked systematic and comprehensive planning to limitations on individual freedom.[26] A Federally funded carrot-and-stick approach to creating state-level comprehensive planning in criminal justice evoked similar concern over control (although it was control of the fragmented, locally administered justice system rather than control of individual rights that seemed to be at issue).

These considerations notwithstanding, the Safe Streets Act evolved most directly out of the conclusions of the President's Commission on Law Enforcement and Administration of Justice (1967), which found a cumbersome justice system greatly in need of comprehensive planning. Indeed, the Commission seemed implicitly to have rejected many of the supposed benefits of decentralization, championing instead some benefits of centralization. Organizational theorist Howard Aldrich notes, among the supposed benefits of decentralization, that organizations become "maximally responsive to heterogenous client demands" and "innovate when local conditions demand," and that "duplication and overlap of functions and domains increases overall system reliability."[27] The arguments for centralization, in Aldrich's terms, include that "indivisible problems require large-scale planned interaction of a magnitude not possible if social service organizations interact only to satisfy their own requirements."[28] It is the latter argument for centralization that seems to characterize the underlying assumptions of the President's Commission. Unfortunately, the Federal initiative was nebulous, except in assuring that planning (however defined) was to precede the disbursement of Federal dollars to states and localities. The more ambitious Safe Streets objective was that this requirement would somehow induce within the states and localities and their agencies a generalized propensity (if not the capacity) to plan for their own needs and to consider the impact of their individual actions on other structures within the criminal justice system.

Doing Comprehensive Planning: 1970–1980

By 1970 several problems were apparent. Federal (LEAA) guidelines for comprehensive plans were only partly instructive about the meanings and applications of comprehensive planning. The guidelines did not distinguish between what was meant by comprehensive planning and what a comprehensive plan should contain. Other problems also emerged. The State Planning Agencies (SPAs), and their commissions created through the 1968 legislation, were dominated by law-enforcement elements, circumstance that largely precluded systemwide considerations, and not intended by the legislation. The annual rush to complete a state comprehensive plan in order to gain Federal block and action grants usually resulted in short-range plans that ignored long-range implications—the opposite of what the legislation intended. And the required state-level review of local plans and Federal review of state plans raised prickly questions about Federal control and encroachment. Indeed, the Federal Safe Streets initiative represented, for many, a particularly virulent form of normative Federal planning.

The more serious consequence of the uninformed rush to establish planning and planning agencies was that state and local planning efforts were not comprehensive but functionally fractionalized.[29] State plans were largely local "wishlists" for equipment and other goodies, reviewed at both state and Federal levels with little regard to systemwide or comprehensive planning issues and linked almost entirely to the disbursement of Federal dollars. As a further impediment to comprehensiveness, the SPAs and LEAA organized divisions reflecting the traditional functional components of the criminal justice system. Thus, not only was comprehensive planning ill defined, but there seemed to be no organizational structure capable even of talking about it.

Testifying before the Senate Judiciary Committee, Mayor Roman Gribbs of Detroit summed up the problem by noting that the Safe Streets process assured only that everybody got something–to the detriment of dealing with the real crime problems that communities faced.[30] Gribbs represented one side of a fairly clear division of opinion between the localities, on the one hand, and the SPAs and LEAA, on the other. This division was exemplified in the 1975 opinion survey of SPAs and units of local government about the objectives of the Safe Streets Act.[31] SPA respondents ranked "provid[ing] states and local units of government with a comprehensive criminal justice planning capacity" as the primary objective, while local governments viewed the primary objective as "provid[ing] funds to supplement state and local criminal justice budgets." Such local views were further reflected in the desire to have LEAA funds follow the more flexible general revenue-sharing format, eliminating what was considered to be the "contrivance" of comprehensive planning.

In 1973, amendments were made to the 1968 Act, and these coincided with several LEAA administrative responses, one of which was to advocate the development of state standards and goals through a nationally funded initiative.[32] The purpose of such state standards and goals was to bring together disparate elements of the criminal justice system and to produce a comprehensive plan (with clear short- and long-range objectives). Unfortunately, the results have been largely ignored by the criminal justice community.

By 1977, a decade of developing planning capability had led to little comprehensive planning. As the Advisory Commission on Intergovernmental Relations noted in January 1977:

> Rarely are the criminal justice activities of state and local agencies planned and coordinated with the activities supported by the SPAs. For the most part, SPA planning in the states visited is project-based and lacks a well-defined set of goals against which to measure individual projects. Although project-based planning can be a very effective means of allocating resources to achieve a successful rate of project implementation, without a broader frame of reference within which to judge the merits of individual programs, the risk of supporting lower-priority objectives or activities with conflicting purposes inevitably arises.[33]

The Commission also noted that the planned disbursement of Federal funds generally followed from one or more of three planning approaches. One approach was *crime-rate driven*, in that criminal statistics were analyzed to single out crime areas for funding. Another approach was *dollar-balance driven*, in the sense of setting minimums and maximums for functional or jurisdictional areas. The third approach was a *bottom-up process* based on cut-and-paste indications from local and state agencies of their needs. None of these approaches seemed in keeping with systematic, long-range, comprehensive, or coordinated planning, but no better alternative seemed on the horizon. The principal difficulty noted by the Commission was "the relatively limited use of criminal justice data and analysis."[34] The problem, it seemed, was not a reluctance by the SPAs to use data but the overall lack of data.

Probably the most serious impediment to defining comprehensive criminal justice planning was the controversy over whether planning should be oriented toward improving systems or toward reducing crime.

> System-improvement planning, the most common approach used by the SPAs, seeks to enhance the quality of the components of the criminal justice system and the management of the flow of cases and people through it. Directing planning efforts toward system improvement rather than crime reduction has been a continuing bone of contention for those concerned about the program. The uneasy compromise eventually adopted by Congress in the 1973 amendments called upon the program to promote planning for "strengthening and improving the criminal justice system" in order to reduce crime.[35]

The controversy clouded how the issue of comprehensive planning was to be operationalized and did little to help differentiate between intermediary and final objectives for planning. And whether system improvement or crime reduction (or a combination of these) was to be the ultimate objective, crosscomponent planning seemed only weakly served.

The term *comprehensive* seemed to have only limited meaning: emphasis was given to the fair distribution of Federal funds among the criminal justice components and to crosscomponent representation on planning boards. But the collection and analysis of data that would permit consideration of the interactions and effects among components were generally ignored. Practice seemed to have little to do with Richard Bolan's notion of planning—planning as both a thinking process *and* a social process.[36] Missing, too, were Gibbon's three "core elements of criminal justice knowledge":[37] a detailed understanding of the underlying causes of crime, the social forces and factors involved, and of crime patterns; a detailed understanding of the criminal justice system in operation, of the networks of linkages, interactions, and decision-making centers; and a knowledge of the internal workings of the system and its components. In the absence of such knowledge, no basis for comprehensive planning appeared to exist.

Indeed, the knowledge base for comprehensive planning is hard—some believe impossible—to amass.[38] Blair Ewing, former acting director of the LEAA National Institute, concluded, for example, that incremental, process-oriented planning is more appropriate for criminal justice than is comprehensive planning, owing to the fragmentation of the system and the lack of a suitable knowledge base.[39] Ewing's remarks are parallel to the views of such system critics as Ida Hoos.

Two later assessments, published in 1979 and 1980, offered more promise for the development of comprehensive planning. In 1979, the National Academy of Public Administrators (NAPA) concluded that "comprehensive criminal justice planning is 'coming of age'— it is an area of state government management where heartening progress and innovation is apparent."[40] NAPA noted that criminal justice planning was really just then beginning in most states, but that it could increasingly be characterized as having systemwide perspectives, policy outputs that went beyond the grant-letting function, and concern for coordination of the criminal justice components within the state. Also, NAPA concluded that SPA personnel were increasingly developing professional planning and research expertise.

In 1980 a study of system manpower planning conducted by the School of Criminal Justice at Michigan State University concluded that development along the lines noted by NAPA were taking place in the SPAs. However, the Michigan State study found the NAPA conclusion that criminal justice planning was "coming of age" to be "premature, or perhaps a misleading choice of terms."[41] Alternatively, it seemed that the development of comprehensive and coordinated planning capability within the various SPAs was still experimental. Yet both studies found evidence of important advancement toward comprehensive planning—which had not been the case just a few years earlier.

IMPEDIMENTS TO COMPREHENSIVE PLANNING

In 1979 a major revision of Federal crime-control legislation included a drastic redesign of the LEAA effort. The new legislation created an Office of Justice Assistance, Research, and Statistics (OJARS) with three subdivisions: LEAA, the National Institute, and the Bureau of Justice Statistics, each of which was to have a specialized role in assistance to operational agencies, research, and data collection.

The new legislation also stipulated that at least 50 per cent of administrative costs for SPAs and coordinating councils would be funded from state and local revenues. (The old formula had been 90 per cent Federal funds and 10 per cent state or local funds.) The fifty-fifty split recognized that many of the SPAs had become established units in state government and were now fully part of the state apparatus rather than being simply Federal creations. Forcing an increase in the level of state support would further encourage an integration of the SPAs into state decision-making networks.

Early in 1980, under increasing pressure to control inflation by balancing the Federal budget, President Carter announced sweeping budget cuts which eventually included all funding for OJARS/LEAA for Fiscal Year 1981. President Reagan continued these cuts. Suddenly, after twelve years of Federal support, there was to be none. Initial appraisals came to catastrophic conclusions, including the view that criminal justice systemic planning was dead. Subsequent appraisals have been less pessimistic.

A September 1980 appraisal, conducted by the National Conference of State Criminal Justice Planning Administrators, suggested that 60–70 per cent of the SPAs would continue during the year without new Federal funds.[42]

The continued survival of many of these SPAs beyond Fiscal Year 1981 was considered more doubtful because part of the financial support for that fiscal year was still Federal—funds reverted from previous years.

The SPAs and local planning councils that survive the 1980s and into the 1990s are likely to have certain characteristics. First, the survivors will have had fairly long-run commitments to activities and responsibilities passing far beyond simple Federal grant-letting functions. In Michigan and Washington, for example, the SPAs have for several years had budget-review powers for state criminal justice agencies. In these and similar states, state-oriented functions have strengthened the SPAs position within the state governmental infrastructure. It is also generally true that these states have also been the ones most consistently to "overmatch" Federal funds from year to year. Both conditions, of course, reflect a commitment to SPA activities beyond the mere attempt to qualify for Federal funds. The demise of LEAA and crime-oriented block grants should, therefore, have less than catastrophic impact on these states.

Second, a few survivors will have had administrative responsibilites for a major state-funded or local-funded program (e.g., administration of a career-criminal program or of a victim-compensation program or of a metropolitan narcotics program). More grandiose notions of state or local comprehensive planning remain under consideration, perhaps assumed to be "buildable" on the base provided by the funded program area.

Third, some states are adopting, or have adopted, a state-funded "grant" program of their own, to support innovation or basic functions. State-level financing of local criminal-justice functions appears to be increasing and may eventually signal greater need for state-level and local-level coordination. The need has already been recognized in some states where funds are being administered by the SPA, working in cooperation with other state agencies (e.g., the SPA working in conjunction with a state jail board in allocating funds to support county jail operations). Innovation grants are being considered by a few states, with the distinct possibility that the SPA will be given administrative responsibility for these grants.

Fourth, it is generally the medium- to larger-size states and the larger metropolitan areas that are most seriously considering the institutionalization of their own planning apparatus. A correlate of this is that a "policy-planning model," emphasizing policy development and systemwide *planning analysis*, is proving to be the most popular function or role adopted for these agencies. The nature of this correlation seems obvious enough: the larger the state or more populous the locality, the more complex its criminal justice apparatus, and the greater the need for coordination and data-based planning analyses.

The demise of criminal justice block grants may have a positive effect on the nature of criminal justice planning in the next few years. Elimination of the Federal grant program will relieve state and local planning agencies of the suboptimizing chore of administering these grants. Survival of these agencies over the next few years will depend on their capacity to treat problems of coordination and dysfunction arising out of the fragmentation of the justice system (an essential capacity, as noted by Blair Ewing and The Council of State Governments). In other words, the survival of criminal justice planning agencies may now depend on their ability to plan.

PROSPECTS FOR COMPREHENSIVE PLANNING

Both the NAPA study and the MSU Manpower Planning Study indicate that substantial building of SPA capacity to conduct planning is in progress. Among the specific indicators mentioned in these studies is the increasing professionalization of SPA staffs in the area of technical planning skills. Also, data bases supportive of coordinated planning, although at present incomplete and uneven in quality, are improving. Recent acquisitions of automated data-management machinery, housed within many of the SPAs themselves and within some local planning agencies, will facilitate manipulation of these data for planning purposes.

These improvements, although necessary for effective coordinated or comprehensive planning, are not sufficient to guarantee its development. By far the most important additional variable is the importance state government officials give to coordinated planning and the support rendered by local criminal justice agencies. Both the NAPA study and the MSU study indicate increasing pressure from state and local government officials for the employment of empirically based planning in criminal justice. But cooperation from local criminal justice agencies, especially in the collection of data, is not assured. The MSU study indicated, for example, varying levels of caution on the part of local agencies concerning state-level data-collection efforts.[43] There seems little doubt that increasing cooperation will be "forced" through state financing and the growing understanding of the importance of empirically based planning and policy development. But real cooperation and support is likely to evolve only as comprehensive or coordinated planning comes to have perceived benefit.

There now appears to be a pervasive understanding that comprehensive planning is not something simply achieved, as was apparently assumed in the 1968 legislation. This is a useful and essential first step. The professionalization of SPA staffs, as reported by NAPA, will also help. The decrease or elimination of Federal funds, may well reorient surviving state and local planning agencies from Federal "grantsmanship" to state and local problem-solving. And the apparent increase in the use of empirical data for planning purposes, as reported by NAPA and as noted in the Michigan State Manpower Study, offers the opportunity for more objective system planning.

Other impediments to comprehensive planning seem more formidable. System fragmentation will probably continue for some time. Although the NAPA and Michigan State studies both point toward contact and discussion among different levels and components of the criminal justice system, there is only scattered evidence to suggest that such contacts have led to pervasive cooperation. The elimination of Federal dollars will almost certainly have some bad effects: the death of some SPAs and local planning bodies, staff cutbacks in others. Funds available to finance data collection will be less, and reductions in staff are likely to decrease data-collection efforts initiated by planning agencies. The most serious impediment—the complicated nature of criminal justice problems—will certainly remain, as will the lack of structural arrangements and techniques that permit cross-sector problem analysis.

Alternative Definitions of Comprehensive Planning

This brings us full circle to the comment that comprehensive planning is an operationally ill-defined concept in criminal justice. Two alternatives seem possible. The first is to define comprehensive planning as *central planning*, the authority for which would be vested in a state-level agency. The other option is to define comprehensive planning as *coordination*, to recognize that fragmentation is a fact of criminal justice, and that decision-making in the system is decentralized and fragmented.

To redefine comprehensive planning as central planning does not appear to be advisable, partly because central planning tends to be associated with control, which runs counter to our basic political beliefs:

> Everything we know about American government, and especially about the separation of powers doctrine, argues against centralized comprehensive planning and in favor of fragmented functional planning located throughout the various branches and subdivisions of government. *Fragmentation is not the problem to overcome: The dysfunctions resulting from fragmentation should be the target.*[44]

Even if central planning were politically feasible, it would remain impractical in the near future: there is little evidence to suggest that planning agencies have enough staff and authority to accomplish such planning. And in a time of economic uncertainty, it seems improbable that additional staff and funds will be made available to state and local agencies. This is ironic indeed, for the lack of funds makes more important the elimination of duplicative or conflicting purpose.

Comprehensive planning as coordination, however, seems to be an option for the future, but it would probably take different forms in the various states and localities. The idea of coordinated criminal justice planning would seem more acceptable to states and localities than that of central planning, and its appeal in a systemic sense has had a substantial history. The contemporary groundwork for viewing comprehensive planning as coordination seems to have been laid in the 1976 publication of the Council of State Governments:

> Planning is not inherently more valuable because it is centralized. A public policy on criminal justice planning should (1) place high priority on developing a sound planning capacity at every significant decision-making point, and (2) supplement those diffused planning capacities with a mechanism for ameliorating the dysfunctions which fragmented power must inevitably produce. . . .
>
> A policy of building a criminal justice planning capacity at strategic points in government does not necessarily mean abandonment of a comprehensive perspective. The need for a systemwide perspective seems now to be so well established among planners that the presentation of policy or program strategies without regard to their impact upon other agencies would in all likelihood be regarded as unprofessional. All planners, wherever situated, can take a comprehensive perspective even though they are typically instructed to develop strategies for the attainment of limited objectives.[45]

The Council points out that, in its view, "coordination is as much a public policy objective as it is a formal process."[46] By this it apparently means to stress the importance of recognizing that system components affect one another and that those planning within each of the components must be cognizant of such effects and plan for them. Findings from the Michigan State study, as well as from the NAPA study, seem to confirm the Council's view that ignoring systemwide implications would be unprofessional.

The basic underlying assumption of systems theory is that maximizing the efficiency and effectiveness of each component of the system does not necessarily maximize the efficiency and effectiveness of the system as a whole. A systemwide perspective makes the efficiency and effectiveness of components conditional on the efficiency and effectiveness of the system. This is an appealing thought, and it has applications in certain production or service-delivery areas. Its application to the criminal justice system, however, presents more problems, owing to the competing values expressed as system and component goals. A full-blown system approach, as might be exemplified in a truly comprehensive and centralized system-planning effort, might well prove to mitigate the effects of fragmentation if competing values were capable of resolution. Experience indicates, however, that such resolution is not easily achieved.

The 1976 Council Report offers an alternative perspective on what may be possible in the future.

> What is needed in order to deal with fragmented decision-making is a method of interfacing the decisions of separate agencies or units of government so that such problems as duplication of services, unequal funding, and discontinuities or conflicts in policies can be minimized.[47]

This appears to focus on dealing with the obvious dysfunctions that result from fragmentation rather than on some notion of a comprehensive response to dysfunction. NAPA findings indicate that this is the nature of the current development of planning capability. The findings of the Michigan State study concur: present development takes this less global and more program-specific or problem-specific approach.

What also seems clear is that value-free and apolitical planning is only wishful thinking—not simply because of the fragmentation of the system, but also because of the nature of planning in social systems and their highly volatile political environments. It should not be surprising, therefore, if comprehensive planning in criminal justice evolves into something less than a purely rational, systematic, and analytical endeavor. The implications for the criminal justice planner have been succinctly put by Robert Cushman:

> [C]riminal justice planners today have a hybrid role to play. Most planners use some form of rational step-by-step planning process as a guide, but they also rely on techniques of brokerage, advocacy, negotiation, and a certain degree of conscious "politicking."[48]

ELEMENTS OF COMPREHENSIVE PLANNING

Comprehensive planning is distinguished from agency planning by its interagency focus and its enhancement of coordination among agencies. It is distinguished from city or county planning by its focus on promoting cooperation across political jurisdictions. In a limited sense, there are levels of comprehensiveness that have an impact not only on the scope of planning issues but also on the pertinent actors involved in the process. The problems and issues involved in statewide and local comprehensive planning are very wide in scope, reflecting the need to coordinate activities of agencies scattered throughout the state bureaucracy and of agencies at both the state and local levels. State comprehensive planning, for example, might well include examining the definition of police roles and the shared and specialized tasks of city, county, and state police agencies throughout the state, as well as the roles of peripheral enforcement agents such as forest or park rangers, firemarshalls, and health inspectors.

The fact is, however, that similar kinds of questions and issues arise at both the local and the state levels. Certainly planners must be cognizant of the political and jurisdictional independence of many participants in local as well as state criminal justice planning. But, further, what criminal justice planners at the state and local levels *do* is not all that different. Indeed, state planning agencies as well as local and regional coordinating councils may each be involved in providing technical assistance to operating agencies, in collecting and analyzing data on system performance, in coordinating the development of system goals, and in securing requisite cooperation among appropriate agencies. In a 1980 LEAA publication about local criminal justice planning, seventeen sample tasks or activities were listed as appropriate for local comprehensive planning agencies.[49] Figure 5-1 shows a portion of the chart displaying these activities and their associated planning objectives. Each of these activities and functions is, however, appropriate to state-level planning agencies, and not only in a theoretical sense. There is ample evidence that these are the things actually done by state-level planning agencies.[50]

Each of the activities listed in Figure 5-1 is no doubt important, but some are more fundamental than others. For example, data-base development and system analysis are keystones of the analysis of system productivity, of the identification of system-level problems, and of the review of agency budgets. All of these activities provide a basis for informed attempts to assess areas needing coordination of policies and programs. Information brokerage plays a key role not only in making these determinations but in organizing coordination among component agencies as well.

If the prime roles of agencies involved in comprehensive planning are taken to include controlling duplication and dysfunction and furthering the achievement of the system's overall goals, then the analysis of productivity and operations is crucial. Such analyses are concerned not only with what agencies do, how they do it, and what costs are involved in doing it, but also with determining where funding imbalances among agencies exist, and in assessing priorities among competing programs and agencies. Such analyses will often have legislative implications, suggesting changes in the missions assigned various component agencies. Analyses of productivity and operations also assist in policy analysis directed toward establishing which major priority areas are in need of improvement. Convening and serving coordinating groups is a prime function of system-planning agencies because establishing program and funding priorities almost always involves negotiated tradeoffs, funds never being sufficient to cover everyone's wishlist. The process of achieving this involves some sort of consensus within

Figure 5-1. Sample Activities of System–Planning Agencies[51]

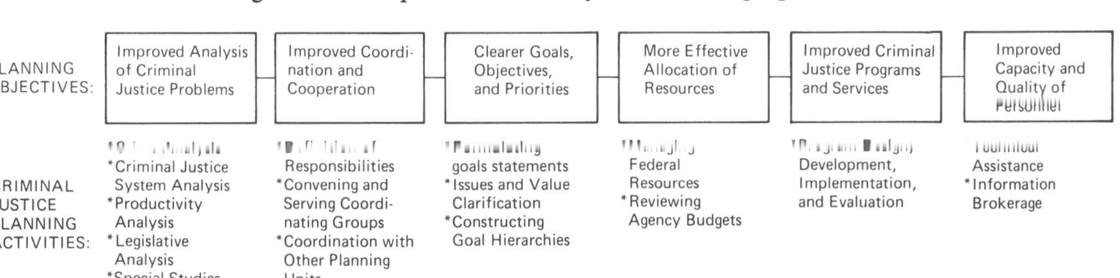

the criminal justice system about the ordering of priorities, with one objective being to find the most effective investment of dollars. Negotiation is, therefore, not only a key activity of planners but a requisite skill as well, because the most effective investment of dollars is not determined in a value-free environment. This confirms Bolan's point that planning is both a thinking and a social process.

An alternative way of visualizing the numerous responsibilities of comprehensive- or system-planning agencies has been offered by the National Conference of State Criminal Justice Planning Administrators.[52] The conference has proposed "eight alternative administrative policy models" for planning agencies at the state level, but the "alternatives" are relevant for local and regional planning bodies as well. Although the Conference proposes the eight as "alternatives," there is nothing to preclude all eight, or combinations of the eight, from being considered appropriate roles for criminal justice planning bodies. Many of the conference's options, with some adaptation and changes, are reflected in Figure 5-2.

1. ***Policy-planning.*** The planning agency is charged with broad responsibilities for assessing the consequences of existing and alternative policies. The role is systemic, offering policy development and staff support to jurisdiction chief executives on issues cutting across the system. This would most directly concern matters of program duplication, assignment of new missions or redistribution of existing missions among component agencies, and the development and assessment of new or innovative programs such as county or statewide narcotics units, career-criminal or organized-crime programs, and the like. Key questions in the policy-planning process include whether a particular function should be carried out by government at all, whether the appropriate agency or combination of agencies is charged with carrying it out, and whether the level of effort should be raised or reduced.

Figure 5-2. Comprehensive Planning Agency Roles

1. Policy-planning
2. Data collection and analysis
3. Legislative analysis
4. Budget analysis
5. Training coordination
6. Technical assistance
7. Futures forecasting and alternative testing
8. Intercomponent communication
9. Fostering agency-based planning
10. Implementation and evaluation

2. ***Data collection and analysis.*** The planning agency is responsible for determining the kinds of data needed to analyze the productivity of the system and for enhancing the component agencies' technical abilities to collect and to provide this data. It is also the planning agency's role to draw together system components in data analysis, to provide a capability for analysis, and to increase the utilization of data in decision-making, both within component agencies and throughout the system. This is an information- or data-brokerage function that includes identifying necessary data, creating the capability for securing the data, ensuring the compatibility of data coming from various criminal justice agencies, and providing the analytical capability for analyzing the data for "systems implications." The compatibility of data is most important because unless data coming from the various component agencies allow for aggregation and subsequent comparison, systems analysis is severely hampered.

3. ***Legislative analysis.*** The planning agency proposes standards and goals for the criminal justice system and its components and follows through with specific legislative proposals when necessary. On the other hand, it also helps to analyze legislative changes proposed by others that may have an impact on the system. For example, legislative proposals for mandatory sentences for certain crimes will cause stress in and among the various components and will require systemwide adjustments. So too, proposals not specifically related to crime or criminal justice, such as for tax rollbacks, may have far-reaching effects on the system. The objective of legislative analysis is to inform decision-makers of the likely impact of these and other proposals and to provide an informed basis on which decision-makers can take a position on the proposals.

4. ***Budget analysis.*** The planning agency can be responsible for providing the jurisdiction chief executive and the budget unit with the

review and analysis of criminal justice agency budgets. The review function is particularly focused on issues of system fragmentation, duplication, inefficiencies, and returns on dollars spent. The review function may include the authority to red-line and otherwise alter agency budget requests, or it can be restricted to reviewing and commenting on agency budgets. Budget-review authority may well be the most effective inducement to promoting and encouraging agency coordination.

5. ***Training coordination.*** The role of the planning agency includes the design, development, and coordination of training for all components of the criminal justice system. Although some training is and must be specific to individual component agencies, many training issues—such as general-management training or first-aid training—cut across component agencies. There is also the need to coordinate training programs within individual components of the systems so that, for example, several law-enforcement agencies might share recruit-training facilities and programs. The idea is not only to eliminate duplication and save dollars, but also to foster a comprehensive view of training needs throughout the system.

6. ***Technical assistance.*** The planning agency's responsibility includes acting as a clearinghouse for information about innovative management or technical applications to components of the system. The agency may actively encourage the adoption of new techniques by sponsoring conferences or hiring consultants and making them available to assist operating agencies. Providing technical assistance for component agencies to adopt and adapt new technologies is a critical function of the planning agency.

7. ***Future forecasting and alternative testing.*** Much of planning in criminal justice component agencies may be described as reactive, partly because the press of daily business often precludes leisurely consideration of the direction of events. Planning agencies, however, are specifically charged with the mission of considering trends and changes in the future, especially as such matters affect *system* productivity and effectiveness. They must develop responses for alternative futures and assess the relative merits and likely effects of various proposals for dealing with or meeting these futures in order to inform decision-makers of the need to consider and to prepare for changes in policies, programs, and the environment.

8. ***Intercomponent communication.*** A major function of planning agencies is to facilitate communication and negotiation among component agencies. More often than not, the planning agency is the chief formally structured and commissioned means of getting the various component agencies to talk with one another about existing and emerging problems and jointly to negotiate solutions. The formation of advisory planning boards and intercomponent task forces to deal with specific issues of duplication and dysfunction are ways of encouraging this form of communication.

9. ***Fostering agency-based planning.*** Cutting across many or most of the other roles and functions of the criminal justice planning agency is the important objective of encouraging and assisting individual component agencies to develop their own planning capabilities. Healthy planning capabilities within component agencies advance the process of system planning because many of the data for system-level planning originate in component agencies, and much of our collective understanding of individual operational problems arises from the experiences of the component agencies.

10. ***Implementation and evaluation.*** Program monitoring and evaluation indicate whether planning-based program recommendations have proven "correct" and effective. Many of the data for subsequent plannng efforts and analyses of system dysfunctions come from accurate and valid evaluation of the system and its components. An important role, therefore, for planning agencies is not only to encourage the collection of evaluation data, but also to help set criteria for performance evaluation. This is an important part of the process of setting and clarifying goals, which, left to component agencies to determine individually, may lead to suboptimization, for goals set without reference to overall system objectives and evaluation criteria may well result in program-evaluation criteria irrelevant to the system as a whole. The process of setting complementary goals and evaluation criteria among the system components is suitably negotiated under the auspices of the planning agency.

INTERAGENCY RELATIONSHIPS IN COMPREHENSIVE PLANNING

An important ingredient in system or comprehensive planning is the ability of planning agencies and planners to form linkages to a variety of agencies both within and without the formal confines of the criminal justice system. The nature of these relationships is complex, stretching to include budget bureaus, civil-service units, citizens' advisory and "watchdog" groups, legislative- and executive-branch politicians, multiple units of government and their administrative machinery, and other government-service agencies (such as welfare), in addition to the full range of criminal justice component agencies. Although Chapter 7 will explore some of these relationships and demands within the context of organizing and staffing the planning apparatus, some general comments are pertinent here.

The complex web of bureaucratic agencies involved in delivering various social services is characteristic of public bureaucracies, not limited simply to criminal justice. Recognition of these complexities by such theorists of public administration as Ira Sharkansky has enhanced our understanding:

> Relationships among administrators of different governments evolve from concrete problems that affect several jurisdictions; they often combine "horizontal" with "vertical" relationships. "Triangular" relations may also develop. . . . Beyond this level of complexity, a variety of "polyangular" relations may evolve among a number of Federal, state, or local agencies that have a common interest in a particular problem.[53]

It is also, in Sharkansky's view, "an oversimplification to assume that the involvement of a 'superior' level of administration permits that organization to control its 'subordinate' associates."[54] The often voluntary and quid pro quo transactions required of agencies in criminal justice makes the exercise of power-based control by comprehensive-planning agencies impractical and nonsensical. The control exercised by a planning agency in a criminal justice system generally depends on the extent to which the relationship between the planning agency and the component agencies allows for and enhances mutual adjustment among bureaucratic entities. The most effective coordinating device at the disposal of planning agencies in criminal justice is one that is based on influence rather than power or authority, on cooperation rather than antagonism between the planning agency and the component agencies.

In a recent survey of criminal justice state planning agencies[55] respondents were asked to characterize the degree of influence and the nature of relationships their agency had with a variety of criminal justice and other bureaucratic actors. More particularly the survey concerned the nature of interaction between the SPA and other actors when issues related to criminal justice were being discussed or decided. Summary responses are reported in Table 5-1.[56]

Although there were no controls for separating socially desirable responses from empirically supportable responses, the results reflect the complex web of interactions facing systems-level planning agencies. Comparatively few respondents indicated that there is "no interaction" between the SPA and the other actors. Respondents were also asked whether SPA attempts to secure coordination and cooperation among component agencies were more effective when based on legislative and bureaucratic authority or when based on voluntarism, influence, and credibility. The vast majority of respondents clearly subscribed to the notion that the ultimate ability of the planning agency to secure cooperation and coordination among component agencies was vitally dependent on influence secured through credibility, and the bureaucratic authority, or power and authority derived from legislative mandate, was hardly sufficient.[57] These findings seem to support Sharkansky's view that cooperation among bureaucratic entitites is based less on formal lines of authority than on credibility and influence.

SUMMARY

Criminal justice agencies exist as parts of a complex system of agencies. These agencies are interdependent and impact on one another in manifold ways. Some of the interactions and impacts are dysfunctional owing to the lack of coordination, the duplication of service functions, and the conflict of purposes and activities among the system's agencies.

Table 5-1. SPA Influence with and Relationships with Other Bureaucratic and Political Actors (Based on Returns from 34 SPAs)

	SPA's Influence With*				SPA/Agency* Relationships			
	Very Influential	*Somewhat Influential*	*Little Influence*	*No Influence*	*Cooperative*	*Competitive*	*Antagonistic*	*There Is no Interaction*
	%	%	%	%	%	%	%	%
Governor's Office	35	38	18	3	82	3	–	6
Legislative or Legislative Committees	12	47	32	3	68	9	6	6
Bureau of Budget or Equivalent	9	32	41	6	56	15	12	12
Civil Service or Equivalent	9	12	29	32	38	9	6	29
Higher Educational Institutions with Criminal Justice Programs	15	35	41	3	77	–	–	18
Employee Unions	–	3	6	71	9	3	–	68
Professional Association (e.g., Chiefs, Sheriffs, Prosecutors)	21	53	21	–	88	3	3	–
State Police or Equivalent	18	50	24	–	74	12	3	6
Local Police Agencies	18	71	9	–	82	6	6	–
State Department of Corrections	21	50	24	3	74	15	8	–
Courts	9	44	32	12	68	12	15	3
Probation and Parole	15	56	27	–	85	9	–	–
Criminal Justice Training Councils	21	32	18	6	71	3	3	6
Prosecutors	15	53	27	3	88	3	3	3
Regional Planning Units, Criminal Justice Coordinating Councils or Equivalents	62	27	–	3	74	9	6	–

*All percentages are rounded to the nearest whole number. Some items do not sum to 100 per cent because of rounding or because of missing data.

System-level planning has as its prime objective the minimization of dysfunction, duplication and cross-purpose activity. A systemwide perspective allows planners to focus on the overall efficiency and effectiveness of the criminal justice system. Such a focus helps to avoid the trap of maximizing individual agency efficiency and effectiveness at the expense of overall system objectives.

Comprehensive criminal justice planning is a principal means by which system-level planning efforts can be engendered. State planning agencies and local coordinating councils, funded initially through the Safe Streets Act of 1968, were intended to be the principal mechanisms for comprehensive planning efforts. The history of these system-level planning agencies has been checkered: there is only scattered evidence that these planning bodies understood the term *comprehensive planning* and attempted to coordinate the goals, policies, and activities of the fragmented criminal justice system. There is some evidence, however, of the further development of comprehensive planning capabilities within the system.

Several impediments to meaningful coordination through comprehensive planning exist: lack of goal consensus among system agencies; disjointed authority arrangements; and insufficient funds for comprehensive planning analyses. These impediments, however, do not obviate the need for comprehensive planning and do not preclude its being undertaken.

Ten prime roles for system-level planning agencies have been presented in this discussion. They include the following systemwide cross-agency endeavors: policy-planning, data collection and analysis, legislative analysis, budget analysis, training coordination, technical assistance, future forecasting and alternative testing, intercomponent communication, fostering agency-based planning, and program implementation and review. Each of those roles represents a specific activity that comprehensive-planning agencies can and should undertake. Effective comprehensive planning in the criminal justice system depends less on formal administrative authority than on the establishment of interagency cooperation, credibility, and influence.

· *Chapter 5* ·
NOTES

1. Samuel Walker, *Popular Justice: A History of American Criminal Justice* (New York: Oxford University Press, 1980), p. 55.

2. Herbert L. Parker, "Two Models of the Criminal Process," in *The Limits of the Criminal Justice Sanction* (Stanford, Calif.; Stanford University Press, 1968), pp. 149-73. Also see Robert Wiebe, *The Search for Order* (New York: Hill and Wang, 1967).

3. Walker, op. cit., p. 172.

4. Institute for Defense Analyses, *Task Force Report: Science and Technology*—A Report to the President's Commission on Law Enforcement and Administration of Justice (Washington, D.C.: Government Printing Office, 1967), Chap. 5.

5. President's Commission on Civil Disorders, *Report of the National Advisory Commission on Civil Disorders* (New York: Avon Books, 1968) pp. 255–57.

6. U.S. Law Enforcement Assistance Administration, *Guide for State Planning Agency Grants Under the Omnibus Crime Control and Safe Streets Act of 1968* (Washington, D.C.: U.S. Government Printing Office, 1969), p. 13.

7. Frederick W. Howlett and Hunter Hurst, "A Systems Approach to Comprehensive Criminal Justice Planning," *Crime and Delinquency*, 17: 4 (October 1971), 345–54.

8. Ludwig von Bertalanffy, *General Systems Theory*, rev. ed. (New York: George Braziller, Inc., 1973), p. 9.

9. See for example, George C. Homans, *Social Behavior: Its Elementary Forms* (New York: Harcourt Brace Jovanovich, Inc., 1961).

10. Walter Buckley, *Sociology and Modern Systems Theory* (Englewood Cliffs, N.J.: Prentice-Hall, Inc., 1967). This is a thorough treatment of the evolution of important systems concepts.

11. Ibid., Chap. 5.

12. For a similar formulation, see Ira Sharkansky, *Public Administration: Policy-Making in Government Agencies* (Chicago: Markham Publishing Co., 1970), p. 153.

13. Walker, op. cit., p. 57.

14. Buckley, op. cit., pp. 8–11.

15. Aaron Wildavsky, "If Planning is Everything, Maybe It's Nothing," *Policy Sciences*, 4(1973), 127–53.

16. Robert Chin, "The Utility of System Models and Developmental Models for Practitioners," in Warren G. Bennis, et al. *The Planning of Change*, 2nd ed.(New York: Holt, Rinehart and Winston, Inc., 1969), pp. 268–312.

17. Ida R. Hoos, *Systems Analysis in Public Policy: A Critique* (Berkeley, Calif.: University of California Press, 1972). Also see Ida R. Hoos, "Systems Techniques for Managing Society: A Critique," *Public Administration Review* (March/April 1973), 157–164.

18. Ibid., p. 101.

19. Ibid., pp. 210–11.

20. For example, Ronald J. Waldron, "Systems Approach to Correctional Institutions," *Federal Probation*, 38: 1 (March 1974), 51–54; James T. Pittman and Paul Gray, "Evaluation of Prison Systems," *Journal of Criminal Justice*, 2: 1(Spring 1974), 37–54; Martin L. Forst, "To What Extent Should the Criminal Justice System Be a 'System'?" *Crime and Delinquency*, 23: 4 (October 1977), 403–16.

21. Gary R. Perlstein, "Criminal Justice: A System or a Myth," *Police*, 16: 10 (June 1972), 3–4.

22. Jan Chaiken, et al., *Criminal Justice Models: An Overview* (Washington, D.C.: National Institute of Law Enforcement and Criminal Justice, U.S. Government Printing Office, April 1976).

23. Ibid., p. 21. Also see J. Belkin, et al., *JUSSIM: An Interactive Computer Program for Analysis of Criminal Justice Systems*, rev. ed. (Pittsburgh: Urban Systems Institute, Carnegie-Mellon University, July 1974).

24. The block grants to control crime were one of the final additions to the Johnson Administration's "Great Society" program; these programs included similar funding arrangements for health, housing, community development, and employment.

25. Don C. Gibbons, et al., *Criminal Justice Planning: An Introduction* (Englewood Cliffs, N.J.: Prentice-Hall, Inc., 1977), p. 3.

26. Friedrich A. Hayek, *The Road to Serfdom* (Chicago: The University of Chicago Press, 1944); Karl R. Popper, *The Open Society and Its Enemies*, (Princeton, N.J.: Princeton University Press, 1950).

27. Howard Aldrich, "Centralization versus Decentralization in the Design of Human Service Delivery Systems: A Response of Gouldner's Lament," in Rosemary Sarri and Yeheskel Hasenfeld, eds., *The Management of Human Services* (New York: Columbia University Press, 1978), pp. 65–71.

28. Ibid.

29. Advisory Commission on Intergovernmental Relations, "Safe Streets Reconsidered: The Block-Grant Experience 1968–1975" (Washington, D.C., January 1977), p. 18.

30. United States Senate, Committee of the Judiciary, Subcommittee on Criminal Laws and Procedures, *Federal Assistance to Law Enforcement: Hearings*, p. 326.

31. Advisory Commission on Intergovernmental Relations, op. cit. p. 52.

32. The National Advisory Commission on Criminal Justice Standards and Goals (six volumes), *A National Strategy to Reduce Crime: The Criminal Justice System; Community Crime Prevention; Police; Courts; Corrections* (Washington, D.C.: U. S. Government Printing Office, 1973).

33. Advisory Commission on Intergovernmental Relations, op. cit. p. 215.

34. Ibid., p. 80.

35. Ibid., p. 78.

36. Richard S. Bolan, "Mapping the Planning Theory Terrain," *Urban and Social Change Review,* 8: 2 (1975), 35–43

37. Gibbons, et al., op. cit., pp. 85–88.

38. Ibid., p. 60, citing Edward C. Banfield. Also see Charles Lindblom, *The Intelligence of Democracy: Decision Making Through Mutual Adjustment* (New York: The Free Press, 1965).

39. Blair G. Ewing, "Criminal Justice Planning: An Assessment," *Criminal Justice Review* (Spring 1976), 130.

40. Report of a Panel of the National Academy of Public Administration (NAPA), *Criminal Justice Planning in the Governing Process: A Review of Nine States* (Washington, D.C.: NAPA, February 1979), p. ix.

41. John K. Hudzik, et al., *Criminal Justice Manpower Planning: An Overview*, U.S. Law Enforcement Assistance Administration (Washington, DC.: U.S. Government Printing Office, 1981), p. 150.

42. National Criminal Justice Association (The National Conference), *Approaches to Institutionalization of State Planning Agencies in Criminal Justice*, September 1980, unpublished.

43. Hudzik, et al., op. cit., Chap. 1.

44. The Council of State Governments, *The Future of Criminal Justice Planning* (Lexington, Ky.: The Council of State Governments, 1976), p. 25.

45. Ibid., pp. 25–26.

46. Ibid., p. 36.

47. Ibid., p. 29.

48. Robert C. Cushman, *Criminal Justice Planning for Local Governments*, National Institute of Law Enforcement and Criminal Justice (Washington, D.C.: U.S. Government Printing Office, 1980), pp. 11–12.

49. Ibid., p. 32.

50. See for example, NAPA, op. cit., and Hudzik, et al., op. cit.

51. Cushman, op. cit., p. 32 (adapted from a chart presented by Cushman).

52. National Criminal Justice Association, op. cit.

53. Sharkansky, op. cit., pp. 270–71.

54. Ibid., p. 271.

55. Hudzik, et al., op. cit., Chap. 5.

56. John K. Hudzik and Steven M. Edwards, *State Planning Agency Survey Results,* Manpower Planning Development Project (East Lansing, Mich.: School of Criminal Justice, Michigan State University, 1980).

57. Hudzik, et al., op. cit., Chap. 5.

• Chapter 6 •

PLANNING IN CRIMINAL JUSTICE ORGANIZATIONS

It is clearly important and instructive to contemplate the police, courts, and corrections as interrelated parts of a single entity. Viewing criminal justice as a system for processing cases, or as a series of related decisions, often yields a better and wider perspective on how crime control, due process, and justice are or are not being provided in society. What appears to be productivity improvement for one agency (say, more drug arrests by the police) may actually be a misleading indicator (if the cases are dismissed by the prosecutor or by the court for insufficient or improperly obtained evidence), or may be a cause of inefficiencies in the system as a whole (if the drug arrests clog the courts, delaying trials of other, perhaps higher priority, offenders). Only by focusing on the several agencies of criminal justice as parts of one system can problems such as these be recognized. By planning for the entire system, such problems can often be prevented, minimized, or even solved.

Although the systemic view of criminal justice is crucial, it is also important to consider criminal justice agencies as single entities. Police departments, courts, prisons, and other criminal justice agencies are organizations with their own boundaries, goals, processes, and personnel. Their behavior is to be understood partly within the context of their participation in the criminal justice system, and partly in terms of their own individual histories and characteristics. Efforts to improve criminal justice require, in part, improvements within the agencies that comprise the system, and one of the major avenues for such improvement is organizational planning.

This chapter will examine some basic characteristics of organizations, as a guide to understanding individual organizations, and particularly to comparing different ones. These characteristics will then be examined in relation to various types of criminal justice agencies, in order to understand the different agencies in organizational terms. With this base of understanding, we will then look at the role of planning in organizations.

SOME CHARACTERISTICS OF ORGANIZATIONS

It is no simple task to summarize current thinking about organizations: the volume of literature is tremendous; the variety of perspectives and disciplines is very wide; and there is not much consensus among experts as to what is important or how things work. In the last thirty or forty years, organizations have probably received as much scholarly attention as any aspect of society. The attention has come from a broad range of academic disciplines: business administration, economics, engineering, political science, psychology, and sociology. Because these observers have different interests and perspectives (and, more important, different vocabularies), they tend to "see" and describe different things, which makes it difficult to integrate their findings and often makes it hard to believe that they are describing the same phenomena.

Writing and research on organizations have varied in level of analysis and in purpose. Some research has focused on behavior *in* organizations; some, on the behavior *of* organizations. Studies of the first sort have focused on the behavior of individuals and groups within organizations; studies of the second type have focused on the actions of the entire organization. Differences in purpose distinguish works that are primarily oriented toward understanding organizations from those that are intended to make organizations work better and more efficiently. The relation between the different levels and the different purposes is illustrated in Figure 6-1.

Organizational behavior is a term usually applied to the behavior of individuals and groups in organizations. The approach of studies aimed at explaining such behavior is largely psychological and social psychological, and emphasizes such considerations as leadership, morale, satisfaction, motivation, and group relations. The organizational-behavior approach is also commonly referred to as the *human relations model*.[1]

The approach to organizations that emphasizes the control of behavior within them is usually called *management*. Its purpose is to devise ways of getting people in organizations to perform in ways that will enhance efficiency and productivity or achieve goals. This is the perspective of business administration and engineering, and this approach also draws heavily upon theories of organizational behavior.

Organization theory is that body of knowledge pertaining to the behavior *of* organizations: how they grow and decline, how they react to changes in their environments, how they secure needed resources, and how they interact with other organizations. Sociology is the discipline most closely associated with organization theory, with contributions also from political science and economics.

Finally, *administration* has to do primarily with the issue of controlling the behavior of organizations. Although *management* and *administration* are often used interchangeably, *management* seems to have a narrower focus, used particularly in the sense of managing people. *Administration*, on the other hand, usually comprehends larger issues such as how to get organizations to pursue public interest goals, how to translate legislative policy into executive action, and how to restrain powerful organizations. The academic discipline most directly involved in such considerations is public administration (and its modern cousin, policy analysis), with political science and economics also involved and largely forming the foundation for public administration.

In organizations, planning is one means of control, one way to get activities and resources arranged efficiently, and to get entire organizations doing what we want. But before turning to planning as an aspect of management and administration, we need to look carefully at a few important characteristics of behavior in and of organizations.

Goals

Goals are important for planning. Sometimes goals are clear and known; sometimes they are vague or in conflict. There are actually two kinds of goal conflict: the several goals of an organization may not be compatible, or there may be substantial conflict over whether or not they are the proper goals. Organizational goals also vary in how controversial they are, how crucial they seem, and how far they can realistically be expected to be achieved.

An important distinction is usually made between the ostensible goals and the operative goals of an organization. Ostensible goals are those the organization is supposed to be pursuing; operative goals are those it actually is pursuing. The movement of organizations from ostensible goals is called *goal displacement*.[2] Frequently, the operative goals of an organization come to be maintenance and survival, in contrast to the loftier notions that serve as the ostensible goals (the overcoming of disease, the elimination of illiteracy, the encouragement of excellence in the arts). Ostensible goals may be kept for public edification, but they often are not the guides to routine organizational activity that their originators intended them to be.

For police departments, for example, one frequently cited set of goals includes law enforcement and maintenance of order. James Q. Wilson pointed out many years ago that these

Figure 6-1. Approaches to the Study of Organizations

Level of Analysis	Primary Purpose: Understanding	Primary Purpose: Control
Behavior *in* organizations	Organizational behavior	Management
Behavior *of* organizations	Organization theory	Administration

two objectives create dilemmas for police organizations.[3] The goal of law enforcement generates consensus and public support, but it is largely unattainable. The police are never even made aware of most criminal offenses, and for those they do learn about, usually little evidence is available and little can be done. The second goal, maintenance of order, inspires consensus only as a very general principle. In practice, the question of what constitutes order or disorder is almost always in dispute, and the police must choose whose definition of proper and seemly conduct to accept. The choice generally dissatisfies some of the disputants. In practice, then, the police goal of maintaining order may create conflict and dissension.

Perhaps the two basic aims of the courts are to protect society and to protect the rights of individuals, or crime control and due process.[4] There is constant tension between the two goals. The balancing of these two goals is one of the crucial issues in judicial decision-making. Certainly the goal of crime control usually has greater public support, but many jurists consider the protection of due process a particularly important function.

Incompatibility among the goals of an organization is even better illustrated by corrections. Custody and treatment, or restraint and rehabilitation, are usually given as the goals of prisons and other kinds of correctional organizations. Almost all kinds of treatment have been shown to be most effective when administered in as normal and open a setting as possible. Normal and open settings are not conducive to the maintenance of custody, however, particularly within prisons. Custody is best achieved, of course, by keeping prisoners in their cells continuously, and in general by limiting freedom and maximizing controls. So the two correctional goals seriously conflict with one another, and this conflict creates strains and problems for correctional organizations.

Structure

A second important characteristic of organizations is structure, the manner in which work and authority are arranged. Organizations in which authority is concentrated in a few are termed *centralized*; those with wide distribution of authority are termed *decentralized*. An organization in which there is a preponderance of different, relatively narrow jobs is said to have a high degree of specialization, particularly if the jobs require special skills or training. Organizations with greater horizontal differentiation (division of labor, specialization), greater vertical differentiation (more levels, more decentralization), and greater spatial dispersion are said to have greater complexity than those displaying fewer of these characteristics.[5]

Basically, *structure* refers to the static characteristics of an organization. Most organizations maintain tables of organization, or organization charts, that reflect their structure. In Figure 6-2, organization charts for two twenty-five-person police departments are shown, one of which obviously has greater vertical differentiation. In Figure 6-3, two more charts are presented, one clearly displaying more horizontal differentiation. One element of structure not highlighted by these charts is size, for the organizations pictured have the same number of personnel. But size can be an important consideration, with implications for other structural characteristics and for management and administration. (The impact of size and structure on organizing and staffing the planning function is discussed in Chapter 7.)

Generalizing about the structure of different types of criminal justice organizations is difficult, because they vary in size and in other basic characteristics. Police departments are the most numerous of criminal justice organizations, and exhibit the widest variations in size. The estimated 20,000 police departments in the United States[6] include many with but one employee, and range upward in size to the almost 30,000-employee New York Police Department. The median for police departments in this country is ten to twenty employees,[7] and the most common structure probably resembles either the less vertically differentiated structure in Figure 6-2 or the less horizontally differentiated structure in Figure 6-3. In organizational structure, then, these departments are not particularly differentiated or complex.

Although the median size of police departments is rather small, most of the police in this country work for larger agencies. Fewer than 2 per cent of the police departments in the United States employ over half of all police employees.[8] These larger departments have personnel complements well in excess of 200, and tend to be considerably more differentiated, both horizontally and vertically, than smaller departments. The use of districts or precincts makes

Figure 6-2. Two 25-Person Police Departments Varying in Vertical Differentiation

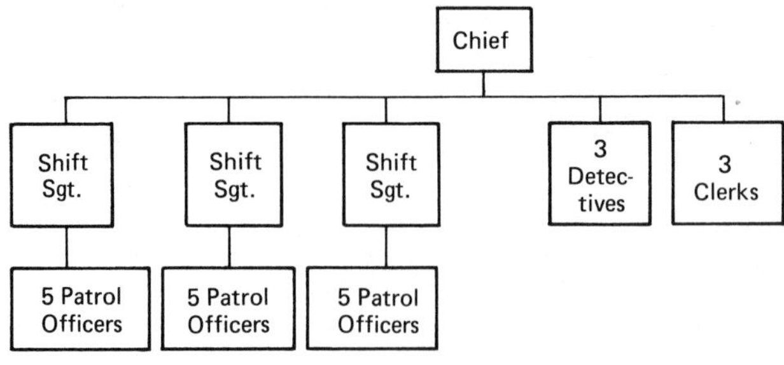

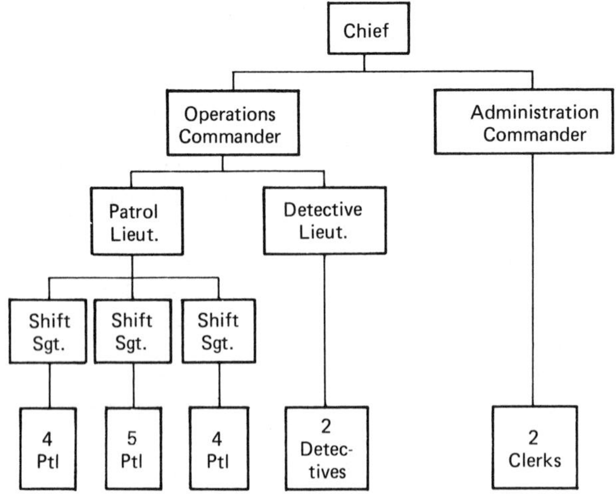

the largest police departments even more structurally complex.

Although their structures often appear fairly centralized, and despite emphasis on chain of command, discipline, and other "military" concerns, police departments are in reality very decentralizied. The lowliest members of police organizations, particularly patrol officers, have considerable authority and are allowed wide discretion in its use.[9] This fact, together with the geographical dispersion of patrol officers throughout the jurisdiction, makes even small police departments structurally more complex than their organization charts sometimes suggest.

Courts are structurally complex for different reasons. In the description of their structure, an initial problem that must be overcome is the designation of their organizational boundaries. The basic issue is whether or not to regard the prosecutor and the defense attorney (often a public defender) as employees of the court: although they routinely do their work in the courts, and many regularly work in the same court, they are neither paid out of the court's budget nor are they hired or fired by the court, and no one in the court is their "manager."[10] Still, their roles fall within the context of the court; they are clearly bound by some of the rules of the court; they may express and exhibit a kind of organizational loyalty to the court; and in some respects the judge is obviously their superior.

Whether or not the prosecutor and the defense attorney are considered part of the court organization, their work and the nature of their relationship to the court is evidence of considerable decentralization: they clearly have a great deal of authority with respect to the work and decisions of the court.

Although this odd form of decentralization

Figure 6-3. Two 25-Person Police Departments Varying in Horizontal Differentiation

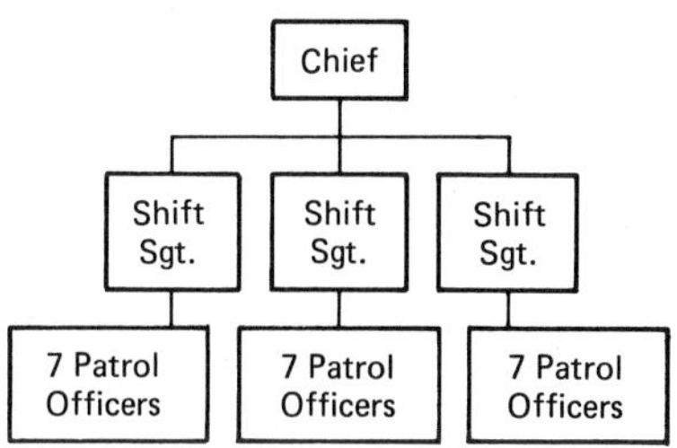

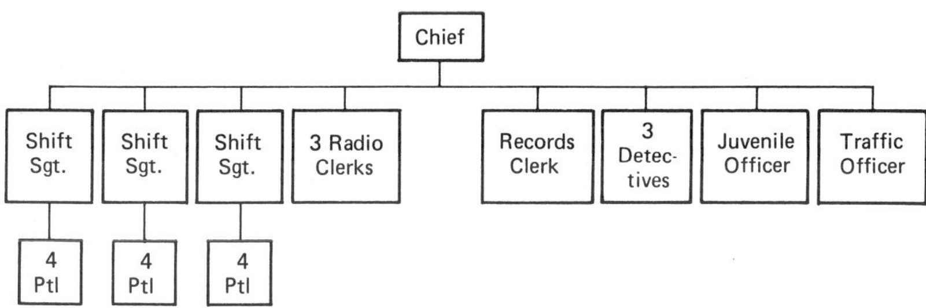

introduces complexity in court structures, the small number of central roles (judge, prosecutor, defense attorney) and the common requirement for each (a law degree) reduces complexity. In this respect, courts are similar to police departments, which also have few basic roles (patrol officer, detective) and a common requirement (basic recruit training). But police departments also have a clear hierarchy of supervisors and managers, while courts do not (the prosecutor and the defense attorney are part of other hierarchies—the prosecutor's office, the public defender's office, a private law firm, and so on). Even within the court, managerial authority is often unclearly distributed between judges and court administrators.

Of course, there are other employees of the court, such as clerks, bailiffs, and stenographers. Courts also often run a variety of programs, so that the court's employees might include bail interviewers, diversion counselors, various kinds of caseworkers, probation officers, presentence investigators, and community arbitrators. Each of these employees is a specialist, doing a kind of work different from that of other court employees. This aspect of the court's organization is similar to that of the more horizontally differentiated police department in Figure 6-3.

Most individual courts are relatively small organizations, but some court systems, even at the substate level, are fairly large. The Detroit Recorder's Court, for example, has seventeen judges, each with his own courtroom and supporting personnel. In addition, there are central court personnel concerned with budgeting, planning, and other managerial functions. For the most part, however, even large court systems are not very differentiated vertically. Often there is one chief judge or administrative judge, with all of the remaining judges arranged on the next lower level. Thus, even large court systems tend to have structures similar to that of the police agency with greater horizontal differentiation (Figure 6-3).[11] (Within state court systems, of course, there are levels of jurisdiction and appeal, but these are not really analogous to managerial levels.)

Prisons, usually the largest correctional agencies, often combine the vertical differentiation characteristic of large police departments and the extreme horizontal differentiation sometimes characteristic of the courts. The custodial staff is usually vertically differentiated, with numerous supervisory and managerial levels. Just about all of the custodial employees do the same kind of work, though. On the other hand, considerable specialization is common among the treatment staff, with various kinds of caseworkers, educators, psychologists, psychiatrists, and so on. This part of the organization often has relatively few levels of management. Within state prison systems, another element of structural complexity is added by the geographical dispersion of institutions, and by the delegation of considerable authority to institution managers.

Probation agencies, parole agencies, and other "community" correctional organizations are numerous and for the most part very small, except in states in which they are parts of departments of corrections or statewide departments of probation and parole. These types of correctional organizations, especially the small ones, tend not to be structurally complex and have relatively little specialization and few levels of hierarchy. Most of the employees are caseworkers, and although the nature of their caseloads may vary, all perform essentially similar tasks within a particular agency. Larger agencies, however, including state agencies, are faced with the complicating factor of geographical dispersion.

Technology and Decision-Making

These organizational characteristics pertain to the basic tasks, including decision-making, undertaken in pursuit of the goals of the organization. In recent years, it has been increasingly recognized that the technology of an organization is an important determinant of other characteristics, including structure and goals.[12] Technology, as a key organizational variable, does not refer to sophistication of equipment, but to the tasks and techniques by which work is accomplished.

Two dimensions of technology are the number of exceptional cases encountered in the performance of tasks, and the nature of these exceptional cases.[13] The interrelation of these two dimensions is illustrated in Figure 6-4. Organizational technology characterized by few exceptional cases which can be resolved with logical, analytical activity falls into the category usually termed *routine*. The opposite situation, involving many exceptional cases that are unanalyzable and require inventive or creative solution rather than simple analysis, is termed *nonroutine*.

Two additional varieties of organizational technology are presented in Figure 6-4. Craft industries provide an example of technology in which few exceptional cases are encountered, but these often pose unanalyzable problems. At the other extreme are engineering situations characterized by many exceptional cases that are susceptible to the logical application of known rules and methods for their resolution.

These varieties of organizational technology have fairly direct implications for organizational structure and management. In routine situations it is possible to establish rules that specify appropriate action. The rare perplexing problem that arises can be referred to managerial personnel or experts. In the engineering situation, exceptions are more common, so that it may be necessary to allow employees more freedon and authority (otherwise everything might be passed up to managers to decide), but the

Figure 6-4. Two Dimensions of the Technology Variable (Industrial Examples) (Adapted from Charles Perrow, "A Framework for the Comparative Analysis of Organizations," *American Sociological Review*, 32:2 [April 1967], 194-208, by permission.)

Nature of Problems Encountered	Exceptional Cases Encountered: Few	Exceptional Cases Encountered: Many
Unanalyzable	Craft industries (specialty glass)	Nonroutine (aerospace)
Analyzable	Routine (tonnage steel mills, screw and bolts)	Engineering (heavy machinery)

problems are still relatively analyzable. So, work (or decision-making) will remain largely the application of known principles.

In the craft situation, relatively few exceptional cases are encountered, so that much of the work activity involves the application of familiar methods to familiar problems. The exceptions that do arise, however, are relatively unanalyzable, requiring intuitive or original solution. Depending upon the timing of these exceptions, the geographical dispersion of activities and other characteristics of the organization, these unanalyzable problems might automatically be referred to experts, or it might be necessary that each worker be equipped to respond to them. In the latter case, a good deal of discretion would be left to each decision-maker.

The nonroutine situation, in which many unanalyzable exceptional cases are encountered, would require that considerable discretion be given to each worker. Because unanalyzable exceptions require creative solution, the simple application of known principles is not possible; because there are many exceptions, they cannot all be simply referred upward or to experts. In this kind of situation, the organization and its executives are clearly most dependent on the resourcefulness and creativity of rank-and-file employees.

These four kinds of situations correspond to some familiar labels often attached to varieties of work (see Figure 6-5). Routine technology corresponds to essentially *bureaucratic* work. Nonroutine activity, calling for intuition, imagination, invention, and artistry, corresponds to *creative* work. Situations involving relatively few, but unanalyzable, exceptions correspond to *craft* activity. Finally, situations involving many exceptions that can be resolved through analysis and the application of a body of knowledge that can be learned corresponds to *professional* activity.

The basic work of the police, patrol work, is probably best characterized as craft.[14] The work primarily involves answering calls, routine patrolling, and generally "handling situations." Most of the situations encountered are reasonably routine, and can be handled according to established rules and procedures. These include enforcing traffic laws, investigating accidents and minor disputes, "taking reports" of minor crimes, and numerous even less serious matters (helping people who need directions, householders who are locked out, and so forth). The occasional exceptions encountered, however, may require instant and ingenious responses, rather than simple application of rules or logical analysis. These exceptions include such problems as serious domestic disputes and a wide range of situations in which individual police officers must decide whether or not to utilize their legal and coercive powers.

Most investigative or detective work undertaken by the police is essentially bureaucratic. Detectives spend most of their time processing documents and information supplied by others (patrol officers, victims, witnesses).[15] Even the more active elements of detective work tend to be routine: interviewing and other forms of information gathering. Some active investigative work, though, particularly completely undercover operations, might be characterized as creative, for it involves many exceptions that cannot be resolved simply by the application of rules or principles.

Most court work is also bureaucratic. The basic work of the courts involves decision-making about the processing and disposition of cases. The principal decision-makers are prosecutors, defense attorneys, and judges. Although these officials are lawyers and normally accorded professional status, most of their decision-making is routine, especially in plea-bargaining, which is used to dispose of a very large proportion of all criminal cases.[16] Most cases are quickly diagnosed and categorized, with dispositions following straightforwardly

Figure 6-5. Four Types of Work Based upon the Technology Variable

Nature of Problems Encountered	Exceptional Cases Encountered: Few	Many
Unanalyzable	Craft	Creative
Analyzable	Bureaucratic	Professional

for each category of "normal" crimes.[17] Even exceptional cases involve primarily logical analysis and application of known principles. Occasionally perplexing cases arise, and court decision-makers are sometimes expected to formulate creative strategies or dispositions, but these instances are quite rare and not characteristic of court work.

Also best characterized as bureaucratic are the custodial aspects of correctional work, particularly in traditional prison settings.[18] The work of prison guards is largely routine, with few exceptional cases, and those problems that are encountered are usually referred upward to supervisors for resolution. Custody is designed to minimize exceptions and to deal analytically with those that do arise. More treatment-oriented correctional work, however, including the work of guards in some treatment prisons, is possibly best described as professional, for all clients are regarded as exceptional cases meriting individualized attention. Client problems are presumed to be analyzable and susceptible to logical solution, but successful treatment is understood to depend on the choice and knowledgeable application of general principles, rather than on mere invocation of standardized rules and procedures.[19] This description reflects primarily the theory of treatment; in practice, however, treatment tends to be much more bureaucratic, at least with respect to the handling of most clients and cases.[20]

Control Process

All organizations employ methods of influencing the work behavior and decision-making of their members. From the standpoint of the organization (or its executives), influence and control are critically important, for individuals must adopt the organization's goals and methods, rather than their own. A variety of control processes may be utilized, as illustrated in Figure 6-6.

Two important dimensions of organizational control are its source and its object.[21] Individual employees may internalize the organization's goals and methods, or those goals and methods may be externally imposed. Even when goals and methods are internalized, of course, the original source of control may have been the organization, but once the individual has adopted the organization's means and ends, he may be "trusted" to take unsupervised actions. The objects of control may be either the means of doing the work of the organization, or the ends that are to be sought.

External control over means is most obviously exercised through direct supervision, with a supervisor looking over the employee's shoulder, giving orders and ensuring that the proper methods are used. Standardized practices in an organization also exert external influence over means, as they prescribe precisely what is to be done in a given situation. The division of labor is another mode of external control, limiting each employee to a specialized portion of the total process, and identifying where in the organization any particular task or decision should be carried out.

External control over ends is primarily exercised through authority and incentives. One function of authority is to specify who chooses the goals to be pursued, and who resolves conflicts over competing ends. A key way in which the organization influences individuals to accept and to pursue its goals is through the offer of incentives for effort. These incentives induce individuals to join and to work for organizations, and the manipulation of incentives also

Figure 6-6. Two Dimensions of Organizational Control (Adapted from Herbert A. Simon, *Administrative Behavior*, 3rd ed. [New York: The Free Press, 1976].)

	Source of Control	
Object of Control	External to Individual	Within the Individual
Ends	Authority Incentives	Socialization
Means	Direct Supervision Standardized Practices Division of Labor	Training

affects their continued willingness to pursue the organization's ends.

When an individual learns the means for accomplishing work, his need for direct supervision is reduced. The general process by which these means are learned is training, although it can take many forms, from apprenticeship through lengthy classroom education. Training may involve learning fairly routine rules and standardized practices, or it may involve learning more general principles and rough guidelines for their application to less predictable situations. For decision-making, a critical element of training is learning to apply the criterion of efficiency to alternative actions or solutions. When the individual learns to use this criterion, the organization can be satisfied that he is capable, within the limits of available information, of choosing that alternative which maximizes benefits over costs. The organization's task then is to ensure that decision-makers get the information needed to make informed choices.[22]

An organization is also interested in having its members internalize its ends, so that the need for coercive control (authority) and expensive incentives is reduced. In fact, people often join an organization, in part, because they identify with its goals, so that they may have started with some internalized control over ends. Through a socialization process, the organization encourages its members to feel increasingly loyal and committed. If the organization can bring its members to identify with its goals, so that the employee willingly strives to achieve organizational ends, a very strong and unobtrusive brand of influence comes into play.

These varieties of control processes in organizations correspond roughly, but not exactly, to the varieties of technology and work already discussed. In organizations that encounter analyzable problems and analyzable exceptional cases, an emphasis on control over means can be expected, for known rules or at least general principles are useful in such situations. For unanalyzable problems, however, the organization must rely on the employee's ingenuity, and the control exercised is likely to be over ends. That is, the organization would seek to convince the employee to pursue its goals, but would allow him considerable freedom in choosing the means to achieve those goals.

Most organizations use at least several kinds of control processes, and vary mainly in the emphasis given each. Police departments certainly use all the forms of organizational control noted in Figure 6-6. For the more routine aspects of patrol work, external modes of control are emphasized, including standardized procedures, reporting requirements, and authority. Patrol officers encounter exceptional cases, however: they often must react quickly; their supervisors are rarely present; and rules and procedures are usually not instructive about what to do, though they may specify at length what *not* to do. Organizational control in these circumstances (if present at all) is primarily internal: the patrol officer draws on training to select appropriate means for handling the exceptional situation, influenced through socialization to pursue appropriate ends. Any external control is usually exercised after the fact, when the officer's behavior may be reviewed and judgment rendered.

Court work is mostly bureaucratic, and certainly several external sources of control are widely used. The division of labor among judges, prosecutors, and defense attorneys is one basic form of control, as it constrains each role and apportions decision-making authority. The law establishes a variety of standardized practices that exert control over court decision-makers. Incentives exert a strong influence as well, especially over the judge or prosecutor desiring re-election, or the defense attorney desiring a winner's fee. A less obtrusive but quite important source of control, though, is internal. Key court decision-makers have been trained in the practice of law, and have been socialized into the legal profession. Through these internalized controls, courts manage to function as organizations even though key participants are not really employees of the organization.

Correctional organizations exercise both internal and external controls. Treatment-oriented organizations usually rely on training to influence employee behavior. Counselors, for example, are taught general principles and methods of rehabilitation, and then are expected to diagnose, to classify, and to treat accordingly. Supervision over the counselor-client relationship is indirect at best, and employees are regarded as professionals capable of self-direction and self-control. At the other extreme, custody-oriented correctional organizations tend to emphasize external control over employee behavior. Supervision is more direct;

standard rules and procedures are more widely used; and the limitations of employees' authority are stressed.

Of course, official organizational control processes are not the only sources of influence over employee behavior. Perhaps the strongest influence of all comes from cultural expectations about appropriate behavior on the part of employees.[23] As a result of these norms, much of the obedience to organizational means and ends is given without reflection and taken for granted. Informal organizational controls can also be important. In police departments, the peer group or "police subculture" exerts considerable influence on officer behavior, often running counter to official preferences.[24] In courts, an informal work group commonly develops among the regular participants or "courtroom elite," and its influence on decision-making is often in conflict with official procedure or policy.[25] In prisons the inmates exercise considerable control, over guards as well as over each other.[26] And in correctional organizations, such as parole agencies, where there is casework, informal influence is exerted by the peer group and by other criminal justice agents, such as judicial and police officials, with whom caseworkers must interact.[27]

Environment

The environment of an organization is everything beyond its boundaries. Whatever is not part of an organization is part of its environment. The most important aspects of an organization's environment, however, are those that affect its goals, activities, and resources. The kinds of relationships that organizations have with their environments vary, and these relationships have important consequences for behavior in and of organizations.

Three components of the environment of organizations are particularly significant. A key characteristic of any organization is its resource environment: the source of an organization's resources, and the relative strength and independence it has in acquiring the resources it needs. Also important is the work environment, the setting within which the basic tasks of the organization are performed, and the extent to which the organization controls that setting and the work itself. Finally, organizations vary in the degree to which they are susceptible to regulation: such regulation may constrain the organization in its choice of goals, in the strategies it can adopt, in its allocation of resources, or in many other ways.

Although attention is usually focused on the effects of the environment on the organization, and although the organization's survival and success usually depend on its ability to adapt to its environment,[28] many organizations are large and powerful enough to affect their environments, so that the environment may be required to adapt. For example, when a major manufacturing plant or business firm threatens to leave a small town unless given tax relief or other advantages, the town is often forced to adapt to the organization's wishes. On a larger scale, Chrysler's apparent failure to adapt to its environment did not lead to the demise of the corporation, but to major changes in its environment designed to ensure its survival. It is probably most accurate to think of organizations and their environments as interdependent, with the relative strength and autonomy of major participants varying.

Public agencies, including criminal justice organizations, acquire their resources primarily through government appropriations. Because public agencies are funded from limited tax revenues, all desires cannot be satisfied, and competition can be fierce. Among the different types of criminal justice agencies, police departments seem to be generally most successful in getting the funding they want.[29] The police receive natural support from adherents of a crime-control ideology, and they can usually mobilize a constituency of concerned citizens when necessary. Correctional agencies, and particularly community-based programs such as halfway houses or probation agencies, have the least advantageous relationship with their resource environments; the general public often views money spent on such activities as providing services and opportunities to people who do not deserve them.

Prisons too do not generally have a strong relationship with their resource environments, except after major crises or at times when prisons seem critical to the protection of society. Frequently, after riots or large-scale escapes, prisons are able to acquire increased resources. In periods when incapacitation is a dominant policy, prisons often come to be viewed as a key part of hard-nosed crime control, and benefit accordingly. At other times, though, when prisons are identified with rehabilitation, their relationship with their resource environments is weakened.

The work environments of different types of criminal justice agencies vary dramatically. The police have little control over the amount or timing of their workload, and little control over the settings in which they are required to act. The work setting of the police is commonly confused and chaotic, and occasionally dangerous. The courts have more control over their work settings and schedules, although they are somewhat dependent on the police and prosecutors for the initiation of cases and thus for the quantity of work brought to them. The work setting of the court is considerably more serene than that of the police, but certainly not totally controlled, especially as many of the key participants (prosecutor, defense attorney, witnesses, jurors, defendant) are not, strictly speaking, part of the court organization. The work environments of prisons are the most controlled. They are, in fact, "total institutions," and by their very nature greatly restrict interference from the environment. In recent years the walls of the prison have become more "permeable," though, so that its independence from the environment is probably not as great as it once was.[30]

The courts are more independent of their regulatory environment than are other types of criminal justice organizations. The judiciary is an independent branch of government, and individual courts are usually rather independent of even superior courts or state court administrative offices. Prisons, on the other hand, though once quite independent, have become heavily regulated by forces in their environments in recent years. The courts have been the source of much of this regulation. Virtually every aspect of prison life and administration has been affected by court rulings as the judiciary has abandoned its "hands off" posture toward postconviction issues and increasingly found due-process guarantees applicable to the incarcerated.

THE ROLE OF PLANNING IN ORGANIZATIONS

Planning, as part of management and administration, has to do with getting organizations, and the people in them, to do the things we want. To accomplish this, it may prove helpful to know something about the organizations that are to be managed and administered. Now that the characteristics of criminal justice organizations have been described, let us consider the role of planning. This section will examine some of the specific organizational applications of planning, broadening somewhat the notions of managerial and organizational planning.

Planning in organizations is part of management or administration. In general, management is that function in an organization that is responsible for seeing to it that things turn out right—that the company make a profit, that quality services be delivered, or whatever. One of the key functions of management is decision-making. Managers are presented with situations in which they must decide, or choose, what to do. To make wise choices, managers need information: ideas, a range of alternatives, good estimates of consequences, a view of the future, and an understanding of the relationships among various choices. The role of planning is to supply this information to the decision-maker. Another key role of organizational planning may be to widen the range of available choices.

Management must maintain a double perspective: the manager must be concerned with what is going on inside the organization, and also with the environment and its effects on the organization. Planning, too, must maintain these two perspectives.

The Internal Focus

The internal focus of management is closely linked with ideas of efficiency. Goals to be achieved or problems to be solved are identified, and the manager's task is to use resources in the best way possible. Attempts to inform decision-making and improve efficiency through planning are often focused on these resources and activities, as well as on their coordination.

Resources. Organizations need and use resources. Part of their resource-related efforts are directed toward their resource environments, and involve the acquisition of money and people. Fiscal planning and manpower planning (see Chapters 13 and 14) include such considerations.

Once the money and people have been acquired by the organization, the manager's concern is to use them efficiently—to spend the money wisely or invest it appropriately, and to elicit maximum productivity from people. In criminal justice organizations, the management of people and concern for their productivity is probably the most important factor in the efficient use of resources.

Three approaches to increasing the productivity of people in organizations are illustrated in Figure 6-7. Of the approaches listed, the last is probably the most closely identified with planning; it might be called the *decision-making approach.* The assumption is that organizational inefficiencies result from a lack of information, or from failure to use information correctly. To rectify this situation, more or better information is provided, and the organization gives more attention to designing decision-making systems and influencing the choices made. The result of these efforts, it is hoped, is greater rationality in decision-making, and improved productivity.

The general phenomenon of information systems in criminal justice organizations reflects this decision-making approach to the improvement of productivity. Many police departments, for example, have elaborate systems that provide regular information about workload, response times, clearance rates, pending cases, staffing levels, and other matters. It is expected that decisions based on such information will result in more efficient use of people. Besides just providing information, of course, the police organization also seeks to influence its use in decision-making. Priorities may be established, ranges of acceptable tolerance prescribed, and computational algorithms provided, all for the purpose of guiding decision-makers in their choice among alternatives.

Parole boards, too, are greatly affected by the decision-making approach, because their basic task is to render decisions. Efforts to improve their decision-making have generally focused on making more information available, and on providing guidance in the use of such information. Sometimes, "guidance" has taken the form of parole-prediction tables and decision formulae that pretty well specify the choice to be made.

The role of planning in the decision-making approach should be obvious. Planning serves to improve the information available, to widen the range of choices considered, to force consideration of the future, and so on. Planning includes much of the preparation for decisions based on informed choices.

The role of planning is less direct and obvious in the other two approaches shown in Figure 6-7, but alternatives still need to be found and considered, consequences estimated, forecasts made, and decisions rendered. The first approach assumes that people are intentionally "goofing off," and that what is needed to improve performance is increased obedience to rules and procedures. The usual response is to emphasize management direction and control, so that employees are clearly told what they are supposed to do, and then required to perform accordingly. This is the *classical management approach.*

The third approach, the *human relations approach*, assumes that people often do not apply their maximum energy to their work; that if they were more committed to their organization, they would work harder and be more productive. Although incentives (more pay, promotion) are often used to get people to work harder, they are always in short supply, particularly in the public sector. In response, managers try to provide better leadership,

Figure 6-7. Three Approaches to Improving Human Resource Productivity in Organizations

Perceived Problem	Management Response		Intermediate Consequence		Desired Outcome
Lack of discipline: rules not followed	Direction and control	→	Obedience	→	Improved productivity
Lack of commitment: full effort not given	Leadership	→	Better morale	→	Improved productivity
Lack of information: decisions not rational	Information and influence	→	Greater rationality	→	Improved productivity

which *may* lead to higher morale and satisfaction among employees, which *may* in turn lead to improved productivity. The word *may* is underscored above because these presumed connections have been challenged.[31] Nevertheless, this is perhaps the dominant approach to management and productivity improvement in both private and public organizations these days, with many ardent adherents.

The classical management approach underlies traditional police and correctional administration, but as a means of productivity improvement has had perhaps its most dramatic success in the courts. Members of the courtroom élite, including judges, prosecutors, and defense attorneys, have often been found to work relatively short hours and to manipulate scheduling to their convenience. Docket control programs that have had the authority to compel obedience from these officials have sometimes been very successful at reducing backlogs of cases in the courts.

The human relations approach to productivity improvement is a cornerstone of team policing and related police programs. Among the assumptions behind these programs have been that police officers find their work less than satisfying, and that they come to be alienated from their organization and their community. By organizing the work differently and providing a different kind of leadership, team policing has been expected to enhance the morale and commitment of police officers, which in turn could lead to better performance.

Activities. Thus far we have considered productivity only in terms of getting more out of resources, through greater effort, more obedience, or improved rationality in decision-making. But it is also important to realize that organizations use resources to *do* something—for their activities—and that there are many ways in which things might be done. Another way in which productivity in an organization might be increased is through the improvement of its activities. This is the *scientific management approach*.

Police departments are currently undergoing study and analysis. The traditional police activity, patrol, has been seriously challenged: doubts have been raised about its effects on crime rates, on public fear of crime, and even on public perceptions of the police presence.[32] Several alternative strategies, including team policing, directed patrol, and saturation patrol, are being considered and tested. The challenge is to determine which of the strategies represents the most efficient or productive use of resources.

Correctional organizations are, with respect to treatment programs, in a similar situation. Many programs have been tried or proposed, including psychotherapy, group therapy, reality therapy, milieu therapy, education, job training, vocational counseling, and so on. The task facing managers is to determine the consequences of each of the alternatives (and the consequences may vary by type of client or setting), and then to choose the most desirable activities—those that will improve the performance of the organization.

When an organization faces choices about what activities to undertake, the role of planning is to enlarge the range of activities (alternatives) from which choices will be made, to estimate the likely consequences of each, to forecast the conditions under which the chosen activities will need to work, and generally to provide ideas and information for decision-making. With or without planning, decisions will be made; with planning, they can be informed decisions.

Coordination. One of the distinctive elements of planning is its focus on comprehensiveness and coordination. In any organization, decisions are made continuously, and often rapidly. Management is often crisis-oriented, treating each new problem as a separate phenomenon to be solved as quickly as possible. Planning frequently provides the only opportunity to consider all the organization's decisions and problems together, and to develop a coordinated strategy for dealing with them.

There is ample evidence of the need for coordination in organizations. Many police departments in recent years have adopted participative management to enhance employee commitment, and have initiated new strategies such as directed patrol, designed to improve the efficiency of activities. But the efforts seem incompatible, for directed patrol greatly limits the discretion and autonomy of the patrol officer. It may be that two problems (poor morale and perceived inefficiency of routine patrol, probably) were dealt with separately, when in fact they are both components of one complex problem.

All kinds of decisions in organizations need

to be coordinated. In a prison, for example, a decision to increase educational opportunities for prisoners, or visitation privileges, must be coordinated with the custody staff, for these programs might require more guards, or a different pattern of assignments. A decision to alter the daily release and lock-in times of inmates would have to be coordinated with counselors, health officials, food-service employees, and other staff whose schedules must be adapted to those of the prisoners. And these are relatively routine examples. The prison considering a major alteration in its basic correctional philosophy, or the construction of a major new facility, is confronted with a multitude of related decisions that need to be coordinated, and the planning process is the most likely context for such coordination.

The key idea behind coordination is that separate decisions and actions in an organization have an impact on one another. Daily pressures, short-sightedness, habit, and factional jealousies tend to encourage decision-makers to treat problems in isolation. The planning process presents the opportunity to consider the interdependence of decisions and actions, and to coordinate the organization's responses to problems.

The External Focus

The external focus of organizations and organizational planning is the environment. The environment is always changing, and it is in the organization's best interests to detect such changes as quickly as possible. The more quickly changes are detected, the more time the organization has to adapt, or to attempt to force the environment to alter its course.

Any organization needs constantly to monitor its resource environment, anticipating the availability of revenues, people, and other important resources. The work environment also must be kept under regular surveillance, as organizational activities may have to be adapted to any changes in the work setting. And the regulatory environment must be monitored for changes that require alterations of organizational goals, resource allocations or activities.

A somewhat different classification of potential changes has been suggested by Theodore Caplow.[33] One important set he identifies as market pressures. These characteristics of the market requiring organizational adjustment include competition, scarcities, rising costs, and declining revenues. Criminal justice agencies compete with each other, and with other organizations, for revenues, manpower, public support, and political influence. They face scarcities primarily in the form of too few high-quality job applicants. Petroleum scarcities, of course, could have serious consequences for police patrols or for the heating of prisons. Market pressure from rising costs affects all agencies in inflationary periods and, combined with stable or even declining revenues, can have significant impact on the performance of an organization. Criminal justice agencies must monitor these market pressures, anticipating them, adapting to them, or influencing them whenever possible.

Moreover, as Caplow notes, "no organization can be completely insulated from the currents of social change in the surrounding society."[34] He specifies demographic shifts and changes in public policy and social values as key components of social change. Demographic shifts—variations in the proportions of population falling into different age categories—strongly affect criminal justice organizations.[35] So does the shift in population from the Northeast to the "sun-belt" states, for some agencies must lay off employees while others have to deal with sharp increases in crime, arrests, court cases, and prison populations.

Changes in public policy include new laws and new regulations, as well as less formal statements. At this very moment for example, new laws are taking effect all over the country, many of them with direct implications for criminal justice agencies. Public policy is also shaped by the courts, as with the *Gideon* and *Miranda* Supreme Court decisions, which had far-reaching effects on the police and on trial courts. New policies may also emanate from other kinds of governmental decisions, as when a governor announces a crackdown on traffic offenders, or when a district attorney advises police that he will no longer actively prosecute certain kinds of offenses. All such changes in public policy require criminal justice agencies to react, and those that have been paying attention to their environments will be more likely to have foreseen the changes and to have adapted in a timely and successful fashion.

Social values include attitudes toward deviance and control, relations between the sexes, and the importance attached to education and religion. According to Caplow, "changes in social values are even more unpredictable in the long run than changes in public policy, but since they are much less abrupt, they permit more intelligent planning and adaptation."[36] Particularly important here is the whole manner in which people view crime, which forms the foundation for society's response to crime, as described by Gresham Sykes:

> [W]e must be concerned not only with changes in the crime rate but also with the meanings and interpretations attached to crime by society. Will crime be seen as a mass of individual harms or as a threat to society itself in the form of a challenge to the normative system? Will crime be thought to be due to a flaw in the individual or caused by a "pathological" social environment? Will crime be viewed largely as a lower-class phenomenon or as something that is to be found at every level of society? The relative strength of perceptions such as these will do much to influence how the nature of the crime problem will be defined in the United States in coming decades and what steps are taken to solve it, and these in turn are likely to have at least some influence on the incidence of criminal behavior.[37]

In addition to market pressures and social changes, a third general category of changes to which organizations must adapt, in Caplow's view, is technological progress. In this electronic, computer age, the pace of innovation and invention is much faster than it ever has been, and it is accelerating.[38] Organizations need to keep abreast of such innovations in order to avoid falling behind their competitors. In fact, organizations are often coerced into purchasing the latest equipment because parts for older models become unavailable. New technology may also be something that has to be dealt with in the work environment, as the police are discovering with respect to computer-related crime, for example.

All these various characteristics of organizational environments and changes call for reactions by organizations. In order to react, organizations need to be aware of the changes going on around them. In order to react effectively, they need to have valid information about the changes; they need to consider a range of alternative ways of responding; they need good estimates of the consequences of alternatives; and, if possible, they need to anticipate the changes before they take place. Planning is intended to satisfy all of these needs. Although we need not fully agree with Caplow that "a nearly magical enhancement of the manager's personal capability can be achieved nine times out of ten by an intelligent emphasis on planning,"[39] there are areas of organizational functioning in which planning seems to offer considerable benefit.

The Need for Integration

Though organizational planning has been discussed as having an internal focus and an external focus, the division is largely artificial. By the same token, planning for resources and for activities cannot, or at least should not, be conceived or undertaken separately. In fact, one of the great strengths of planning is that it provides the opportunity to integrate functions. In an organization, each manager and employee tends to develop a narrow focus, to pursue suboptimal goals. Any mechanism that reintegrates thinking and activity is of great value.

The overall consideration of goals, activities, and resources, and of the internal and external foci, is really in the domain of *strategic planning*. Lorange and Vancil acknowledge this breadth when they state that "a strategic-planning system has two major functions: to develop an integrated, coordinated, and consistent long-term plan of action, and to facilitate adaptation of the corporation to environmental change."[40] The connection between internal and external perspectives is also noted by Gringer: "[S]ince business strategic planning is essentially a matter of searching for opportunities, evaluating them, and selecting a set as a basis for action, surveillance of the environment plays an important part in the entire process."[41] The connection is made even more explicitly by Marks, who also emphasizes the role that planning can play:

> [T]he achievement of a good fit—of congruence—between the external challenges and opportunities and the internal organization of the firm is one of the crucial factors in long-term survival. . . . Planning in its broadest sense can make an important contribution to this adaptive process.[42]

Crises, routine, and simple narrow thinking

have a way of taking over in organizations. Most organizations are desperately in need of an integrated, strategic view: what are we here for? what have we got to work with? how can we use it to best advantage? Planning is one means, and sometimes the only means, for achieving a broad perspective and harnessing the energies of an organization.

SUMMARY

The organizational level of analysis is important to criminal justice and planning, as contrasted with the systems level explored in Chapter 5. Despite the interdependencies that give rise to system considerations, criminal justice agencies are organizations in their own right, with their own characteristics and their own interests to pursue.

Among the important characteristics of any organization are goals, structure, technology, decision-making, control processes, and environment. These organizational variables were used to make some generalizations about types of criminal justice agencies. Although there are substantial diversities to be found within such categories as "police departments" or "courts," some of the fundamental features of each type of agency, and some of the basic types of distinctions between different types, have been highlighted.

This foundation and vocabulary are essential to a discussion of planning in organizations. The organizational setting immediately establishes two crucial foci, an internal one oriented toward efficient use of resources and productive activities, and an external one intended to facilitate adaptation to environmental constraints and contingencies.[43] In each case the role of planning is to anticipate problems and opportunities, to widen and clarify choices, and generally to provide information in advance of decision-making. Organizational planning presents the opportunity to integrate the internal and external orientations, to integrate resource and activity considerations, and to coordinate the many decisions being made at different times and places within any organization. The dynamics of most organizations foster fragmentation, suboptimization, and goal displacement; planning provides one way of countering these pressures and keeping the operation on track.

• *Chapter 6* •
NOTES

1. Charles Perrow, *Complex Organizations: A Critical Essay*, 2nd ed. (Glenview, Ill.: Scott, Foresman, and Company, 1979), pp. 90–138.

2. Robert K. Merton, "The Unanticipated Consequences of Purposive Social Action," *American Sociological Review*, 1 (1936), 894–904.

3. James Q. Wilson, "Dilemmas of Police Administration," *Public Administration Review* (September/October 1968), 407–17.

4. Herbert Packer, *The Limits of the Criminal Sanction* (Stanford, Calif.: Stanford University Press, 1968).

5. Richard H. Hall, *Organizations: Structure and Process*, 2nd ed. (Englewood Cliffs, N.J.: Prentice-Hall, Inc., 1977), pp. 130–51.

6. *The National Manpower Survey of the Criminal Justice System: Volume II* (Washington, D.C.: U.S. Government Printing Office, 1978), p. 5. The President's Crime Commission in 1967 estimated 40,000 police departments in the United States, a figure that was accepted and widely cited for a decade. It has recently been determined, however, that a serious error was made in the computation of the 40,000 figure, and recent estimates of the number of police departments in the United States have varied between 17,000 and 25,000.

7. Ibid. Also see National Sheriff's Association, *County Law Enforcement: An Assessment of Capabilities and Needs* (Washington, D.C.: National Sheriff's Association, 1978).

8. See John K. Hudzik, et al., *Criminal Justice Manpower Planning: An Overview* (Washington, D.C.: U.S. Law Enforcement Assistance Administration, 1981), p. 101, n. 33.

9. This condition has achieved the status of conventional wisdom, suggesting that it probably needs to be carefully re-examined. The basic argument is presented in James Q. Wilson, *Varieties of Police Behavior: The Management of Law and Order in Eight Communities* (Cambridge, Ma.: Harvard University Press, 1968).

10. Lawrence B. Mohr, "Organizations, Decisions, and Courts," *Law & Society* (Summer 1976), 621-42.
11. For a general discussion of court organization and structure, see Herbert Jacob, *Justice In America: Courts, Lawyers, and the Judicial Process*, 3rd ed. (Boston, Ma.: Little, Brown and Company, 1978), pp. 149-67.
12. Perrow, op. cit., pp. 139-73.
13. Charles Perrow, "A Framework for the Comparative Analysis of Organizations," *American Sociological Review*, 32 (April 1967), 194-208.
14. Wilson, "Dilemmas of Police Administration," op. cit.
15. Peter W. Greenwood and Joan Petersilia, *The Criminal Investigation Process, Volume I: Summary and Policy Implications* (Santa Monica, Calif.: Rand Corporation, 1975).
16. Arthur Rosett and Donald R. Cressey, *Justice By Consent: Plea Bargains in the American Courthouse* (New York: J. B. Lippincott Company, 1976).
17. David Sudnow, "Normal Crimes: Sociological Features of the Penal Code in a Public Defender Office," *Social Problems*, 12 (1964), 255-76.
18. Donald R. Cressey, "Prison Organizations," in James G. March, ed., *Handbook of Organizations* (Chicago: Rand McNally & Company, 1965).
19. Ibid.
20. See Richard McCleary, *Dangerous Men: The Sociology of Parole* (Beverly Hills, Calif.: Sage Publications, 1978).
21. Herbert A. Simon, *Administrative Behavior*, 3rd ed. (New York: The Free Press, 1976).
22. Ibid. pp. 172-97.
23. Perrow, *Complex Organizations*, op. cit.
24. The best illustrations of this can be found in the novels of Joseph Wambaugh, such as *The Choirboys* (New York: Dell Publishing Co., 1975).
25. Rosett and Cressey, op. cit.; James Eisenstein and Herbert Jacob, *Felony Justice: An Organizational Analysis of Criminal Courts* (Boston: Little, Brown and Company, 1977).
26. See Gresham M. Sykes, *The Society of Captives* (Princeton, N.J.: Princeton University Press, 1958).
27. McCleary, op. cit.
28. Perrow, *Complex Organizations*, op. cit.
29. Hudzik, et al., op. cit., pp. 180-208.
30. See James B. Jacobs, *Stateville: The Penitentiary in Mass Society* (Chicago: University of Chicago Press, 1977).
31. Perrow, *Complex Organizations*, op. cit.
32. George L. Kelling, et al., *The Kansas City Preventive Patrol Experiment: A Summary Report* (Washington, D.C.: Police Foundation, 1974). See also Kevin Krajick, "Does Patrol Prevent Crime?" *Police Magazine* (September 1978), 4-16.
33. Theodore Caplow, *How to Run Any Organization* (New York: Holt, Rinehart and Winston, 1976), pp. 185-99.
34. Ibid., p. 189.
35. See Gresham M. Sykes, *The Future of Crime* (Washington, D.C.: National Institute of Mental Health, U.S. Government Printing Office, 1980).
36. Caplow, op. cit., p. 191.
37. Sykes, *The Future of Crime*, op. cit., p. 69.
38. This was one of the themes of Alvin Toffler, *Future Shock* (New York: Random House, Inc., 1970).
39. Caplow, op. cit., p. 202.
40. Peter Lorange and Richard F. Vancil, "How to Design a Strategic Planning System," *Harvard Business Review* (September/October 1976), 78.
41. Peter H. Gringer, "The Anatomy of Business Strategic Planning Reconsidered," *The Journal of Management Studies* (May 1971), 208.
42. Maurice Marks, "Organizational Adjustments to Uncertainty," *The Journal of Management Studies* (January 1977), 1.
43. James D. Thompson, *Organizations in Action* (New York: McGraw-Hill Book Company, 1967).

• Chapter 7 •

ORGANIZING AND STAFFING CRIMINAL JUSTICE PLANNING

Planning is labor intensive and, thus, vitally dependent on human resources. Although a competent staff of sufficient size, properly organized and commissioned, will not guarantee high-quality planning, it is difficult to imagine competent planning without such a staff. This chapter discusses some pertinent issues in designing and staffing a planning operation, the relationships among various staffing alternatives and the factors that influence the location and function of planning and the ways in which various staffing and organizing patterns provide different kinds of information to decision-makers when they need it. It is organized into three major sections: the first focuses on planning in the individual operating criminal justice agency; the second addresses some special issues in the organization of system-level planning agencies; the third takes up several issues related to planning staff, both in the individual operating agency and in system-level planning agencies.

THE OPERATING AGENCY: PLANNING STAFF AND ORGANIZATION

Given the great diversity in size and function of criminal justice agencies, no single organizing and staffing arrangement for planning can be recommended. The number of planners and their placement in the organization depends on numerous factors, five of which seem particularly important:

1. Size and type of organization
2. Managerial style of top management
3. Money available for planning
4. Amount and kind of support services available
5. Functions and responsibilities assigned to planners

Each of these factors influences planning throughout the criminal justice system and among component operating agencies. Although these factors will be discussed in relation to the operating agency, there is little question that they influence the course and organization of system-planning agencies as well (e.g., state criminal justice planning agencies and regional and local criminal justice planning units and councils).

Size and Type of Organization

The size of an agency affects the extent to which the planning function is given formal and specialized recognition. Certainly, it would be ridiculous for the one-man police department to employ a full-time planner. There is no clear rule specifying that when organizations reach a certain size, planners should be hired and planning units should be organized. However, the 1973 Task Force on Police of the National Advisory Commission on Criminal Justice Standards and Goals suggested that every police agency with seventy-five or more employees should establish a planning unit staffed by at least one person whose full-time responsibility would be the administration and coordination of planning.[1] The Task Force further suggested that the size and composition of the planning unit should be "proportionate to the size of the agency and the magnitude of the present and anticipated planning task,"[2] The Task Force later noted that "many agencies will realize this need while far below a personnel strength of seventy-five; and many agencies with under fifty personnel now have such a planning unit."[3] A 1980 LEAA publication noted that the Task Force recommendation could be interpreted to mean that agencies with annual budgets in excess of $1 million should employ full-time planners.[4] Examples of such agencies included police departments with sixty officers, and prosecutors' offices with forty to seventy full-time attorneys.

The larger the agency, the clearer the necessity for some kind of planning unit. In large agencies, the question tends not to be whether a planning unit is required but how large the planning unit should be and whether specialized "branches" of the planning unit should be located in various operational units of the agency. For example, large state departments of corrections may choose to have a central executive-planning unit, as well as planning units at each major prison. A large police department may have specialized planning units for the patrol division and for the investigation division; very large city police departments may set up separate planning units for each command district.

Thus, agency size will influence not only the number of planners, but also the organizational configuration of planning. Although agency size, number of planners and configuration of planning do not correlate perfectly, certain patterns can be expected. The four categories of agencies discussed next are divided according to size and are based on a similar division presented by Douglas Gourley.[5]

1. The Moderately Small Agency: 25–100 Employees. In moderately small agencies there is usually no separate planning unit; rather, the planning function is located within an administrative-services division responsible for budget preparation, inspections, records maintenance, public information, and the like. The staff of such a division tends to share responsibilities for each of the assigned functions, including planning. It is unusual to find a professional planner among the personnel (usually between one and five, not counting clerical personnel) assigned to administrative services.

2. The Medium-Size Agency: 100–400 Employees. Separately structured planning units, or research and planning divisions are usually found in medium-size agencies. The head of the planning division usually reports to the agency head, and one or two members of the unit may have had formal training or education in research and planning. Other members of the staff have usually been assigned to the planning unit, perhaps on a rotating basis, from various parts of the organization. The size of the unit (usually four to ten people, not including clerical employees) depends on the functions assigned it. For example, in addition to general planning responsibilities, the unit may be charged with planning budgets, collecting data about agency workloads and performance, and producing year-end reports.

3. The Large Agency: 400–1000 Employees. The pattern of the medium-size agency is found in large agencies. But in agencies that approach the 1000 mark, the head of the planning unit may report to a deputy agency head. And some of the more laborious functions (such as basic agency data collection) may be assigned to a separate unit, leaving the planning staff more time to engage in such matters as strategic planning and basic research and development. Moreover, the unit tends to have two or more professionally trained planners or researchers. Finally, divisions of the planning unit may be created to deal with specific parts or functions of the agency. There may thus evolve a central planning division that reports directly to the agency head or deputy head, and separately functioning special planning units located in the major operating divisions[6] of the agency, reporting to both the central planning division and to the respective operations heads.[7]

4. The Very Large Agency: Over 1000 Employees. Very large agencies tend to have specialized planning units, more professionally trained planners, and a larger planning staff. In some of the largest agencies, professional staff assigned full-time planning duties may exceed twenty, and structures specializing in certain aspects of the planning process itself may evolve (see Figure 7-1).

The development of specialized planning units within the formal organizational structure does not obviate the need for planning in all levels and areas of the agency. This point is made explicit by Wilson and McLaren:

> The student of police administration should understand that the planning function is part of the larger process of administration. The

activity is found throughout the organization. The idea of a staff planning unit carrying out all planning in the department is no more sensible than suggesting the creation of a "direction" division for carrying out all activity related to direction.[8]

Wilson and McLaren's point is applicable to large and to small agencies and to agencies other than the police–indeed, to any organizational entity.

Administrative Style of Top Management

The nature and function of a planning apparatus depends on the administrative style of top management. Ronald Lynch has identified four classes of managerial style: purposeful, traditional, entrepreneurial, and crisis-oriented (see Chapter 1); each greatly affects the structure and function of planning.[9]

For example, the crisis-oriented manager might be expected to view planning as of use only in dealing with emergencies. The traditional manager would tend to accept the value of planning for both the long run and the short run, but primarily for purposes of maintaining stability and perhaps preserving the status quo. The purposeful manager is the one most likely to develop a planning unit capable of undertaking long-range, short-range, and emergency planning both in order to maintain stability and to assure adaptability.

Purposeful and traditional managers, more than crisis-oriented or entrepreneurial managers, tend to create climates that stress the importance of long-range planning. This in turn encourages the institutionalization of data collection and on-going analysis, and leads to the establishment of formalized planning and research units staffed with professionally trained personnel.

Crisis-oriented and entrepreneurial managers tend to discount, or perhaps to ignore, the relevance of formalized long-range planning and the value of on-going data collection. Their planning operations tend to be less stable and to rely on "bright people" or those skilled in organizational surveillance rather than on profesionally trained planners. The planning unit tends to be spread thinly across many organizational areas, shifting from one organizational problem to another and not concerned with planning in any comprehensive sense.

Alternative Structures Dependent on Managerial Style and Agency Size

There are several alternatives for structuring the planning enterprise, including the use of planning committees, executive management committees, planning task forces, and formally structured planning units or divisions. Which of these is used, or which combination of options is used, depends on management style and agency size. In very large organizations it is not uncommon to find all these options used in one way or another, or at different times. Figure 7-1 depicts one such complex arrangement.

The planning and research division specializes in organizing and collecting data and in con-

Figure 7-1. A Multidimensional Agency-Planning Structure

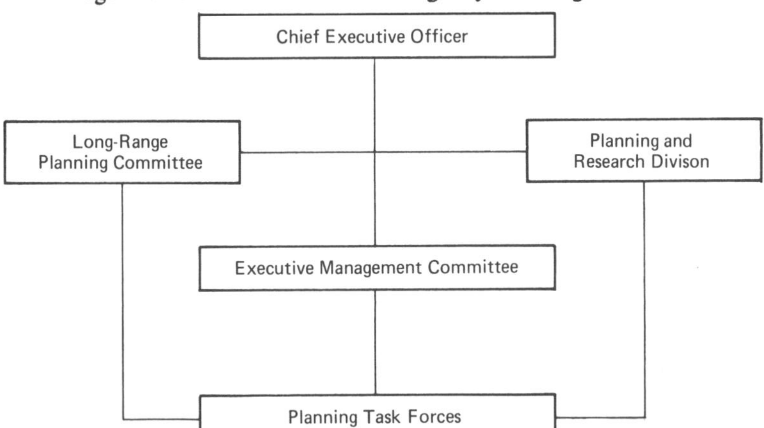

ducting analyses of such data to support both long- and short-range planning. These functions provide analytical support for the planning functions of the other units. To perform this specialized function, the division tends to be staffed with people skilled in computer programming, statistical analysis, operational gaming and simulation, and other specialized research procedures, who become the skilled technicians of the planning apparatus and are not normally expected to be the only, or even the primary, source of alternative policy directions for the agency. The other planning units of Figure 7-1 may tend to specialize in providing such directions, although the technical features of testing alternatives (see Chapter 10) would be a responsibility of the planning division.

The long-range planning committee may be compared to a "think tank." Its specific purpose is to consider the future of the agency. Its primary function is to forecast and to set (or at least to discuss) goals (see Chapters 8 and 9). The committee tends to be stable, its members drawn mainly from top agency management and top agency thinkers (the two are not necessarily synonymous). It is not uncommon, however, to find outsiders—community leaders, business executives, and academics, for example—in the long-range planning committee. The long-range planning committee is often a prime force in commissioning special studies or special data summaries relating to the long-term development of the agency. The planning division may provide the data and analysis essential to the "thinking" of the long-range planning committee.

The planning task force can be used for a variety of purposes and can take many forms. A task force may focus on either broad or narrow issues, although a task force is usually commissioned for a specified period to deal with a specific problem.[10] For example, a task force may be formed in a particular jail or prison to oversee the development of a new manual of policies and procedures.[11] Or a task force may be established in an agency to analyze alternatives and to propose new policy about a particular problem (e.g., to devise an appropriate agency response to increased narcotics traffic).

The objective in forming a task force is to bring together the best combination of experts to deal with a specific problem within a specific time.[12] The best combination may include personnel from several divisions and several ranks or levels in the agency. It may also team agency personnel with outsiders. For example, a few years ago a task force was formed to develop policy for a large metropolitan jail. The task force included personnel from every major jail division and from all ranks, and two academics with research-oriented expertise not then found within the agency. The task force functioned for about six months and went out of existence after issuing a report and recommendations to the sheriff.[13]

It is also not unusual to find two or more task forces operating within an agency at one time. When overall reviews of the agency and its functions are taking place (as when goals are being examined or alternative programs are being generated), management may elect to divide the tasks among several specialized task forces. Under such circumstances, a planning division might collect and analyze data in support of the activities of the task forces. For purposes of coordination, the various task forces may report directly to the agency head, to the executive management committee, or to the long-range planning committee. One such recent overall review, undertaken by the Michigan Office of Criminal Justice (the state planning agency), included the creation of several task forces, each responsible for analyzing priorities and goals in a given policy area (i.e., systemwide training and education, police-role definition, systemwide data management, corrections policy).[14]

The executive management committee has numerous responsibilities—among them, coordination of the units of the agency. The executive management committee is primarily concerned with the coordinated implementation of plans generated by the planning divisions, the long-range planning committee, and the task forces.

The complex arrangement shown in Figure 7-1 is not likely to be found in many criminal justice agencies today. Several examples of the use of task forces are available, and the development of a planning and research division increasingly characterizes the nature of agency organization. Long-range planning committees tend to be found in the larger agencies, but in smaller and medium-size agencies, long-range planning tends to be undertaken—if at all—by top management, perhaps within the confines of an executive management committee.

The planning task force is probably the most

adaptable to any of the four managerial orientations. Managers, regardless of orientation, tend to find varying uses and purposes for planning task forces. Certain political advantages can also accrue from using a task force: the public tends to notice the appointment of a special task force, and the appointment and the charge given the task force draw attention to management's concern about a problem and imply that something is being done about the problem. The normal operations of a research and planing division are usually less noticeable.

Resources Assigned to the Planning Function

The size and structure of an agency's planning operation depend on the resources made available to it. But it is often difficult, and sometimes impossible, to determine the resources an agency actually devotes to its planning operation. There are, of course, the dollars directly allocated to a planning and research division or to a task force. Except for such relatively identifiable expenditures, however, the calculation of resources applied to agency planning functions is quite difficult. For example, the informal use of agency personnel at various levels to assemble information, to provide insight into a particular problem, or to act as sounding boards for ideas coming from the planning division or a task force, represents an allocation of resources to the planning effort, but such allocations are not usually formally recorded.

Moreover, many planning-related activities are deliberately assigned to other units of the agency. Some of the basic data collection required in agency planning may be undertaken by a records unit or by a personnel unit or division. Such data serve various purposes, as in compiling reports for audits and outside reviews. This suggests that the size and structure of the planning operation are not defined by the resources formally devoted to planning units but may include other agency-funded activities that are not formally recorded as expenditures for planning.

The Availability of Support Services

Support services provided by other units of an agency, and the availability of these services for planning purposes, influence the size and structure of the planning operation. For example, a multifunction agency computer, workload data collected by operational units, or personnel data collected by the personnel division can provide important inputs to the planning operation and greatly influence not only the size of the planning operation, but the scope of planning as well.

An analogous situation would be the establishment of a new college of medicine at a university. The size of the new medical college, the breadth and depth of its teaching and research, will be vitally dependent on whether certain other academic units already exist at the university. If the university has departments of physiology, anatomy, and biochemistry, for example, the new college can be structured to take advantage of these existing units. If they do not exist, the new medical college will require more resources and entail higher formal costs.

Comparable factors influence the size and structure of planning units in agencies.[15] Figure 7-2 depicts a hypothetical set of relationships between the formal planning operation and other units in the agency that might offer support to planning.

There are complex reciprocal relationships among support services, management orientation, the nature and scope of planning structures, and agency size. Managerial style influences the importance and support given to collection and analysis of data, and the objectives ascribed to planning. Similarly, planning activities themselves may generate additional interest in and support for information, thereby raising the level of support for activities of other staff-support units. These factors thus feed on one another, producing effects throughout the agency.

Functions and Responsibilities Assigned to Planning

Finally, the purposes, functions, and responsibilities assigned to the planning apparatus influence its size and staffing. There have been numerous attempts to catalog the potential functions assigned to a planning unit. According to Burt Nanus, these functions are to

1. Provide staff services to the top management of the agency in the development of strategies for achieving the agency's objectives. . . .
2. Conduct special planning studies to assist

Figure 7-2. The Formal Planning Apparatus and Other Agency Units

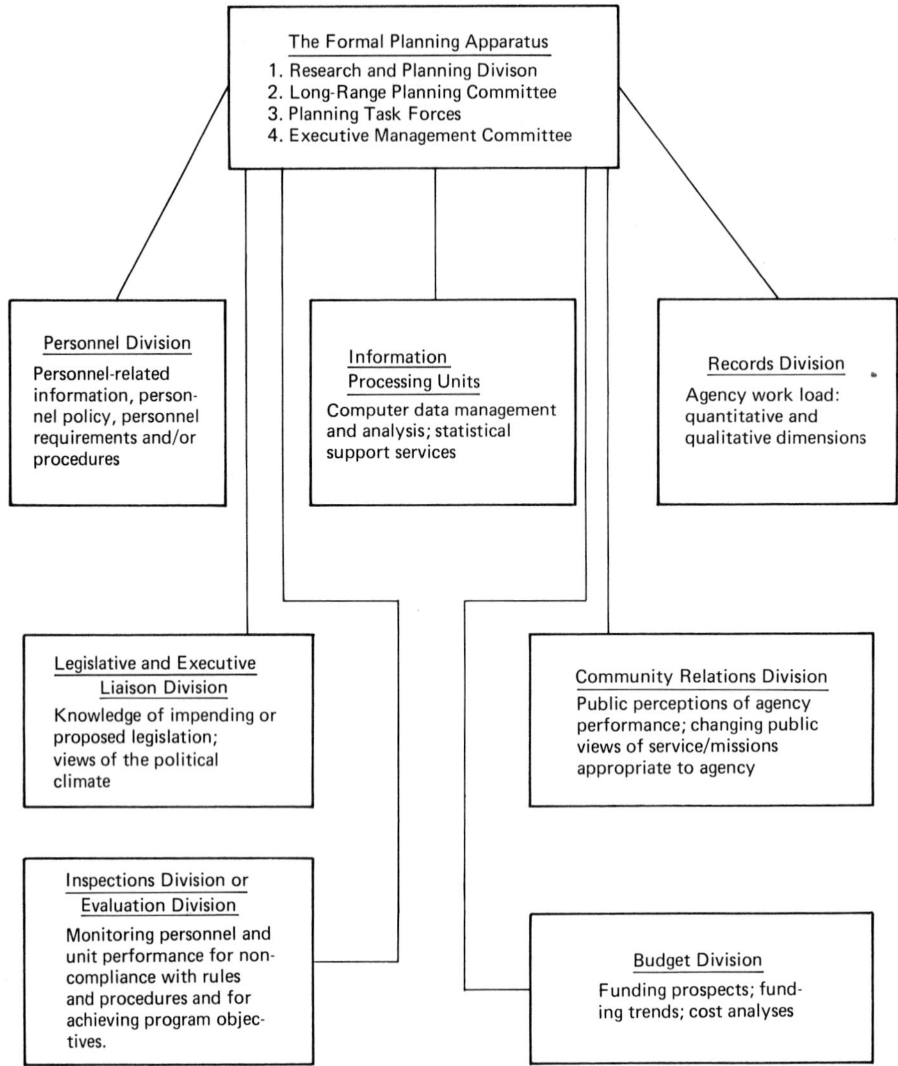

top and middle management of the agency[,] . . . continuously survey evolving trends in major environmental forces[,] . . . analyze local crime trends[,] . . . forecast the future of the agency[,] . . . conduct special studies of new methods, techniques, and procedures[,] . . . analyze and develop new approaches[,] . . . investigate new organizational alternatives. . . .

3. Assist the divisions and bureaus in the agency in the effective development of formal long-term planning for their own functions[,] . . . provide analytical problem-solving skills[,] . . . coordinate the plans of the divisions into an overall agency plan. . . .

4. Coordinate the planning efforts of the agency with those of interfacing agencies at the Federal, state, and local level.[16]

The categories implied in this general statement of the potential responsibilities of a planning unit relate to the basic steps in the planning process as discussed in Chapters 1, 2 and 3.[17] A more concrete description of the potential duties and responsibilities associated with planning is presented in Figure 7-3, which points out relatively specific chores that might be assigned to the planning staff. Of course, the existence of specialized units might mean

Figure 7-3. Potential Duties of the Planning Staff

1. *Departmental Budgets*: To analyze fiscal needs with regard to workloads and goals and objectives; to prepare required budget forms, to prepare supporting documentation in support of budget requests.
2. *Grants*: To write grant applications; to supervise or to monitor activities under the grant for compliance; to seek additional sources of grant funding.
3. *Service Sector Indicators:* To analyze (and possibly collect) data that relate to agency workloads (e.g., crime rates, offender characteristics); to determine changes in trends, or simply to note trends and their effect on the agency.
4. *Policy and Training Manuals*: To determine the need for policy, personnel, and training materials; to write policy and training manuals; to update manuals on a constant basis.
5. *Departmental Records and Forms*: To prepare and to update departmental records and forms of all types (personnel, complaint, workload, and so on); to monitor the use of these forms by departmental personnel, measuring quality control.
6. *Report Writing*: To act as a clearinghouse and report-writing center for special studies or reports required by top management, by outside bodies, or by units of the agency.
7. *Social and Community Indicators*: To determine the nature of community service needs and community expectations of the agency; to note trends and changes in expectations and needs arising from changes in the service population, in the economy, or in geographical distributions; to determine required changes in agency response.
8. *Program Evaluation*: To collect and to analyze data related to the achievement of agency goals and objectives; to monitor program efficiency and effectiveness; to assist in setting and defining program evaluation criteria and goals.

that they, rather than the planning staff, would undertake these chores. Yet it is not uncommon, even in large agencies where one would expect a proliferation of specialized units, to find many of these specific chores assigned to the planning unit or shared by the planning unit with other agency units. In a recent survey of the 250 largest police agencies in the nation, the fifty state departments of corrections, state juvenile authorities, and 125 of the largest local probation agencies, a high percentage of respondents reported that planning units are assigned or participate in many of these responsibilities. Table 7-1 summarizes findings from these surveys in relation to ten categories of duties.[18]

It should be remembered that Table 7-1 is based on returns from the largest criminal justice agencies in law enforcement and corrections. In smaller agencies, not surveyed in the study, a planning unit (where there is one) might be even more heavily involved in many of these specific chores. Nonetheless, whether in a small agency or a large one, the responsibilities of a planner may be wide indeed and, following Wildavsky's logic, if the planner is expected to be everything, no real planning may be found.

The principal role of planning—whether by a task force, a long-range planning committee, or a formal planning unit—is to provide information that is useful to management, and to provide ideas that will help in formulating the agenda of the agency. As Sharkansky has noted, that information and those ideas provide management with the materials necessary to shape environmental responses to the agency:

> Administrators send many of their "informational" outputs to other branches of government. Indeed, many of the inputs that come to administrators from the legislative and executive branches of government actually got their start as the outputs of the administration. . . . These outputs of the administration are so important in the deliberations of other branches

Table 7-1. Sample Duties of Planning Units: Percentages of Agency Respondents Indicating Planning Unit Is Assigned Various Duties

	Law-Enforcement Agencies		Corrections Agencies	
	State: N = 34	Local: N = 115	State: N = 46	Local: N = 9
Updating agency forms and policies	76	74	32	11
Aiding in development of agency budget requests	30	36	36	11
Preparing grant applications	68	77	56	56
Developing new agency programs	65	75	39	44
Evaluating agency programs	56	64	55	33
Anticipating future employment needs (e.g., numbers of personnel needed)	44	43	21	22
Collecting and analyzing agency workload data and analyzing agency operations	50	73	49	67
Collecting and analyzing agency personnel data	18	33	18	11
Responding to outside requests for information	59	69	49	33
Overseeing and/or analyzing training needs and programs	12	14	18	22

that–to some observers–they permit administrators to dominate other officials.[19]

Planning-derived information also provides the essential data for shaping the agency's agenda in responding and adapting to the environment. Thus, the role of planners is not simply to produce information and ideas that can serve to shape the environment; it includes the processing of information from that environment. It is probably this exchange between agency and environment, and planning's role in analyzing the exchange, that makes planning roles and functions so complex.

THE SYSTEM-LEVEL PLANNING AGENCY: SPECIAL ORGANIZATIONAL ISSUES

The essential feature of agencies engaged in system-level comprehensive planning (see Chapter 5) is that their activities are intended to affect and to coordinate aggregates of criminal justice agencies. Although in operating agencies planning is usually understood to be a "staff support function," in systems planning agencies planning is, by definition, the prime and central mission. These differences affect the organizational and staffing arrangements required to further system planning.

In the operating agency, planning focuses on providing information directly to agency decision-makers and only indirectly to others; at the system level the purpose is to provide information not only to decision-makers within numerous operating criminal justice agencies, but also directly to political and bureaucratic decision-makers whose interests and responsibilities span criminal justice organizational boundaries and, indeed, include much more than criminal justice.

Another difference concerns the scope of missions, goals, and objectives of the several criminal justice agencies that must be considered by system-level planning bodies. Coordination of diverse agencies and missions is the prime function of such bodies, but often coordination is only a minor consideration for operating agencies, whose prime focus is on the particular missions and objectives of the individual agency.

Despite these differences, many of the factors and issues that affect operating agencies apply to system-level planning agencies as well. Certainly managerial style within the system-level planning agency and that of the jurisdiction chief executive will greatly influence the form and scope of system planning.[20] The heads of affected criminal justice operating agencies will also do much to determine the latitude, responsibilities, support, and expectations of the state and local planning agency. Fiscal resources and the availability of support services for system planning will depend on these, and on whether planning in general is supported by the state or local unit of government. The various planning options (task forces, executive management committees, and long-range planning committees) all have their application and use in system-level planning agencies, and often the circumstances governing their use and their composition are comparable to those in the operating agency.

Thus, many of the prime factors that affect the organization and function of planning in individual operating agencies also have an impact on the structure and function of systems-planning bodies. But other factors and considerations are also important in influencing the organization and staffing of systems-planning agencies.

Jurisdiction Level and Administrative Placement

The need for systems planning occurs at various jurisdictional or governmental levels (individual cities, counties, combinations of cities and counties, regions, and the state as a whole). An important consideration has been whether systems planning at each of these levels has had a "top-down," "bottom-up," or independent orientation. For example, one effect of the 1968 Safe Streets Act and subsequent LEAA administrative arrangements was to control many state and local planning bodies through Federal money and programs, thus imposing a "top-down" orientation on some state and local criminal justice planning bodies. A resulting charge was that these bodies were located in the community, but not oriented toward community or state problems or to special issues or coordination at each of these levels.[21] With the termination of Federal funding, this has become a less salient issue and attention can now be focused instead on the options available in organizing and staffing state, regional, county, and city criminal justice planning efforts.

1. At the State Level. Administrative placement of a state planning agency has proven significant in determining not only the structure and function of the planning agency, but also its relative impact on the criminal justice system at both the state and local levels. In 1980 the National Governors' Association Committee on Criminal Justice and Public Protection signalled the importance of the governor in promoting system coordination by noting that, "no individual in state government is more suited to this role than the governor."[22] Indeed, the state planning agency's access to the governor and to his or her executive apparatus is critical,[23] and such access is often an issue of appropriate administrative placement. Equally important is the governor's interest in, and support for, criminal justice planning.

There are several administrative-placement options, each with slightly different implications for system planning at the state level. One option is placement within the executive structure of the governor's office, which provides direct access to the governor and the opportunity for direct policy and legislative advice to the chief executive's decision-making process. The attractiveness of this option depends, however, on the governor's interest in being directly involved with issues confronting the criminal justice system—an interest which has by no means been even among governors.

Another option is to house the planning agency within the budget bureau of state government, which acknowledges the importance and centrality of budget review to achieving effective coordination.[24] A third option is to create a state-level independent "board of regents" for criminal justice, with powers to propose and implement criminal justice policy on a statewide basis.[25] In this arrangement, the state planning agency becomes the principal planning arm of the independent agency.

A fourth option, related to the third, is to establish an "umbrella" state-level criminal justice administrative agency, with the state planning agency serving the criminal justice planning function. In New Mexico, for example, most executive department criminal justice functions have been brought under one such department.[26] Such a development is parallel to one presented by Skoler. In his view, concerns over mounting costs, proliferation of programs, and duplication have led to an increasing trend within the states to reorganize structurally.[27] The course of state-level reorganization, in Skoler's view, is toward the creation of superagencies, the combining of agencies with related service functions in "umbrella" cabinet- or secretariat-level units. Criminal justice is one such service-delivery area.

There are natural disadvantages when the state planning agency is not placed within, or does not report directly to, the governor's office. Placement within a "superagency" of justice or in a state budget office serves to isolate the planning agency from direct and influential contact with the chief executive. Placement within an operating state criminal justice agency may bias the planning agency toward one or more state agencies and the state level,[28] and divert attention from coordination with local criminal justice agencies. Indeed, the question of the relationship between state and local criminal justice has perplexed most state planning agencies, and is not resolved simply through administrative placement.

Although placing the state planning agency within the governor's executive apparatus may offer an opportunity for greater "impartiality" and "comprehensiveness" in dealing with the broad spectrum of policy and legislative coordination, it may nonetheless serve to isolate the planning agency from the real world of operating agencies. Unfortunately, these also are concerns that cannot be settled simply through administrative placement alone.

2. At the Local Level. There are various options for the administrative placement of the local criminal justice planning agency. One option is to attach the agency to the city or county executive's office or to the city or county general planning office. Another is to establish an "independent" city/county planning and coordinating council, or to establish a regional criminal justice planning unit. Several variations on such options exist, but these are the principal options.[29]

None of these options is ideal for all or even most situations, owing to the vagaries of local politics and the substantial differences in local governmental structure. For example, under a strong mayor or a strong county executive system, placement of the criminal justice planning agency within the executive's office may offer the agency an opportunity to influence policy and legislation. If, however, the chief executive is not interested in criminal justice planning or if the executive system is weak, such placement may yield comparatively few benefits.

Placement of the criminal justice planning agency or function in a county or city general-planning department may bring additional expertise and support to bear on criminal justice planning, but it may isolate criminal justice planning from operating criminal justice agencies, and criminal justice planning may itself get buried or lost in the wider-scope planning activities of the city or county general-planning unit.

A greater difficulty in the administrative placement of the local planning agency has to do with the fact that criminal justice agency jurisdictional boundaries often overlap or do not coincide with political jurisdictional boundaries. Additionally, criminal justice agencies in different political jurisdictions often share the clientele they serve. Thus, for example, a county-based criminal justice planning unit may not include city criminal justice agencies even though the need for coordination between city and county criminal justice agencies is imperative. One potential solution is to create multijurisdictional planning bodies in the form of regional planning units or city-county coordinating councils.

Although there are differences between regional planning units and coordinating councils in their creation and use, both are planning units jointly created and funded by several affected political jurisdictions to foster comprehensive planning and review of the activities of city and county criminal justice agencies as a whole. Some regional planning units are multicounty in scope, reflecting, for example, the need to coordinate activities throughout sprawling metropolitan areas or, alternatively, the inability of some small counties to fund all services by themselves.

Regional planning units and coordinating councils have the potential for resolving some of the difficulties arising from jurisdictional inconsistencies, yet they are usually voluntary creations of multiple and independent governmental jurisdictions. As such, they may have a tenuous existence. Indeed, the competing desires of independent political jurisdictions sometimes preclude any comprehensive planing. These problems have led many to conclude that the local criminal justice planning unit should parallel the jurisdictional boundaries of the local criminal justice system.[30] Unfortunately, this is not always possible.

An Ancillary Administrative Arrangement: The Planning Commission

The need for input from, and coordination among, diverse elements of the criminal justice system is central to systems planning. Because administrative placement of systems planning agencies does not sufficiently meet these needs, an additional administrative structure has emerged: the planning commission. Planning commissions, mandated by the 1968 Safe Streets legislation, encompassed the notion that state and local-level comprehensive planning efforts should be directed and advised by commissions that represented all relevant types of criminal justice agencies, the general public, and local and state political jurisdictions.

The idea was that if planning was to be comprehensive, a comprehensively representative supervisory board should be constituted to guide the activities and recommendations of the planning agency. These ideas have received important support from outside criminal justice. For example, the National League of Cities and the National Conference of Mayors endorsed a model, broadly representative, membership list for local planning commissions: the local chief executive, representatives of city councils and county boards, city and county police chiefs, the county sheriff, the district attorney, the public defender, the chief juvenile probation officer, representatives of the juvenile court, correctional facility officials, and administrators of "other public and private criminal justice-related agencies."[31]

At both the state[32] and local levels,[33] most commissions or supervisory boards are today broadly representative and include not only representatives of criminal justice agencies but pertinent representatives from the system's environment as well (e.g., the general public, budget analysts, legislators, and so on). Yet broad representation, although it widens the scope of perspective and information brought to the systems-planning effort, has not always brought consensus about coordination, duplication, or dysfunction. Though members of commissions may discuss pertinent issues and problems, they do not always agree on solutions. Several factors account for this, including interagency rivalries, disagreements over priorities, and jurisdictional disagreements and rivalries among affected governmental units. Moreover, not all such differences are resolvable through consensus achieved within representative planning commissions. An important factor in achieving coordination and controlling duplication has been the presence or lack of strong leadership from the jurisdiction's chief executive.

Leadership of the Jurisdiction Chief Executive

Numerous studies have concluded that the leadership exercised by the jurisdiction chief executive (governor, mayor, city or county manager) is crucial to comprehensive systems planning.[34] The tone set by the chief executive determines how seriously system planning is taken by participating criminal justice agencies and will do much to mediate interagency rivalries and disputes. And strong chief executive support for systems-level planning and coordination often encourages the expansion of agency-based planning within individual criminal justice agencies.[35]

There is evidence that increasing attention is being devoted by chief executives to the issue of coordination and system-level planning, and that their interest in raising the level of commitment to planning and coordination is also increasing.[36] One governor, for example, so testified before the Senate Judiciary Committee:

> Our system costs approximately $400 million annually. Planning costs three tenths of one per cent of the annual cost of our criminal justice system. Do you know of two successful businesses with an annual $400 million income, with the kinds of responsibilities of the criminal justice system, which only uses [sic] three

tenths of one per cent for planning and coordination?[37]

The Importance of Enabling Legislation

For both state and local criminal justice planning units, appropriate enabling legislation is important. Such legislation addresses such issues as the function and scope of planning, funding for planning, and the powers and authority of the planning agency and planning commission.[38] Legislative authorization increases recognition of the importance of systems planning; legislative establishment of clear powers and authority for planning agencies may help promote cooperation and discourage the divisiveness among component agencies that is so typical of informal and voluntary planning efforts. Also, some jurisdictions have attempted to establish an independent financial base for system-planning agencies through dedicated millage or line-item appropriations; when these attempts have been successful,[39] the local or state planning agency has been placed on a much firmer footing than that of the agency sustained through purely voluntary contributions from affected criminal justice agencies. Naturally, legislated powers and authority are not sufficient to establish credibility and influence, but appropriate enabling legislation is often crucial in providing a basis for subsequent efforts to build credibility and influence through action.

Association with the Budget Process

Resource allocation, as part of the overall budget-planning process, is most effective in promoting coordination and controlling duplication. State and local systems-planning efforts divorced from budget review and allocation processes may well resemble those of a toothless lion, and be no more effective than the thoughtful meanderings of a philosopher king. The responsibilities of planning agencies should not be restricted to reviewing budget proposals in order to balance resources or redress inequities; they should give form to, and improve the content of, the process by which agencies prepare their budgets. Widened and formal responsibility for the budget process is often a key to establishing appropriate linkage between systems planning and budgetary decision-making.

THE PLANNING STAFF

Ideally, the planning operation should be staffed with "Renaissance men"—individuals widely informed and broadly skilled and capable of dealing with all of Nanus's planning functions or with all the duties of planners listed in Figure 7-3. Then, the only problem would be to determine how many such individuals were necessary to undertake the planning effort. Unfortunately, such people are hard to find. As Ansoff points out:

> [T]he list [of planning responsibilities] suggests that it is no longer helpful to characterize "the planner" in the singular, that there is more planning work than an individual can handle, and, most important, that the range of work now requires a wide variety of skills rarely found in a single individual. The traditional systems designer-expediter is still needed, but so is the entrepreneurially minded new venture analyst, so is an analytic diagnostician-controller, so is a skilled forecaster-analyst, so is a computer-model builder.[40]

Not only are individuals with all these skills rare, but the task of planning is so complex that it requires the selection of individuals whose different skills complement one another. It may be that only the largest of criminal justice operating agencies have the luxury of hiring enough individuals with special skills to form a truly complete and complementary planning unit. On the other hand, the medium-size and smaller agencies, serving smaller populations, have less need for such complex planning structures. Regardless of size, however, the agency must seek a *balance* in skills and knowledge in staffing its planning operation.

These points apply as well to the staffing of the systems-planning agency—perhaps more so, because the scope of coordination required of planners at the systems level is wide and the range of substantive issues arising out of the various operating agencies is complex. In most state and local criminal justice planning agencies, this complexity has been recognized as requiring specialization among planning staff. In one pattern of specialization, planners divide responsibilities according to the major functional components of the system: police, courts, corrections and juvenile. The objective is to develop individualized expertise in dealing with issues arising out of the component operating agencies, and planners who have had previous work experience in one or more of the component agencies are considered more eligible for these assignments than planners who have not. The danger in this arrangement is that planners so specialized may lose sight of systemic issues, focusing primarily or exclusively on the component agencies within their purview or on their special area of knowledge.

Many state and local planning agencies have also recognized the need for specialized staff to deal with such tasks as the collection and management of data (including computer applications), budget analysis, operations analysis and management studies, evaluation-research skills, and legislative analysis. But it is difficult enough to find individuals with experience in one or more of the component operating agencies and with one or more of these analytical skills without insisting that they each possess all of the requisite experience and analytical skills. Thus, the goal of the operating agency and the system-planning agency should be to develop a planning *team* which, as a group, possesses the range of requisite skills.

The general idea of staffing balance has been addressed by Jack Rothman within the context of staffing an agency research unit; his comments, however, seem equally relevant to the issue of staffing an agency planning unit and to that of staffing the systems-level planning agency. In Rothman's view, the "unit should be made up of personnel with combined competence in research (design, statistical analysis, computer technology) and in application or operations (knowledge of planning process, of services, of social change, and of the functioning of the organization)."[41] A simplification of Rothman's view leads to the conclusion that two broadly defined sets of skills are required: analytical research-oriented skills, and practical experience and understanding of the missions and work of criminal justice. This kind of breakdown is also explicitly recognized by Souryal:

> Police planners must, therefore, be selected from among the most competent, educated, and trained personnel. A combination of a background in behavioral sciences with adequate training in quantitative research and ample police experience seems exemplary.[42]

Requisite Analytical Skills

Within the broad category of analytical skills, specific capabilities can be identified as potentially relevant to the planning operation. Knowledge of statistical and research methods, of problem-identification methodologies, of methods of generating and weighing alternative solutions, and of forecasting seems relevant. So too, it seems essential that a planner understand the legal and professional standards for conducting planning research, that he or she be able to synthesize findings so that proper conclusions can be drawn from them, and that he or she have the skill to communicate those conclusions. A good planner ought to know how to identify needed data, how to collect them, how to analyze them, how to draw conclusions from them, and how to communicate those conclusions orally and in writing.[43]

Opinions differ about the level of these skills the planners in operating agencies need possess. The size and complexity of the agency and its missions, the orientations of top management toward planning, and the level of sophistication of analytically based information demanded of the planning operation will all influence these opinions.

In systems-planning agencies, the interest of state or local government, and especially that of the jurisdiction chief executive, in analytically based planning greatly influences the need for planners with appropriate analytical skills. Unless the jurisdiction is truly interested in "objectively" measuring and considering its criminal justice system, and unless changes suggested by analytically based planning can be implemented,[44] the analytical skills of planning staff may well be superfluous. If the interest and the potential for implementation exist, hiring planners with these skills may be useful and rewarding to the jurisdiction. Such differences are often reflected in job descriptions for planning positions. In the 1974 publication of the American Society of Planning Officials, "Job Descriptions for Planning Agencies," the sample job descriptions for a variety of positions in city planning agencies indicate wide variance of opinion.[45] Some of these job descriptions reflect detailed and specific expectations of applicants, such as thorough knowledge of pertinent laws and regulations, or detailed knowledge of field-survey techniques; others reflect far less specific expectations.

In a study conducted by Anderson and Ball, forty-four acknowledged experts in the field of educational evaluation responded to a request to rate the importance of a lengthy list of skills thought to be relevant to the conduct of evaluation research.[46] Although it may be argued that the analytical and research skills required to conduct evaluations do not precisely parallel those required to conduct planning, many of the categories of knowledge and skills singled out by Anderson and Ball are similar to those often associated with planning. There is, of course, a fundamental relationship between evaluation and planning: the former provides information for the latter. The findings of Anderson and Ball, although their study focused on evaluation skills rather than directly on planning skills, suggest that numerous specialized understandings and capabilities are widely held to be important. Table 7-2 summarizes findings on sixteen of thirty-two skill and knowledge areas listed by Anderson and Ball.[47]

Table 7-2 also shows that there is a difference of opinion about what kinds of knowledge and

Table 7-2. Importance of Content Areas and Skills (Rated by Number of Persons Responding to Each: $N = 44$)

	Importance			
Content Area	Essential	Desirable	Not Very Important	No Response
Statistical analysis	35	9	0	0
Data preparation and reduction	33	11	0	0
Method of controlling quality of data collection and analysis	32	10	1	1
Alternative models for program evaluation	31	9	4	0
Techniques of setting goals and performance standards	23	16	4	1
Reactive concerns in measurement and evaluation	21	16	3	4
Field operations [field research]	21	15	1	7
Cost benefits analysis	19	20	4	1
Contracts and proposals	17	20	5	2
Legal and professional standards for empirical studies	15	24	4	1
Professional and ethical sensitivity	37	4	1	2
Expository skills (speaking and writing)	32	10	0	2
Sensitivity to concerns of all interested parties	31	5	0	8
Interpersonal skills	28	12	3	1
Public-relations skills	17	20	6	1
Management skills	14	26	3	1

Source: Scarvia B. Anderson and Samuel Ball, *The Profession and Practice of Program Evaluation* (San Francisco: Jossey-Bass, 1978), pp. 172–173. The sixteen content areas presented here were culled from a larger table with 32 content areas presented by the authors. Used with permission.

skills are "essential" and what kinds are merely "desirable." It is possible that not all the "essential" skills would need to be possessed by agency planning staff–they could be provided, when needed, by consultants. But members of a planning staff ought to be at least informed enough to act as intelligent and critical "consumers" of the activities or recommendations of consultants or experts. The general understandings gained through undergraduate courses in research and statistics may provide the basis for intelligent "consumerism." And an agency that had frequent need for certain specific knowledge and skills might switch from using consultants to hiring its own planners.

Requisite Agency Experience

Analytical and research skills are one thing, substantive knowledge about an agency and its mission is quite another. Indeed, the planner in the operating agency who does not understand the work of the agency and its particular problems and procedures risks basing his or her planning on mistaken premises. The same may be said of systems planners who understand little of the work and interrelationships of the system and its components.

Some argue that knowledge of the agency and its problems can be gained only by working one's way up through the organization, that criminal justice systems planners should have broad line and staff experience.[48] Others argue that lack of experience can be offset by heightened sensitivity to "learning" about the agency and the system and its problems.[49] And, of course, some individuals with on-the-job experience may never have really come to understand what the job has been about or may have been socialized through line-job experience in such a way that they never learned or soon forgot the underlying reasons for standard operating procedures.

There seems to be little doubt that planners in police agencies would profit from the experience of "working on the street," and that planners in correctional agencies would profit from work experience in inmate custody and services or in supervising parolees or probationers. Ideally, all systems-level planners should have relevant work experience; in practice, at least *some* of those assigned to the planning task should have such experience.

The relatively rare combination of analytical skill and experiential knowledge is particularly desirable in the director of an operating planning and research division or in the head of a state or local planning agency. As Rothman noted, the head of the operating agency division would ideally, be skilled in analytical techniques and have work experience in the business of the agency.[50] In practice, a difficult choice must often be made between a candidate with analytical skills and one with an intimate knowledge of the agency who can deal with the agency and its personnel. Of course, a director who is analytically skilled but inexperienced in the business of the agency may nonetheless have the requisite ability to put management and line personnel at ease–thus coming to be viewed as a nonthreatening "egghead." But being perceived as an "egghead"–threatening or not–carries negative consequences, not the least of which is that the planning unit may be viewed by other agency personnel as a pie-in-the-sky operation, irrelevant to the day-to-day work of the agency. Thus, the balance between analytical skills and experience affects not only the quality of planning, but also its acceptance and implementation within the agency.

Similar considerations arise in the selection of the head of a system-level state or local planning unit. It may, however, be especially important that those who head state and local planning agencies be familiar with the system and its components, be perceived as familiar, practical, and nonthreatening eggheads. The ability of the head of a planning agency to achieve compromise and coordination through negotiation with semi-independent component agencies will be vitally dependent on these qualities.

Attempts to resolve such difficulties include selecting individuals, or a group of individuals, who not only understand the principles of planning and the techniques of research but who also are sensitive to the organization or system environment in which planning takes place. Another possible solution lies in training planners to appreciate these things. Finally, as noted by Wilson and McLaren, the "planning process really involves a state of mind rather than an adherence to a rigid set of principles to guide the activity."[51] This may suggest that individuals should be selected who, although technically skilled in planning, do not plan simply to plan but, rather, who also see the instrumental value of planning in addressing practical agency and system concerns.[52]

Work experience alone in an agency is probably not a good primary measure of relevant knowledge and understanding of the system or any of its components. More relevant is the individual's level of performance (evaluated by some set of valid measures) in certain line functions or jobs. Experience in agency line-supervisory or managerial positions can provide the necessary broadly based substantive knowledge about the agency. In systems-level planning agencies, individuals with appropriate kinds of agency-based experience may be selected to fill the specialized planning positions for police, corrections, and juvenile programs.

Staffing the planning agency with individuals who have analytical expertise, agency experience, and an appropriate mind set is difficult but not impossible. In police agencies, this difficulty may be resolved by selecting individuals from the ranks who also have a relevant college education. Their numbers can be supplemented by civilians specially trained and educated in research and analytical techniques. In corrections, similar combinations can be made, with particular attention devoted to making sure that both custodial and treatment/rehabilitation work experiences are represented.

Selecting the Planning Staff

The process of selecting planners normally focuses on several criteria: certain types of educational backgrounds and experience as well as certain personal characteristics. Formal training and education seem clearly essential to an initial understanding and appreciation of most of the analytical techniques associated with planning. Formal undergraduate or graduate training in criminal justice provides an introduction to the field. Thus, one criterion but not necessarily a limiting one, is that planners be sought from among those with college degrees. Candidates with degrees in behavorial sciences or criminal justice offer particular promise. Courses in planning, research, and statistics, and field practica in planning and evaluation research can be particularly pertinent.

An appropriate mix of organizational and system "insiders" and "outsiders" must be achieved when forming *and* maintaining the apparatus—whether for operating-agency planning units or for systems-level planning agencies. The experienced view of insiders may be devoid of fresh approaches or new ideas; the truly fresh ideas of outsiders may need to be tempered by organizational realities. Therefore, selection of the planning staff and maintenance of the planning apparatus should be designed to balance the infusion of the new ideas provided by outsiders with the continuity provided by the experience of insiders.

Teaming Line and Staff Personnel. Selecting a number of insiders who have had work experience in the agency or system does not guarantee the long-term relevance of what the planning agency does. Indeed, such experience is usually only partly conducive to an understanding of current conditions and realities. There is the risk of what Daniel Katz calls "positional lag": the longer the planner is isolated from the "real" work of an agency or the system, the less "experienced" he or she becomes in the present nature of work.[53] One solution in the operating agency is to fill some positions in the planning unit with individuals rotated from line positions for deliberately short terms. In system-planning agencies some individuals might be rotated from component operating agencies. This allows, in theory, for a constant influx of *current* work-related experience and understanding. Other solutions, used separately or in conjunction with rotation, include establishing task forces that team operational personnel with planning staff, creating planning liaison groups in operational units, and holding regular planning seminars for operations units.[54] Each of these solutions regularizes interchange between the planning apparatus and field operations.[55]

All these measures seek to facilitate the flow and interchange of information between those whose jobs *are* operations-oriented and those whose jobs *are* planning-oriented. The numerous advantages that presumably accrue include the widening of the spectrum of information brought into the planning, the blending of idealism and realism, and the easing of the plans' implementation. Actually, all these advantages are interrelated and are primarily a matter of melding ideas produced through the planning exercise with realities imposed by the system, its component agencies, and the environment.

Planners naturally tend to think of agency problems at one or another level of abstraction, while operational personnel more often think of problems more concretely. The two orientations are potentially complementary especially if there exists a structure for interaction—if, for example, planners and operational personnel are teamed in task forces or working groups. The consequences of insufficient contact between planners and operational personnel have been addressed by Brown:

> Practitioners [will not be] knowledgeable about research. . . Researchers [will] tend to do research of little interest for practitioners and practitioners continue to run programs with disproved or unproved methods. Linkage, however, between these two has been shown to improve relevancy of research and produce programs incorporating methods of proven merit. . .[56]

Aside from making planning relevant and agency practices valid, there is the issue of making plans acceptable to the operational components of the agency. Some might view this as deliberate cooptation of operational personnel into the process of planned change, under the assumption that planners are oriented toward change while operational personnel prefer the status quo. This is, of course, not necessarily the case: planning, under the traditionalist managerial approach, may be chiefly concerned with preserving the status quo; often operational personnel are the first to perceive the need for change. Nevertheless, implementation of a plan is often eased if planners first submit it to operational personnel for "trial by comment." This process blends the planning-derived "should do" with operational estimates of "can do."

Implementation of change can be impeded when planning has been undertaken in secret, leading to operational-level suspicions about the real purpose of the plan and fears about a "hidden agenda". The inclusion of operational personnel in the planning process helps to offset worries about "hidden agendas." When the "practical" concerns introduced by operational personnel are taken into account during the planning process, the likelihood increases that the plan will be viewed by operational personnel as a forthright attempt to deal with agency problems.

Teaming Agency Planners with Consultants. The use of consultants on a temporary or part-time basis offers great potential for supplementing in-house planning expertise. Consultants can infuse fresh ideas into the organization, and often can provide a greater degree of objectivity than might be provided by agency personnel. Consultants are also particularly useful when an agency is confronting substantial change or new problems with which the in-house planning staff has had little experience.

Certain disadvantages pertain to the use of consultants, however. Consultants in highly technical areas may speak in technical jargon, thereby confusing the transfer of information or alienating operational personnel. Consultants may also not fully appreciate the nature of the agency, the system, or its environment, so there is a risk that their recommendations may be unrealistic. And consultants are often not around long enough to confront the hardest part of planning—that is, attempting to put the plan into effect. Consultants are, therefore, hardly a cure-all. They should supplement the planning efforts of operating and systems-planning agencies rather than substitute for them. It is for the infrequently occurring condition that the use of consultants seems most appropriate, while the usual or frequently occurring condition requiring planning ought more appropriately to be staffed in-house.

SUMMARY

No single model can be recommended for the design and implementation of the planning apparatus within an agency. The specific structure and functions assigned to organizational planners depend on numerous factors: the size of the organization, the administrative style of top management, the resources available to planning, the support structures available within the agency, and the specific responsibilities assigned to planning. Most of these factors influence the function and structure of planning agencies at the system level as well.

These factors influence not only the number of professional planners needed but also the way planning is organized within the agency. Organizations need to determine which combination of the following planning structures are appropriate to their needs: the long-range planning committee, the planning task force, the planning and research division, the executive management committee. Each of these structures has slightly different capabilities and objectives; each can make unique contributions to the overall planning effort.

Special organizational issues also influence the nature and placement of system-level planning bodies. Chief among these factors are administrative placement within the jurisdiction's political and administrative machinery, the support of the jurisdiction chief executive, the existence of enabling legislation, and the provision for budget-review authority. These factors, and the level of cooperation between the system planning agency and the component criminal justice agencies, crucially affect the nature and scope of planning activity permitted to, and undertaken by, a planning agency.

A central concern of staffing and organizing is the balancing of analytical skills and experiences. Both analytical skills and experience in criminal justice are essential: it is less important that each planner hired have a full range of such skills and experiences than that the planning staff as an entity have them. Also, the teaming of line personnel and planning staff is advisable when developing and implementing plans and the teaming of agency planners with outside consultants is one means of providing some critical planning-related skills and experience not available within the agency.

· *Chapter 7* ·
NOTES

1. National Advisory Commission on Criminal Justice Standards and Goals, *Police* (Washington, D.C.: U.S. Government Printing Office, 1973), p. 122.
2. Ibid.
3. Ibid., p. 124.
4. Robert C. Cushman, *Criminal Justice Planning for Local Government* (Washington, D.C.: U.S. Department of Justice, Law Enforcement Assistance Administration, National Institute of Law Enforcement and Criminal Justice, 1980), p. 28.
5. G. Douglas Gourley, *Effective Municipal Police Organization* (Beverly Hills, Calif.: Glencoe Press, 1970), pp. 30–37.
6. O. W. Wilson and Roy C. McLaren, *Police Administration*, 3rd ed. (New York: McGraw-Hill Book Company, 1972), pp. 156–57. Also see Robert Sheehan and Gary W. Cordner, *Introduction to Police Administration* (Reading, MA.: Addison-Wesley, 1979), pp. 164–69.
7. John P. Kenney, *Police Management Planning* (Springfield, Ill.: Charles C. Thomas, Publisher, 1959), esp. pp. 32–54.
8. Wilson and McLaren, op. cit., p. 153.
9. Ronald G. Lynch, *The Police Manager: Professional Leadership Skills*, 2nd ed. (Boston: Holbrook Press, 1978), pp. 121–26.
10. Peter H. Nash and Dennis Durden, "A Task-Force Approach to Replace the Planning Board," *Journal of the American Institute of Planners*, 30: 1, (February 1964), 10–22.
11. John K. Hudzik and Jack R. Greene, "University Collaboration in Agency Problem-Solving: A Short Introduction to the MSU-WCSD Policy Development Project." Criminal Justice Systems Center, Michigan State University, East Lansing, Mich., 1976.
12. Nash and Durden, op. cit.
13. Hudzik and Greene, op. cit.
14. The task forces functioned for about a year. One task force remained in existence for an additional year owing to continuing business.
15. Kenney, op. cit., see pp. 27–31.
16. Burt Nanus, "A General Model for Criminal Justice Planning," *Journal of Criminal Justice*, 2 (1974), 352–53.
17. Also see H. Igor Ansoff, "The State of Practice in Planning Systems," in William R. Dill and G. Kh. Popov, *Organization for Forecasting and Planning: Experience in the Soviet Union and the United States* (New York: John Wiley & Sons, Inc., 1979), p. 176.
18. John K. Hudzik, et al., *Criminal Justice Manpower Planning: An Overview* (Washington, D.C.: U. S. Law Enforcement Assistance Administration, U. S. Government Printing Office, 1981); adapted from data presented in Chaps. 2 and 3.
19. Ira Sharkansky, *Public Administration: Policy-Making in Government Agencies* (Chicago: Markham Publishing Co., 1977), p. 284.
20. Hudzik, et al., op. cit., see Chap. 7.
21. Cushman, op. cit., p. 53.
22. National Governors' Association, Committee on Criminal Justice and Public Protection, *Criminal Justice: A Governor's Guide* (Washington, D.C.: National Governor's Association, Center for Policy Research, 1980), p. 4.
23. Panel of the National Academy of Public Administration (NAPA), *Criminal Justice Planning in the Governing Process: A Review of Nine States* (Washington, D.C.: NAPA, February 1979), pp. 45–47.
24. The States of Michigan and Washington

have had the longest experience with SPA budget-review authority.

25. National Criminal Justice Association (The National Conference), *Approaches to Institutionalization of State Planning Agencies in Criminal Justice*, September 1980. Unpublished.

26. *A Governor's Guide*, op. cit., p. 14.

27. Daniel L. Skoler, *Organizing the Nonsystem* (Lexington, MA.: Lexington Books, 1977), p. 266–67.

28. NAPA, op. cit., pp. 34–35.

29. Cushman, op. cit., pp. 53–64.

30. Nancy Loving and John W. McKay, *Criminal Justice Planning: Five Alternative Structures for Cities* (Washington, D.C.: National League of Cities and U.S. Conference of Mayors, 1976), p. 14.

31. Gordon Raley, *Criminal Justice Planning: The Coordinating Council* (Washington, D.C.: National League of Cities and U.S. Conference of Mayors, 1976), pp. 15–16.

32. NAPA, op. cit.

33. Cushman, op. cit., p. 69.

34. *A Governor's Guide*, op. cit., Hudzik, et al., op. cit., NAPA, op. cit.

35. Hudzik, et al., op. cit., see Chap. 7.

36. Ibid.

37. *A Governor's Guide*, op. cit., p. 6.

38. Arthur D. Little, Inc., *Local Criminal Justice Planning and Analysis: Activities and Capabilities* (Washington, D.C.: Law Enforcement Assistance Administration, 1976).

39. It appears, for example, that this has been the case in Kalamazoo, Michigan, for voters gave approval to a millage specifically to support the Regional Criminal Justice Planning Council (1979–80).

40. Ansoff, op. cit., p. 176.

41. Jack Rothman, *Using Research in Organizations: A Guide to Successful Application* (Beverly Hills, Calif.: Sage Publications, 1980), p. 51.

42. Sam S. Souryal, *Police Administration and Management* (St. Paul, Minn.: West Publishing, 1977), pp. 282–83.

43. For a general discussion of these issues, see Herbert A. Simon, *Administrative Behavior*, 3rd ed. (New York: The Free Press, 1976).

44. Cushman, op. cit., p. 74.

45. Daniel Lauber, *Job Descriptions for Planning Agencies*, American Society of Planning Officers, Planning Advisory Service, *Report No. 302* (May 1974).

46. Scarvia B. Anderson and Samuel Ball, *The Profession and Practice of Program Evaluation* (San Francisco: Jossey-Bass, 1978).

47. Ibid., pp. 172–73. The table presented here is adapted from findings reported by Anderson and Ball.

48. Cushman, op. cit., p. 77.

49. Anderson and Ball, op. cit., p. 184.

50. Rothman, op cit., pp. 51–52.

51. Wilson and McLaren, op. cit., p. 153.

52. Carol H. Weiss, *Evaluation Research: Methods of Assessing Program Effectiveness* (Englewood Cliffs, N.J.: Prentice-Hall, Inc., 1972).

53. Daniel Katz, "Field Studies," in Leon Festinger and Daniel Katz, *Research Methods in the Behavioral Sciences* (New York: The Dryden Press, 1953), p. 71.

54. Rothman, op. cit., pp. 41–51.

55. Ibid., p. 43.

56. Rothman, op. cit., p. 46, quoting Timothy Brown, "Guidelines for Integrating Program Evaluation with Administrative Decision-Making." Paper presented at APA Convention, Washington, D.C., 1976.

· Part III ·

THE PROCESS OF CRIMINAL JUSTICE PLANNING

Chapters 8, 9, and 10 finally get down to the nitty gritty of how to do planning. You may recall that at the end of Chapter 3 we presented a revised planning model that included three basic stages. The chapters in this section each cover one of these stages in the planning process.

In Chapter 8 the planning stage of goal and problem identification is discussed. Planning is undertaken to achieve goals or resolve problems—these things provide the targets, the ends toward which planning efforts are directed. Identifying goals and problems is not always a simple task, however. Goals are too vague or controversial, and multiple goals often conflict with each other. Certain conditions may appear as problems to part of the citizenry, but not to others. This aspect of planning is perhaps the least analytical and most political of the three stages.

Chapter 9 deals with forecasting. All implemented decisions and plans take effect in the future, and so decision-makers and planners need to forecast the relevant characteristics of the implementation setting. Usually, of course, a default assumption is made that the future will be just like the present. One need not look far, though, to realize that the world is changing quickly these days. Especially for decisions with long-term implications (such as prison construction), forecasting is a crucial component of the planning process.

Generating and testing alternatives, the third stage in the planning process, is discussed in Chapter 10. Having identified goals or problems, and having taken the future into consideration, what remains is to generate alternative means for achieving chosen ends, and to test the alternatives in order to determine their likely consequences. When generating alternatives, the common tendency, which must be resisted, is to consider only well-known, readily available means. A wider search is highly recommended. Testing of alternatives is principally an analytical activity, using many of the same techniques as in forecasting.

•Chapter 8•

GOAL AND PROBLEM IDENTIFICATION

This chapter and the next two examine how to do planning. This examination is based on the foundation of information and knowledge laid in earlier chapters. In general those chapters discussed the *sociology* of planning, criminal justice, and organizations, aiming to explain and understand them. The remaining chapters, however, will be taking a managerial, rather than sociological, perspective. Their focus will be on action, on making things work—in other words, on *doing* planning.

Chapter 3 introduced the planning process. It was easy to demonstrate that the eight-step "modern-classical" model of planning made demands far in excess of the cognitive and resource capacities of individuals and organizations. In short, the model demanded objective rationality when, in fact, even subjective rationality (maximum achievement relative to actual knowledge) is hard to achieve. These demands and limitations, and the fact that human behavior and decision-making are at least intendedly rational (within a variety of real-world constraints), led to a proposed three-stage planning process—identifying goals and problems, forecasting, generating and testing alternatives—the rationality, detail, and sophistication of which depend on a variety of factors affecting the organization and the planner.

This chapter is concerned with the first stage of the planning process: the identification of goals and problems. It begins by considering these things called goals and problems. Then it describes how goals and problems are found, and some of the goals that guide criminal justice. The third section discusses how, from among the possible goals and problems, those meriting major planning effort can be selected. This is followed by a discussion of what is involved in studying and analyzing the planning issues that have been selected, and of the role of citizen participation in planning.

GOALS VERSUS PROBLEMS

Most discussions of planning focus on goals and their attainment. Planning is undertaken to achieve goals; it starts with setting or identifying goals. The rest of the process consists of figuring out the most efficient and effective means of attaining those goals.

Although most ideal models of the planning process begin with the setting of goals, real-world planning often does not, and perhaps for good reasons. Because the goals of an organization or a system can create confusion, controversy, and conflict, they may not be too helpful as guides for a planning process. Another aspect of the general situation has been described by Hirschhorn:

> Groups that face genuinely new and confusing situations often find that their values and goals lack meaning and relevance. They face a "mission crisis." They do not know what is important. It often happens in these situations that when people specify their goals, they are doing so defensively and hastily to reduce the psychological costs of genuine uncertainty. Goal specification may thus prove premature and the group, organization, or agency may very well produce a goal statement that is not consonant with its context.[1]

The major alternative to goals as the focus of planning is problems. Problems tend to be more concrete and down-to-earth than goals, and so may be more useful as guides to planning. It is possible to agree about the undesirability of a problem, even when it is impossible to agree about the desirability of a particular goal.[2] People might agree that they are dissatisfied with where they are, even when they do not agree about where they would like to be.

Problem-oriented planning gives rise to two related difficulties, however, one practical and the other more philosophical. The practical difficulty is that problem-orientation provides no guidance in the identification of solutions. Without some notion of goals or desired ends, the planner is without guides for choosing which solution is best.[3] Agreement that a problem exists does not tell the planner anything about what would constitute a solution, or even a mitigation.

The more philosophical difficulty to which purely problem-oriented planning gives rise is that goals, values, or some other notions of desired ends are still at work, indirectly or implicitly. It is the sense of how things should be that gives rise to the disappointment in how things are—the "problem."

It seems reasonable to conclude that neither goals nor problems suffice as guides to planning. As the planning context varies (see Chapter 3), the relative importance of goals and problems will vary, but both are always involved, at least implicitly. Clear and consistent goals may provide primary guidance for generating and testing alternatives, but when goals are unclear and/or conflicting, planning may focus more directly on problems.

These general ideas about goals and problems in planning are fully supported by the results of a recent study by Robert C. Cushman, who found that effective criminal justice planning was focused on "problem-oriented goals."[4] Goals were regarded as very important: "efforts to establish clear goals, objectives, and priorities have a positive effect on local decision-making. Setting clear goals, in fact, is the heart of effective policy-making."[5] Traditional goal-setting was not found to be sufficient, however:

> A problem-oriented approach to planning, which relies heavily on the problem identification and analysis phase of the planning cycle, can help policy-makers to formulate goals and priorities in terms that are focused on specific problems and solutions.[6] Criminal justice planners have found it easier to galvanize cooperative efforts around problem-oriented goals and priorities rather than more abstract notions. It is easier to mobilize efforts toward the goal of reducing the number of commercial burglaries in the central city than around the more amorphous goal of "reducing crime and delinquency." It is more meaningful to attack specific problems, such as school truancy or inadequate emergency response times, than to "enhance respect for the law." This is not to say that such abstract goals are unimportant, but only that it is difficult to act on them. The evidence suggests that the goal-setting process must provide concrete direction for planning activities designed to solve specific problems.[7]

It is not necessary to choose between goal-oriented and problem-oriented conceptions of planning, for planning involves both goals and problems. In criminal justice planning, goals may be unclear or divisive, but they have an important role to play in conjunction with problems.

Some Problems with Problems

The planning process encounters difficulties caused by goals that are vague, controversial, or in conflict with one another, and goals that generate conflict among interested parties. Formal goals may be presented for public consumption, while the individual or organization really pursues other aims, such as survival and self-interest. These characteristics of goals affect their role in planning. Problems, too, have different characteristics that bear implications for planning: the mere specification of a concrete, consensual problem does not necessarily simplify the planning process.

Timothy J. Cartwright has provided a classification of problem types.[8] One characteristic that he finds important is the number of variables needed to define the problem, and in particular whether the number can be specified or must be left open-ended. The second trait he considers is the nature of these variables, especially whether they are known and calculable. The result of putting these two problem characteristics together is the four types of problems presented in Figure 8-1.

Cartwright characterizes the four types as follows:

> *Simple* problems are problems which are completely understood: they are defined in terms of a specified number of calculable variables.
>
> *Compound* problems are the problems some, but not all, of whose parts are known: they are defined in terms of an unspecified number of calculable variables.
>
> *Complex* problems are problems which look like simple problems but are not: they are defined in terms of a specified number of vari-

Figure 8-1. Four Types of Planning Problems

(Adapted from T. J. Cartwright, "Problems, Solutions and Strategies: A Contribution to the Theory and Practice of Planning," by permission of the *Journal of the American Institute of Planners* [May 1973], 183.)

	Number of Variables	
Nature of Variables	Specified	Unspecified
Calculable	Simple Problem	Compound Problem
Incalculable	Complex Problem	Metaproblem

ables, but the variables are incalculable rather than calculable.

Metaproblems, on the other hand, are the least precise of all: they are defined in terms of an unspecified number of incalculable variables.[9]

Though the typology establishes different kinds of problems, it does not imply that one type is better, more scientific, or even necessarily easier to solve, than the others. Simple problems may be well understood, but their solutions might be too costly, technologically unattainable, or perhaps unthinkable. Conversely, there may exist solutions to some metaproblems, although metaproblems may not be very well understood. Certainly this is the contention of behavior-modification enthusiasts, who employ positive and negative reinforcements to correct abnormal behavior, without much concern about its causes.

The characterization of a problem in terms of the number and calculability of its component variables depends heavily on perception. The same problem might seem simple to one observer, complex to another. This is particularly true of social problems, as Cartwright suggests:

As a simple problem: poverty means having an annual income of less than three thousand dollars.

As a compound problem: proverty means having an annual income of less than three thousand dollars, having an education below the level of grade eight, living in substandard housing (according to some specific criteria), and/or other characteristics.

As a complex problem: proverty means the inability to obtain for oneself the minimum basic necessities of life (i.e., adequate food and shelter).

As a metaproblem: poverty means relative social deprivation.[10]

Crime too could be perceived in such dramatically different ways, and in fact this difference accounts for much of the controversy surrounding what should be done about it.[11]

What this clearly demonstrates is that problems, too, can fail as clear guides to planning. Simple problems, like situations with clear goals and well understood relationships between means and ends (see Chapter 3), lend themselves to rational planning and maximization. At the other extreme, metaproblems, like situations with vague or conflicting goals and poorly understood relationships between means and ends, encourage disjointed incrementalism in pursuit of "successive approximations" or "partial improvements." In Cartwright's terms, compound problems have "disjointed rationality" as the appropriate solution strategy, while complex problems should be approached with "comprehensive incrementalism."[12]

IDENTIFYING GOALS AND PROBLEMS

Both goals and problems serve as guides to the planning process, but both can introduce confusion and conflict. Despite their clarity or simplicity, goals may be unattainable, problems insoluble. Given that, what goals are to be pursued and what problems confronted? And where are they to be found?

General Public-Policy Goals

A few general goals apply to all public policies and agencies: efficiency, equity, participation, predictability, and procedural fairness.[13] These five desired ends are all in addition to the specific goals of particular public policies. For example, an urban-renewal program might be designed to "renovate or replace all substandard buildings in the central city." A recreational program might be aimed at "providing organized activities for all age groups and for residents of all neighborhoods." In addition to these goals, though, such programs would also generally be expected to pursue efficiency, equity, participation, predictability, and procedural fairness.

Before going any further, we should identify these five goals a little more specifically.

Efficiency—benefits over costs; costs per unit of service, outcome, or impact

Equity—equal distribution of costs and benefits

Participation—involvement of general public or relevant interests in decision-making

Predictability—use of objective or agreed upon criteria; universalistic rather than particularistic decision-making

Procedureal Fairness—authority invoked, or costs and benefits distributed, according to a fair process that includes reasonable notice, a right to present evidence, a right to confront accusers, an impartial and detached arbiter, and an opportunity to appeal[14]

It might be argued that these "general" goals are really means, not ends, but there is considerable evidence that these things are desired in and of themselves, and not merely as means to some other goals. If participation were only a means to the good life, for example, we should willingly accept benevolent authority. We often do not, of course, because participation seems to be an element of the good life, not merely a means to it.

These five goals indicate some of the features of a desired end-state, some of the things that planning tries to achieve. They also serve as criteria for judging the relative desirability of alternatives or solutions. The decision, for example, that one urban-renewal plan is better than another rests in part on an estimate of the effects of each on efficiency, equity, participation, predictability, and procedural fairness. Knowing these effects will not completely settle the issue, of course, in large part because the effects are likely to be mixed, so that priorites and weights may be needed.

Criminal Justice Goals

In addition to the five general goals applicable to all public policy, criminal justice has some substantive goals of its own. In his recent study of planning, Cushman identified five criminal justice system goals: to protect the integrity of the law; to control crime and delinquency and/or root out the causes of crime; to improve the quality of justice; to improve the criminal justice system and related programs; and to increase community support for the criminal justice system.[15] Some of these goals, however, seem to be means, or at least of a lesser order than the general public-policy goals presented earlier.

A set of criminal justice goals more consonant with the five general public-policy goals has been suggested by Levine, et al.: crime prevention, public tranquillity, justice, due process, efficiency, and accountability.[16] The goal efficiency in criminal justice corresponds with the goal of efficiency applicable to all public policy. Due process corresponds with procedural fairness. Accountability includes the public-policy goal of participation, and perhaps extends the concept to include other respects in which decisions and officials should be accountable to the public.

The goals of crime prevention, public tranquillity, and justice are the ones most specific to criminal justice. The goal of justice is broader than the notions of equity and predictability. Although costs and benefits should be equally distributed, the ideas of retribution and of mercy are inherent in conceptions of what is fair and just. And though objective, universal criteria should be used in making decisions about the distribution of benefits and costs, each individual case is different, and justice must be tailored to situational considerations.

Crime prevention, or crime control, involves constraining the incidence of criminal law violations in society. This is certainly one of the principal reasons for a criminal justice system, criminal justice agencies, criminal justice policies, and criminal law. These components of criminal justice are not the only means employed in pursuit of crime control, nor perhaps the most important means, but they clearly have crime control as one of their major goals.

Public tranquillity refers to the desire for a relatively undisturbed, peaceful, orderly environment in which individuals can come and go as they please, sleep and read in reasonable quiet, and not be constantly offended as they travel about. Public tranquillity is very relative, though: things can be too quiet, too sterile, too peaceful, too orderly, at least for some. But there is probably a minimal level of tranquillity that all would agree is desirable, even though some would want far more.

Combining the general goals of public policy with those of criminal justice results in six goals of criminal justice:

Crime control
Public tranquillity
Justice
Due process
Accountability
Efficiency

These are the ultimate goals of criminal justice. Some might argue that the ultimate goal is human happiness or the quality of life, but this is too vague to be of help in planning. In fact, the six goals specified are rather vague, and additional guides may be needed for meaningful criminal justice planning.

Goal Hierarchies

Goals form a hierarchy. Actions, means, are designed in order to attain a goal. That goal, in all likelihood, is in turn a means to an even higher goal, and so on. In this sense all but a very few goals are instrumental: they are means to other desired states.

Some prefer to label the various levels of goals, in order to distinguish among them, but the labels are far from consistent. For example, some refer to terminal goals as *objectives;* others use that term for subordinate goals. Let us retain the term *goal* for all the desired ends and aims that guide planning and decision-making, using *basic purposes* for the broadest and most terminal goals, and *missions* for goals that are somewhat more specific. Subordinate to missions will be *long-range objectives,* and subordinate to long-range objectives will be *short-range objectives.*[17] This hierarchy is illustrated in Figure 8-2.

The six criminal justice goals—crime control, public tranquillity, justice, due process, accountability, efficiency—are basic purposes, terminal desired ends that provide general guidance to the planning process. They are somewhat vague, though, and on a day-to-day basis do not provide much specific guidance to planners or decision-makers. What are needed are more specific goals that are logical or empirical components of these basic purposes.

Any listing of the missions of criminal justice is highly subjective. Like basic purposes, missions are fairly vague. Steiner has noted that statements of purposes and missions "are not designed to express concrete ends but to provide motivation, general direction, an image, a tone, and/or a philosophy to guide the enter-

Figure 8-2. Hierarchy of Goals

(Adapted from George A. Steiner, *Strategic Planning: What Every Manager Must Know* [New York: The Free Press, 1979], p. 150.)

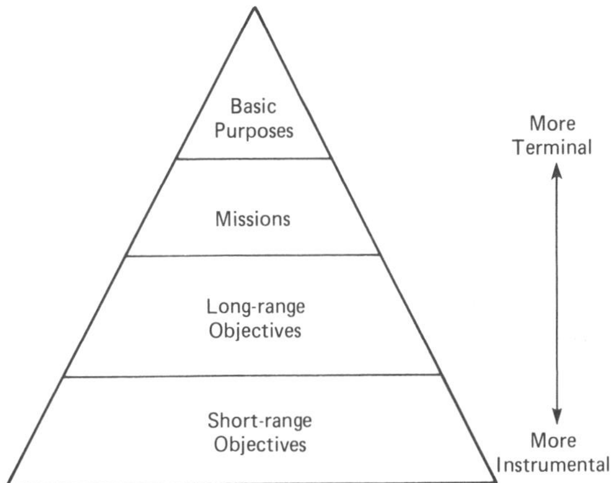

prise."[18] A list of the missions of criminal justice that is consistent with its basic purposes might be

Prevention of crime	Protection of life and property
Detection of crime	Preservation of the peace
Apprehension of offenders	Protection of the integrity of the law
Adjudication of offenders	Respect for freedoms and liberties
Punishment of offenders	Respect for public preferences

This list of missions is only one among many, many possibilities. But these missions seem to derive logically from the six basic purposes of criminal justice and to support them.

Long-range objectives are more specific than missions. For example, the mission "adjudication of offenders" might lead to the following long-range objectives: provision of reasonable bail opportunities for arrested suspects; assurance of the right to counsel for suspects and defendants; assurance of the presentation of all relevant evidence; protection of all rights and liberties of defendants; conviction or acquittal on the basis of proof beyond a reasonable doubt; conduct of adjudicatory processes in a timely manner; and so on. These objectives are designed to contribute to the achievement of the "adjudication of offenders," and they take into account other missions and basic purposes (such as due process) that should guide criminal justice planning.

Short-range objectives are even more detailed, and logically or empirically connected to long-range objectives and, through them, to missions and basic purposes. It is at this point, too, that problem-oriented goals are encountered. Consider, for example, these objectives: provision of judicial bail review within twenty-four hours of arrest; provision of counsel for indigent defendants within twenty-four hours of arrest; provision of preliminary hearings within fourteen days of arrest; provision of misdemeanor trials within ninety days of arrest; and provision of felony trials within 180 days of arrest. Alternatively, we might prefer problem-oriented objectives: reduction of the number of prosecution-requested trial date postponements by 25 per cent; reduction of the district court case backlog by one third; or reduction by 50 per cent of average number of nontrial days required by jury duty.

Although these short-range objectives are rather detailed, it is possible to get even more specific. More specific objectives, though, begin to move into the realm of means, and attention turns more toward alternatives than toward goals. But it is important to realize that means and ends are really connected—points along a continuum rather than items in separate categories.

The usefulness of long-range objectives and short-range objectives, Steiner suggests, depends on the extent to which they exhibit certain characteristics:

Suitable: An obvious requisite for an objective is that its achievement must support the enterprise's basic purposes and missions.

Measurable over time: To the extent practicable, objectives state what is expected to happen in concrete terms and when.

Feasible: Objectives should be possible to achieve.

Acceptable: Objectives are most likely to be achieved if they are acceptable to people in the organization.

Flexible: It should be possible to modify the objective in the event of unforeseen contingencies.

Motivating: Generally, objectives that are out of reach of people are not motivating nor are objectives that are too easily achieved.

Understandable: Objectives should be stated in as simple and as understandable words as possible.

Commitment: Once agreement is reached about objectives there should be a commitment to do what is necessary and reasonable to achieve them.

People participation: Best results are achieved when those who are responsible for achieving objectives have some role in setting them.

Linkage: First, objectives should be linked to basic purposes, as previously noted. Second, objectives in different parts of the company should be examined to see that they are consistent with and meet, in the aggregate, top management objectives.[19]

Criminal Justice Organizational Goals

This discussion of the general goals of criminal justice has used labels somewhat different from those used for the goals of specific criminal justice agencies discussed in Chapter 6. Any inconsistency is merely semantic. The six basic purposes of criminal justice (crime control, public tranquillity, justice, due process, accountability, efficiency) also serve as the basic purposes for each type of agency, though the relative importance of each may vary from one kind of agency to another. The agency goals discussed in Chapter 6 were simply versions of the missions of criminal justice.

Subordinate to the missions of each type of criminal justice agency would be long- and short-range objectives, some of which might be shared by more than one agency. For example, "assurance of the presentation of all relevant evidence" might be an objective of the police, the prosecutor, the public defender, and the court, though each might interpret and pursue the objective somewhat differently. Similarly, a problem-oriented objective such as "reduction of the incidence of school truancy" might be shared by several criminal justice organizations, though their efforts to attain it would differ.

Sources of Goals and Problems

Where do goals and problems come from? How are they found? Identifying goals and problems is sometimes difficult and/or controversial, sometimes not. In general, it is probably easier to find and to reach agreement on basic purposes and missions, more difficult to get consensus on long- and short-range objectives.

Nagel has suggested that there are two basic ways to identify and justify ultimate ends:

> One approach is a traditional philosophical approach that talks in terms of the inherent nature of human beings, divine authority, intuitive obviousness, or other such criteria. The other approach is more associated with social science and survey research. It defines an ultimate value as something which people observably or empirically seek as or at least advocate as an end in itself. . . .[20]

The discussion up to this point has leaned toward the philosophical orientation described by Nagel: public-policy goals, and the basic purposes, missions, and objectives of criminal justice have been justified primarily on the basis of logic and intuition, as well as by observations of criminal justice planning and practice. This approach is certainly legitimate, but in the public sector it is important to determine what the citizenry thinks the problems are, and what the goals of public policy should be. For planners, this means looking to public opinion, relevant interest groups, legislation, elected officials, case law, and other such sources of guidance for information about what is desired and what is perceived as less than perfect now.

It is easier to say that planners should go to the public to find out about goals and problems than it is for planners to do it. People disagree about goals and problems; information is inadequate, insufficient, and uncertain; and the public interest is rarely obvious. Planners *are* often required to choose among competing individual and group interests, or at the very least to exert influence. Although the public interest is not ordinarily obvious, it remains the appropriate criterion for the evaluation of public policies, and planners are often, by virtue of their position, capable of transcending narrower interests. Richard Klosterman has argued the point well:

> [I]t is not unreasonable to suggest that an individual may err in choosing between available alternatives and be well advised to rely on the advice of doctors, financial advisors, and other professionals to determine which course of action is, in fact, in his interest.
>
> Thus, while it is objectionable for planners to evaluate the wants and preferences of private individuals, this does not mean that they must be prohibited from determining whether a proposed policy will be in an individual's interest. Individuals and groups must of course be given the opportunity to help define the policies of government which affect them; however, this does not eliminate the need for specialized knowledge and informed opinion. The determination of whether a policy is in an individual's or group's interest requires the evaluation of the policy's long- and short-term impacts on their welfare. Identifying these effects for complex policy choices concerning, for example, regional economic development and environmental protection will often require specialized substantive knowledge and analytic techniques which only planners and other specialists will

possess. As a result, planners will often be better able to determine whether a proposed policy is in an individual's or group's interest than those who will be directly affected.[21]

As Klosterman indicates, planners can more legitimately exercise authority in the choice of alternatives than in the identification of goals. But because the real distinctions between means and ends are blurred, planners do become involved in identifying goals and problems, not merely reacting to the public will. Planners need to realize this, and to exercise restraint. As "planning is a sublime power," so too is it an "awesome responsibility."[22]

Among other sources of criminal justice goals and problems, perhaps the most noteworthy are the national and state standards and goals commissions of the last decade, and the American Bar Association standards project.[23] The various task forces of the National Advisory Commission on Criminal Justice Standards and Goals were comprised of criminal justice personnel, elected and appointed public officials, and members of the general public. They produced a large number of objectives,

Table 8-1. Objectives and Priorities Identified By the National Advisory Commission on Criminal Justice Standards and Goals in 1973

Sector	Guides
Total System	*Goal:* a 50% reduction in high-fear crimes by 1983.
	Priorities: The highest attention must be given to preventing juvenile delinquency and to minimizing the involvement of young offenders in the juvenile and criminal justice system, and to reintegrating juvenile offenders into the community.
	Public and private service agencies should direct their actions to improve the delivery of all social services to citizens, particularly to groups that contribute higher than average proportions of their numbers to crime statistics.
	Delays in the adjudication and disposition of criminal cases must be greatly reduced.
	Increased citizen participation in activities to control crime in their community must be generated, with active encouragement and support by criminal justice agencies.
Police	*Objectives:* Fully develop the offender-apprehension potential of the criminal justice system.
	Get the police and the people working together as a team.
	Get the criminal justice system working together as a team.
	Clearly determine and act on the local crime problem.
	Make the most of human resources.
	Make the most of technological resources.
	Fully develop the police response to special community needs.
Courts	*Priorities:* Speed and efficiency in achieving final determination of guilt or innocence of a defendant must be increased.
	Upgrade performance of the prosecution and defense functions.
	Ensure the high quality of judges.
	Study and evaluate the exclusionary rule.
Corrections	*Priorities:* Equity and justice in corrections must be achieved.
	Exclude sociomedical problem cases from corrections.
	Shift correctional emphasis from institutional to community programs.
	Unify corrections and total system planning, develop manpower.
	Increase involvement of the public.

Adapted from four reports of the National Advisory Commission on Criminal Justice Standards and Goals: *A National Strategy to Reduce Crime; Police; Courts;* and *Corrections* (Washington, D.C.: U.S. Government Printing Office, 1973).

priorities, standards, and recommendations that were intended to guide criminal justice planning and programs for a decade or more. Some of the principal normative guides produced by the Commission are presented in Table 8-1.

Some of the objectives and priorities shown in Table 8-1 are clearly problem-oriented; others are not. The Commission also promulgated a wide variety of more detailed and specific standards. The intention was that local and state jurisdictions could compare their current conditions and practices to the standards, and thus identify "problems" (i.e., substandard present-states). Other standards intended to be used in the same way have been established by such groups as the American Bar Association and the American Correctional Association, as well as by numerous state-level criminal justice advisory commissions.

Citizen participation, which will be discussed later in this chapter, can also help identify goals and problems. As Koberg and Bagnall observe:

> The problem-solving process begins in a combination of several basic ways:
>
> 1. Someone brings a problem to us and says: "I'd like you to solve/consider/think about/do something to help me out of this situation."
> Example: "What color do you think I should paint my car?"
>
> 2. We detect that something in our environment requires replacement, alteration or repair in order to be improved.
> Example: "Mom's pie was always so good. I wonder what the secret was."
>
> 3. Some prior experience gnaws at us to deserve our concern.
> Example: Finding a way to affect the city council to save the shoreline.
>
> 4. We intentionally or inadvertently become enmeshed in a series of problems.
> Example: We took the course in order to learn to type and now we've got to learn to spell also.[24]

Goal and Problem Priorities

Usually, there are so many goals and problems, and such limitations on time and resources, that priorities are needed to guide our planning efforts. Moreover, the achievement of some terminal end depends first on the achievement of a more instrumental end, or the solution of some lower-level problem.

The identification of priorities differs little from that of goals and problems. Priorities may be based on logic or guided by the public or other representative interests. It is a relatively simple matter, using the research techniques of social science, to find out the importance attributed by the public to various goals and problems (see Chapters 11 and 12). At times, though, the public's preferences may not seem logical or consistent, or the divergence of opinion may be great, or such information may simply not be available. It is in such instances that the expertise of the planner, and the planner's ability to identify the public interest, are most seriously challenged.

SELECTING PLANNING ISSUES

An aspect of the identification of goals and problems that is often overlooked is the decision to invoke full-fledged planning. Merely identifying a goal or a problem does not necessarily or automatically lead to application of the entire planning process. As Wiseman has recently noted:

> Some of the issues that arise are such that they can quite adequately be dealt with by an administrative rather than an analytical approach and some will be so urgent that no option exists anyway about the degree of investigation they receive. Since adopting a systematic approach to an issue is expensive and involves a considerable commitment of skilled resources, a decision to tackle any issue in this way requires careful consideration of the likely benefits to accrue.[25]

Wiseman has reported on a process for selecting planning issues that was developed out of a major study of public-sector planning in Britain. The discussion that follows draws heavily on his report.

Selection Criteria

There are some criteria by which the importance of issues can be judged. Within the general categories of size, nature, future implications, and political setting, Wiseman suggests twelve such criteria:

Size of the Issue

1. Resources committed: quantity and quality of resources involved, rate of change in resources committed

2. Projected need or demand: future demand for and need of services to be delivered

Nature of the Issue

3. Range of choice: amount of discretion available in choosing future courses of action

4. Complexity: extent of interdependence with other issues and degree of uncertainty about effects

Future Implications of the Issue

5. Innovation type: whether change is likely to be incremental or more substantial

6. Resource implications: whether resource commitments extend far into the future and are substantial

7. Flexibility retained: whether decisions and actions have irreversible future implications

8. Outcome significance: possibility of achieving improvements in output and/or outcome

Political Setting of the Issue

9. Level of urgency: time available for analysis, perceptions of urgency of action

10. Decision-making consistency: need to consider other commitments and links to other decisions and agencies

11. Strategic relevance or sensitivity: relevance to agency's central role, whether issue is too hot to touch

12. Pressures for change: who stands to gain from change, who supports the status quo[26]

Naturally, complete and certain information on these criteria as they apply to any particular planning issue is never available. The criteria are useful, though, in deciding whether to initiate a planning process in response to a problem.

Problem Formulation

The first stage in determining which issues should receive full planning attention, *problem formulation,* is an informal effort by an ad hoc group to answer the question, "What is the problem?" The issue may have arisen in any number of ways: the organization may be reacting to a problem thrown at it, or it may have identified a goal or problem apparently in need of some attention. In formulating the problem, the group needs to interpret the issue in terms of current perceptions, history, and political setting; it must consider the aims behind problem resolution and the constraints limiting action; it must test alternative statements of the problem; it must develop a working formulation of the issue; and it must come to a preliminary assessment of the eligibility of the issue for further planning effort.[27]

Issue Analysis

When problem formulation results in agreement that an issue may be eligible for full planning treatment, more information and more analysis are needed. An individual or a small group is assigned the task of looking into the problem more carefully and developing a more detailed problem statement centered on the twelve selection criteria as they apply to the issue under consideration. Also important to document are any assumptions that have been made about the nature of the problem and its context.[28] In general, the intention of this stage is to determine, "What is known about the problem?"

Issue Filtration

The results of issue analysis must be more systematically examined and considered. The basic question to be answered is, "What is the issue's planning importance?" The individual or group analyzing the issue must more explicitly compare information about the problem to the selection criteria. At this stage only the first eight criteria (all but the political ones) are applied. The assessment should follow a systematic procedure such as that outlined in Figure 8-3, which illustrates one way of thinking about and discussing the importance of a planning issue.[29] The results of this comparison, and other information gathered during analysis, are then presented to the ad hoc group in the form of a discussion paper.

Final Assessment

At this point the ad hoc group must answer the question "What should be done?" This question is not so much how to solve the problem, as how best to address it. The options available include doing nothing, dealing immediately with the issue in a routine manner, requesting minor additions to the information about the problem, or submitting the issue for full-scale plan-

Figure 8-3. Systematic Procedure for Assessing the Importance of a Planning Issue

(Adapted from C. Wiseman, "Selection of Major Planning Issues," *Policy Sciences*, 9 [1978], 83, with permission of Elsevier Scientific Publishing Company.)

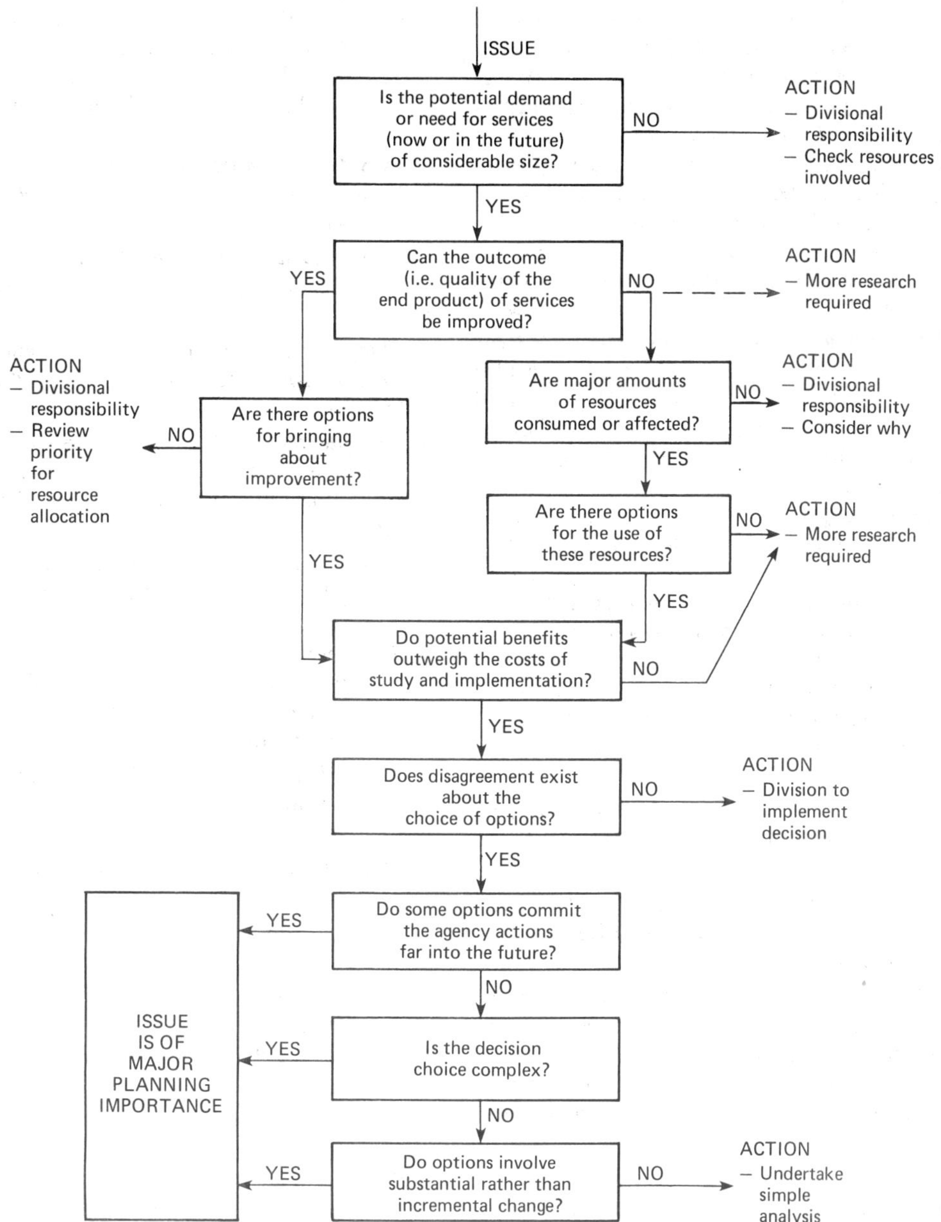

ning attention. The ad hoc group has the discussion paper on which to draw, but must also consider the issue in terms of the four political criteria specified earlier. It is quite conceivable that an issue deemed low in importance on the basis of rational criteria might nevertheless be scheduled for major planning effort because of its political implications, and the reverse is also very conceivable. These kinds of decisions have to be made by the ad hoc group on the basis of the potential costs and benefits associated with each option.[30]

An Example

Consider the following hypothesis: the judicial council (an advisory group of trial and appellate judges) in a state has been hearing criticism about the pervasiveness of plea bargaining, and is wondering what to do about it, if anything. In conjunction with the state court administrative office, the judicial council might want to consider acting immediately, engaging in a major planning exercise, ignoring the issue, or taking some other course of action.

The initial task would be to roughly formulate the problem: What is it? Where did it come from? Who seems to care about it? By what criteria is it a problem? It might be important to determine whether the problem really is plea bargaining, or disenchantment with judicial leniency, for example. Is the criticism that offenders are getting off too lightly? that defendants are pressured to plead guilty? that the wishes of victims and the police are ignored? or that the legal system is made a mockery? Also important are the constraints that operate with respect to plea bargaining, such as guarantees of due process, judicial resources, and human dislike of uncertainty.

Alternative statements of the problem, based on this preliminary information, should be considered. These might be some possibilities:

–Too many defendants are pressured by their lawyers to plead guilty in exchange for reduced sentences.

–Too many defendants are allowed by prosecutors to plead guilty to lesser offenses than originally charged.

–In too many cases, the result of plea bargaining is that there seems little connection between the legal ceremony in court and what the defendant actually did, so that few of the parties involved have any sense that justice was served.

These initial statements can be important, because they set the stage for much of what follows, suggesting what is relevant and what is not. Consider the third of these statements and imagine that the preliminary assessment is that the issue does deserve further consideration.

The next step is issue analysis, involving an initial determination of what is known about the problem. Some information will already be available from the problem formulation. A planner or analyst with the court administrative office might be assigned to clarify and systematize that and other readily available information. With this additional and more organized information, the issue could then be considered in terms of the selection criteria. A brief and hypothetical attribution might go as follows:

1. *Resources committed:* considerable–judges, prosecutors, defense attorneys, other court personnel, witnesses, and so on

2. *Projected need or demand:* number of court cases has been increasing and should continue to

3. *Range of choice:* the prosecutor and judge both have considerable discretion, as does the defendant

4. *Complexity:* unclear what the effects would be if plea incidence was altered, would depend on numerous legal and bureaucratic policies and interests

5. *Innovation type:* incremental may be more likely, but substantial change is quite conceivable

6. *Resource implications:* substantial changes in resource requirements are possible; could also have major resource implications for other sectors (corrections)

7. *Flexibility retained:* would not seem to have irreversible implications except for individual defendants

8. *Outcome significance:* real possibility of improved outcomes

9. *Level of urgency:* perceived as urgent by general public and some interest groups; should be sufficient time to study, though

10. *Decision-making consistency:* would have to coordinate with defense attorneys and prosecutors; would have to consider effects on corrections

11. *Strategic relevance or sensitivity:* very relevant to central role of court, but may not want to take on entrenched judicial interests (judicial autonomy, and so on)

12. *Pressures for change:* law-and-order-type groups and elected officials vying for votes seem to be most in favor of a change; courtroom elite most in favor of status quo

These attributions do include uncertainties (e.g., whether outcomes would really differ) and assumptions (e.g., that reducing plea bargaining really is possible) that would also have to be taken into account.

The stage after issue analysis would be issue filtration: the systematic determination of the problem's importance in terms of the selection criteria. If the procedure illustrated in Figure 8-3 is used to apply rational criteria to the plea bargaining issue, there seems little doubt that the issue is of major importance. A discussion paper, presenting the basic information about the plea bargaining problem along with the conclusion about its importance, would be prepared.

The judicial council (or a subcommittee) would then make a final assessment about how to deal with the plea bargaining issue. Judgments reached on the basis of political criteria would be combined with those reached on the basis of rational criteria. Quite possibly, a decision to do nothing could be reached, because of unwillingness to tackle entrenched judicial interests, or a belief that nothing would really change as a result of reform. But let us imagine that the plea bargaining issue was submitted to the complete planning process. What would that entail? The remainder of this chapter, and the next two chapters, address that question.

ANALYZING CONDITIONS AND PROBLEMS

Once a problem has been deemed a major planning issue, the next step is to study it more exhaustively. If the problem is to be resolved, or the goal attained, the issue first must be very clearly understood. Such an understanding will be crucial to forecasting, to generating alternatives, and to estimating the consequences of alternatives.

The basic steps involved in analysis are these:

–Collecting information
–Stating the problem
–Explaining the problem

Though these steps may seem to duplicate those undertaken in the selection of planning issues, they extend earlier efforts substantially. The aim is to reach an understanding of the situation that will contribute to its improvement.

Collecting information involves gathering data about the problem, about its environment or context, about its history, and about other relevant conditions. One requires a theory of the problem in order to know what data are relevant, yet prior to analysis theory is likely to be tentative and fragmentary. It is tempting to try to collect all possible data, but this is never practical: the process would be too costly, and the data would never all be used anyway. Basically, the need is to collect information that an initial understanding of the problem indicates is relevant, and as more is learned about the problem, what is perceived as relevant information may alter.

Once most of the relevant information about the planning issue has been gathered, the problem must be stated explicitly. During issue selection, several alternative statements of the problem were developed, and one tentatively chosen on the basis of the information then available. At this point, more information should be available, and the nature of the problem may be understood differently. The problem should be restated, based on all the information now available.

When some agreement about what the problem is has been reached, the problem must be explained. How did it come about? What causes it? Why does it persist? This is by no means a simple task. It is one thing to *describe* a problem and the conditions surrounding it, and quite another to account for it, to explain *why* it is the way it is. And an important point here, of course, is that finding covariation is not the same as finding causes and effects. That is, if one finds that school truancy is highest in schools with fewer bathrooms, that does not prove that too few bathrooms causes truancy (or that truancy causes fewer bathrooms). Great care must be taken in drawing causal inferences (and policy implications) from the relationships observed among data.

Despite these difficulties, it is necessary to seek explanations for problems. Consider the theory-building process: we have notions about how things work; we compare these notions with data and make any necessary modifications; we test these adjusted notions against new data, and on and on. We may never prove that our problem is caused in the way we think, but we may become increasingly confident that our theory is correct. And make no mistake about the importance of theories: no matter how practical we are, we all operate constantly on the basis of theories about how the world

Table 8-2. The Increase in Motor Vehicle Theft in Montclair, N.J.

	1972	1973	1974	1975
Motor Vehicle Thefts Reported to the Police	79	88	128	145
Vehicles Recovered Locally	41	67	88	115
Vehicles Recovered in Other Jurisdictions	22	9	19	12
Total Local Vehicles Recovered	63	76	107	127
Vehicles Stolen From Other Jurisdictions and Recovered Locally	59	46	58	–

works. The choice is not between being theoretical or practical, but between the use of implicit or explicit theories and between untested or tested assumptions. The planner is well-advised to test rigorously and explicitly the theories and assumptions used in the identification, explanation, and resolution of problems.

An Example. A down-to-earth illustration of problem analysis is provided in a case described by Dorothy Guyot. The planning issue concerns motor vehicle theft, the perspective is that of a police agency, and the issue has been selected as worthy of some planning effort.[31] (Table and footnote numbering have been adjusted from the original.)

Table 8-2 shows the actual figures on motor vehicle theft in Montclair, New Jersey, a town of 44,000.[32]. . . The rate of the rise can be seen more clearly when the initial year of the series, 1972, is given the index number of 100 and subsequent years are calculated as increases on the initial year, much the way cost of living in creases are calculated. The planner examines how effective the department has been in diminishing the damage caused by this rising river; in other words, how many of the cars are recovered? Table 8-3 converts the raw figures into percentage of cars recovered, indicating a consistently high recovery rate and a substantial increase in recoveries made locally.

As the planner circles the problem, he asks two further questions: Is Montclair's experience part of a broad trend? And who is stealing the cars? The planner checks and finds that motor vehicle theft has barely increased nationally. The more appropriate comparison is with the rest of New Jersey, since the ease of crossing state lines contributes to high rates of vehicle theft. Since New Jersey publishes a state uniform crime report, Montclair's rise can easily be contrasted with the slight decline statewide shown in Table 8-4. The planner could obtain a more precise picture of Montclair's exceptionally rapid rise in auto theft by making comparisons with similar towns. However, this extra effort is probably not worthwhile, for the planner has already established that an unusual trend exists. The purpose of circling the problem is to state it sufficiently accurately so that its seriousness can be judged and so that solutions can be planned. The planner should proceed to questions about the seriousness of the problem, both for the victims and for those who take the cars.

The seriousness for the victim is diminished by the department's excellent recovery rate. The department strictly enforces a local ordinance forbidding overnight parking and thus

Table 8-3. An Index of Increases in Motor Vehicle Theft and Percentages of Recovery in Montclair, N.J.

	1972	1973	1974	1975
Motor Vehicle Theft Index (1972 = 100)	100	111	162	184
Percentage Recovered Locally	52	76	69	79
Percentage Recovered Elsewhere	28	10	15	8
Total Percentage Recovered	80	86	89	87

Table 8-4. Motor Vehicle Theft Rates (Per 100,000 population)

Area	1972	1973	1974	1975
Montclair	179	200	291	309
New Jersey	586	565	541	528
United States	424	440	461	469

quickly recovers abandoned vehicles. Insurance spreads the burden of loss. A telephone call to a major auto insurance company confirms that Montclair's base rate for full coverage comprehensive auto insurance has not risen in comparison with the state average, but runs about 10 percent less.

The final step in circling the problem is to discover who has been committing the auto thefts. A partial answer comes from arrest records which show that those apprehended were primarily juveniles or young adults. Another part of the answer comes from comparing local recovery rates that are averaging 70 percent with the state rate which averages 45 percent. This disparity suggests that the cars were taken by local people, presumably for transportation.The problem appears to be one of joyriding.

Now the problem statement can be made.

1. The 87 percent increase in motor vehicle theft over the last four years has been a local problem and is not reflected in state or national trends.
2. The very low rate of auto theft in1972 was less than one third the state average, and the rise has reached somewhat over half the state average.
3. The increase in auto theft has not pushed up insurance rates.
4. Apparently youths have committed the increased auto thefts.

In turning to the analysis, the planner asks, "Why has joyriding increased? Have the individuals who take cars stepped up their frequency? Has a greater proportion of the age group begun to take cars? Are there more youths these days?" The answer to the last question is a clear, "Yes".

Population trends are easy to verify through the census.[33] The 1970 figures show a bulge in the population pyramid—boys who were ages 10 to 14 then are 17–21 now. Teen-agers and youths in their early twenties are more numerous now than ever before and will continue to increase into the early 1980s and then decline. In 1961, the largest number of American babies ever was born. Now they are 16 years old.

Further, the town has a magnet attracting youths, Montclair State College. A call to the registrar reveals that since 1971 total enrollment has increased steadily from 12,400 to 15,800, about two thirds of whom are in their late teens and early twenties. Even if all 3,000 local men and women of college age were attending Montclair State, the influx about triples the number in town of this age group.

The answers to the questions of frequency and proportion are harder to find. An excellent recent study of self-report of delinquent behavior shows that total delinquent behavior changed little between 1967 and 1972.[34] Car theft, which was admitted to by about 10 percent of the 13- to 16-year-old boys, had not increased significantly except in the suburbs, which suggests that Montclair is not alone. Thus, the planner can conclude his analysis with the insight that if the police department does nothing different, car theft will continue to increase in the next few years as the number of teen-agers in town increases.

Scenario Writing

The secret to analyzing a problem, and particularly to explaining it, is clear, rigorous thinking. Some planning techniques have been developed to aid in the conceptualization and solution of problems. One of the more promising is developmental scenario writing, which seeks to construct and link together cause-and-effect sequences in order to describe a "history of the future."[35] This procedure is designed to clarify the present-state; it also aids in forecasting and in testing alternatives (see Chapters 9 and 10).

Scenario writing involves identifying key variables or events, and estimating their cause-and-effect relationships. Usually there is no attempt to completely quantify the elements of the model, however, or to engage in formal computer simulation. Rather, an attempt is made to use logic and common sense to perceive the causal sequences and their interrelationships. And it is usually *not* a solitary attempt, but a process of argument and debate among the members of a planning group or task force. The process of developing a scenario is every bit as important as the scenario itself. A planner experienced with the process reports that "scenario writing can help people clarify goals by providing them with broad theories, concepts, and information about the interaction of their organization and their context."[36]

The first step in developmental scenario writing is to create a series of causal chains—independent statements about the organization and its environment, and the relationship between them. As described by Hirschhorn, these chains consist of five components: the environment, a problematic or driving force, agency action, failure modes, and alternatives in the event of failure or further problems. He describes the components as follows:

The environment sets the overall context. The problematic is a joint product of the environment and the agency (i.e., it is the part of the environment that is most relevant to the agency's activity); the activity is produced by the agency itself. The failure modes are again joint products of the agency and its environment, and the alternatives are joint products of the agency and the environment, which might in turn lead to a new general environment.[37]

Table 8-5. Chain Chart for a Police Department

Environment	Problematic: Driving Force	Police Dept. Actions	Failure Modes	Alternatives
1. A. High unemployment	B. Increased street crime	C. More aggressive patrol	D. Lack of $ E. Low morale F. Community resentment	G. PCR approach H. Team policing I. Publicize social causes
2. A. High unemployment B. Increased crime	C. Increased demand for services	D. Directed patrol E. Managed investigations	F. Low morale G. Inadequate data H. Poor coordination I. Public resistance to priorities	J. More police K. PCR Approach L. Team policing M. Participative management
3. A. Poor city finances B. Higher pay in other agencies	C. Police labor strife D. Poor morale	E. Tighter discipline	F. Strike G. Low productivity H. High turnover	I. Participative management J. Higher pay K. More open labor relations
4. A. Few jobs for teenagers B. Public fear of youth crimes	C. Antagonism between police and kids	D. Diversion programs E. Special youth unit	F. Reduced deterrence G. Widened net H. Alienation of regular patrol personnel	I. Push for social programs J. Push for tougher juvenile code K. Generalist programs
5. A. Inflation	B. Supplies and equipment cost more	C. Conservation	D. Increased demand E. Cuts in resources F. Conservation fails	G. More resources H. New modes of service delivery
6. A. Women's movement	B. Demands that more women be hired	C. Special recruiting	D. High turnover among women E. Women fail to pass physical tests F. Pay too low to attract qualified women	G. Special training H. Lower physical standards I. Alter selection devices J. Offer special opportunities or other inducements

Causal chains are not intended as predictions but as explanations of how things currently work. Their main purpose is to expand viewpoints and to organize and clarify thinking about the planning issue, not to forecast.

Table 8-5 illustrates some causal chains. The focus of the chains is a police department. An understanding of the organization and its relationship to its environment would be needed to fully explain any planning problem and, later, to forecast, to generate alternatives and test their effects.

The second step in developmental scenario writing is to explore ways of combining the causal chains in plausible, sensible sequences of events. The chains themselves are independent statements about different facets of the planning issue or situation. In the real world, though, things are often more interrelated. If each of the chains made sense, then it ought to be instructive to combine them in various ways, searching for plausible explanations of problems and insights into their solution. One sequence constructed from five of the chains in Table 8-5 would look like this:

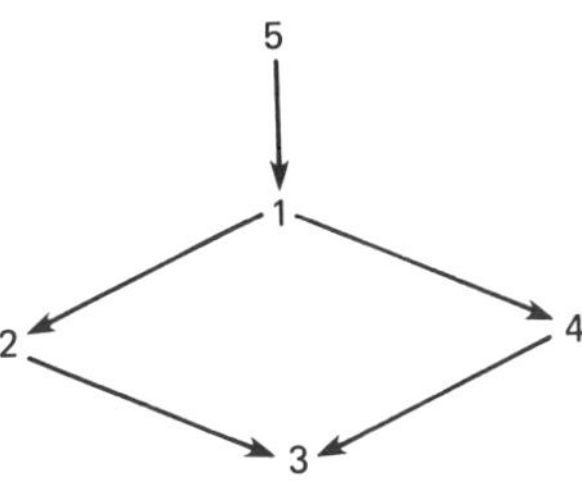

In the construction of such sequences (or "developmental trees") of causal chains, it is quite permissible to adjust characteristics in order to make the events seem more plausible. Because the scenario-writing process is intended to encourage hard and clear thinking, the components of the chains, and the chains themselves, should be juggled around into as many different combinations as possible; the best combinations will be those that provide insight and explanation, those that are surprising yet plausible.[38]

CITIZEN PARTICIPATION

Permeating the entire process of identifying goals and problems in public agencies—and, in fact, the whole planning process—is the matter of citizen participation. Clearly, criminal justice is a public concern, and citizens expect to play a major role in determining what ends are pursued and by what means.

In a recent article, James Glass has noted that although the need for citizen participation in planning is widely recognized, such participation is more often sought than achieved. He argues that there are actually a variety of reasons for seeking citizen participation, and that the appropriate techniques for achieving it depend on the particular objectives being sought. He identifies five important objectives of citizen participation (information exchange, education, support building, decision-making supplement, and representational input) and describes them:

> Information exchange may be defined as bringing planners and citizens together for the purpose of sharing ideas and concerns.
>
> Education, an extension of the information-exchange objective, refers to the dissemination of detailed information about a project, about proposed ideas, or about citizen participation itself.
>
> Support buildings would involve such activities as creating a favorable climate for proposed policies and plans or the resolution of conflict among citizen groups or between citizen groups and the government.
>
> The decision-making supplement objective refers to efforts that are designed to provide citizens an increased opportunity for input into the planning process.
>
> Representative input may be defined as an effort to identify the views of the entire community on particular issues in order to create the possibility that subsequent plans will reflect community desires.[39]

The relationship between different methods of getting citizen participation and the objectives of such participation is illustrated in Table 8-6. Information exchange is well provided through unstructured techniques such as drop-in centers, neighborhood meetings, agency information meetings, and public hearings. With these methods there is little control over what information actually is produced or who participates. Education and support building are more likely to be achieved with structured techniques such as citizen advisory committees, review boards, and task forces. With these approaches the planners have considerably more

Table 8-6. Objectives and Techniques of Citizen Participation

	Objectives			
	Information Exchange	**Education and Support Building**	**Decision-Making Supplement**	**Representational Input**
Technique Categories	**Unstructured**	**Structured**	**Active Process**	**Passive Process**
Techniques	1. Drop-in 2. Neighborhood meetings 3. Agency information meetings 4. Public hearings	1. Citizen advisory committees 2. Citizen review boards 3. Citizen task forces	1. Nominal group process 2. Analysis of judgment 3. Value analysis	1. Citizen survey 2. Delphi process

Adapted from James J. Glass, "Citizen Participation in Planning: The Relationship Between Objectives and Techniques," by permission of the *Journal of the American Planning Association* (April 1979), 183.

control over who is involved and what takes place.

Supplements to decision-making are best provided by such active process methods as nominal group process, analysis of judgment, and value analysis. These specialized techniques permit planners to gather specific information from a relatively small number of selected participants. These are termed "active" methods because planners interact in-person with the small group of citizen participants. More representative input can be attained from such passive processes as citizen surveys and the Delphi method. Though participating citizens have less opportunity to actively communicate with the planners through these methods, large numbers of citizens can be involved so that the sentiments of the entire public can be estimated.

The key point of Glass's discussion is that different techniques of citizen participation are associated with different reasons for seeking such participation. Planners, then, should first decide the kind of participation they need, and then choose an appropriate method for attaining it. In planning for criminal justice, though, many kinds of participation are needed in order to ensure that planners are responsive to the public, and that the public understands the reasoning behind policies and practices. For such a situation, Glass concludes that "if a firm commitment to citizen participation exists, what seems necessary is not the selection and implementation of one particular technique, but the development of a continuous, multifaceted system of citizen participation."[40]

For achieving citizen participation in the identification of goals and problems each of the four categories of techniques might be appropriate. Unstructured methods could give planners some rough preliminary information about what kinds of things are on people's minds. One of the structured techniques, such as a citizen advisory committee, could be used to test alternative definitions and statements of problems. Both the active- and passive-participation methods could be used to get more reliable information about goals, values, problems and priorities perceived by the public.

These techniques for achieving citizen participation would also be useful at other stages in the planning process. Expert opinion on likely future events, and public preferences regarding alternative means of attaining goals, could be important contributions to planning. At all planning stages, it is crucial to match citizen participation techniques with the objectives of such participation and the kinds of information desired.

SUMMARY

The initial stage in the planning process, the identification of goals and problems, provides the ultimate purpose and the normative framework for the planning enterprise. But goals and problems can be difficult to identify and troublesome to work with. Consequently, their identification is not a simple or straightforward undertaking, especially in an area as controversial as criminal justice.

Nevertheless, six goals (crime control, public tranquillity, justice, due process, accountability, efficiency) seem to apply to the entire criminal justice system, as well as to its policies and component agencies. They are very general goals, though. About their specific meaning, their subordinate objectives, or their order of importance, consensus is more difficult to obtain. Nevertheless, because specificity is needed to guide later planning stages (forecasting, generating and testing alternatives), clear, careful thinking about goal hierarchies is essential.

Of course, identifying goals and problems requires more than thinking by planners. The appropriate goals are presumably those of "the people," and the problems can only be found "out there" in the community. Citizen participation in identifying goals and problems is required, though there are many "publics" and rarely clear public interests.

Having somehow initially identified a goal or problem, planners must consider whether the issue deserves planning attention at all. For some kinds of goals or problems there simply might not be the time to plan; for others, the costs of planning might not be justified by the likely benefits. The decision whether or not to fully plan is based on preliminary problem analysis.

· *Chapter 8* ·
NOTES

1. Larry Hirschhorn, "Scenario Writing: A Developmental Approach," *Journal of the American Planning Association* (April 1980), 180.

2. Charles E. Lindblom, "The Science of 'Muddling Through,'" *Public Administration Review,* 19 (Spring 1959), 81; John R. Seeley, "What is Planning? Definition and Strategy," *Journal of the American Institute of Planners,* 28 (May 1962), 91-97.

3. Horst W. J. Rittel and Melvin M. Webber, "Dilemmas in a General Theory of Planning," *Policy Sciences,* 4 (1973), 169; Herbert C. Kelman and Donald P. Warwick, "The Ethics of Social Intervention: Goals, Means, and Consequences," in Bertram H. Raven, ed., *Policy Studies Review Annual* (Beverly Hills, Calif: Sage Publications, 1980), p. 52.

4. Robert C. Cushman, *Criminal Justice Planning for Local Governments* (Washington, D.C.: Law Enforcement Assistance Administration, 1980).

5. Ibid., p. 41.

6. Mark Hoffman, "Criminal Justice Planning," *ASPO Planning Advisory Service Report No. 276,* January 1972, p. 26. As footnoted in Cushman, Ibid.

7. Cushman, op. cit., pp. 41, 43.

8. T. J. Cartwright, "Problems, Solutions and Strategies: A Contribution to the Theory and Practice of Planning," *Journal of the American Institute of Planners* (May 1973), 179–87.

9. Ibid., p. 183.

10. Ibid., p. 184.

11. Gresham M. Sykes, *The Future of Crime* (Washington, D.C.: National Institute of Mental Health, U.S. Government Printing Office, 1980), p. 69.

12. Cartwright, op. cit., pp. 185–86.

13. Stuart S. Nagel, "The Means May Be A Goal," *Policy Studies Journal,* 9, Special Issue #2 (1981), 567–78.

14. Ibid., p. 568.

15. Cushman, op. cit., p. 32.

16. James P. Levine, et al., *Criminal Justice: A Public Policy Approach* (New York: Harcourt Brace Jovanovich, 1980), pp. 21–35.

17. Adapted from George A. Steiner, *Strategic Planning: What Every Manager Must Know* (New York: Free Press, 1979), pp. 149–64.

18. Ibid., p. 160.

19. Ibid., pp. 164–68.

20. Nagel, op. cit., p. 570.

21. Richard E. Klosterman, "A Public Interest Criterion," *Journal of the American Planning Association* (July 1980), 326.

22. Richard S. Bolan, "Mapping the Planning Theory Terrain," *Urban and Social Change Review,* 8 (1975), 43.

23. See American Bar Association, Section of Criminal Justice, *Comparative Analysis of Standards and Goals of the National Advisory Commission on Criminal Justice Standards and Goals with Standards for Criminal Justice of the American Bar Association* (Washington, D.C.: American Bar Association, 1974).

24. From Don Koberg and Jim Bagnall, *The*

Universal Traveler: A Soft-Systems Guide to Creativity, Problem-Solving, and the Process of Reaching Goals (Los Altos, Calif.: William Kaufman, Inc., 1972), p. 34. Copyright ©1972. All rights reserved.

25. C. Wiseman, "Selection of Major Planning Issues," *Policy Sciences,* 9 (1978), 73.

26. Ibid., pp. 75–79.

27. Ibid., pp. 79–81.

28. Ibid., pp. 82–83.

30. Ibid., pp. 83–85.

31. Dorothy Guyot, "Planning Begins with Problem Identification," *Journal of Police Science and Administration,* 5 (1977), 331–32. Reprinted by permission of the *Journal of Police Science and Administration,* copyright 1977 by Northwestern University School of Law.

32. Ibid.; data provided to Guyot by Chief James J. Reardon and Lt. John F. Haas of the Montclair Police Department.

33. Data derived by Guyot, op. cit., from the U.S. Department of Commerce, Bureau of the Census, *Census Tracts, Newark, N.J. SMSA* (Washington, D.C.; U.S. Government Printing Office, April 1972).

34. Martin Gold and David Reimer, *National Survey of Youth,* Report No. 1: *Changing Patterns of Delinquent Behavior Among Americans 13 Through 16 Years Old* (1967–1972), Institute for Social Research, University of Michigan, Ann Arbor, 1974; reprinted in *Crime and Delinquency Literature,* 7 (December 1975), 483–517; footnoted in Guyot, op. cit.

35. Hirschhorn, op. cit., pp. 172–83.

36. Hirschhorn, op. cit., p. 180.

37. Hirschhorn, op. cit., p. 177.

38. Hirschhorn, op. cit., pp. 180–81.

39. James J. Glass, "Citizen Participation in Planning: The Relationship Between Objectives and Techniques," *Journal of the American Planning Association* (April 1979), 182.

40. Ibid., p. 188.

Chapter 9

FORECASTING

The identification of goals and problems brings into focus the purposes of planning—ends to achieve or problems to resolve. It is followed by a crucial stage in the planning process: forecasting. Whenever we consider taking some action, we are considering a future act. Whether that act will have the effects we intend depends, in part, on whether we have correctly imagined the future context in which it will be carried out. Imagining that future context is forecasting.

The first section of this chapter provides some general information about forecasting and its role in planning. The second section examines five basic forecasting methods. In the next section, an examination of some recent and very useful evidence on the strengths and weaknesses of the various forecasting methods forms the basis for some fairly specific and confident recommendations about when to use what methods. The final two sections discuss general futures studies, and some speculations about the future of crime and criminal justice.

FORECASTING AND PLANNING

"It is a commonly stated truism that everyone makes forecasts," wrote William Ascher recently. "Every deliberate action, from the pettiest to the most significant, rests on the actor's expectations of the results of his action."[1] When considering which job to take, which car to buy, or which pair of shoes to wear, one is considering, in part, the future effects of the choice.

Considering future effects of choices (the consequences of each of the possible alternatives) represents only one aspect of forecasting, the aspect known as the testing of alternatives (see Chapter 10). But forecasting has other aspects, too. For example, one may want to forecast goals and values, in order to know what aims will be cherished at some point in the future, what means will be valued above others, what characteristics will be associated with "the good life," or simply what the public will like and dislike. Problem-oriented forecasting, on the other hand, is an attempt to anticipate major crises and problems—and, thus, possibly to prevent them or at least to prepare an appropriate reaction to them.

The kind of forecasting that will be the focus of this discussion might be termed *contextual.* When a goal to be achieved or a problem to be solved has been identified, various alternatives have to be considered and the likely consequences of each determined. Information is therefore needed about the context or situation in which the alternatives will *actually be implemented*. What will be the values of key variables?

Suppose, for example, that the problem identified is a high turnover among correctional guards at a particular prison. A number of possible solutions might be under consideration: higher pay, more predictive selection tests, increased promotional opportunities, restructuring of the job, and so on. If the lasting effects of these alternatives are to be estimated, some information on relevant future conditions in the prison and in its environment is needed. What will the physical structure of the prison be like? What will the inmates be like? What resources will the prison have at its disposal? What activities will be mandated by law, binding standards, union agreements, or court order? What will supply (the manpower pool from which the prison must recruit) be like? What will demand (the competition from other employers) be like? What will the community (as a place to live, as a source of employees, as a source of other support) within which the prison is located be like?

Why worry about such questions? Because planned actions take effect in the future. Between now and then, important things may change. Change is a dominant characteristic of the modern world and, as David Ewing has pointed out, "almost every organization in a changing world must take forecasts and use them in its planning."[2]

Lots of planning is done without any real forecasting, of course. In such instances, those doing the planning are implicitly predicting that the future will be the same as the present, or that any differences will be so minor as to not matter. Making such assumptions is sometimes not disastrous, but always dangerous. There is really no excuse for not thinking about the future context and then designing and choosing alternatives accordingly.

Some people equate (or confuse) the terms *forecasting* and *planning*. Ewing argues forcefully that "planning is not forecasting," that forecasting is often a part of the planning process.[3] The distinction between the two activities is emphasized by J. Scott Armstrong, who suggests that "forecasting is concerned with determining what the future *will* look like, rather than what it *should* look like. The latter is the job of planning."[4] He goes on to say that "the forecast is an input to the planning model. The forecasting model can be used to try to find out what the world will look like if you leave it alone . . . or what the world will be like if you make different assumptions about the future . . . or what the world will look like if you make changes."[5]

By providing information about what the future will look like, forecasting seeks to reduce the uncertainity always involved in decision-making. The task is not always a simple one, however, as Sylvan and Thorson note:

> Forecasts are made in part to reduce uncertainty about the future. This is a relevant observation since if there were no uncertainty as to the future there would be no need for forecasts. But this suggests a rather basic dilemma. Forecasts are most needed in precisely those situations in which they are most likely to be wrong; those areas in which uncertainty is highest. As an example, weather forecasters are much more important (in general) in Minnesota than in Hawaii. They are also more likely to be wrong in Minnesota.[6]

The fallibility of forecasts is certainly an important consideration. The future is never really knowable. Ascher has pointed out that "of all the information used by policymakers, projections are the least rooted in discoverable facts."[7] The plausibility of forecasts used as inputs to the planning process needs to be carefully assessed. After reviewing numerous unpredictable developments in American business and industry, David Ewing concluded by recommending "great humility on the part of decision makers who would try to outline the shape of things to come so clearly and accurately that they can justify choosing a precise strategy for the organization on the basis of this information."[8] It is hard to imagine a better recommendation for criminal justice forecasters and planners than humility.

There is another very important sense in which forecasts are not definitive. Although forecasts are concerned with determining what the future will be like, the desire for this information is not disinterested. Planning is, in fact, an attempt to change the world in intended ways, an attempt to intervene and affect the future. Forecasting and futurology, writes Gresham Sykes, are "best thought of not as the study of the inevitable course of society in the decades to come but as the construction of a chart upon which the course has yet to be drawn."[9] The task of planning is to help draw the course. As part of planning, forecasting helps provide the chart on which the journey will be taken.

FORECASTING METHODS

There are at least as many aspects of the future as there are of the present and, as one might expect, there are quite a few varieties of forecasting. Fowles, for example, speaks of social forecasting, which is "concerned with the most sweeping and ineluctable features of sociocultural change."[10] Ascher's recent appraisal considered the narrower categories of population, economic, energy, transportation, and technological forecasting.[11] Just as there are substantive varieties of planning for each and every facet of society, so too are there numerous types of forecasting.

Other distinctions among varieties of forecasting can be made. Sylvan and Thorson distinguish between mere intuition about the future and "scientific" forecasts, which they define as "statements about future events which are based upon assumptions which are either explicit or able to be determined."[12] Similarly, Ascher focused his appraisal on "distinct, explicit forecasting efforts made available to decision-makers by people of specialized expertise," rather than on the everyday sort of forecasting in which everyone engages.[13] The length of time over which predictions are to be made also distinguishes types of forecasting. In particular, long-range forecasting (much like long-range planning) is often regarded as involving more difficulties and more uncertainty than short-range forecasting. Armstrong, struggling to define *long-range*, suggested that "it is the length of time over which large changes in the environment may be expected to occur."[14] Thus, the actual time-span qualifying as long-range would vary from one context to another.

Different varieties of forecasting may require different methods. There are five general methods of forecasting, ranging from simple to very sophisticated, from subjective to objective, from qualitative to very quantitative and mathematical, from a priori to empirical. Whereas political and communicative skills are involved in identifying goals and problems, and imagination and creativity are required to design alternatives, some forecasting methods require considerable analytical and statistical competence.[15] The ability to reason clearly is probably even more important, however, and the "simpler" forecasting methods frequently outperform more complex ones.

Judgmental Methods[16]

Judgmental forecasting methods are subjective, in that few, if any, specific rules or procedures are explicitly used in making predictions about the future. "Judges" of some kind are asked to draw upon their expertise, experience, insights, or intuition in order to make judgments about future conditions. But although the *method* of reaching predictions is subjective, completely quantified data may be used as part of the process. For example, ten criminological experts might be supplied with historical data on crime, population, economic conditions, and other social factors, and then simply asked to predict crime levels for the next twenty years. The experts would be free to take into account any information they believed relevant, and to use that data in any manner they thought reasonable. This would represent a judgmental, subjective method, even though objective data might be used.

Two important categories of judgmental forecasting focus on intentions and on opinions: the former concerns what judges "intend to do"; the latter, what judges presumably "know something about." Judgments and forecasts of intentions are often overlooked in planning, but could have some very useful applications, particularly in an interdependent and fragmented system such as criminal justice. For example, corrections officials might want to periodically gather information from trial court judges on their sentencing intentions, in order to forecast probation caseloads and prison inmate populations. Similarly, state-level police training commissions might be interested in the hiring and promotion intentions of police department administrators, so that the demand for training programs could be forecast. Here are some of the general conditions that make intentions data useful and meaningful:

1. The intended event should be important.
2. Responses can be obtained from those with the intentions.
3. The respondent must act intentionally.
4. The respondent must report correctly.
5. The respondent must be able to carry out the act.
6. The respondent's action must not be too easily altered by new information.[17]

The focus on opinions in judgmental forecasting is probably more common than the focus on intentions. It is certainly easier, in many situations, to elicit opinions than to elicit expressions of intentions. Asking criminologists to predict future crime levels would be, in effect, asking them for their opinions. It would be difficult, although perhaps not impossible, in forecasting crime levels to meet the six general conditions that would make intentions data useful. (One would have to identify those with criminal intentions, obtain their responses, assume that they were not influenced by the questions, and so on).

Several problems arise out of the subjectivity of judgmental forecasting, particularly when opinion data are used. Basically, they arise from the fallibility of human judgment. Many of the types and sources of bias are readily recognizable—selective perception, conservatism, habit, social pressure, wishful thinking, probability errors, and logical fallacies are only a few examples.[18] Bias has the effect of introducing error in judgmental forecasts. The problem is complicated by the fact that when judges are informed of their errors and biases, their forecasts improve hardly at all. So any judgmental forecast must be viewed with a certain amount of skepticism.

There are several specific methods of obtaining judgmental forecasts: surveys, the Delphi technique, traditional meetings, structured meetings, scenario writing, and role playing. (These judgmental forecasting methods correspond with the techniques, noted in Chapter 8, for getting citizen participation. The reason for the similarity is simple: in both instances an attempt is made to gather information from people about what they think.) The most common of the methods, and probably the least effective, is to gather a number of experts and hold a traditional meeting. The criteria relevant for evaluating the different judgmental methods are summarized in Table 9-1. Space does not permit detailed discussions of the various methods, but these can be found in the literature.[19]

An Example. In a study reported in 1974, Terry Cooper used the Delphi method to make a long-range forecast of police issues and values.[20] The Delphi method is basically a multiround survey of expert opinion, with anonymous feedback. In this instance, a panel of educators, police administrators, and other experts was selected for an open-ended three-item questionnaire that probed their opinions about recent and future significant trends in police attitudes and values. The responses to these open-ended questions were then reduced to 164 statements about past and future trends. A closed-ended questionnaire was developed that asked for agreement or disagreement with the statements, and an estimate of the probability of their coming true; it was administered to the same panel of experts, as well as to a group of veteran police officers. The responses to the second-round survey were compiled, and respondents were again sent the closed-ended questionnaire, along with information about average responses and distribution of responses to each item. In this way, respondents could compare their responses to those of other experts, and had the opportunity to maintain or to change their original opinions.

At the conclusion of this process, Cooper attained what he regarded as "substantial consensus" on well over half the items. His findings are too lengthy to fully report here, except for three future-trend items and one of his conclusions:

	Percentage of Agreement	
	Panel A	*Panel B*
Younger policemen who have perfected their education and training will begin to replace the "old guard" and their more traditional approach to law enforcement.	92%	98%
Emphasis on productivity and efficiency due to rising costs will continue to be important to law enforcement administrators.	96%	87%
Police unions will become increasingly involved in the political arena and will adopt an "antiliberal" posture.	77%	74%

It is possible to envision a situation in which the future shape of law enforcement teeters precariously between a trend toward professionalization, on the one hand, which could be encouraged by substantially increased salaries, a larger role in decision-making and increased social status, and a trend toward unionization, on the other, fed by continued social alienation, undiscriminating public demands for tax reduction and cost cutting, and resistance by short-sighted, efficiency-oriented police leadership to the granting of substantial rewards and recognition for becoming "professionalized."[21]

These forecasts and Cooper's conclusion were made in 1974; nearly a decade later, they seem quite on the mark.

Extrapolation Methods

Extrapolation methods of forecasting are objective and naïve. They are objective in that there are firm rules to follow in using data to make predictions about the future. They are naïve in that no attempt is made to explain why things change as they do, or what causes or is associated with changes in the phenomenon of interest. Instead, the trend of the phenomenon (gross national product, automobile sales, crime rates, or whatever) is simply extended into the future.

Table 9-1. Strengths and Weaknesses of Judgmental Forecasting Methods
(1 = least favorable, 5 = most favorable, n.a. = not applicable)

Method	Cost	Speed	Situation Involves Interaction Among Conflicting Parties Plus High Uncertainty	Questions Cannot Be Well Defined	Sampling Error Is Important	Nonresponse Error Is Important	Judges Are Concerned About Evaluation of Their Responses
Personal Interview	3	4	1	4	5	5	2
Telephone Interview	5	5	1	3	3	3	2
Mail Questionnaire	5	2	1	1	4	4	4
Delphi	4	2	2	2	4	4	4
Traditional Meeting	1	5	2	3	1	n.a.	1
Structured Meeting	2	4	2	5	1	n.a.	3
Group Depth Interview	2	3	4	4	2	n.a.	2
Role Playing	2	3	5	3	2	n.a.	5

Adapted from J. Scott Armstrong, *Long-Range Forecasting: From Crystal Ball to Computer* (New York: John Wiley & Sons, Inc., 1978), p. 122, with permission of the publisher.

An important initial consideration is that extrapolation should make sense. For example, a police department probably would be misled if it extrapolated work load data for June, July, and August to forecast demands for the rest of the year: seasonality should be taken into consideration. For extrapolation to be valid, the system surrounding the phenomenon to be forecast must be reasonably stable. For example, it would not make a great deal of sense to forecast consumption of coal by simply extrapolating historical trends without taking into account trends in the availability and use of other sources of energy. Extrapolating coal consumption naïvely in 1900 would have produced incredible overestimates of coal consumption in this century: coal consumption was affected by increases in the use of petroleum and of hydroelectric and nuclear power.[22]

"The basic strategy of extrapolation is to find data that are representative of the event to be forecast," writes Armstrong. "The assumption is made that the future event will conform to these data."[23] This assumption is important and must be carefully examined. It is often reasonably valid, though. When the assumption can be made, the extrapolation of historical, comparative, or simulated data can provide quite accurate forecasts, especially of the short-range future.

Several techniques may be used in extrapolating longitudinal data. If the data are plotted along a time line, it may be satisfactory simply to "eyeball" the trend and extend it. Figure 9-1, for example, shows ten years of data for Part I (most serious) and Part II (less serious) crimes and miscellaneous police calls for service in Pontiac, Michigan.[24] The trends for all three phenomena seem fairly steady, and especially for short-range forecasting it might be reasonable to make rough extrapolations by hand, as shown in Figure 9-1. Such rough forecasts might be useful for budget requests, grant applications, or internal planning for the allocation and utilization of resources. Forecasts could also be made of the range of probable values in order to identify the set of conditions for which contingency plans would be needed.

"Eyeball" extrapolation is largely a subjective exercise, however, and it is usually better to apply some specific rules when extending historical data. These rules and techniques provide guidance on how to weigh recent as compared to distant data points, what to do with extreme events (out-liers) that probably are not part of any trend, how to extrapolate data that "jump around" a lot, and for other problem situations frequently encountered. The techniques that are often used include Markov chains, exponential smoothing, moving averages, the Box-Jenkins method, curve-and cycle-fitting, and regression (with time as the independent variable).[25] All these methods require mathematical manipulation of the data; moving averages is probably the simplest technique to understand. The strengths and weaknesses of the four most common extrapolation methods are presented in Table 9-2.

An Example. Chiu and Chang recently reported on the use of extrapolation methods to forecast calls for police service in Seattle.[26] Using both the exponential smoothing and Box-Jenkins methods, they sought to forecast calls in order to aid in police operational planning. They first collected historical data for sixty-five four-week periods from 1970 through 1974 (four-week periods standardize the number of days, weekdays, and weekends, and are thus often used instead of months). Using these data and using both methods, they projected calls for service two years into the future (twenty-six four-week periods). They examined the fit achieved by each method to the historical data, and also the accuracy of the forecasts produced by each. Overall, they found that the less complicated exponential smoothing method yielded better results than the Box-Jenkins method. For the fourteen forecast periods for which data were available at the time they wrote their report, the average percentage error of their forecasts was only about 3.5 per cent. They noted that errors of this magnitude were "considered acceptable to the operations personnel in the Seattle Police Department."[27]

Econometric Methods

The econometric method of forecasting is objective, causal, and linear. It is objective because firm rules are followed in producing the forecasts from data (the data are also ordinarily objective). Econometric forecasting is causal because independent variables are used to predict the values of the phenomenon of interest. These independent variables are selected on the basis of their theoretical or empirical relationship with the dependent variable, such

Figure 9-1. Reported Part I and Part II Crimes and Miscellaneous Calls for Service, Pontiac, Mich., 1968-77 with Simple "Eyeball" Forecasts (Adapted from Gary W. Cordner, et al., *The Pontiac Integrated Criminal Apprehension Project: A Final Evaluation Report*, School of Criminal Justice, Michigan State University, East Lansing, Mich., 1979, p. 95.)

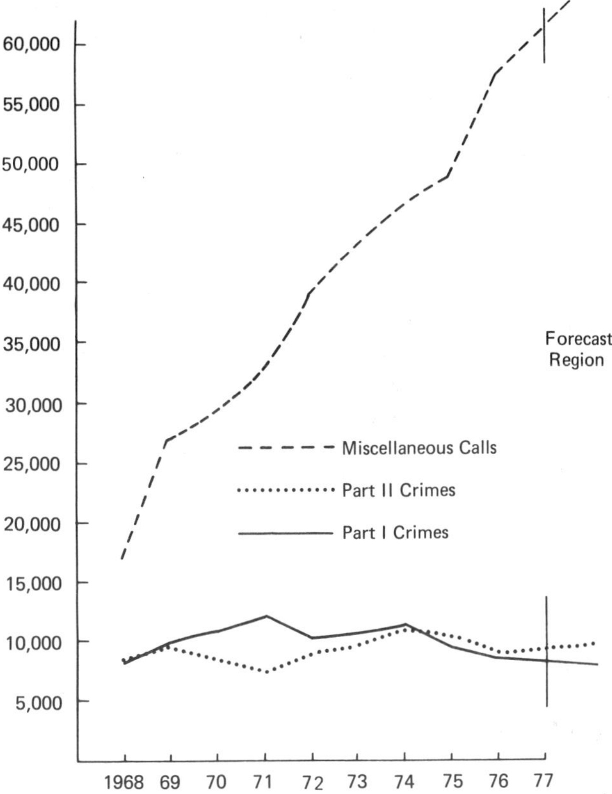

that changes in the former are believed to cause or at least to predict changes in the latter. This method is linear because "linear combinations" of the independent variables are used in making predictions about values of the dependent variable.

There are three general forecasting conditions that tend to favor the use of econometric

Table 9-2. Strengths and Weaknesses of Four Common Extrapolation Methods (1 = best ranking)

			Forecast Accuracy	
	Cost	Understandability	Short-Range	Long-Range
Exponential smoothing	1	2.5	2.5	1.5
Moving averages	2	1.0	2.5	1.5
Box-Jenkins	4	4.0	2.5	4.0
Regressions	3	2.5	2.5	3.0

Adapted from J. Scott Armstrong, *Long-Range Forecasting: From Crystal Ball to Computer* (New York: John Wiley & Sons, Inc., 1978), p. 161, with permission of the publisher.

methods.[28] First, information on causal relationships must be available; the forecaster must be able to identify one or more independent variables that have some predictive value. Second, the situation must involve substantial change in the variables (if only small changes are expected, extrapolation is a much simpler and probably more accurate method). Third, the forecaster must be able to predict reasonably well the changes that will occur in the independent variables, as these values are needed to forecast the dependent variable, which is the real interest. For example, it would be of little use to use automobile sales and new housing starts to forecast general economic conditions, if such sales and starts could not themselves be predicted with any accuracy. Nor would it help the owner of a baseball team to forecast attendance on the basis of the team's won-loss record and the weather, if neither team success or the weather could be accurately predicted.

The basic issues involved in econometric forecasting concern selecting the variables to be used, and figuring out how to use them in generating the forecast. The best guide to selection of variables is good theory; previous studies, expert advice, experience, and common sense are also useful. Probably the worst approach is crass empiricism, in which one collects data on *every*thing and then selects predictors simply on the basis of correlation coefficients or regression weights. The folly of this approach was vividly demonstrated by a study in which it was found that, using data from the *Historical Statistics for the United States*, "for a randomly selected series of twenty-five years, it was usually possible to explain 50 per cent of the variance by regressing the series against two to six other randomly selected time series."[29] This clearly illustrates that theoretical, rather than empirical, considerations should dominate the selection of predictor variables for econometric forecasting.

Once predictor or independent variables have been selected, what is done with them? If there are more than one independent variable, they must be combined. The most common approaches are to add them or multiply them—and the choice should depend on theory. It must also be decided whether the independent variables are equally important—if not, they might be assigned different weights reflecting their relative importance. Probably the dominant approach to the combination and weighting questions is regression analysis. Independent variables are usually additively combined, and regression weights are computed for each variable in order to minimize errors in fitting the historical data. This "best fit" equation for the historical data could then be used to forecast, by first predicting future values of the independent variables and then using them in the equation to compute the forecast value.[30]

Less sophisticated methods may also be employed in the use of causal variables for predicting a dependent phenomenon. For example, in predicting whether a crime will be solved, one might simply take note of the presence or absence of, say, ten different kinds of evidence. Previous analysis of crime investigation might have led to the belief that at least three pieces or kinds of evidence must be available at the time of initial reporting, for a favorable investigative outcome to be likely. One could then predict whether the crime would be solved based on whether at least three kinds of evidence were reported following the patrol officer's preliminary investigation. Though crude (especially as equal weight would be being given to different kinds of evidence, ranging from partial fingerprints to eyewitness identifications), a simple prediction scheme such as this one might prove fairly accurate. It might be improved by applying some rough weights based on experience and judgment, to account for gross differences in the utility of the types of evidence.

An Example. Nowhere in criminal justice is prediction a more explicit and pervasive undertaking than in decisions concerning parole. When prison inmates become eligible for parole, the crucial criterion is often a prediction about their likelihood of rearrest, reconviction, recidivism, or return to criminal behavior. Such predictions may be made purely judgmentally, but it is also common to use econometric methods. One such approach was reported by Daniel Glaser in 1954.[31]

The importance of Glaser's article lies in his use of theory to identify predictor variables. Whereas earlier parole prediction studies had tended to rely on whatever quantifiable data were available in prison files, Glaser developed hypotheses about parole experience, adapting Sutherland's differential association theory to the parole situation.[32] As a result, he was able to identify a priori a small set of factors theoretically linked to success or failure on parole. He then chose operational variables that represented his theoretical factors, and examined the empirical relationships between the variables and rates of parole violation. (His predictor variables were as follows: age at first leaving home; social development pattern; work record; most serious previous sentence; total criminal record; schooling; and use of prison time.) In order to develop weights for his variables, he first calculated their prediction efficiency, using the mean cost rating measure,[33] and later transformed these coefficients to a five-unit weighting scale. He reported very small prediction error when applying his scheme to the historical data.

Later parole prediction studies have often used multiple regression or other multivariate statistical techniques to help in the choice of predictor variables and/or the assignment of weights. Interestingly enough, however, the use of such sophisticated techniques does not always increase either explanatory or predictive power. In an English study, for example, Frances Simon found that multiple regression, a "deviance score" computed similar to Glaser's method, and probation officers' judgments of "delinquent tendencies" performed equally well in predicting probation failure (defined as reconviction within one-year and three-year periods).[34]

Segmentation Methods

Segmentation methods of forecasting can be either objective or subjective, naïve or causal. They can incorporate judgmental, extrapolative, or econometric methods in their forecasting. The defining characteristic of these methods is that separate subsets of the population are expected to act differently, and an attempt is made to forecast for each of these subsets, rather than for the population as a whole. In the parole prediction situation, for example, separate prediction equations might be calculated for drug offenders and nondrug offenders, or for married and unmarried offenders, or even for married drug offenders, unmarried drug offenders, married nondrug offenders, and unmarried nondrug offenders.[35] By forecasting for subsets such as these, problems of nonlinearity and interaction among variables that plague econometric methods can more easily be dealt with. Causal priorities can also be ordered, providing another advantage over many traditional econometric methods.[36]

An important consideration in using segmentation methods is the extent of interaction between segments. If the segments are independent, that is, if behavior in one does not affect behavior in another, then the strategy is to forecast separately for each segment, and then to sum the forecasts for an overall prediction, if that is desired. The parole prediction situation suggests independence of segments—the parole success or failure of married drug offenders would not be expected to appreciably affect that of unmarried nondrug offenders, and so on. When segments are dependent, however, forecasting becomes more complicated. Rather than separate forecasts for each segment, simultaneous equations or formal simulation models might be used to capture the interactions between segments. For segmented economic forecasting, for example, extremely complex models of the interactions between components of the economy are often used, and the outcome of the forecasts is even more determined by model specification than usual.[37]

The crucial decision involved in segmentation methods is the choice of segments. Several sophisticated analytical techniques are available for identifying segments on the basis of empirical relationships, including cluster analysis and factor analysis. As in the choice of variables for use in econometric forecasting, however, it is strongly recommended that a priori and theoretical information be used as the primary guides for the definition of segments. It is more appropriate and generally more effective to use observed relationships in the data to check and adjust theory and judgment, rather than vice versa. This is true for research in general, and for forecasting in particular.[38]

An Example. Another parole prediction study provides a good example of independent segmentation.[39] Sampson first used stepwise multiple regression for an entire sample of 200 releases from the Florida Division of Corrections. This data-driven approach selected three predictor variables (race, bad influences in the home, and whether the current term was being served for parole violation) that together best accounted for the success or failure of a parolee within two years of release. For the total sample, this prediction equation accounted for only about 10 per cent of the variance in success or failure. Sampson then used cluster analysis to segment the sample, and identified one homogenous group of forty-eight releases. He then repeated his stepwise regression analysis for just this segment, and found three different predictor variables most powerful: I.Q., length of sentence, and size of immediate family. This prediction equation accounted for 45 per cent of the variance in the segment. This is a good illustration of how forecasting may be improved by segmentation, although the purely empirical approach to variable selection and segment identification is not recommended.

Another Example. Dependent segmentation often takes the form of simulation modeling in which the decision-making processes and workflows of a system are examined and described in order to construct a model of the real-world phenomenon. To the extent that the model is accurate, it may be used to predict the consequences of various alternative practices or policies, or simply to forecast future conditions should everything remain the same. A number of criminal justice models are in common use, including the JUSSIM simulation of the entire criminal justice system, and several models of police patrol allocation and deployment.[40]

One application of modeling sought to specify arrest, court disposition, and recidivism rates for the District of Columbia.[41] These were viewed as interacting segments in a model that sought to predict inmate populations. The rationale for this approach was stated by Stollmack:

> The most common method for predicting incarcerated populations appears to be extrapolation of linear trends determined by linear regression techniques. This model relies totally on past data of the number incarcerated and is of little use in predicting the effects of recent changes in arrest rates, court policy, release policy, etc. In fact, total reliance on linear regression is a tacit admission that we know nothing about the process which creates the phenomenon—in this case, incarcerations. The models we are concerned with here describe the result in terms of other observable phenomena which in turn may be predicted, based on either "linear extrapolation of past trends" or other descriptive models.[42]

The linear regression referred to by Stollmack would be that using time as the independent variable, rather than regression in the econometric sense, with true causal variables.

The model that was developed took the basic case-flow (or input-output) approach. The number of arrests specified the initial magnitude of the case flow, along with parole violations. The paths taken by cases after arrest were investigated and mathematically represented. A recidivism probability was also incorporated which, along with rates of population and arrests, helped to determine changes in system input. The result was a formal, mathematical representation of actual case flow and decision-making, which was then used for forecasting purposes. It is interesting that Stollmack suggested modeling subsets of the population (by sex, age, and so on) as a next step in refining his forecasting model. In effect, he was arguing for independent as well as dependent segmentation.

Bootstrapping

The bootstrapping method of forecasting is essentially an attempt to "objectify" more subjective approaches to forecasting. This is done by making explicit the decision-making processes used by judges—to create, in effect, a model of the judge. This would not seem a noteworthy method, except that such models consistently outperform the judges themselves in terms of forecast accuracy. One explanation for how this can be so is offered by Armstrong:

> The decision maker thinks that he knows how to make the forecasts, and he wants things done his way: in fact, his inputs are used to do this. The objective model does the repetitive work by applying the judge's rules without getting tired or irritable. This consistency seems to outweigh the losses that occur in going from a complex judgmental method to a simple objective method.[43]

The two basic approaches to bootstrapping are inductive and deductive. The inductive method uses the evidence of the judge's past decisions and forecasts to identify causal variables that account for these past actions, often by way of a regression model. The model can then be used to predict future decisions or forecasts of the judge, using the same general techniques as in econometric forecasting. The deductive approach, by contrast, seeks information directly from the judge about the rules that are used in making decisions or forecasts. To the extent that these rules can be identified and communicated, a model of the judge may be easy to create.

An Example. A very interesting illustration of bootstrapping, mainly of the deductive variety, was provided by Kort in 1957.[44] He examined the opinions in twelve U.S. Supreme Court right-to-counsel cases, and identified the "pivotal factors" cited by the justices themselves. Through a somewhat involved mathematical process, he calculated values for each of these factors, based on their apparent importance in the twelve cases. He was able to show that those of the twelve cases scoring above a certain mark had all been ruled in favor of the original defendant, while those below the mark had all been decided against the original defendant. Then he used his scoring method to predict the outcomes of twelve subsequent right-to-counsel cases. These cases had already been decided by the Supreme Court, but they had not been used by Kort in his model. His predictions were correct for all twelve cases in the validation sample. He concluded as follows:

> The results indicate that the Court has been willing to tolerate factors detrimental to the interests of the defendant in state criminal proceedings to a certain critical point, located within the zone separating the numerical ranges of the composite values here identified. Beyond that critical point, the Court has invalidated the state criminal proceeding as deficient in the essentials of a "fair trial." It should not be inherently surprising that a gradually changing group of justices, acting over the years in an instititutional as well as an intellectual tradition, should, when confronted with the necessity of saying yes or no in the presence of a complex body of competing considerations that are individually recurrent, behave according to statistical regularities of which they are unaware, and which they may . . . emphatically disavow.[45]

It seems unlikely that, before actually voting, any of the Supreme Court justices could have predicted the outcomes of the twelve cases as accurately as this model did. Certainly none could have done any better, and it seems highly probable that many would have done worse.[46]

CHOOSING A FORECASTING METHOD

The choice of a forecasting method is a relative, rather than an absolute, question.[47] The methods discussed thus far have strengths and weak-

Table 9-3. Costs and Benefits of Forecasting Methods
(5 – most favorable rating)

	Costs			Benefits		
Method	*Development*	*Maintenance*	*Operation*	*Uncertainty*	*Alt. Futures*	*Learning*
Judgmental						
Intentions	3	4	1	3	3	1
Opinions	4	4	3	3	3	2
Delphi	3	4	2	3	3	2
Traditional Meeting	5	5	2	2	2	2
Structured Meeting	4	4	2	2	3	2
Group Depth Interview	4	4	2	1	4	1
Role Playing	3	4	2	2	5	1
Extrapolation	3	4	5	3	1	1
Econometric						
A priori	3	4	4	3	4	3
Updated	2	3	4	5	5	5
Segmentation						
Independent	1	2	4	4	4	4
Input-output	1	2	3	3	4	3
Simulation	2	3	3	3	4	3
Bootstrapping	3	4	4	3	4	3

Adapted from J. Scott Armstrong, *Long-Range Forecasting: From Crystal Ball to Computer* (New York: John Wiley & Sons, Inc., 1978), p. 339, with permission of the publisher. The ratings may be compared only within columns (e.g., a 4 on alternative futures is not related to a 4 on maintenance costs).

nesses in terms of costs, data requirements, complexity, accuracy, and other characteristics. Although in any particular situation one method, on the whole, is preferable, the choice may not always be clear. Certainly the choice must always depend on the situation.

Information on the relative costs and benefits of the various forecasting methods is summarized in Table 9-3. As one might expect, some of the methods offering greater benefits are also more costly. On the other hand, the most sophisticated and costly forecasting methods often have produced no better predictions than much simpler and cheaper meth-

Figure 9-2. Guide for Selecting Methods on the Basis of Forecast Accuracy (Adapted from J. Scott Armstrong, *Long-Range Forecasting: From Crystal Ball to Computer* [New York: John Wiley & Sons, Inc., 1978], p. 388, with permission of the publisher.

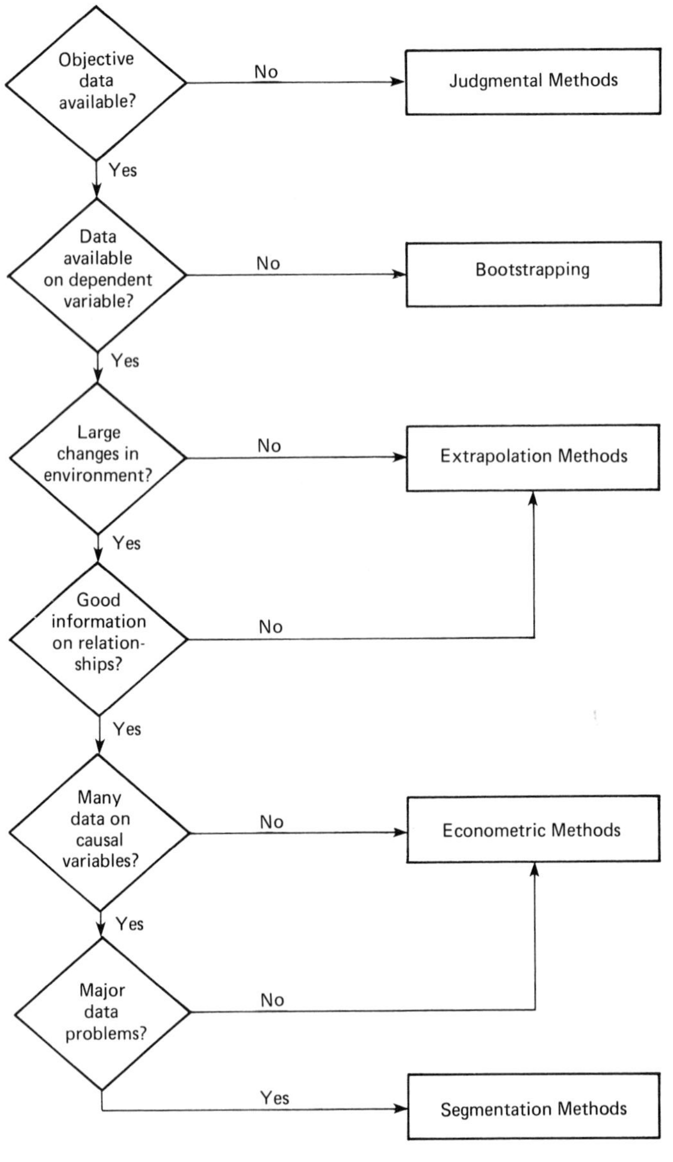

ods, partly because sophisticated methods are frequently used with grossly inadequate data, thus undermining their promise.[48]

A guide to selecting the appropriate forecasting method is presented in Figure 9-2. Although other factors (such as those in Table 9-3) must be taken into consideration, the advice presented is very useful, and summarizes the careful evaluation of forecasting methods undertaken by J. Scott Armstrong.[49] As progressively more information is available in forecasting situations, more objective and sophisticated methods are generally recommended. Even the most complex methods, using appropriate data, are no better, however, than the theory, common sense, and basic assumptions underlying them. In his appraisal of forecasting in several fields, Ascher found that faulty assumptions caused the greatest inaccuracies.[50] He used the term *assumption drag* to describe the common situation in which forecasts continued to be based on unexamined and clearly outdated premises. No forecasting method, simple or complex, can overcome such fundamental sources of error and bias.

A strongly suggested practice in significant forecasting situations is the utilization of multiple methods. This entails additional cost, but the benefits may be substantial. If separate forecasts can be made using several methods, a consensus—or at least a range of likely outcomes—can be identified, and more confidence may be justified. This is particularly true if the forecasts really are independent, and not based on common assumptions.

A final consideration in the choice of forecasting methods and in the evaluation of forecasts is the range of the prediction (see Figure 9-2: the question "large changes in environment?"). In general, less sophisticated methods work better in short-range forecasting; more complex ones, in long-range forecasting. This assumes, of course, that the long-range forecasting attempted with sophisticated methods is done carefully, with adequate data and explicit, up-to-date assumptions. The overall experience, Ascher found, was that "the time horizon of the forecast is the most important factor: the more distant the forecast target date, the less accurate the forecast is expected to be."[51] So one must be very skeptical of any long-range forecasts, and whenever possible use multiple methods and regularly revise the forecasts in the light of new information.

GENERAL FUTURES STUDIES

This discussion of forecasting methods has focused primarily on fairly narrow predictions. Though narrow, these kinds of forecasts are often of crucial importance in planning. The extrapolation of calls for police service, for example, would be very helpful in police strategic and operational planning. The police agency would have forecasts of its work load on which it could base resource needs and the design of activities. Similarly, the use of dependent segmentation to forecast inmate populations would be of obvious utility in correctional planning.

Another form of forecasting is general futures studies. These are attempts to describe the broader features of future society, as opposed to the prediction of the specific values of one or a few variables. Futures studies are concerned with "the larger context within which volition may be exerted and alternatives effected, if desired."[52] They seek to map the unfolding landscape upon which the future will be discovered and shaped. Beyond providing information about what the terrain will probably look like, studying the future is valuable in that "we are encouraged to think explicitly and systematically about the range of future possibilities."[53] That is, thinking about what the future *will* be also encourages thinking about what it *could* and *should* be.

Futures studies are, for the most part, wide-ranging versions of judgmental forecasting. One of the most popular approaches is scenario-writing.[54] Using approaches similar to those described in Chapter 8, experts write stories about the future in which the logical implications of current and foreseeable trends are spun out to their conclusions. Obviously, a great deal of subjective judgment is involved. As in most scenario-writing, the success of the effort is primarily gauged by the plausibility, but yet surprising nature, of the future events and conditions that are described. If the forecasts are not viewed as plausible, it is unlikely that planners or decision makers will take any action in response to them. If the forecasts are not surprising, the general reaction will be, "We already knew that," or, "So what?"[55]

The Delphi method is often used in broad efforts to describe the future.[56] Whereas scenarios are sometimes the product of one person or a very few people, the Delphi method uses a large number of experts to forecast. As has been described, the method involves several stages, and allows the experts first to offer their judgments independently, and then to alter their views according to the responses of others. The Delphi study of police attitudes and values, already discussed, was rather broad, and there would seem to be no limit to the specificity or generality of forecasts that could be obtained with this method. Of course, the accuracy of the forecasts might vary, particularly as the breadth of the forecast begins to exceed the real expertise of the participants.

Jib Fowles has drawn an interesting distinction between two approaches to general futures studies that transcends the question of method.[57] One basic approach is to forecast the characteristics of the system; the other is to forecast the characteristics of its elements (this is somewhat analogous to segmentation). In social forecasting, Fowles's particular interest, this means predicting the behavior of the social system, as opposed to predicting individual behavior. Studies of the latter type have focused on the changing images, values, aspirations, and needs of individuals, as the basis for predicting where society is heading. This approach is heavily psychological, obviously. The contrasting approach, which focuses on forecasting the characteristics of the social system itself, is principally sociological.

In practice, many futures studies combine the two approaches, and they are not clearly separable. Many futures studies also do not incorporate any judgmental forecasting methods, but instead represent largely the intuition, insights, and clairvoyance of solo futurists or, at most, the joint conclusions of a few collaborators. No respectable gambler would be inclined to bet on long-range forecasts produced with so little scientific rigor, but they are not without value: they stimulate the imagination, help to overcome outdated assumptions, and suggest the range of possibilities that the future will or could present. Such socially acceptable mind-expanding experiences are particularly useful at the stage of generating alternatives.

An Example. A brief example of the futures studies approach, as well as some general information on methods, was presented in a 1975 article by Willis Harman.[58] His approach was very broad in scope: he reviewed other major forecasts to identify what seemed to be basic trends in society, and updated them to reflect the very latest developments in economic, environmental, social, and technological areas. Then, from this rather long list of basic trends and issues, Harmon and his colleagues outlined five basic dilemmas facing the United States and other industrialized nations. As they saw it, the future would largely be shaped by these dilemmas and by the actions taken in response to them:

1. We need continued economic growth but we can't live with the consequences.
2. We need guidance of technological innovation but shun centralized control.
3. Ever-closer coupling between individuals and organizations appears to lead inexorably in the direction of reduced liberties and system fragility.
4. Possession of a societally supported work role is essential to the individual's sense of self esteem, yet the economy seems increasingly unable to provide enough satisfactory work opportunities.
5. The industrialized nations will find it costly to move toward a more equitable distribution of the earth's resources; not to do so may be even more costly.[59]

Harman argued that none of the three most likely reactions to this set of dilemmas—preservation of the status quo, humanist-environmentalist reaction, "new socialism"—could be expected to ameliorate all five dilemmas. He forecast "a time of troubles and social disruption in the mid-1970s" and found that "the only practical paths that led to a generally desirable future seemed to require a monumental task of social learning and a major transformation of social institutions to be substantially accomplished in the period before the mid-1980s."[60] Several years later, the dilemmas he outlined still seem quite relevant to our social condition, but it is not clear either that his forecast was accurate or that his recommended "practical path to a desirable future" has been adopted.

THE FUTURE OF CRIME AND CRIMINAL JUSTICE

The kinds of trends and dilemmas identified by Harman would certainly have implications for the future of crime and criminal justice.

His rather bleak economic forecast, especially regarding the shortage of fulfilling jobs, might indicate increases in traditional crime (thefts, assaults, and so on). At present, unemployment levels among some groups in our society, particularly young black urban males, are tremendously high. Some European countries have long experienced a condition that is now affecting the United States: too few jobs that meet the expectations of the large numbers of college graduates. Both conditions could be exacerbated by the use of tight-money policies to combat inflation. Sykes suggests that "it is possible, then, that we face the prospect of a social order that will be chronically unable to create sufficient places in the world of work for both the most and the least educated."[61] This combination could well lead to higher levels of traditional crime, as well as to frustration, alienation, and anomie.

Major slowdowns in economic growth could also lead to increased crime. As long as the economy pie was expanding, everyone could have more and more without seeming to take anything away from anyone else. But "if economic opportunities in the United States no longer expand as they have in the past," Sykes suggests, "we may witness an intensifying competitive struggle for the available economic rewards."[62] Social mobility could become much more limited, and commitment to equal opportunity could be seriously threatened.

The "humanist-environmentalist" reaction to these economic problems is that all can learn to make do with much less. Proponents of this view passionately argue that through conservation, the use of alternative forms of energy, cooperative associations, less materialistic values, and other means, Americans can adapt to slower or even zero economic growth. Sykes supplies the more pessimistic possibility:

> If the economy should fall into a period of long decline, . . . if America enters an era of diminishing resources and shrinking opportunities, the picture is likely to change markedly. The theme of success may be in fact transformed, not in the direction of a growing allegiance to modest achievements sensibly integrated with less material ends, but in the direction of a "root-hog-or-die" philosophy. Getting ahead may be replaced by staying even—in an increasingly harsh competitive struggle with economic survival as the overriding goal. The anomic character of American life, with its attendant strain toward deviance including various forms of criminality, would grow worse rather than better.[63]

This "root-hog-or-die" philosophy is most dramatically exemplified now in the survivalist movement, whose adherents are storing food and weapons in preparation for major economic collapse and civil strife.

If economic growth is maintained, it will undoubtedly be owing to technological innovations and a willingness to risk environmental hazards. But new technologies generally introduce either new crimes or new means of perpetrating old crimes (think about cars, credit cards, telephones, recording equipment, computers). In general, "white-collar" crimes may be expected to increase. On the other hand, more action may be taken against the more generalized harms that accompany innovation and continued growth. Coates suggests that "there may be greater recognition of a new class of crimes: the crime with the multivictims and the uncertain victims."[64] These would include the victims of pollution, unsafe products, price-fixing and other commercial schemes, and perhaps even major government boondoggles. The law and the government typically react rather ineffectively toward these kinds of crimes, though, so that direct citizen action and demonstrations may also become more common.

If these are some of the possibilities for the future of crime, what can we expect for criminal justice? Coates forecasts the legalization or at least decriminalization of "social pathologies" such as alcoholism, drug addiction, sex crimes, and suicide. He also expects much less enforcement action against such crimes without victims as gambling and prostitution.[65] Trends such as these did seem evident in the late 1970s, but in the 1980s moral crusaders are flexing their political muscles. The trends toward decriminalization may be reversed or slowed down.

If economic and social problems lead to increases in traditional crimes against persons and property, Sykes believes, the "get-tough" approach to criminal justice will probably be continued.[66] There seems to be a sense that the efforts at social reform in the 1960s failed, at considerable expense, to solve any of the social problems, including crime, that were their target. Thus, any "social-welfare" approaches are tainted. Within criminal justice, theories of rehabilitation are viewed with skepticism, and the prevailing mood is that "nothing works" in corrections. Consequently, the get-tough approach, emphasizing incapacitation, has become popular.

If middle-class criminality (including white-collar crime) also increases, however, it seems likely that an alternative to incapacitation will be sought. Most people seem more willing to get tough with armed robbers than with embezzlers, even when the latter can be shown to have wreaked greater havoc. These nontraditional crimes that often involve middle-class offenders will lead, Sykes suspects, to an emphasis on deterrence and prevention.[67] Such offenders are not perceived as hardened recidivists or as truly dangerous, and perhaps most people can see a little of themselves in them. Rather than incapacitating, punishing, or attempting to "reform the internal moral character of the law violator," society may shift to attempts to "modify the external social environment, presumably with a greater hope of success."[68] A very great danger is that this enlightened correctional philosophy might be applied to middle-class offenders, while incapacitation is reserved for lower-class offenders. If that were to happen, equality before the law would be diminished, and the perceived legitimacy of the criminal justice system eroded.

The probable emphasis on deterrence and prevention raises additional undesirable possibilities. Leslie Wilkins anticipates that "these methods will produce rather unpleasant conditions for those who are protected."[69] Deterrence and prevention are more subtle limitations on freedom than incapacitation or punishment, but they constrain nevertheless. Increased police patrols, increased use of locks, bars, lights, alarms, and similar devices, the use of public embarrassment to deter middle-class offenders, and safety-oriented lifestyle changes are all likely strategies. So are increased electronic surveillance and data-gathering in the name of internal security. Because of possibilities like these, Coates suggests that the Bill of Rights may need to be strengthened and updated in order to retain some semblance of present liberties.[70]

This gloomy view of the future of crime and criminal justice dominates the forecasts and futures studies that have been published. But this future is not predetermined: it is one possibility among many. It is the more likely to come about if we do nothing. But we have the opportunity now to do something, to make choices and devise strategies that will lead to a more hospitable future. How? By planning, of course. But we will need more imagination and creativity than we have demonstrated in the past. As Wilkins suggests, "the majority of the current planning in the criminal justice system, which is not regressive, seeks solutions by means of more-of-the-same."[71]

SUMMARY

Forecasting is an often neglected but important aspect of the planning process, because planned actions are always carried out in the future and sometimes have major long-term implications. To assume that the future in which plans are to be implemented will be very much like the present is, in this day and age, clearly risky.

The forecasting methods available include judgmental, extrapolative, econometric, segmentational, and bootstrapping techniques. The choice of method depends on the kinds of data available, the degree of forecast accuracy needed, and the costs that can be afforded. In many situations, the use of costlier and more sophisticated methods does not lead to more accurate forecasts. Particularly crucial are the basic assumptions underlying any forecasting effort: no sophistication of method or abundance of data can overcome faulty premises about the fundamental structure of the problem and how it changes.

In addition to forecasts of the values of specific indicators (crime rates, gross national product, inmate populations), there are general futures studies. These are based on less formal methods and provide broader views of what the future will be like. Done well, futures studies can be particularly helpful by forecasting the shape of things to come *if* nothing is done. The value of such studies for planning is that future crises and problems may be identified, and thus perhaps prevented, avoided, or at least ameliorated. Also, such studies provide a glimpse of the landscape of the future, beneficial in designing policies and programs with which we will have to live for years to come.

• *Chapter 9* •
NOTES

1. William Ascher, *Forecasting: An Appraisal for Policy-Makers and Planners* (Baltimore: The Johns Hopkins University Press, 1978), p. 16.

2. David W. Ewing, *The Practice of Planning* (New York: Harper & Row Publishers, 1968), p. 45.

3. Ibid., p. 16.

4. J. Scott Armstrong, *Long-Range Forecasting: From Crystal Ball to Computer* (New York: John Wiley & Sons, Inc., 1978), p. 6.

5. Ibid.

6. Donald A. Sylvan and Stuart J. Thorson, "Choosing Appropriate Techniques for Socio-Political Forecasting," *Policy Sciences*, 12 (1980), 269.

7. Ascher, op. cit., p. 1.

8. Ewing, op. cit., p. 48.

9. Gresham M. Sykes, *The Future of Crime* (Washington, D.C.: National Institute of Mental Health, U.S. Government Printing Office, 1980), p. 2.

10. Jib Fowles, "An Overview of Social Forecasting Procedures," *Journal of the American Institute of Planners* (July 1976), 253.

11. Ascher, op. cit.

12. Sylvan and Thorson, op. cit., p. 265.

13. Ascher, op. cit., p. 16.

14. Armstrong, op. cit., p. 5.

15. Robin M. Hogarth and Spyros Makridakis, "Forecasting and Planning: An Evaluation," *Management Science*, 27 (February 1981), 116.

16. The discussion of the five general forecasting methods follows that of Armstrong, op. cit., very closely. See especially pp. 66–269 of that volume. The reader interested in further information on forecasting is strongly encouraged to consult Armstrong's book, which is very informative and also very readable. For a concurring opinion, see a review of the Armstrong book by William A. Nisakanen in *Policy Analysis*, 6 (Summer 1980), 371.

17. Armstrong, op. cit., p. 75.

18. See Hogarth and Makridakis, op. cit., for an extensive review of these and other sources and types of bias as they affect planning and forecasting.

19. For an overview, see Armstrong, op. cit., pp. 100–35. On surveys, see Earl R. Babbie, *Survey Research Methods* (Belmont, Calif.: Wadsworth Publishing Co., Inc., 1973); and Harper Boyd and Ralph Westfall, *Marketing Research* (Homewood, Ill.: Irwin Publishing Company, 1972). On the Delphi method and structured meetings, see Andre L. Delbecq, et al., *Group Techniques for Program Planning: A Guide to Nominal Group and Delphi Processes* (Glenview, Ill.: Scott, Foresman and Company, 1975). Also see Norman R. F. Maier, *Problem-Solving Discussions and Conferences* (New York: McGraw-Hill Book Company, 1963). On the group depth interview, see Alfred E. Goldman, "The Group Depth Interview," *Journal of Marketing*, 26 (July 1962), 61–68. For an application of role playing to criminal justice, see Philip Zimbardo, "The Pathology of Imprisonment," *Society* (April 1972), 4–8.

20. Terry L. Cooper, "Professionalization and Unionization of Police: A Delphi Forecast on Police Values," *Journal of Criminal Justice*, 2 (1974), 19–35.

21. Ibid., pp. 32–33. Reprinted by permission of Pergamon Press, Ltd.

22. Example drawn from Armstrong, op. cit., p. 139.

23. Armstrong, op. cit., p. 138.

24. From Gary W. Cordner, et al., *The Pontiac Integrated Criminal Apprehension Project: A Final Evaluation Report*, School of Criminal Justice, Michigan State University, East Lansing, Mich., 1979, p. 95.

25. For an overview of these extrapolation methods, see Armstrong, op. cit., pp. 142–65. He strongly recommends the exponential smoothing method, and suggests Robert G. Brown, *Statistical Forecasting for Inventory Control* (New York: McGraw-Hill Book Company, 1959), as a good guide.

26. John S. Y. Chiu and Samson K. Chang, "Forecasting Calls for Police Service in Seattle," *Journal of Police Science and Administration*, 6 (March 1978), 105–14.

27. Ibid., p. 107.

28. Armstrong, op. cit., p. 174.

29. E. Ames and S. Reiter, "Distributions of Correlation Coefficients in Economic Time Series," *Journal of the American Statistical Association*, 56 (1961), 637–56, as cited in Armstrong, op. cit., pp. 493–94.

30. See Charles Ostrom, *Time Series Analysis: Regression Techniques* (Beverly Hills, Calif.: Sage Publications, 1977, for a concise treatment of this method, as well as Armstrong, op. cit., pp. 172–224.

31. Daniel Glaser, "A Reconsideration of Some Parole Prediction Factors," *American Sociological Review*, 19 (June 1954), 335–41.

32. See Edwin H. Sutherland and Donald R. Cressey, *Criminology* (Philadelphia: J. B. Lippincott Company, 1978).

33. For an explanation of this measure, see

O. D. Duncan, et al., "Formal Devices for Making Selection Decisions," *American Journal of Sociology*, 58 (May 1953), 573-84.

34. Frances H. Simon, "Statistical Methods of Making Prediction Instruments," *Journal of Research in Crime and Delinquency*, 9 (January 1972), 46-53.

35. See James A. Inciardi, "The Use of Parole Prediction with Institutionalized Narcotic Addicts," *Journal of Research in Crime and Delinquency*, 8 (January 1971), 65-73.

36. Armstrong, op. cit., pp. 228-29.

37. See Donella H. Meadows, et al., *The Limits to Growth* (New York: Universe Books, 1972), the so-called Club of Rome report.

38. Armstrong, op. cit., pp. 46-51, 235-38.

39. Allan Sampson, "Post-Prison Success Prediction: A Preliminary Florida Study," *Criminology*, 12 (August 1974), 155-73.

40. J. Chaiken, et al., *Criminal Justice Models: An Overview* (Washington, D.C.: Law Enforcement Assistance Administration, U.S. Government Printing Office, 1976).

41. Stephen Stollmack, "Predicting Inmate Populations from Arrest, Court Disposition, and Recidivism Rates," *Journal of Research in Crime and Delinquency*, 10 (July 1973), 141-62.

42. Ibid., p. 142.

43. Armstrong, op. cit., p. 252.

44. Fred Kort, "Predicting Supreme Court Decisions Mathematically: A Quantitative Analysis of the 'Right to Counsel' Cases," *The American Political Science Review*, 51 (March 1957), 1-12.

45. Ibid., pp. 11-12.

46. For some insight into the uncertainty surrounding U.S. Supreme Court voting and decisions, see Bob Woodward and Scott Armstrong, *The Brethren: Inside the Supreme Court* (New York: Avon Books, 1981).

47. Hogarth and Makridakis, op. cit., p. 131.

48. Armstrong, op. cit., Ascher, op. cit.

49. Armstrong, op. cit.

50. Ascher, op. cit.

51. Ascher, op. cit., p. 199.

52. Fowles, op. cit., p. 253.

53. Sykes, op. cit., p. 2.

54. See, for example, Herman Kahn and A. J. Wiener, *The Year 2000* (London: Macmillan & Company Ltd., 1967).

55. Larry Hirschhorn, "Scenario Writing: A Developmental Approach," *Journal of the American Planning Association* (April 1980), 172-83.

56. See, for example, Olaf Helmer and Paul de Brigard, *Some Potential Societal Developments 1970-2000* (Middletown, Conn.: Institute for the Future, 1970).

57. Fowles, op. cit., pp. 253-63.

58. Willis W. Harman, "On Normative Futures Research," *Policy Sciences*, 6 (1975), 121-35.

59. Ibid., pp. 128-29.

60. Ibid., p. 126.

61. Sykes, op. cit., p. 32.

62. Sykes, op. cit., p. 33.

63. Sykes, op. cit., p. 43.

64. Joseph F. Coates, "The Future of Crime in the United States from Now to the Year 2000," *Policy Sciences*, 3 (1972), 40.

65. Ibid., pp. 32-36.

66. Sykes, op. cit., p. 68.

67. Sykes, op. cit., pp. 68-69.

68. Sykes, op. cit., p. 69.

69. Leslie T. Wilkins, "Crime and Criminal Justice at the Turn of the Century," *The Annals of the American Academy of Political and Social Science*, 408 (July 1973), 22.

70. Coates, op. cit., pp. 42-43.

71. Wilkins, op. cit., p. 15.

• Chapter 10 •

GENERATING AND TESTING ALTERNATIVES

This chapter discusses the third and final stage in the planning process: the generating and testing of alternatives. At this stage, goals and/or problems have been identified, important conditions have been forecast, and information about the present and the future (including information on the desired ends to be sought or the problems to be ameliorated) has been collected. What remains is to identify the different paths that might be taken and to determine where each would lead. In other words, alternative *means* for achieving the goals (or for solving the problems) must be generated, and the likely consequences of each must be estimated. The final task will be to choose the alternative with the effects which most closely achieve the goal or solve the problem.

First, some general considerations that greatly affect the generating and testing of alternatives will be discussed and methods of identifying alternatives will be presented. Then the methods for testing alternatives (many of which are similar to the forecasting methods presented in Chapter 9), will be examined. The final section of this chapter will briefly discuss implementation and evaluation, which, although not actually part of the planning process, are necessary components of rational action, and, together with feedback, comprise the principal activities engaged in by organizational management.

GENERAL CONSIDERATIONS

As shown in Chapter 3, planning in the real world often varies considerably from textbook descriptions of how planning should be done. Perhaps nowhere in the planning process is this gap between ideal and real more pronounced than at the stage of generating and testing alternatives. A wide variety of alternatives should be considered in the planning process, but usually only a very few even come to mind.[1] Alternatives should be rigorously tested, in order to get good estimates of their likely consequences, but in fact it is not uncommon to find little more than hunches and guesses being used.

To be completely rational one would have to consider all possible alternatives, but it would be physically and fiscally exhausting to attempt to identify and consider every conceivable alternative; besides, decision-makers would normally be required to act long before all alternatives could be fully compared.

Although rationality may be constrained by limitations of time and energy, it is certainly reasonable and desirable to consider as many alternatives as possible. Even this lowered expectation, though, sets a higher standard than is achieved in practice. As James L. Adams notes:

> Few people like problems. Hence the natural tendency in problem-solving is to pick the first solution that comes to mind and run with it. The disadvantage of this approach is that you may run either off a cliff or into a worse problem than you started with. A better strategy in solving problems is to select the most attractive path from many ideas, or concepts.[2]

If pure rationality is beyond reach, it is possible to strive for a higher level of rationality than that associated with picking "the first solution that comes to mind." The next section will discuss practical, down-to-earth methods for enlarging the range of ideas considered in the planning process.

Traditionally, little attention has been given to the generating of alternatives, though the testing of alternatives has been closely scrutinized and highly developed. Though we have failed to devote much effort to learning how to get more and better ideas, we have gotten very sophisticated when it comes to analyzing and evaluating the few ideas that we usually come up with.[3] Oddly enough, this situation parallels one found in the field of personnel administration. In personnel work, efforts at recruiting (generating alternative employees) tend to be underdeveloped, but a great deal of energy and talent is devoted to selection (testing alternatives). In the personnel field, the pool of candidates sets the boundaries for selection and thus for employee quality; in planning, the range of generated alternatives forms the pool of ideas from which a strategy will be chosen. The wider the pool, the more the alternatives that are initially identified, and the more likely that a truly satisfactory alternative will emerge.

GENERATING ALTERNATIVES

Three recent studies of planning help explain why some organizations generate and consider many alternatives while others do not. These studies have some important implications for any efforts to widen the range of choices available to decision-makers.

Jansson and Taylor examined "search activity" among managers of social-service agencies in Los Angeles County.[4] By *search activity*, they meant the extent to which managers considered a variety of alternatives (especially those not already in use in their organizations) in the course of their planning efforts. The managers surveyed generally reported that both they and their organizations treated search activity as an important part of planning. Depending on the area (personnel, agency clientele, and so on), however, from 36 per cent to 53 per cent of the managers rated search activity as either unimportant or only somewhat important in their planning activities. Also, one third of the managers reported having only "some involvement" or less in planning.

Jansson and Taylor were primarily interested in accounting for variations in search activity among agencies. They found that certain formal characteristics of the social-service agencies (ratio of clients to staff, proportion of staff who are professionals, ethnic and economic characteristics of clientele) were *not* associated with extent of search activity, nor were such personal characteristics of the managers as length of administrative experience, sex, or level of education. They found that very small agencies engaged in less search activity, but that there was little difference between medium-size and large agencies.

The extent of search activity undertaken in the organizations was most strongly related to such factors as the commitment of resources to planning, the integration of planning in agency decision-making, and the general organizational climate toward change and innovation (see Chapter 7). They summarized their findings as follows:

> [S]earch activity . . . may be directly stimulated by earmarking organizational resources, by recruiting change- and policy-oriented executives, and by drawing into the planning process a variety of diverse organizational participants. . . . [It] may be indirectly stimulated by making organizational tasks more complex, by providing leeway in budgets for planning, by inducing organizational change, and by integrating planning with decision-making processes. Technical competence in planning, as well as personal orientations of executives toward it, may be important factors, but data from this survey suggest that planning strategy for the future must be integrated with the complexity of institutional realities, realities that may serve as preconditions both for search activity and systematic planning.[5]

A recent national study of manpower planning in criminal justice examined many of these same issues.[6] Among the factors found to be related to the extent of planning and searching for alternatives in criminal justice agencies were the general climate of rationality in the jurisdiction and its government, the extent to which agencies felt capable of influencing and anticipating changes that affected them, the extent of change actually encountered, and the degree to which agencies felt constrained by external forces beyond their control (such as equal employment opportunity pressures or dominance by civil service decision-making). There was also some evidence, though far from conclusive, that police agencies undertook more manpower planning than did correctional agencies, and that state agencies were more likely than local agencies to plan and search widely for alternatives.

Several consistent themes emerge from these two studies. A wide range of alternatives seems more likely to be identified and considered when an organization is oriented toward change and innovation. Obviously a reciprocal or cyclical process is at work here: orientation toward change encourages the consideration of more alternatives; consideration of more alternatives reduces resistance to change, makes change more likely, and encourages a more positive orientation toward change. Generating more alternatives also seems more likely when planning is integrated with decision-making, so that it is seen not as an academic or idealistic exercise but as an important part of setting the organization's direction. Also helpful is a perception of rationality in organizational and environmental decision-making, which gives planners reason to believe that alternatives will be fairly and honestly considered, and not rejected summarily on the basis of political criteria or narrow self-interest. And although organizational size and technical-planning expertise may not be of crucial importance, it does seem that search activity and planning are enhanced when resources are committed on their behalf, and when individuals are involved who have the knowledge and breadth of vision required to see beyond day-to-day crises.

The third study is a very interesting one that examined the relationship between generation of alternatives and other stages in the planning process.[7] Ernest R. Alexander examined the effect that identifying goals and problems had on the generation of alternatives and the effect that the testing and evaluation of alternatives had on their generation. He noted that the literature "suggests that the greatest openness for the uninhibited design of alternatives is offered by the 'rational' approach, where goal or problem definition interacts with design but judgment is deferred."[8] Certainly the identification of goals and problems should guide and set the stage for generating alternatives, and testing and evaluating should not be undertaken until a wide array of alternatives is produced.

Alexander was interested in determining whether real-world planning matched this prescription. He found, perhaps not surprisingly, that it often does not. Instead, judgments about the feasibility of alternatives are usually made quite early, substantially limiting the range of alternatives actually considered. Premature evaluation of alternatives is usually very informal and subjective, so that it is entirely likely that deserving alternatives meet an early and undeserved end. Alexander noted that "the review of alternatives, then, seems to be an integral part of their development, and an indispensable 'focusing' process which narrows down the range of options long before they are forwarded for systematic evaluation."[9]

The relationship between the generation of alternatives and the identification of goals and problems also turned out to be somewhat at odds with the rational model of planning. Alexander found that the generation of alternatives was guided not so much by the goals or problems previously identified as by a more concrete objective or criterion that somehow emerged. This had a limiting and inhibiting effect on the range of alternatives identified and considered. The reduction from broad aims to narrower ones resulted from convenience, a desire to decrease ambiguity, and also from perceptual, ideological, and organizational assumptions about what was really possible and feasible. The narrowing, usually implicit, greatly constricted the set of alternatives that was generated.

The net result of premature evaluation of alternatives, and of the narrowing of goals and problems, Alexander found, was that alternatives considered were usually well-worn and accepted ones. The range of options narrowed very rapidly in the planning process, so that few alternatives actually were submitted for formal testing and evaluation. The "importance of systematic search in the organization and its immediate environment to elicit unconventional and novel alternatives"[10] is not openly repudiated, but there is a strong tendency for other considerations to impinge upon and restrict the generation of alternatives in real-world planning applications.

These, then, are some of the "realities" of generating alternatives. It is difficult to say which can be overcome by concerted effort. Certainly time and resources are always limited, so that pure rationality is unachievable. By encouraging an openness to change, however, by devoting some resources to planning, by making planning an integral part of agency decision-making, and by maintaining a constant wariness about unrecognized limiting assumptions, it seems reasonable to expect something more than picking "the first solution that comes to mind."

It also seems reasonable to expect that the effort and sophistication applied to generating alternatives will depend upon the saliency, novelty, and difficulty of the planning issue being addressed. When goals are clear and the relationships between means and ends is well understood (see Chapter 3), or when the problem is a simple one (see Chapter 8), it may be possible to identify a wholly satisfactory alternative relatively quickly and inexpensively. Situations involving less certainty might require more hard thinking and more time to identify alternatives that seem likely to achieve desired effects.

Three general levels of activity associated with generating alternatives are reviewing, searching, and designing. They are arranged in an ascending order of effort, innovation, and sophistication. Ordinarily, the attempt to generate alternatives begins with a review of known alternatives; if one that promises to be satisfactory if found, the search may cease right there. If the review is unsuccessful, the search for promising alternatives widens, beginning close to home and moving farther as necessary. Prolonged failure to find a satisfactory alternative may lead to a decision to scale down expectations and criteria of satisfaction rather than continue searching.[11] In other situations, though, the search may be quite extensive, or it may be decided to undertake to design a brand-new alternative that meets the criteria. These successive stages of reviewing, searching, and designing will now be discussed in greater detail.

Reviewing

Initially, generating alternatives usually involves reviewing strategies and activities that are already in use or that have been used in the past. For example, a police agency may identify a problem (or have it identified for them by others) of inadequate representation of minorities among their employees. As a first step toward attempting to solve the problem, the agency would want to review its present and past recruitment and selection activities, to see whether any of these alternatives might yield a satisfactory solution. A review might indicate that the department's one minority recruiter is proficient at attracting successful minority applicants, suggesting that an increase in the number of minority recruiters might increase the number of minority employees. Or it might reveal that a particular current activity, such as recruiting at predominantly black colleges, has been productive in attracting desirable applicants, suggesting that an increase in such an activity might be successful. It might also have been the case that the agency confronted a similar problem some time in the past, or avoided such a problem, so that reviewing past practices might provide an alternative solution for the present problem.

A review of present and past alternatives usually begins with alternatives in the planner's or the organization's own repertoire: these tend to be close at hand and come readily to mind. The personnel director, when trying to solve the problem of securing more minority employees, will naturally focus on current and traditional methods of recruitment and selection. If a present method seems likely to solve the problem, the review probably will go no further. If no current methods seem promising, however, the personnel director is likely to review his or her experience and that of coworkers and of the organization, in hope of identifying an alternative of merit. Past practices tend to be somewhat harder to identify than present ones, of course, because memories fade and records are rarely comprehensive. An alternative that worked well before in a similar situation may be completely forgotten or inaccurately recalled.

The definition of a goal or problem, and the criteria of success, have a strong influence on attempts to generate alternatives (see Chapter 8), and the Alexander study, discussed earlier in this chapter, reinforces the point. For example, a goal of a police agency might be to have its personnel closely reflect the racial composition of the community, and to have its personnel practices truly offer equal opportunity without regard to race. The guiding objective behind personnel planning, though, might well be narrower and more concrete, such as having 25 per cent of each recruit training class composed of minorities, or simply complying with minimal affirmative-action requirements. For narrow objectives, a review of present or past practices might provide promising alternatives, whereas the achievement of the broader goal might necessitate a more extensive effort at generating alternatives.

The generation and the choice of alternatives depends on the conception of the goal or problem, and on the criteria for satisfactory achievement or solution. It is therefore essential in the planning process to think carefully and first about ends, before going headlong after means: "If someone tosses an idea in your way before you have a definite direction you might be misled into taking a trip to someone else's destination instead of your own," or, perhaps worse, "You may take a trip to nowhere."[12]

Searching

Searching for alternatives involves going beyond past and present practices of the organization; it involves an attempt to identify alternatives already in use by other organizations or at least discernible in the existing stock of knowledge. Another organization may have faced a similar problem, for example, and found a way to solve or minimize it. It may have spent considerable money and time devising the solution, or benefitted from a stroke of genius in discovering it. In either case, borrowing the organization's solution may be much easier than attempting to reinvent the wheel.

There are a variety of standard approaches to the search for alternatives. One is to contact other organizations that may have faced, or are known to have faced, the same problem or sought the same goal. An alternative is to contact an association of such agencies, such as the American Correctional Association, the National Center for State Courts, the International Association of Chiefs of Police, or the Police Executive Research Forum, which may suggest alternatives or at least provide referrals to other agencies likely to be of assistance. Trade journals (such as *The Police Chief*) are also good sources of alternatives, as many of their articles report the successful programs and innovative practices adopted by organizations. Scholarly journals, research reports, books, and the library in general are also sources of alternatives. These may require somewhat more energy and ingenuity to decipher and transform into practical alternatives, but they are also more likely than most other sources to suggest really new ideas that depart significantly from present practice.

Particularly during the latter part of its existence, the Law Enforcement Assistance Administration (LEAA) sought to aid criminal justice agencies in the search for alternatives through technology transfer and through model programs and exemplary projects.[13] When LEAA-sponsored projects resulted in programs that were deemed successful and worthy of emulation, attempts were made to publicize the programs and to recommend them to other jurisdictions and organizations facing similar circumstances. This is the process known as *diffusion of innovation*. LEAA's attempts to diffuse innovations were aided by the ability to offer grants to agencies that agreed to adopt certain programs, as well as by the ability to prepare and distribute printed documents through the National Criminal Justice Reference Service (NCJRS). In addition, agencies and individuals could query NCJRS (and still can, for a fee) on a particular topic and receive an annotated listing of pertinent LEAA and other publications.

The search method of generating alternatives is aimed at locating existing ideas that lie outside the present knowledge and repertoire of the planner or organization. A wide range of ideas and alternatives is desired, among which it is hoped will be a satisfactory solution to the problem or a satisfactory means to goal attainment. Herbert Simon has described a remarkably effective method that he uses when searching for information:

> I pick up the phone and call the person, among my acquaintances, whose field of expertness is as close as possible (it need not be very close at all). I ask him, not for the answer to the question, but for the name of the person in his circle of acquaintance who is closest to being an expert on the topic. I repeat the process until I have the information I want. It will be a rare instance when more than three or four calls are required.[14]

In planning applications, and particularly during the generation of alternatives, it may not be possible or wise to seek *an* expert from whom to glean *a* best alternative. However, Simon's simple technique can be used to identify the person or persons most knowledgeable about a given problem or a given set of alternative strategies. A range of ideas, as well as their judgments about the likely consequence of each, can then be sought from such experts. Alternatively, these experts may be able to identify organizations facing similar situations or suggest pertinent publications. This search method is probably less costly and more productive than most other, more sophisticated methods.

Designing

Sometimes problems are so significant as to demand resolution, but no promising solutions are found through review and search activity. In such situations, an attempt must be made to fashion a new solution. This is *design*, though it might also be termed *creation*, *discovery*, or *invention*. It is a very tricky business, and not one easily described.

One aspect of design is clearly scientific. Any sorting out, explanation, and understanding of how the world works and what causes the present problem aids the effort to decide what action to take to improve things. Even if actual design choices are guided by little more than trial and error, choices about what to try, and interpretations of errors, should be informed by knowledge about how things work.[15]

There is also a sense in which design involves craft. Christopher Alexander has described design as the creation of "forms" that "fit" their contexts or environments.[16] One criterion for design is the minimization of "misfits." Though this conception of design perhaps most readily brings to mind such fields as engineering, architecture, or interior design, it could just as easily be used to describe the design of police strategies or correctional programs. But the very terminology used suggests the applicability of aesthetic considerations as well as of scientific principles.

Another characteristic frequently associated with design is imagination or creativity. Design is often thought to involve not only logic and aesthetic appreciation, but also the ability to transcend usual ways of looking at problems and thinking about solutions. Successful design may require the planner to develop a completely new way of conceptualizing the problem, for example, which then yields a surprising but successful solution.[17] Most successful designers are often rather unusual people, who think about and look at the world differently from others, who are not limited by the conventional categories and assumptions that bind most people, and who can therefore come up with ideas that astound and amaze.[18]

A commonly used method for generating new ideas and alternatives is *brainstorming*.[19] This is a group or individual effort to list as many solutions to the problem, or means for attaining the goal, as possible. The key to successful brainstorming is to seek a large quantity of ideas, to defer judgment, to let the imagination run free, and to seek new ideas from old ones by altering one or more components. When these guidelines are followed, brainstorming can usually provide many alternatives in a relatively short period.

Another sometimes helpful approach to generating new ideas is through *morphological forced connections*.[20] This involves identifying several attributes of the problem or goal situation, and then listing alternatives with respect to each attribute. All possible combinations of the attribute alternatives are then created. Some of these may make little sense, of course, but others may present real and innovative responses. Suppose, for example, that a police agency felt a need to improve information handling. Attributes of the situation and their alternatives might include the following:

Information Type	**Medium**
Call for service	Direct voice
Lookout	Telephone
Inquiry	Document
Report	Radio
Memo	Printer
Order	CRT
Sender	**Receiver**
Operator	Operator
Dispatcher	Dispatcher
Patrol officer	Patrol officer
Crime analysis	Crime analysis
Patrol supervisor	Patrol supervisor
Top management	Top management

Combining alternatives in various ways presents some interesting possibilities. Operators might relay calls for service to dispatchers by direct voice communication. One patrol officer might make an inquiry to another patrol officer by sending the message from one CRT (Cathode Ray Tube: visual screen terminal) to another (perhaps an in-car terminal). Patrol officers might compose their reports in their cars, type them onto their CRT screens, check and proofread them, and then transmit them to remote printers in the records division, the crime-analysis division, and the patrol-supervisor's office. Top management might transmit its memos and orders to all members of the organization via regular messages over the police radio system.

Brainstorming and morphological forced connections are just two of many possible methods for identifying new ideas and alternatives. The most important general rules to obey when generating alternatives are to defer judgment and to seek as many alternatives as practical. Some alternatives will naturally seem too bizarre or too costly, and it is inevitable that some judgments and some winnowing will limit the range of alternatives identified and considered. The time and resources available for generating alternatives will also be limited, so that all possible alternatives can never be located. Still, the planner is well advised to err on the side of too many, rather than too few, alternatives. The human tendency toward provincialism and conventionalism, which often results in picking the first alternative that comes to mind, should be avoided at all costs. A principal purpose of planning, one that sets it apart from other managerial activities, is to widen the range of choices available for decision-making. The decision, the choice, will be made soon enough. At this stage, the planner should be looking for options, not dismissing them.

TESTING ALTERNATIVES

The testing of alternatives should also precede judgment. Before alternatives can be judged, their probable effects must be estimated. The alternatives that have been identified are simply proposed means to some end; the planner needs to determine where each of the means would lead in order to select the one that comes closest to achieving the desired end.

The testing of alternatives does not always involve the use of formal or sophisticated techniques. This activity is often carried out very informally, on the basis of hunches and guesses. Nevertheless, alternatives must be tested to estimate what would probably happen if they were adopted.

The effects of alternatives are tested, or estimated, in order to determine which come closest to achieving the goal (or solving the problem). Estimated effects are then compared to the goals or to the criteria for problem resolution. Suppose, for example, that the planner is helping a state legislature to formulate broad-scale policies to deal with crime. He will have identified goals and generated alternatives in earlier stages of the planning process. Assume that the goals and alternatives are those shown in Figure 10-1. The task now is to test the alternatives to "fill in the blanks." That is, he would need to estimate the effects of each alternative policy on each goal. Once these effects have been estimated, the planner will then be in a position to compare alternative policies and determine which promises the greatest possibility of attaining the goals.

As another illustration, suppose a prison is concerned about the problem of recidivism. Before alternatives can be tested and compared, the criteria for problem resolution must be

Figure 10-1. Goals, Alternatives, and the Domain of Alternative Testing for Broad-Scale Criminal Justice Policy (Adapted from James P. Levine, et al., *Criminal Justice: A Public Policy Approach* [New York: Harcourt Brace Jovanovich, 1980].)

Alternatives / Goals	Deterrence	Rehabilitation	Diversion	Decriminal-ization	Social Welfare
Crime Control					
Public Tranquillity					
Justice					
Due Process					
Efficiency					
Accountability					

formulated. This would be very important in this instance because recidivism can be defined in a variety of ways. Assume that recidivism has been defined as reconviction within three years for any offense punishable by imprisonment, and that the criterion for problem resolution is any decrease in the recidivism rate of former inmates. There would be little difficulty in generating a wide range of alternatives: educational programs for inmates, vocational training, psychiatric treatment, behavior-modification programs, work-release programs, halfway houses, job placements, and parole. The testing of alternatives would involve estimating the effects of all these options on the recidivism rate.

This seems a simpler planning situation than that described in Figure 10-1, mainly because it involves just one criterion of problem resolution, rather than six general goals. In reality, though, other considerations similar to the six goals shown in Figure 10-1 would come into play: halfway houses, for example, might reduce recidivism but be unacceptable to many neighborhoods–in other words, they might have a negative impact on public tranquillity; early parole might reduce recidivism (by avoiding drastic prisonization) but fail to satisfy the desire of many for retribution, their concept of justice; forced treatment might violate the inmates' right to due process; and indeterminate sentencing might be unacceptable because it reduces accountability to the public.

In addition, all alternatives would be judged in relation to their efficiency, their potential benefits and costs. An alternative might, for example, promise a one per cent decrease in recidivism, but at a cost of $10 million. The alternative might also have the benefit of ensuring inmates' right to due process, but at the cost of contributing to public fear about ex-convicts roaming the streets. The decision that a particular alternative really represented an improvement over present practice would require consideration of all these costs and benefits.

Once some alternatives have been generated and before any can be selected for implementation, information about their probable effects is needed. How does the planner get that information? The sections that follow discuss some of the methods that can be used for obtaining that information.

Informal Estimation

The most common approach to testing alternatives is informal estimation, which corresponds to judgmental methods in forecasting (see Chapter 9). Informal estimation of the effects of alternatives is based on personal or collective opinion, judgments, everyday knowledge, guesses, and hunches. Informal estimation would "fill in" Figure 10-1 with opinions and judgments about the effects of the policies on the six goals of criminal justice.

Informal estimation probably works best when the effects of alternatives are very obvious or when the people doing the estimating are particularly knowledgeable in relevant areas. Like judgmental forecasting, informal estimation is a subjective method, not because the data used are necessarily subjective but because there are no formal rules about how to use the data. When people rely on their judgment, instead of formal rules, to make estimations, they are susceptible to wishful thinking, selective perception, and a host of other biases.[21]

Several techniques can be used for informal estimation. All basically ask the same question: "If we implemented Alternative A, what would most likely happen?" Sometimes the planner asks himself the question, sometimes he asks other people, who may be chosen because their judgments would be well informed. Interaction among judges, and discussion, may be generated if the question is posed to a group in a meeting. Alternatively, the question might be posed by the Delphi method (see Chapter 9), in order to get individual judgments first, with judges then able to revise their estimates according to the judgments of others. To get a really large sampling of informal estimates, the survey method could be used to pose the question to hundreds or thousands of people.

There is a close correspondence between forecasting and the testing of alternatives. Both look to the future. Forecasting focuses on the future behavior of a particular phenomenon (the crime rate, or inflation), or the future shape of society as a whole. When forecasting, the planner asks, "Given the way things are now, and the way they seem to be going, what will the future be like if we don't do anything differently?" In testing alternatives, he asks, "What will the future be like *if* we do something differently—specifically, if we implement Alternative A, or Alternative B, and so on?"

The principal benefits of informal estimation are, of course, convenience and low cost. The method is easy to use, comfortable, quick, and cheap. When the effects of alternatives are fairly obvious and well known, informal estimation may be the preferable method. If the alternative in question was identified through a review process, if it is already working well, or if it has worked well in the past and conditions have not changed much, it may be reasonable to assume that it will work well in the current application. If the alternative was located through search activity, and there is evidence that it worked well elsewhere in a comparable situation, it may be reasonable to assume that it would work well in the present instance. But already a lot of assumptions have been made; "working well" does not describe specific effects; and only one alternative has been dealt with. A planning situation is more likely to generate several alternatives, each with several important effects. To sort all these out, it is usually desirable to go beyond informal estimation.

"Soft" Formal Estimation

The methods described in this section are largely judgmental and subjective, but they attempt to overcome serious biases, to make assumptions explicit, and to consider available data carefully. These methods incorporate some rules for estimating, and also some rules for evaluating past experiences.

Perhaps even more than other methods for alternative estimation, the "soft" formal approach relies heavily on past research and current theory. A concerted effort is made to assemble what is known about the particular question. Past studies are collected and evaluated to determine what they contribute to the present attempt to estimate the effects of identified alternatives. Current theories are also examined as ways of explaining how things work and how they change.

Consider the recidivism problem presented earlier. One step toward testing the effects of the numerous possible alternatives might involve reviewing reports of research on the various treatments and programs. There have been hundreds of studies of different correctional practices and their effects on recidivism.[22] These studies would need to be carefully examined: some may not have been conducted according to reasonable scientific standards, so that their internal validity is in doubt; others might have been conducted in such a way as to render doubtful the applicability of their findings to other settings. Evaluating these studies means applying scientific standards in order to limit the subjectivity of one's conclusions about what the research has to say on correctional practices and their effects.

In order to sort out and organize the many research findings on correctional effectiveness, some theories about why people become criminals and about how to induce behavioral change are needed. In truth, everyone has such theories, but in a planning situation, it may be advisable to make them explicit, to ask more objectively whether the theories are supported by the research findings that have been collected. Research findings and theory are thus interdependent: the findings help to evaluate the theories; the theories help to organize the many pieces of knowledge that the findings represent.

Few are naturally inclined to make their theories and assumptions explicit. It is tempting to fit any and all research findings within our favorite, and largely unexamined, theories. One technique that has been developed to counteract these tendencies is scenario-writing (see Chapters 8 and 9). Scenarios can be written by individuals, but are usually better done by groups, so that the theories held by each person are challenged.

In testing alternatives the first step is to describe the salient features of the present situation, which would correspond to a discussion of the environment in scenario writing for forecasting. The next step is to specify whatever it is that is not right in the present situation. This is the problem that needs to be solved, or the goal that is not being attained. It is important to be careful and explicit in describing the present situation and the problem, for they are the basis for the rest of the scenario. The third step is to identify the alternative under consideration. The fourth, and most important, step in writing the scenario is to estimate the most likely, the best, and the worst consequences of the alternative, *and* to specify precisely why these effects will follow from the alternative. This is the stage in which previous research and theory are drawn on most heavily. If the group is required to write out what they think will result from the implementation of the alternative, and why, more careful thought is usually brought to bear.

Two additional questions are sometimes added to the scenario-writing process: "Given these estimated effects, how will the environment be likely to react? Given this reaction, will we be in a position to respond reasonably?" The intention of these questions is to encourage consideration of more than simply the immediate effects of the alternative, and to sensitize planners to the fact that they are dealing with systems that react when they are altered.

The first two steps in the scenario-writing exercise, the description of the present situation and the specification of the problem, will remain the same as each additional alternative is tested. The testing of each additional alternative also generally becomes easier because assumptions, relevant variables, and expected relationships have already been identified. There will usually be less that has to be "invented" with each new alternative, although occasionally the estimation of an alternative's effects may challenge and upset previously recorded scenarios, requiring reconsideration of the earlier cases.

Another "soft" formal method for estimating the effects of alternatives, similar to scenario writing, is *counterfactual analysis*.[24] This method involves a retrospective view of what might have happened had a different alternative been implemented at some point in the past. What actually did happen is known, and information about the period in question, because it is in the past, is available. The method, however, does not explicitly take any account of the future, so that it "cannot be used for prediction, for it is based upon a fiction. Nevertheless, it can serve as the basis for informed and vigorous speculation, providing both an understanding and a feel for a sequence of events."[25]

The process of counterfactual analysis is like scenario-writing. A period is chosen for consideration, and the actual experience of the phenomenon is established. Then, at key branching points at which choices were made, alternative choices are posited and their probable effects are estimated. In this way several chains of events can be hypothesized, based on alternatives different from those that were really implemented. Following the chains of events suggests how things might have been different had other choices been made. This information can then be used to inform present decisions about what kinds of alternatives to implement.

The state of Maryland, for example, is faced with a severe problem of prison overcrowding, and is considering major prison construction. Several years ago the problem was similar, though perhaps slightly less severe, and the alternative of prison construction was rejected. Instead, other alternatives, including increased use of parole, work-release programs, and community corrections centers, were chosen. A counterfactual analysis could review that prior decision, and speculate about the effects had prison construction been chosen then. Information would be available about inmate populations, sentencing practices, crime rates, population characteristics, and the costs of the various alternatives. The counterfactual analysis could use this information, although judgments would also be required. As in scenario-writing, however, research findings and explicit theory could be used to minimize, or at least make clear, the subjectivity employed. The results of the analysis would not "prove" what will happen if Maryland now decides in favor of prison construction, but they would provide useful information.

The primary advantage provided by "soft" formal estimation, as compared with informal estimation, is the reduction in subjectivity. Further reductions are offered by formal models and simulations, described in the next section.

Models and Simulations

Formal models and simulations are as dependent as informal and "soft" formal estimation on the validity of information about how things work in the real world. Models and simulations may take a physical, mechanical form, or may be contained within and operated by computers. In these forms they may seem rather intimidating; and at the very least their complexity tends to evoke respect. It is therefore crucial to realize that models are nothing more than representations of theories "which are designed to answer questions about how the real world will react to changes in conditions and policies."[26] Computer models are used to test alternatives, not because they are wiser than people are, but because "they perform the most monotonous and repetitive tasks at high speed and with absolute mechanical accuracy."[27]

What distinguishes models from less formal methods of estimation is that the rules for using information and data are contained within the model. Models are thus more formal, more complete representations than those discussed in the last two sections. They contain information about the present states of components in the system under study, and also about the relationships among components. By hypothesizing an alteration to one component, the planner can then examine the effects on other components, and on the system as a whole. In undertaking scenario-writing and counterfactual analysis, the planner hypothesizes the implementation of an alternative and then subjectively estimates its effects; in constructing a formal model, the planner "plugs in" the alternative and lets the model specify the effects. The procedure is clearly much more objective, but the model estimates on the basis of instructions given it, and these instructions are based on theories and assumptions about how the world works. The human element, or subjectivity, is therefore not removed, but its influence is reduced, especially in the actual processing of data.

Models and simulations for testing alternatives correspond closely to econometric methods in forecasting (see Chapter 9). As in forecasting, testing alternatives with models may or may not involve segmentation. That is, the effects of the alternative on the entire population or system of interest may be estimated, or effects on different subsets may be examined. The segmented approach requires more detailed information to establish the model, but then will provide more detailed and often more accurate estimates of what would happen upon the implementation of each alternative.

An example of a very elaborate econometric model has recently been published by the National Institute of Justice.[28] This model included several simultaneous equations in an attempt to portray the interactions between crime rate and aspects of the public sector such as property values, property taxes, and criminal justice expenditures. Each separate equation specifies the effects of several factors on a dependent variable. The model employs dependent segmentation: the several equations in the model interact. Thus, for example, although increasing criminal justice expenditures might be expected to reduce the crime rate, it might also increase property taxes, which would affect property values and perhaps cause population shifts, which might then influence the crime rate in some other way. These direct and indirect relationships in the model were based on extensive analysis of existing data, with parameters estimated so as to give the best possible fit of the model to the data.

This model was developed primarily for the purpose of explaining the relationships between crime and components of the public sector. Once developed, though, it could be used to test alternatives. For example, criminal justice expenditures could be increased by 5 per cent, with other factors left initially unchanged, and then the model could be "run" for several iterations (years) to test the consequences of such a move. Or an increase in property taxes could be postulated, and the effects of that condition estimated.

A model designed more for the purpose of testing alternatives, and one containing more criminal justice variables that can be manipulated, is JUSSIM.[29] This is a case-flow model of the criminal justice system that takes into account various types of crimes, their volume, the routes followed by those cases through the system, and the resource requirements created by the case flows. A later version of the model, JUSSIM II, also takes into account recidivism, and allows the planner to use the model interactively. In this mode, the computer program prompts the planner at various points to specify whether existing practices are to be changed or left as they are. Following the prompting, the computer calculates the consequences of the planner's decisions, presents them to the planner, and begins a new prompting for the next year. Thus the planner can choose a strategy and maintain it for several years, monitoring the effects on the input (arrest rates) and case flows, or can alter strategies in response to each year's effects.

The JUSSIM model could be used to test the effects of abolishing plea bargaining. To do this, court "branching ratios" would be altered so that guilty pleas were entered for a considerably smaller portion of cases, while more cases went to the trial stage.[30] A change in the overall sentencing pattern might be specified, because of the altered mix of cases, or the assumption might be made that guilty pleas and trial convictions would still get the same kinds of sentences as in the past. Actually, both alternatives could be tested: no plea bargaining, with altered sentencing; no plea bargaining, with unchanged sentencing. Then we could run the model to estimate the consequences of both alternatives over, say, a five-year period. The model would provide information on resource requirements for judges, prosecutors, jails, and prisons, and also information about changes in the volume and pattern of arrests each year. Initially, one would probably expect the abolition of plea bargaining to impose additional court and prison costs, while reducing the number of crimes and arrests, owing to incapacitation, and perhaps deterrent, effects. The model would provide a means of checking these expectations.

But models, no matter how sophisticated, are no better than the theories and assumptions on which they are based. If the underlying theory is not a good representation of reality, a computer model based upon it will relentlessly and efficiently produce results that probably will be completely erroneous. Models also do not eliminate the need for judgment in testing alternatives. They may standardize much of the data-processing involved in trying to determine the effects of alternatives, but common sense and interpretation are still required. This was illustrated in the plea bargaining example, when we, the planners, had to estimate the effects of abolishing plea bargaining on sentencing, before the highly sophisticated JUSSIM II model could spin out the rest of the story. The general situation has been described by Chaiken, et al.:

> Reliance on judgment and intuition is crucial to every decision. This reliance permeates every aspect of analysis in isolating the question to be analyzed, in limiting the extent of the inquiry, in deciding which hypotheses are likely to be more fruitful, in selecting what factors to include, in determining what the "facts" are, and in interpreting the results. A great virtue of models and model building is that they provide a systematic, explicit, and efficient way to focus the required judgment and intuition, particularly that of experts and specialists on whom analysts must usually depend for practical knowledge and experience.[31]

Limited Implementation

An often overlooked but very reasonable method for testing alternatives is to try them out, on a small scale. This approach involves some costs, and also may consume somewhat more time than other methods. It provides an actual field test, though, and if the setting for the test is representative, the results may be a very reliable indication of the effects of the alternatives were they to be fully implemented.

A logical and cost-effective approach to testing alternatives might be to utilize limited implementation as the final stage, after the wide range of alternatives initially generated has been pared down to a smaller number of "most promising" alternatives. One or more of the other approaches to testing alternatives (informal estimation, "soft" formal estimation, models and simulations) could be used to whittle down the full set of alternatives to a few which would then be tested by limited implementation.

Edward Suchman has termed limited implementations *demonstration programs* and has identified three types: pilot programs, model programs, and prototype programs.[32] He describes pilot programs as flexible and revisable to suit a trial-and-error period when solid information about what should work is not available. A model program, by contrast, is the end result of pilot programs and their revisions. Information about the effects of the program alternative is still somewhat tentative, but there are some grounds for hypothesizing success. The model program should be implemented and operated with rigid adherence to its features, so that the hypothesis is tested. If the model program test is successful, then a prototype program should be developed and tested. This is a version of the model program designed so that it can be implemented in a wide variety of real-world settings, on a large scale if necessary, with all the usual practical constraints that confront social programming. This is necessary because the model program probably will have been implemented on a small scale in a single setting, and may have benefited from special resources and attention.

Limited implementations help planners to discover the effects of alternatives under consideration. The effects of each will still need to be compared to the goals or to the criteria for problem resolution, in order to determine which alternative is the best means to the desired ends.

An important complication is introduced when alternatives are tested by limited implementation. Informal and "soft" formal estimation provide subjective but clear estimates of the effects of alternatives. Computer models produce the effects and print them out. In limited implementation, however, the effects are out there in the real world. In order to find them, the planner must go out into the field and determine what happened as a result of the program–in other words, he must conduct evaluation research in order to test the alternative. This does not impose impossible burdens, but it is a different and probably more difficult undertaking than other methods of measuring effects.

On the other side of the ledger, of course, is the possibility that limited implementation provides the most valid indications of the effects of alternatives. It is difficult and costly, but an informative method for testing alternatives. That is why it should not be used until the truly promising alternatives have been separated from the rest: choosing from this smaller set, especially when choosing will commit substantial resources and/or set in motion major changes, may more readily justify the costs and trouble of limited implementation.

A NOTE ON CHOICE, IMPLEMENTATION, AND EVALUATION

It is often hard to decide where to draw the boundary around a process, in order to differentiate it from other activities. Such is the case with planning. Planning extends through the generation of alternatives and the testing or estimation of their effects, as this chapter has suggested. The next logical step is to choose one or more of the alternatives, to commit the resources of the organization or the system to a course of action. We prefer to regard this stage of choice or decision-making as a separate process, rather than as a part of planning. In our view, planning is primarily concerned with widening the range of choices and providing information, whereas decision-making is the use of information to narrow the range of choices.

In some respects the act of choosing might seem a mere formality, for, through the planning process, the alternatives, their effects, and their relationships to goals or criteria will have been specified. It ought to be obvious which alternative to choose, given this information. Occasionally that is the case, but not often. More frequently, there remains considerable uncertainty, particularly about likely effects; also, each alternative will have multiple effects, so that it is necessary to weigh costs and benefits in order to choose. A particular criminal justice policy, for example, might be estimated to produce a 10 per cent decrease in some kinds of crimes, but to have no effect on other types of offenses, to constitute a serious threat to the right to due process, to decrease accountability to the public, and to cost $20 million. These are disparate costs and benefits, not easy to weigh or to reduce to a common denominator. And if there are, say, ten such policies with multiple effects, the situation becomes even more realistic. And there would be further complications, for all of the effects would be estimates, perhaps with varying probabilities or confidence intervals. These are the kinds of characteristics that pervade real-world decision-making, even when the way has been smoothed by competent planning.

Economists and management scientists have developed some very sophisticated methods for choosing in complicated, uncertain situations such as those commonly encountered in the real world.[33] These methods are well beyond the scope of this book. Interested readers and practicing managers are certainly encouraged to venture into the decision sciences to complement their other skills.

Once a choice is made, the next logical step is to implement the chosen alternative or alternatives. Implementation is obviously a key step in the sequence of rational actions but, oddly enough, until recently it has received relatively little attention. It is fast becoming clear, however, that the translation of plans and decisions into actions cannot be taken for granted. The title of a recent book captures the essence of our findings: *Implementation: How Great Expectations in Washington are Dashed in Oakland; Or, Why It's Amazing that Federal Programs Work At All.*[34]

The importance of implementation is obvious. When considerable time and energy have been invested in figuring out what to do, it is a shame to do something else, or to do nothing at all. Basically, implementation requires sound administration and management. To put plans and decisions into action requires organization, resources, staff, direction, and control. The reader can learn more about these processes and about implementation from just about any management book or course.

Rational action is completed by evaluation. Were the goals achieved? Were the problems resolved? What were the effects of the alternative chosen and implemented? Did that which was intended or planned get implemented? This information is needed for the next round of planning and deciding, for considering alternatives and estimating their effects. It is also needed for identifying the problem: Does the original problem still exist or was it solved? Is there a new problem? Evaluation completes the cycle of rational action:

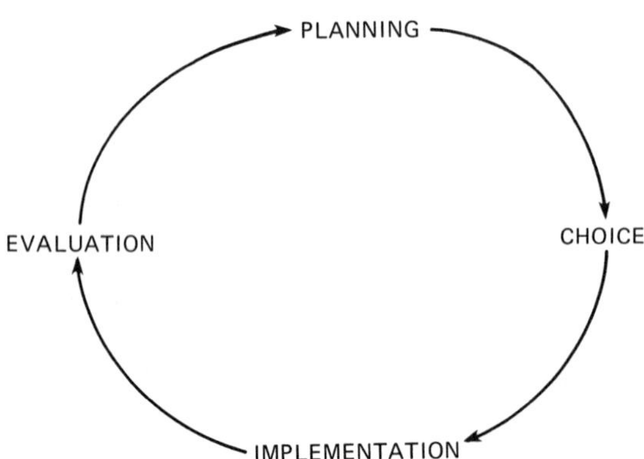

Evaluation was briefly discussed with respect to testing the effects of limited implementation. Basically, evaluation requires research—generally, field research—and it is rarely a simple undertaking. Within all the complexity of the real world, one small change was implemented, and it is a tremendous challenge to try to figure out what, if anything, happened as a result. Rarely does evaluation benefit from the kinds of controls that characterize true scientific experiments. Absent these controls, evaluation findings are often tentative, which is unfortunate, for the result is tentative information to feed into later planning and decision-making. Some evaluation methods are better than others, though, and in the last decade evaluation research has been one of the most popular and most closely scrutinized subjects in the social sciences. The interested reader will have no difficulty locating additional materials on this topic.[35]

One point that must be made with respect to evaluation is that it is absolutely necessary to look very carefully at what was actually implemented.[36] What gets implemented is often different from what the planner and decision-maker intended. The effects will be those of what was really implemented. Too often conclusions are drawn from the evaluation about the desirability of the planner's proposed alternative, when in fact it may never have been put into effect. As one rough example, some people conclude from the present crime situation that the policy of deterrence is a failure: the criminal justice system, they argue, is based on deterrence, but crime continues to increase, so deterrence does not work. Others contend, however, that deterrence has not been given a fair chance, because the present criminal justice system does not provide certain punishment for those who commit crimes. The real problem is to identify what has actually been implemented, and then what its effects have been. Any evaluation of the effectiveness of the deterrence policy would undoubtedly lead to tentative conclusions, both because of uncertain findings about effects and also because of incomplete implementation of the policy.

SUMMARY

It is very important in the planning process to identify and develop a wide range of alternatives. Though there are numerous practical constraints on the generation of alternatives, which inevitably limit the number of ideas considered, alternatives can be generated through review, search, and design. Reviewing involves considering alternatives already within the organization's or system's repertoire; searching seeks alternatives that have been developed and perhaps tried elsewhere; design, the most demanding approach, requires the development of wholly new solutions for problems or of means for attaining goals. Ordinarily, the generation of alternatives begins with review, proceeds to search if necessary, and continues to design only when more routine efforts do not suffice and the problem is serious enough to warrant such an expenditure of time and energy.

Once some alternatives have been identified, an attempt must be made to figure out what would happen if they were implemented. The methods for testing alternatives bear some resemblance to those for forecasting, which is natural for both testing alternatives and forecasting involve an element of prediction. Four general approaches to the testing of alternatives were discussed: informal estimation, "soft" formal estimation, models and simulations, and limited implementation. The first two are the most subjective of the methods. Limited implementation provides the most "realistic" test of an alternative; it is also the most costly, however, and determining the effects may be difficult. The use of models reduces the subjectivity involved in the informal and "soft" formal estimation methods, but the planner must be careful not to forget that the model itself is based upon assumptions and theories that never completely represent the real world.

The chapter concludes with a few comments on choice, implementation, and evaluation, which with planning constitute the cycle of rational action.

Chapter 10 NOTES

1. Herbert A. Simon, *Administrative Behavior*, 3rd ed. (New York: The Free Press, 1976), p. 81.
2. James L. Adams, *Conceptual Blockbusting*, 2nd ed. (New York: W. W. Norton & Company, Inc., 1980), p. xi.
3. Julian Feldman and Herschel E. Kanter, "Organizational Decision Making," in James G. March, ed., *Handbook of Organizations* (Chicago: Rand McNally & Company, 1965), p. 620.
4. Bruce S. Jansson and Samuel H. Taylor, "Search Activity in Social Agencies: Institutional Factors that Influence Policy Analysis," *Social Service Review* (June 1978), 189-201.
5. Ibid., p. 199.
6. John K. Hudzik, et al., *Criminal Justice Manpower Planning: An Overview* (Washington, D.C.: U.S. Law Enforcement Assistance Administration, U.S. Government Printing Office, 1981).
7. Ernest R. Alexander, "The Design of Alternatives in Organizational Contexts: A Pilot Study," *Administrative Science Quarterly*, 24 (September 1979), 382-404.
8. Ibid., p. 385.
9. Ibid., p. 398.
10. Ibid., p. 396.
11. James G. March and Herbert A. Simon, *Organizations* (New York: John Wiley & Sons, 1958), pp. 179-80.
12. Don Koberg and Jim Bagnal, *The All New Universal Traveler* (Los Altos, Calif.: William Kaufman, Inc., 1976), pp. 66, 68.
13. With respect to technology transfer, see Juanita L. Rubinstein, "Office of Technology Transfer," in Susan O. White and Samuel Krislov, eds., *Understanding Crime: An Evaluation of the National Institute of Law Enforcement and Criminal Justice* (Washington, D.C.: National Academy of Sciences, 1977), pp. 156-63. For a program model example, see Terry W. Koepsell and Charles M. Girard, *Small Police Agency Consolidation: Suggested Approaches* (Washington, D.C.: U.S. Government Printing Office, 1979). For an exemplary project example, see Carol Holliday Blew and Robert Rosenblum, *The Community Arbitration Project: Anne Arundel County, Maryland* (Washington, D.C.: U.S. Government Printing Office, 1979).
14. Herbert A. Simon, "Applying Information Technology to Organization Design," *Public Administration Review* (May/June 1973), 272.
15. See Herbert A. Simon, *The Sciences of the Artificial* (Cambridge, MA.: Massachusetts Institute of Technology, 1969), for a very

illuminating and challenging discussion of the science of design.

16. Christopher Alexander, *Notes on the Synthesis of Form* (Cambridge, MA.: Harvard University Press, 1964).

17. See Adams, op. cit., for a discussion of this sort of activity.

18. Thomas Kuhn, *The Structure of Scientific Revolutions*, 2nd ed. (Chicago: University of Chicago Press, 1970), argues more generally that major scientific progress results from episodic transcendence of established "paradigms."

19. Alex Osborn, *Applied Imagination* (New York: Charles Scribner's Sons, 1953).

20. Koberg and Bagnall, op. cit., p. 72.

21. Robin M. Hogarth and Spyros Makridakis, "Forecasting and Planning: An Evaluation," *Management Science*, 27 (February 1981), 116.

22. Douglas Lipton, et al., *The Effectiveness of Correctional Treatment: A Survey of Treatment Evaluation Studies* (New York: Praeger Publishers, Inc., 1975).

23. Larry Hirschhorn, "Scenario Writing: A Developmental Approach," *Journal of the American Planning Association* (April 1980), 172–83.

24. William C. Baer and Skye M. Fleming, "Counterfactual Analysis: An Analytical Tool for Planners," *Journal of the American Institute of Planners* (July 1976), 243-52.

25. Ibid., p. 244.

26. Britton Harris, "Plan or Projection: An Examination of the Use of Models in Planning," *Journal of the American Institute of Planners*, 26 (November 1960), 272.

27. Ira S. Lowry, "A Short Course in Model Design," *Journal of the American Institute of Planners*, 31 (May 1965), 159.

28. Daryl A. Hellman and Joel L. Naroff, *The Urban Public Sector and Urban Crime: A Simultaneous System Approach* (Washington, D.C.: U.S. Government Printing Office, 1980).

29. J. Chaiken, et al., *Criminal Justice Models: An Overview* (Washington, D.C.: U.S. Government Printing Office, 1976), 21–30.

30. Jacob Belkin, et al., *JUSSIM II: An Interactive Feedback Model for Criminal Justice Planning* (Pittsburgh: Urban Systems Institute, Carnegie-Mellon University, 1973).

31. Chaiken, et al., op. cit., p. 6.

32. Edward A. Suchman, "Action for What? A Critique of Evaluative Research," in Carol H. Weiss, ed., *Evaluating Action Programs: Readings in Social Action and Education* (Boston: Allyn & Bacon, Inc., 1972), pp. 59–62.

33. See, for example, Howard Raiffa, *Decision Analysis: Introductory Lectures on Choices Under Uncertainty* (Reading, MA.: Addison-Wesley Publishing Co., Inc., 1970), and George P. Huber, *Managerial Decision-Making* (Glenview, Ill.: Scott, Foresman and Company, 1980).

34. Jeffrey L. Pressman and Aaron B. Wildavsky, *Implementation* (Berkeley, Calif: University of California Press, 1973.

35. See Carol H. Weiss, *Evaluation Research: Methods of Assessing Program Effectiveness* (Englewood Cliffs, N.J.: Prentice-Hall Inc., 1972), for a good introduction to methods and literature in evaluation.

36. Ralph G. Lewis and Jack R. Greene, "Implementation Evaluation: A Future Direction in Project Evaluation," *Journal of Criminal Justice*, 6 (Summer 1978), 167–76.

· Part IV ·

DATA FOR CRIMINAL JUSTICE PLANNING

This part examines several issues related to identifying and collecting the data necessary for criminal justice planning. Chapter 11 is focused on answering two prime questions: What does the term *data* mean in relation to planning? What major types of data are important for criminal justice planning? The answer to the first question involves examining the difference between data and information and examining also concepts of operationalization and validity. These two concepts are central to the process of identifying and collecting data useful for planning purposes. Qualitative and quantitative data and levels of data measurement will also be discussed.

The second part of Chapter 11 presents the major categories or types of data important to criminal justice planning. These data are arranged and discussed under three broad headings: environmental data, organizational data, and system data. Each of these major categories and their principal components are defined, along with their uses or applications in criminal justice planning.

Chapter 12 examines the alternative sources of criminal justice planning data and the principal means or methods available for collecting these data. The chapter begins with a general review of relevant research principles: research design, methods of data collection, operationalization and measurement, validity and reliability, sampling, and basic alternative modes for data collection. The principal alternative methods for collecting environmental and organizational data are presented in the second part of Chapter 12, along with some of the chief difficulties confronted by the attempt to secure valid and reliable data. A crucial point made throughout Chapter 12 is that determining what data needs to be collected and how to collect it is governed by research design. Without good research design and attention to research principles, any attempt to provide planning with useful empirical data is hampered.

Chapter II

DATA AND CRIMINAL JUSTICE PLANNING

As noted in Chapter 1, thinking about or conceptualizing the future is a principal aspect of planning. The central processes associated with planning (setting goals and identifying problems, forecasting, and testing alternatives) are not, however, simply a matter of thinking about the future. An essential element in planning is data—data about past and present conditions, about goals, forecasts, and alternatives for the future. It is important to ground understandings on observational data rather than purely on intuition, imagination, and abstraction.[1] What is needed is empirically based planning—planning based on observational data and information. This chapter and the next discuss this aspect of planning, particularly the kinds of observational data that are important in criminal justice planning and their alternative sources.

The kinds of data important for criminal justice planning depend on the problem or issue being addressed, and a full treatment of data and their relationship to criminal justice planning could well occupy several volumes. The objective in this chapter is to provide an overview of the principal issues involved, and to deal with two major questions: What does the term *data* mean in relation to planning? What are the principal kinds or types of data that are important to criminal justice planning?

Although *data* is a popular term, certain fundamental aspects of the term need to be summarized. A consideration of some of the more important and basic notions about the term *data* will reveal that data can take many forms—and form, more often than not, has implications for what can be done with the data used in planning.

GENERAL NOTIONS ABOUT DATA

In its simplest form, *data* means *records of observations.*[2] Examples of data include the temperature at noon, the size of a door opening, the inmate count at 12:01 A.M., or the number of traffic citations issued last year. Data are records (written or mental) of observations of events in the physical or real world. But, as Abraham Kaplan points out, "we do not observe everything that is there to be seen."[3] Thus, the collection of data is a conscious act.

Another basic notion about data is that a datum has no meaning by itself; it derives meaning from its relation to something else. In "A Theory of Data," Clyde Coombs advances the proposition that observations become data only when they are interpreted in some way, within some set of conceptual referents.[4] The implication is that an observation is given meaning by relation to a concept (to an abstract thinking process), and that when this is done, observations become data and also measures of concepts. Mayer and Greenwood say that concepts are broken into subconcepts or variables, that these in turn are broken down into indicators, and that data are measures of indicators.[5] Figure 11-1 illustrates a similar set of distinctions.

The consequence of viewing data in this fashion is that a simple observation can have different meanings, depending on the concepts being measured.[6] For example, the meaning of an unemployment level in a city will depend on what concepts, variables, or indicators the observation is assumed to be

Figure 11-1. Levels of Abstraction

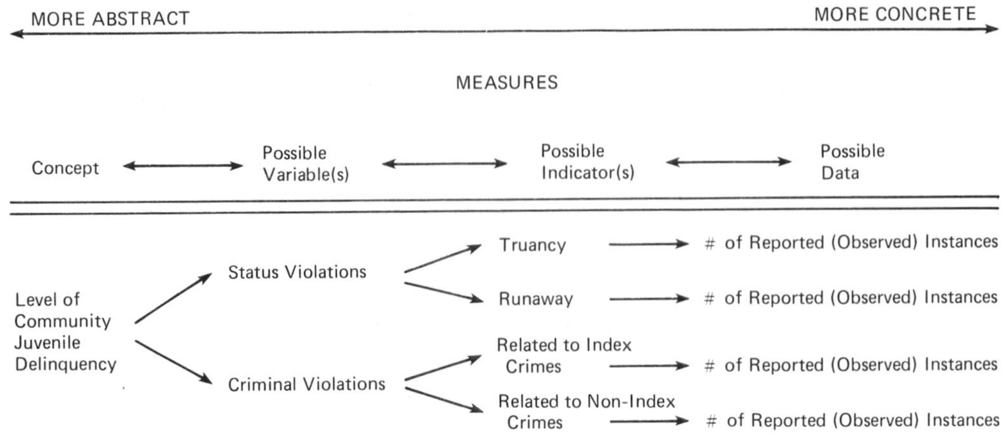

measuring. Two possibilities come readily to mind. One is that unemployment level is measuring the availability of workers in the local labor market: the higher the unemployment level, the greater the availability of workers and, hence, the greater the city's potential for absorbing new business and industry. Or unemployment level may be a measure of economic health: the higher the unemployment level, the less healthy the economy. Both or either of these interpretations may have implications for criminal justice agency planning: a larger pool of labor available for employment in the agency; higher crime levels.

A distinction is often drawn between data and information: data are a record of observation; information is "interpreted data."[7] For Bassett, *information* is "reserved to mean knowledge for the sake of purposeful action."[8] Referring to the example of unemployment data, Bassett would say that these data become information when, for example, they are interpreted to mean the existence of a certain state of economic health or disease.

If observations derive meaning from their relationship to concepts, it is also true that concepts are given meaning through observation of concrete things or events that are *chosen* to "represent" the concept and allow it to be measured. For example, intelligence is a concept: it cannot be observed directly; rather, it is observed only indirectly, perhaps through the use of a test. The higher the score an individual gets on a particular intelligence test, the greater—presumably—his intelligence. Naturally, there is the problem that different tests may measure different aspects or components of intelligence: reasoning, recall, assimilation, handling information, solving problems, and so on. Also, the validity of any test as a measure of intelligence or any of its components is open to great debate. The point in this example, however, is that by employing a *particular* test, a researcher *chooses operationally* to define intelligence in *that* particular way.

Paul Reynolds defines operational definition as

> a set of procedures that describes the activities an observer should perform in order to receive sensory impressions (sound, visual or tactile impressions, etc.) that indicate the existence, or degree of existence, of a theoretical concept.[9]

Another example of operationalization involves the concept of juvenile deliquency. Figure 11-1, if read from right to left, shows one example of how concrete operational indicators and data can serve to "operationalize" a concept. The concept, *level of community juvenile deliquency*, is defined by a certain set of indicators and data to be collected. Imagine the effect on the operational definition of the concept if all pieces of the Figure involving status violations were eliminated: the operational definition of *level of community juvenile delinquency* would be changed, and rather dramatically. Thus, as a single observation may have different meanings, depending on the concept(s) related to it, concepts may come to have different meanings depending on how they are operationally defined.

To identify and to collect data for planning, it is particularly important to understand how concrete measures and recorded conscious observations relate to concepts. For example, the planning goal may be to improve agency performance, but it is a matter of choice how *performance* will be operationally defined and how data about it will be collected. Is *performance* for a corrections agency operationally defined as number of prison disturbances? as recidivism rates among released inmates? as a combination of these? The operational definition will determine what data must be collected.

There are also considerations of the various types of data available for both general research and planning. There are also questions of the validity and reliability of data as measures of concepts. These questions are briefly considered in the short sections following (and further discussed in Chapter 12).

Quantitative and Qualitative Data

By definition, quantitative data are expressed in numerical form and have mathematical properties. Qualitative data do not have mathematical properties but only categorical properties (e.g., black or white; rich or poor; Catholic, Protestant, or Jewish; student or worker, male or female, and so on). Many sophisticated statistical techniques have been developed that are useful only with quantitative data and, thus, a tendency has developed of late to ignore the use of qualitative data.[10] Nonetheless, qualitative data should not be ignored for they comprise some of the most important kinds of data in social research and in planning-related research. For example, in criminal justice planning, categorical data related to the distribution of ideological persuasion among community members may be important for understanding the kinds of policies that will receive community support.

Quantitative and qualitative data may be divided into four groups or types of data: nominal, ordinal, interval, and ratio data. These distinctions are important because specialized kinds of statistical and analytical techniques have been developed for each. Each type is different and is based on different assumptions.

Nominal Data. Nominal data are qualitative or categorical data having the properties of mutual exclusivity and exhaustiveness. That is, every datum collected on some variable fits in one and only one category, and there is a category appropriate for every datum. For example, concerning the variable "sex," the categories of male and female are technically exhaustive and mutually exclusive. Nominal data does not, however, allow any mathematical ordering or measuring of the categories—for example male is not "more" than female or "less" than female.

Ordinal Data. Data collected on variables having qualities that can be mathematically ordered (e.g., height or length, quantity, age, and so on) permit a ranking of the categories within which the various data are fit. For example, suppose that there were a way of measuring and collecting data on the *degree* to which people agreed with or disagreed with the idea of funding a community halfway house. Suppose further that this question were put into a survey that allowed people to indicate that they strongly agreed, agreed, were neutral, disagreed, or strongly disagreed with the idea. The five categories of answers have an order to them—they range from more to less—and the nature of community response to this survey item can be summarized in terms of more or less agreement. What ordinal data do not show, however, is whether the amount of difference between strong agreement and agreement is the same as between agreement and neutrality. Only interval data begins to allow this kind of determination.

Interval Data. Some variables and the kinds of data collected about these variables measure the actual distance between categories. The difference between 56°F. and 57°F., for example, is the same as the difference between 95°F. and 96°F.; the difference between ten and twenty years of age is the same as the difference between fifty and sixty years of age. Budget data expressed in dollars, often used for planning purposes, are another example.

Ratio Data. When the interval scale used to determine the categories within which the data are placed has a true zero point or origin, the data scale is said to be ratio. Examples include Kelvin-scale readings because they have a true zero-degree point. Age or budget data also have true zero points and are thus ratio data.

Picking a Level of Measurement of Data

Both qualitative and quantitative data are important in planning. If quantitative-data collection is structured in a way that permits use of interval and ratio levels of measurement rather than ordinal, then analytical and statistical possibilities are thereby increased. Some variables, of course, do not allow anything but ordinal measurement. Nonetheless, there is a choice in many instances. Suppose, for example, that an attempt is made to collect information about past agency budgets, the objective being to get some idea of budget history as an element in forecasting future budget treatment. One option is simply to record whether from one year to the next the budget has increased, stayed the same, or decreased. Such data are only an ordinal measurement because they do not indicate *how much* the budget has changed. Another option is to collect interval or ratio data—the actual dollar amount of increase or decrease from one year to the next. This interval measure provides more powerful data, but such data are also usually more expensive to collect and record. Indeed, securing "better" data is often more costly, so the quality and utility of data must be considered against the cost of collection.

Primary Data, Secondary Data, and Ecological Fallacy

Primary data are those collected by the researcher or planner firsthand and usually for a specific purpose. Secondary data are those which have been collected for one purpose, but are now used for another purpose or to answer different questions. Primary data have the advantage (theoretically at least) of being uniquely suited to the concepts, variables, and indicators pertinent to the issue at hand. Secondary data have the advantage of costing less in time and money because the data are already collected.

Many data in criminal justice, especially those used for planning purposes, are secondary. For example, public records of agencies as well as internal organizational records (more often than not kept because of general "record-keeping" requirements rather than any specific research- or planning-oriented reasons) provide substantial data for planning purposes. Other examples of secondary data, often useful for criminal justice research and planning, include *Expenditure and Employment Data for the Criminal Justice System*,[11] the U.S. Census, reports from large survey-research centers[12] and public-opinion polling corporations, and data from previous criminal justice studies.

One of the difficulties in using secondary data, however, is that the data from previous studies are reported in summarized or aggregated format—that is, the data describe groups.[13] More particularly, such reports describe aggregate characteristics of one or more groups, but the groups described by such existing data may not be the groups of interest with regard to a particular planning issue; more important, the planner may need the individual data upon which the aggregate data were formed. For example, *Expenditure and Employment Data of the Criminal Justice System* reports aggregate data in a variety of forms—one form being groupings of criminal justice agencies by size. There is a danger, however, in assuming that group patterns reflect corresponding patterns of individual agencies within these groups.

This difficulty, referred to as the *ecological fallacy*, is principally found in secondary data, but it may also occur in the use of primary data if the researcher is not careful to consider the appropriate unit of analysis for recording and arranging the data.

For example, data about a police department might indicate no relationship between response time and likelihood of arrest. It might be the case, though, that substantial differences among precincts, shifts, individuals, and times of day are masked by the overall finding. Unless the data can be broken down according to these criteria, there is little way of determining whether such differences exist and are being masked. Or, consider a situation in which data have been collected on conviction rates for the fifty states. The data might show similar rates among the states but might mask big differences among localities within each state or among conviction rates for certain types of offenses or types of offenders.

Data Validity

Validity is a multifaceted problem in research and data collection and there are also numerous threats to it.[14] Two of its more important aspects involve whether the operational definition of a concept actually measures opinions about the concept in question and whether the right opinions are being measured. For example, if the aim were to survey people's opinions about halfway houses, but questions about minimum-security prisons were asked instead, there would be an obvious validity problem: the measurement device (questions about prisons) cannot, at face value, collect data about the concept (halfway houses). The easiest way of testing validity is "face value": does the measurement device "sensibly and accurately" measure what is meant to be measured?[15] Other ways to check for validity include the criterion, pragmatic, concurrent, predictive, and construct tests of validity.[16] Although the ultimate validity of a measure and its associated data can never be demonstrated,[17] the objective of validity tests is to make measures and data as valid as possible, to think carefully about the concept being investigated and to choose the measurements that would appear to have the best validity (see also Chapter 12).

TYPES OF DATA FOR CRIMINAL JUSTICE PLANNING

The types of data, measures, and indicators potentially useful to criminal justice planning efforts, if fully detailed, would yield volumes of printed material. Indeed, a 1977 book dealt just with the data and indicators necessary to treat the measurement of the "performance of prosecution, defense, and court agencies involved in felony proceedings."[18] The objective of this section is to describe the major categories within which variously detailed observational data useful for planning can be fit, and to discuss a few of the major pitfalls and problems associated with these data and data sources (see also Chapter 12).

It is possible to view the important categories of planning-related data in terms of the central processes of planning: identification of goals and problems, forecasting, and generation and testing of alternatives. Data needs include information related to agency goals, missions, and performance (what they are, ways of measuring them, and observational data about how much they are being met or have been met). Data in this category might well include assessments of community needs, or opinions from community and political leaders about missions, performance, and goals.[19]

Also needed are pertinent data on variables which would allow forecasting of agency and environmental conditions. In criminal justice these might include data on trends in population, crime, the economy, service demands, budgets, and a host of other variables. For example, Volume 6 of the *National Manpower Survey of the Criminal Justice System* included these variables and several others in its attempt to forecast criminal justice manpower needs.[20] The generation and testing of policy and program alternatives would require *agency-based* data and information of a wide variety, and also data and information on findings from previous organizational experiments or from management- and policy-oriented publications.[21] These sources of data and information can provide ideas for new policy and program alternatives, can indicate whether they have been tried and have worked in other places, and can show which circumstances appear necessary to make them viable.

Another way of categorizing data for planning is according to the basic and important variables usually associated with planning analyses. Although the categories are not exhaustive, they are generally recognized as the most important ones:

Environmental Data:

Agency Missions and Goals

Data in this category are usually qualitative and subjective. Data and information collected on missions and goals may come from several sources, including both internal agency and public and political sources. Information on missions and goals provides an anchoring mechanism for planning agency programs and for evaluating agency performance.

Crime

Data in this category often are expressed quantitatively in terms of levels of crime within detailed categories as well as in terms of crime trends, mathematically expressed. Information related to crime provides a principal input to organizational and system planning and can be seen as a measure of demand placed on criminal justice agencies and systems.

Economic and Budget Conditions

In their typical form, data on these variables are expressed quantitatively, and often as trend data/information. Economic and budget data are principal means of measuring the level of potential and actual environmental support for the criminal justice system and its agencies.

Population Characteristics
Demographic data about the population served are often expressed quantitatively along dimensions involving socioeconomic mix, income, housing, education, race, and so on. Information on demographics may serve as indicators for determining the quantitative and qualitative nature of demands placed on the system and its agencies–namely, numbers and kinds of people with associated needs for service.

Public and Political Values
Data and information on public and political values are subjectively derived and affect not only agency missions and goals but agency and system program options. Information may focus on the qualitative aspects of political and public ideology and program preferences, or on quantitative expressions of degree of political and public support for various ideological positions and program alternatives.

Labor-market Conditions
The availability of labor and the qualitative characteristics of the labor pool from which the agency recruits its personnel are primary among these data.

Organizational Data:

Work loads
Data in this category measure the amount and kind of work performed by the agency. The data are usually expressed quantitatively in terms of amount of work performed of various types or in various areas of the agency. Specific forms of data expression include number of work-units performed in various categories, number of personnel manhours consumed per work-unit, and the like.

Job-focused Data
Data and information here concern the nature of the work done in an agency and can be defined and divided into jobs that are collections of roles, tasks and activities. Job-focused data are often qualitatively based and appear as descriptions of job characteristics. There may also be quantitative elements in job-description data–such as the requirement of shooting at the 80 per cent level, or of running a mile in ten minutes or less. Some aspects of job-focused data are quantitative expressions as in specifying the number of jobs within certain categories, or in specifying the number of people needed with certain skills and knowledge to fill certain jobs.

Employee-Focused Data
Data and information in this category are quantitative and qualitative expressions of the characteristics of employees–characteristics relevant to the performance of agency jobs and missions. One typical data expression involves the number of people within the agency who have various kinds of knowledge and skills. This information provides a basis for estimating the work and job potential of the agency, and is important given that criminal justice is largely a labor-intensive field.

Performance
Agency-performance data are vitally concerned with measuring and determining the degree to which the agency is meeting its missions and goals. Performance data may be quantitatively oriented as in law-enforcement agencies traditional calculation of clearance rates. Subjective but quantitatively expressed ratings of agency performance by citizens or by clientele served can act as measures of performance.

System Data:

Simulations of Rate and Flow
Principally, these are data and information about the intake and processing of offenders and cases through the various stages of the criminal justice system. Data may focus on types of cases, types of offenders, or both. Calculations are usually made about rates of flow from one sector to the next, dependent on both initial intake and ratios of the frequency with which various decision options are exercised in each stage.

System-transaction Data:
These are data related to tracking offenses and offenders through the entire system.

Each of the categories of data is considerably more complex and contains numerous, more specific versions of data than have been indicated. The sources of these data vary greatly, as do their form and content.

Environmental Data

Data about conditions and forces largely external to the criminal justice agency are important in planning. An important class of information concerns the missions and goals of an agency. Attempts to state goals in measurable ways often fail (precisely what does "enforcing the law" or "keeping inmates safe and secure" mean?). But knowing what the prime missions and goals are, how to measure them, and when they change is important for planning. For example, if providing education to inmates so as to promote minimal levels of literacy becomes a new mission of a correctional agency, important programmatic, resource, and personnel consequences will ensue. Clear knowledge and understanding of such a mission, with its attendant goals, begins the planning process.

Sources of information about missions and goals include official documents, pronouncements by public officials, and views of the public as recorded through, for example, citizen surveys. These are also the principal existing sources of other forms of environmental data (crime data, economic and budget data, population data, and public- and political-values data).

Data concerning labor-market conditions and demographics are important because criminal justice employees are part of the larger local, state, and national labor markets. The characteristics of the local labor pool, the competition from both public and private employers for qualified personnel, obviously influence both the numbers and kinds of personnel available to the agency. No matter how essential skills and knowledge are defined and no matter what the workload of the agency, criminal justice agencies must compete with others for qualified employees. Data related to sources of competition for employees are important, and can be secured in part through exit interviews with employees to find out where they are going and why. Knowledge of competitive wage-and-benefit scales, of perceptions of the "attractiveness" of occupations in criminal justice compared with that of occupations offered by competitors, of unemployment rates (and their effect on the opportunity for alternative employment) is information that may at one time or another be important to understanding not only the relative availability of people for jobs in the agency, but also what needs to be done in order to attract qualified individuals in sufficient numbers.

Basic characteristics of the population served will influence not only the amount and kind of service expected of an agency, but also the need for numbers and kinds of agency personnel. So will data on the economy and on budgets. The percentage of juveniles in the population, unemployment rates, per capita income, the percentage of in-migrants in the population, the cultural and racial composition of the population (to name a few characteristics) variously influence the amount and kind of crime and ultimately the kind of services expected of law-enforcement agencies.[22] Changes in population may well require adjustments in agencies—changes in basic missions, in allocation of resources, and in programs. Collection of primary data on population and economics is not normally a responsibility of criminal justice agencies, because several official, public, and private sources of such data exist (U.S. Census, chambers of commerce, banks, survey-research bureaus, corporations, and so on). The use of such secondary data risks the attendant problems of inappropriate aggregation and ecological fallacy (see also Chapter 12).

Crime Data

The principal existing forms of crime data are the *Uniform Crime Reports* (UCR), the victimization survey, and internal agency records. An examination of each of these provides more substantial insight into the kinds of crime data available and relevant to criminal justice planning efforts. Crime data are particularly important in many models of, and approaches to, criminal justice planning.

The rates and the nature of crime greatly influence an agency's need for resources, as well as the kinds of resources needed. Obviously, the higher the crime rate, the greater the load on criminal justice agencies, and the greater their need for resources and personnel. Also, however, the changing nature of crime coupled with changing public attitudes about what kinds of crime the system should concentrate on, can affect the types of employees needed. For example, increased emphasis on stopping white-collar crime may lead a law-enforcement agency to hire greater numbers of employees trained in accounting and computers. Conversely, when the greater emphasis is on dealing with street crime, an entirely different mix of agency resources and personnel may be needed.

At least two sets of crime data are important for planning purposes: the first concerns actual levels of crime; the second, public perceptions about crime—the public's fear of crime, and the public's views about which crimes are most serious and menacing. Of course, not all the work of criminal justice agencies is crime-related; the police, for example, have increasingly adopted various social-welfare roles. Nonetheless, the amount and the kind of crime are central pieces of information in criminal justice.

UCR Data. Traditional forms of crime data are the *Uniform Crime Reports* (UCR) which began as early as 1924 under the auspices of the International Association of Chiefs of Police and are now put together by the FBI.[23] The primary data are organized around "index offenses," including criminal homocide, forcible rape, robbery, aggravated assault, burglary (and breaking or entry), larceny-theft, and motor-vehicle theft and arson. The sources of such data are local police agencies, which "voluntarily" submit data on crime *reported* to them. (In some states, reporting is mandatory under state-level requirements.)

Other forms of data collected in similar fashion under the UCR program include clearance rates (arrests of one or more individuals for an index offense); the value of property stolen and recovered; the number of arrests by age, sex, and race; the number of law-enforcement officers killed and assaulted; the disposition of cases (the number of persons charged and the results of the charge); the number of sworn and civilian fulltime employees; and bomb information (not formally a part of the UCR program, but more recently collected as part of the UCR program).

These UCR data form the basis for a number of reports that include rates and trends in reported criminal offenses; trends in arrest broken down by age, race, sex; data on repeat offenders through the Computerized Criminal History (CCH) File; the number of law-enforcement employees according to size of population served; various tabulations by region, division, state, Standard Metropolitan Statistical Area, and cities over 10,000 in population; correlational data on clearance, arrest and disposition; and trend tables of offenses, clearances, and arrests.

UCR data provide a wealth of information potentially useful not only for law-enforcement agencies, but also for corrections, courts, and prosecution. This information can be useful not only in understanding and planning for demands put on the agency, but also for providing a measure of how well the problem of crime is being handled (e.g., decreases in offenses, or increases in clearance rates, or "improvement" in final dispositions).

UCR is not without problems, however, and many of the problems are rather severe. The principal difficulty is that UCR reflects only reported crime subsequently recorded by the police. Yet, much crime goes unnoticed or unreported, and even reported crimes may not be recorded as crimes by police.[24] Particularly in areas where public confidence in the criminal justice system's ability to do something about criminal behavior is low, victims may not bother to report the crime. In cases of rape, with its attendant psychological shock and social denigration, the victim is postively discouraged from reporting. Given these kinds of problems, UCR often may not provide accurate data for planners.

Another problem is that not all criminal behavior is systematically collected or reported in UCR. Don and Michael Gottfredson have made special reference to this problem:

> [I]t may be noted also that many offenses that may be thought quite serious are not included—for example, arson, kidnapping, child molestation, simple assault, extortion, combination in restraint of trade, trusts, monopolies; or weapons offenses. Similarly, some nonindex crimes, such as fraud or embezzlement, may be quite significant in dollar loss to victims. . . .[25]

Offenses such as those cited by the Gottfredsons consume great amounts of the resources of the criminal justice system. A planner without information about them will hardly have a complete picture of the workload placed on the agency. Compounding the problem is the fact that even if crimes are reported, police agencies may manipulate the data in recording them because there is wide variation among jurisdictions and situations in the labelling of a particular criminal act.[26]

Agency Records on Crime. UCR data illustrate the problems inherent in relying on a single source or type of data to measure a concept. UCR data usually need to be supplemented by additional data from other sources in order for the planner to get a more accurate picture. An agency's own records on criminal activity are one obvious supplement. Although UCR data are based on the records of individual police agencies, nothing precludes individual agencies from collecting, keeping, and analyzing data on crime beyond those required under UCR reporting procedures. For example, nonindex offenses, such as those on the Gottfredsons' list, can be recorded, along with concomitant data on clearance, arrest, disposition, demographic characteristics of offenders and victims, and information on the offenses themselves.

If agency-based data are properly kept and stored for retrieval, the agency can produce its own reports, categorizing data according to type of offense, type of offender, type of victim, time and place of offense, and trends in these variables. This is useful as planners attempt to determine what resources the agency needs, and how those resources should be assigned; it also helps to counteract the fact that UCR data are not easily or satisfactorily disaggregated from individual agency reports. Figure 11-2 provides an example of the kinds of crime-related data that an agency may choose to keep as a part of its own records system.

The categories of data in Figure 11-2 are not all that may be important. With automated information systems—systems not now possessed by all or even by most agencies—the task of keeping such data in a manageable and retrievable form is considerably eased. But even just

Figure 11-2. Data on Crime Reported or Observed (Partial Listing of Data that can be Collected)

1. About the Offense

   Classification ______

   Time of day ______

   Location ______

   Property value loss ______

   Victims injured and killed ______

   Source of report ______

   Officer injury ______

   Response time ______

   Arrest ______

   Final disposition ______

2. About the Victim (crossreferenced to offense)

   Demographic data ______
   (e.g., age, race, sex, occupation)

   Data related to the crime ______
   (for example, what was the victim doing, was he/she alone, did he/she witness the crime, and so on)

3. About the Offender (crossreferenced to offense)

   Demographic data ______
   (e.g., age, race, sex, occupation)

   Modus operandi ______

   Previous arrests

   Previous convictions ______

these data will permit planners to analyze the occurrence of offenses by time and place, and correlate that information with types of victims and types of offenders. This in turn would have obvious implications not only for assessing trends in types of crime, but also for assigning agency resources to particular times and places, or for directing agency resources toward certain kinds of offenders, offenses, or victims.

Victimization-Survey Data. Although agency records may supplement UCR data, the problem remains that agency records, as well as UCR, require that a crime be observed and reported. Victimization-survey data, first formally provided by LEAA in 1974, is an attempt to alleviate this problem by circumventing nonreporting and by permitting examination of patterns of nonreporting.[27] Through the use of random-survey techniques, individuals throughout the nation are asked about their experiences with crime, their reactions to crime, their evaluation of the performance of criminal justice agencies, their characteristics, and the circumstances surrounding criminal acts. Victimization-survey data is not necessarily error-free (as will be discussed in Chapter 12), but it is a valuable addition to UCR and agency-records data.

A startling revelation uncovered by initial victimization-survey attempts was that UCR estimates of crime nationwide should be doubled, and more than doubled for certain crime categories (e.g., rape).[28] Although it has been argued that crime may have been overreported in victimization surveys,[29] most observers tend to view victimization-survey data as one of the most sensitive measures of serious crime.

The survey data also allow study of the details surrounding crime and perhaps isolate factors that will allow the deterring of similar crimes. High-risk subgroups of victims can be identified and agency resources can be reassigned to their protection. Data on the experiences of victims in dealing with various criminal justice agencies can be taken as a partial measure of levels of satisfaction of clientele and public.

Victimization-survey data, unlike UCR and agency-based crime data, concentrate on the victim rather than on offenses or offenders. So these data supplement UCR and agency-based crime data by providing an entirely different perspective on the nature and effects of crime. Victimization-survey data can be particularly helpful in directing agency resources and efforts toward those to be served rather than simply toward offenses and offenders.

The Public View of Crime. Actual crime levels are important crime data. Also of immense importance are public perceptions about crime. A single instance of a particularly heinous crime, a flare-up of a type of crime, press coverage of a single criminal event will often shape public opinion about which crimes are most serious, which are to be most feared, and which ought to have the greatest amount of criminal justice resources devoted to them. The difficulty confronting the planner is that actual crime levels and what they imply for the allocation of agency and system resources may often be at odds with public perceptions. However, because criminal justice agencies are public-service agencies, the views of the public are not to be ignored.

Citizen surveys—concentrating on people's attitudes, perceptions, and beliefs about crime—are an attempt to provide data about these views. Several citizen-survey/public-opinion polls regularly measure general perceptions of crime levels and personal safety.[30] Surveys have also been used to determine public attitudes about which crimes are most serious. In one study, 140 different kinds of criminal acts were listed on separate cards given to residents of Baltimore; respondents were asked to place each card in one of nine categories according to the seriousness (in their judgment) of the crime.[31] The planned killing of a policeman was ranked most serious; public drunkenness, the least. Rankings of some of the other 140 criminal acts included: hijacking an airplane (8th), selling LSD (10th), armed robbery of an armored truck (44th), selling marijuana (49th), bribing a public official to obtain favors (103rd), engaging in homosexual acts with consenting adults (123rd), refusal to pay alimony (133rd).

Such data provide insight into public perceptions of the seriousness of various crimes, of morality, of the psychological costs and physical destruction involved in various crimes.[32] This can provide the planner with at least one way of defining serious crime, and the planner may choose to use such information as one criterion in allocating agency resources. Of course, public-opinion rankings may change: fifteen or twenty years ago airplane hijacking would probably not even have made the list; selling LSD might not have either, as few people would have even known what it was. More recently, and as a result of activities of the "moral majority," homosexuality might receive higher ranking than it got in the Baltimore study. Also, the planner must be careful to distinguish between seriousness of crime and volume of crime: for example, petty theft, typically high in volume and in consumption of system resources, is generally not ranked by citizens as a "serious" criminal event.

Organizational Data

Data on workloads, jobs, employees, and performance are the principal types of organizational data important for planners. Although there are other types of organizational data important for planning, these four types are central to most planning efforts.

Workloads. Gathering workload data involves both determining the categories or types of work being performed and measuring the amount of work performed in each category. Workload data are particularly important in planning, particularly in manpower planning (see Chapter 14), because workload measures and data are one of the principal indicators of the demand being put on the agency. For example, John Bramham in *Practical Manpower Planning* notes the importance of workload factors and their ultimate conversion into forecasts of manpower needs:

> It is often helpful to think of workload when considering manpower requirements. . . . Basically, the workload factor method means separating the work to be done into its discrete parts. . . . Each part is then forecast and converted into manning requirements by a conversion factor. This might be the number of man hours required to do each job which can be multiplied by the number of jobs and thus the total requirement for man hours obtained. It is not difficult to convert this into the number of employees required.[33]

Developing adequate measures of workloads and adequate data about workloads is not as straightforward as it may seem. For example, in the law-enforcement field there are great differences between what is officially recognized as the work of the police and what the police actually do. It is often presumed that police enforce the law and prevent crime; yet, any experienced officer knows that great portions of his time are spent doing other things—arbitrating domestic disputes, providing emergency services, rendering first aid, counseling and advising citizens, and the like. Measuring the work actually done by an agency and its personnel, or that expected of agency personnel, should include collecting data related to *all* of the more time-consuming duties.

Accurate measurement of the kinds and amount of work actually performed can itself be a significant task. Thus, some balance must be struck between securing sufficient data and being cost efficient in doing so. Because official descriptions of job duties and statements of agency mission may differ from what individuals actually do, a starting point in securing data about workloads is to develop categories into which the actual work of the agency can be placed. Job-focused data, secured through, say, a job analysis will help to substantiate the *kinds* of work, tasks, and roles performed (see also Chapter 14).

Workload categories should be made to yield a reasonably accurate picture of the work actually performed, but other considerations are involved in making the collection of data about workload efficient and effective.[34] Among these are the following:

1. The kinds of work categories devised should permit something to be counted: number of cases, number of calls for service, number of inmates processed, and so on. Each instance or occurrence becomes one work-unit. The number of work-units performed becomes the workload in that category.
2. The potential or actual volume of work performed in each category should be sufficient to make it worth counting. It may not be worth counting infrequently recurring activities, especially if little personnel time is spent handling them.
3. Work categories should allow, where necessary, for distinctions being made that work performed within certain subcategories of a workload category varies both in the kind of and amount of work performed per work-unit. For example, the amount and kind of workload involved in supervising fifty low-risk probationers may well differ from that involved in supervising fifty high risk probationers.

Differences within types of workload categories are important. In a law-enforcement agency, for example, one traditional measure of agency workload is the number of calls for service; this gross statistic is used as one measure of demand-induced workload. Yet a call involving a noisy stereo is, on the average, less time-consuming than, say, a call involving a homicide. Although the number of man-hours required for a work-unit will differ in different instances, the point in measuring these differences is not to split hairs so finely that every discrete work-unit has its own associated man-hour equivalent, but to recognize that, broadly speaking, there are significant differences in the types of demands placed on an agency in performing certain types of work, even within a given work category.

The distinctions made among kinds of work-units within a given workload class, however, must be valid, and they must have some basis in fact. For example, a correctional classification system that involved categories of high-, medium-, and low-risk inmates should validly represent real differences affecting consequent man-hour requirements. Defining inmates with life sentences as high-risk may lead to the assumption that custody of them will entail more problems because they have nothing to lose in attempting to escape; yet, many experienced corrections managers will testify that "lifers" are often easier to deal with than are "short-termers."[35]

It is important that agency records of workloads and work-units provide valid and consistent measurements. For example, the dispatch records of law-enforcement agencies reflect what citizens think the problem is, but Reiss has found that the police officer on the scene more often than not redefines the problem.[36] Thus, dispatch records and calls for service may not accurately reflect either the real nature of the call for service or the subsequent work of the agency in dealing with it.

The number of work-units performed does not by itself give the measure of a workload. Many people and many man-hours may be involved in disposing of a particular work-unit. For example, a call for service involving a UCR-index crime could involve patrol, detective, clerical, and forensic personnel, each performing a variety of specific tasks. The reception and diagnosis of a single inmate involves custodial, medical, and clerical personnel. A work-unit (one call for service or one intake of a new inmate) is meant to stand for all these things. A good job analysis allows an agency to determine how many people, doing what kinds of things, over what period of time are required on the *average* to dispose of a particular work-unit. This kind of "average" analysis of the work involved in a particular work-unit is usually sufficient for planning purposes, and allows the planner to estimate changes in personnel and resource requirements, dependent on changes in workloads as measured by work-units performed or demanded.

Figure 11-3 shows sample workload categories for monitoring the level of demand placed on a court or a court system. These sample categories are not exhaustive, but merely illustrative of some of the types of measures useful for keeping track of and categorizing court workloads.

Job Data. Some of the data most basic for planning are about the jobs or work within the organization. Without data about the jobs performed, there is little quantitative or qualitative basis for understanding what personnel are needed, and for planning how to get them. And there is little basis for understanding whether what is actually done in the agency is consistent with the organization's goals and objectives. The work done in an agency can be defined as and divided into jobs; the jobs in the agency can be seen as collections of roles, tasks, and activities. Information about these indicates either what goes on or what is supposed to go on in the agency.

A related and important kind of job-focused data concern the skills and knowledge required of people who fill these jobs or perform the various roles, tasks, and activities of the agency. Data about roles, tasks, and activities are related to, but different in form from, data about the skills and knowledge required to do a particular job.

Some data indicate what the jobs of the agency *are* and some indicate what the jobs *should be* or *will be*. Sometimes this difference is ignored and data describing the current jobs are used inappropriately to imply what the jobs should be, or what the jobs will always be (and vice versa). This is dangerous because, over time, the nature of most jobs changes, and with this comes change in the kinds of skills and knowledge required to do the job. For example, the job of a prison custodial officer in a nontreatment-oriented setting differs from that of an

Figure 11-3. Sample Workload Measures in Courts

General Category	Subcategories
Criminal proceedings	Cases filed Arraignments Pretrial motions Uncontested court trials Contested court trials Jury trials Bench time
Civil proceedings	Cases filed Pretrial motions Jury trials Bench time
Juvenile proceedings	Referrals Petitions Cases Bench time

officer in a treatment-oriented setting; if the basic prison mission moves from nontreatment to treatment, the skills and knowledge required to do the job will also change. Job analysis (discussed in Chapter 14) is an empirically based technique that, properly used, can help avoid some of these problems and can help define the responsibilities of the jobs. Other techniques and specially designed job analyses can be used to help decide what jobs should be.[37]

Figure 11-4 summarizes these points, indicating that job-focused data most generally fall into four main categories, each with different purposes and with different contributions to make to manpower planning.

Job-focused data are often qualitative: they take the form of descriptions of certain qualitative attributes of jobs. But job-analysis techniques may also be quantitatively oriented: they may attempt empirically to measure job-related behavior. Thus, each of the cells in Figure 11-4 can have quantitative as well as qualitative types of data associated with it.

Employee Data. An important distinction between job-focused data and employee-focused data is that the former indicate what is demanded in numbers and kinds of personnel while the latter indicate the supply of those numbers and kinds of people. Some types of employee-focused data can be particularly important.

Figure 11-4. Basic Types of Job-Focused Data

	Jobs defined in terms of roles, tasks and activities	Skills and knowledge required for each job
About the way jobs currently are	Nature of present job	Currently required skills and knowledge
About what jobs should be or will be	Nature of future jobs	Skill and knowledge required in future

1. Number of Agency Employees.
When gross statistics concerning numbers of employees are broken down, they take on greater importance. For example it may be important to know how many people are assigned to various job classifications, or how many people in the agency have certain kinds of skills, or how many people are in each age bracket, or how many people have had multiple job experiences in the agency. The issue of multiple-job experience is interesting because knowing how many people have had multiple experiences may give some indication of potential flexibility in reassigning agency personnel from one job to another.

Thus, data on numbers of employees must be associated with something, such as numbers in a particular job classification or numbers with a particular skill. Here are some of the ways in which data on numbers of employees can be categorized for planning purposes:

a. *According to age brackets* (this may be important to estimating retirement dates, turnover, availability of certain personnel to do certain kinds of jobs)

b. *According to types of jobs* (for determinations of the distribution of personnel across jobs and tasks, for laying the foundation for understanding where there are shortages or duplication, and so on.)

c. *According to experience or skill categories* (for estimating the qualitative dimensions of the agency labor force)

2. Skill-Bank Data
An important aspect of understanding the nature of personnel supply in the organization is knowing how many people, with which kinds of skills, knowledge, and experience are currently available to the organization. These data can be important for any of several reasons. First, they provide the basis for estimating agencywide supply of these skills and experiences; this information may be useful, for example, in estimates of the flexibility of the agency to assign personnel. Second, these data lay the basis for determining whether the individuals holding various jobs (requiring certain skills and knowledge) are in the right jobs; this kind of information may become important and necessary in reassigning people to different jobs. Third, these data are important in determining weak spots in the organization, the skills and experiences that are lacking among the present personnel; this information may help to redirect recruitment efforts and to reform selection practices, and to design training programs.

The kinds of information kept in a skills bank vary greatly from agency to agency, depending not only on the type of agency (e.g., law enforcement or corrections), but also on its particular mission (e.g., custodial or rehabilitative). Aside from the general categories of information that every agency needs, each agency must add the specific categories that are peculiar to its jobs and its missions. Here are some of the more general categories of data that are included in skills banks:

a. *Education and training programs completed by employees*: a record of training and education undergone can become an indicator of the kinds of skills and knowledge possessed by the employee.

b. *Certifications and licenses held by employees*: this relates to legal authorizations for employees to perform certain tasks.

c. *The employee-skills questionnaire*: a questionnaire, updated periodically and administered to employees, may request that they, by self-report, indicate a variety of skills or knowledge that they think they possess.

d. *Prior job Experience*: like records of education and training, this information can provide indicators of specific skills and knowledge; to be complete, the prior job history should include information on jobs held both inside and outside the agency.

e. *Job-Performance evaluations*: this may be helpful in providing a qualitative measure of the degree to which employees have been able to display and to utilize various skills and knowledge (assuming, of course, that performance evaluation measures are valid).

A skills data-bank cannot be developed without regard to the jobs or work of the organization and the skills and knowledge those jobs are supposed to require. The basis, therefore, for designing a useful skills data-bank (and particularly a skills questionnaire) is having enough job-focused data. In the employee-skills questionnaire, the questions ought to dovetail to some degree with the list of skills and knowledge taken from job-focused data. If the agency has identified, say, 100 important skills as a part of a job analysis, each employee might be asked to indicate the extent to which he possesses each of these skills.

One problem with skills data-banks is that of "controlling" the amount of information placed within them; the range of conceivably relevant employee skills can be so wide that the skills data-bank becomes unwieldy. Indeed, many organizations which have had experience with keeping skills data-banks report infrequent use,[38] in part because of unwieldiness and in part because union-contract and civil-service constraints may make the use of most of the information irrelevant for recruitment, selection, and assignment.[39]

A 1971 publication of the American Management Association, *Personnel Systems and Data Management*, proposed eighteen general categories of information, with 182 subcategories, each of these with a myriad of additional categories of information to be kept on employees.[40] Taking such requirements seriously would discourage both the collection and use of such data. Nonetheless, some basic data about employee skills should be kept as a means of estimating supply.

3. Employee Job and Career Preferences

Data on employee job preferences and career aspirations are often useful in understanding the dynamics of motivating personnel in the job; this would in turn presumably have some effect on productivity. Information of this type secured and entered into planning-related exercises can be useful in the recruitment, selection, and assignment of personnel. Conversely, not having such information makes it difficult to know whether a productivity problem is related to inappropriate skills among employees or to insufficient motivation.

Performance Data. The performance of the agency and the performance of individual employees, properly and validly conceived, provides the operational measures of goals and missions; performance data provide concrete indicators of the achievement of goals and missions. This is essentially the idea presented in Figure 11-1, which indicates the relationship between data and concepts. For example, one goal of a sheriff's department may be to provide a physical environment and supportive services that protect and contribute as much as possible to the physical and mental well-being of inmates. This may be a laudatory goal but it needs some concrete reference. One set of concrete references is provided by indicators meant to measure the provision of a proper physical environment for inmates' well-being.

1. The number of crimes committed by inmates and having other inmates as victims
2. The percentage of inmates attempting and/or committing suicide
3. The number of sustained inmate grievances about threats to inmate health
4. The number of reimbursed room thefts
5. The number of critical incidents involving dangerous contraband (weapons and drugs)[41]

Although other measures may be more appropriate within a given jail, and although there may be some question about the validity of these particular performance measures, they provide an example of how concrete performance indicators begin to describe the meaning of an abstract goal. A different set of performance indicators not only might produce different results, but would differently describe the meaning of the abstract goal as well.

Although performance measures are important, developing adequate and fair measures of the performance of criminal justice agencies has been most difficult. The problem is much more severe in the public sector than it is in private industry where profit provides a convenient and ultimate measure of performance. In criminal justice agencies, as in all public agencies, the measures are dependent on people's values, and values often differ from one person to the next. For example, some people hold that the mission of institutional corrections is incarceration; under this value system, a measure of good performance might be an absence of escapes and disturbances in the prison environment. Others hold that the mission of institutional corrections is rehabilitation; under this value system, a measure of good performance might be low levels of recidivism among released inmates. Finally, many hold that the mission of institutional corrections includes, but is not limited to, incarceration and rehabilitation; under this kind of value system a measure of good performance might be both the absence of escapes or disturbance and the absence of recidivism (see Chapter 6: these may not necessarily be complementary in achieving the ends desired).

If not properly interpreted, performance criteria are often conflicting. For example, law-enforcement agencies may be perceived as having the duty of enforcing the law *and* of preventing crime. One performance measure for "crime prevention" is how much the crime rate drops. A measure of "law enforcement" might be clearance rates. But if these measures are not properly interpreted, an improvement in one area may give the appearance of deterioration in the other: increased arrests may be interpreted by some evidence of higher crime levels and, hence, of poorer crime prevention. The problem is that performance data are not always, or perhaps even usually, clear in what they mean. They are highly dependent for meaning on what goals or missions they are held to measure. Traditional performance indicators of "law enforcement" include "cases cleared or solved." This concept is, however, not quite as straightforward as it may sound. Cases cleared by arrest are different from cases cleared by conviction. Conviction is not wholly within the power of the police. And an arrest does not necessarily mean (in the eyes of the law) that a case has been solved. Thus, although clearance-rate data may be "objective" and reliable, the meaning of the data is open to debate.

Another indicator of law enforcement performance sometimes used is the number and severity of complaints brought against the department and its personnel by others. This too, however, requires interpretation because not all complaints are necessarily about the performance of the agency in meeting its prime missions. In other words, some complaints derive from mishandled public relations instead of the agencies' central efforts to achieve their goals and missions.

In measuring performance and in collecting data about it, distinctions must be made between workload data as a measure of performance and performance in the sense of accomplishing missions and doing the job well. Workload measures indicate only *how much* work has been done. They do not indicate *how well* the job was done, which is the more relevant to what performance is typically supposed to mean. Answering calls for service or accepting new inmates are measures of *how much* work is done. Clearance rates and lack of complaints (even given the problems with these) begin to measure *how well* the work was done. Similarly, low levels of prison disturbances and inmate suicides may be measures of how well the institution is doing its job, although they are crude measures and sometimes misrepresent the achievement of other missions, such as rehabilitation.

Ratings of agency performance by client groups or the general public can sometimes be used to measure agency performance. Surveying citizens about their perceptions of service levels and quality of service rendered can provide such data. Evaluations of police and other services by victims are another source of such data. Such data are largely attitudinal (based on people's perceptions, beliefs, and attitudes) and should be distinguished from data based on official records. This is not to say that official records are less subjective measures of performance: accurate though they may be, they are nonetheless subject to gross interpretation. Client-attitude surveys may be valid and reliable—objective measures either of people's attitudes or of their experiences.

Thus far, performance data have been discussed at the level of the agency; performance data about individual employees is also important as a basis for determining where particular problems may lie: How well is a particular job being done? How well is a particular position being filled? Performance data on individual employees may be aggregated in various ways to provide estimates about how well various parts or divisions of the agency are performing.

Evaluations of individual performance must be distinguished from evaluations of overall agency performance. Presumably, the sum of individual performances equates in some fashion with overall performance, but not precisely. Data on individual performance are as important as data on overall agency performance, because the individualized data may be used to pinpoint trouble spots, either in certain jobs or in certain individuals. Data on overall agency performance may serve to mask some of these trouble spots, and may lead to the neglect of extant or developing problem areas.

System Data

The development of system-level data has had several foci, from that of providing a national information system on crime and criminals to that of developing data bases that permit analyses of system agencies and their processing of offenders and offenses. Examples of the former include the National Crime Information Center (NCIC), with its computerized search for answers to inquiries about fugitives, wanted persons, stolen cars, and the like, and its computerized criminal history (CCH) files with their emphasis on offenders. These and similar systemwide information systems do not provide exactly the kind of system data needed for planning purposes. More to the point are two other kinds of data bases, now being developed, which permit analysis of system functioning. One gathers data for system-simulation models; the other tracks system performance by gathering offender-based transaction statistics. JUSSIM I and II are examples of the former; OBTS is an example of the latter.

As most recently described by Alfred Blumstein,[42] JUSSIM consists of a number of data inputs that permit subsequent use of JUSSIM for simulation purposes. The empirical data characterize the user's criminal justice system:

1. Number of crimes of each type
2. The decision options available at each stage in the criminal justice system (police, prosecution, courts, corrections, and so on) and the ratios representing exercise of these options according to crime type
3. Resources available at each stage expressed both in terms of dollars and of time
4. Tabulations of cost (expressed in dollars and in time) per unit workload for each type of crime

With these data, suitably placed within the JUSSIM model, simulations can be made to analyze the effect on the system and on each of its stages by varying the decision option ratios or the input of crime, or both; effects can be measured in costs (dollars and time) for each stage of the system. JUSSIM is, of course, an analytical model and not simply an information system. The overriding objective of JUSSIM and similar models is to view and to analyze system-level effects, especially those involving flows through the system. The data provide a basis for estimating changes in the system and its components resulting from simulated changes in any of its parameters.

OBTS is more nearly an information system designed to track "the arrested person through the criminal justice system from the first encounter with the arresting officer until the final disposition of the case."[43] OBTS not only assembles facts but retains them in a format that permits examination of the relationships among events throughout the criminal justice process. Figure 11-5 lists the more common data elements appearing as part of the OBTS system.[44]

An inspection of the data elements in Figure 11-5 indicates that several basic kinds of questions can be answered through analysis of the data collected under the OBTS format. Among the most basic are decisions reached at each stage about what is to happen to the individual offender, and the time involved. Manipulation of these basic data permits generalized statements about what happens to certain types of offenders or to certain types of offenses as they are tracked through the system, and an examination of the nature of the total system response to crime, what happens at each stage, and where the bottlenecks are. Additional information that can be generated includes the relationships among sentences, offenses, and characteristics of offenders. The frequency of guilty pleas, jury trials, and bench trials can be examined, controlling for type of offense and for characteristics of offenders. With the wealth of data collected through OBTS, important discoveries are possible about which factors influence various alternative outcomes.[45] Susan Katzenelson has summarized many of the uses of OBTS data in answering questions about characteristics of the system. The following list is drawn from her longer list:

1. What is the direction of change in most serious charges, from arrest to disposition? What is the relationship between police charges and those pressed by the district attorney? In

Figure 11-5. OBTS Data Elements

IDENTIFICATION ELEMENTS

- State Identification No.*
- FBI No.*
- State Record No.
- Sex
- Race
- Date of Birth

POLICE/PROSECUTOR ELEMENTS

- Arresting Agency No.*
- Sequence Letter
- Date of Arrest
- Charged Offense (Most Serious)
- Police Disposition
- Prosecutor Disposition
- Police/Prosecutor Disposition Date

LOWER CRIMINAL COURT ELEMENTS

- Court Identification No. *
- Initial Appearance Date
- Disposition Data
- Charged Offense (Most Serious)
- Lower Court Disposition
- Release Action
- Release Action Date
- Final Charge (Most Serious)
- Type of Charge
- Plea (At Trial)
- Type of Trial
- Date of Sentence
- Type of Sentence
- Confinement Term (Days)
- Probation Term (Months)
- Type of Counsel

COUNTY PROSECUTOR

- Prosecutor Identification No.*
- Date of Filing
- Type of Filing
- Filing Procedure
- Date of Arraignment
- Charged Offense (Most Serious)
- Initial Plea
- Release Action
- Release Action Date

FELONY TRIAL ELEMENTS

- Court Identification No.*
- Trial Date
- Trial Type
- Final Plea
- Trial Ending/Disposition Date
- Final Charge (Most Serious)
- Type of Charge
- Court Disposition
- Sentence Date
- Sentence Type
- Confinement – Prison (Years)
- Confinement – Jail (Days)
- Probation (Months)
- Type of Counsel

CORRECTIONS ELEMENTS

- Agency Identifier*
- Receiving Agency
- Date Received
- Status
- Date of Exit
- Exit

*Data element should be in data base at state level but is not required to be reported to LEAA in Comprehensive Data Systems Program.

what way would plea-bargaining be reflected in the charges? In what types of cases are the reductions most significant?

2. What are the most common release types? In what way do release status and amount of bond relate to charges and defendant types? What changes occur in release status throughout the process?

3. How does recidivism (defined as rearrest, or reconviction) relate to actions taken against that individual as recorded in previous OBTS cycles: Was he convicted in his previous case(s)? incarcerated? treated?

4. What is the "attrition rate" of cases? at what phase? What types of crimes are most likely to drop out (e.g., dismissals)? How are these factors related to caseloads at each agency?

5. Is there a clear and consistent interagency policy to put more resources in certain types of cases: for example, more police work, special prosecution, and speedier trial directed into the handling of violent crimes, recidivists, major misdemeanors?[46]

The sources of OBTS data are the individual component agencies of the criminal justice system. This has both advantages and disadvantages. The advantage is that the data, when collected and stored, retain agency and offender identification sequences that permit aggregation and disaggregation of the data from the level of individual offender and agency to that of overall system summaries. This helps in avoiding one of the problems mentioned in connection with UCR data. The major disadvantages are in securing cooperation from agencies in collecting and providing the data, and in uniformly adhering to a set of procedures and definitions governing the meaning of requested data. Compatibility of data can be a major problem when numerous semiindependent agencies are the sources of data. But a review of the data elements shown in Figure 11-5 indicates that the requested data are probably kept by each of the component agencies as part of their existing records system. OBTS, therefore, is oriented toward making use of existing data rather than toward requesting the collection of huge amounts of new data. This has certain obvious advantages in securing cooperation from the agencies involved.

SUMMARY

This chapter has surveyed several aspects of data as they relate to criminal justice planning. It has examined several general notions about data and applied these to a consideration of some of the more important kinds of data useful in criminal justice planning: environmental data, organizational data, and system data. Chapter 12 will consider several important and related issues—among others, the sources of data for criminal justice planning, and alternative methods for securing these data.

· *Chapter 11* ·
NOTES

1. For a discussion of logical and inductive approaches to analysis, see Michael Quinn Patton, *Qualitative Evaluation Methods*, (Beverly Hills, Calif.: Sage Publications, 1980), pp. 306–26.
2. Philip J. Runkel and Joseph E. McGrath, *Research on Human Behavior: A Systematic Guide to Method* (New York: Holt, Rinehart, and Winston, 1972), p. 250.
3. Abraham Kaplan, *The Conduct of Inquiry: Methodology for Behavioral Science* (San Francisco: Chandler Publishing, 1964), p. 133.
4. Clyde H. Coombs, *A Theory of Data* (New York: John Wiley & Sons, Inc., 1964), pp. 4–6.
5. Robert R. Mayer and Ernest Greenwood, *The Design of Social Policy Research* (Englewood Cliffs, N.J.: Prentice-Hall, 1980), p. 201.
6. Runkel and McGrath, op. cit., p. 250.
7. Glenn A. Bassett and Harvard Y. Weatherbee, *Personnel Systems and Data Management* (The American Management Association, 1971), p. 22.
8. Ibid., p. 23.
9. Paul Davidson Reynolds, *A Primer in Theory Construction* (Indianapolis: Bobbs-Merrill Co. Inc., 1971), p. 52.
10. Mayer and Greenwood, op. cit., p. 201.
11. For example, U.S. Department of Justice, Law Enforcement Assistance Administration and U.S. Bureau of the Census, *Expenditure and Employment Data for the Criminal Justice System: 1976* (Washington, D.C.: U.S. Government Printing Office, 1978).
12. These include sources such as survey results from the Survey Research Center at the University of Michigan, Harris and Gallup polls, or polls and surveys conducted by the media.
13. Earl R. Babbie, *The Practice of Social Research* 2nd ed. (New York: Wadsworth Publishing Co., Inc., 1979), p. 255.
14. See Donald T. Campbell and Julian C. Stanley, *Experimental and Quasi-Experimental Designs for Research* (Chicago: Rand McNally & Company, 1966).
15. Kenneth D. Bailey, *Methods of Social Research* (New York: The Free Press, 1978), p. 57.
16. See Bailey, op. cit., pp. 57–60, for examples.
17. Babbie, op. cit., p. 585.
18. Sorrel Wildhorn, et al., *Indicators of Justice* (Lexington, MA.: Lexington Books, 1977), p. xix.
19. For examples of how to collect community-needs-assessment data, see Keith A. Neuber, et al., *Needs Assessment: A Model for Community Planning*, Sage Human Services Guide, Vol. 14, (Beverly Hills, Calif.: Sage Publications, 1980).
20. The National Manpower Survey of the Criminal Justice System, *Criminal Justice Manpower Planning* (Washington, D.C.: National Institute of Law Enforcement and Criminal Justice, Law Enforcement Assistance Administration, U.S. Government Printing Office, 1978), Vol. 6.
21. Examples of these include the many Law Enforcement Assistance Administration Prescriptive Packages disseminated in the last several years.
22. See Charles R. Welford, "Crime and the

Police: A Multivariate Analysis," *Criminology*, 12 (August 1974), 195-213.

23. For a history of the Uniform Crimes Reports, see Michael D. Maltz "Crime Statistics: A Historical Perspective," *Crime and Delinquency*, 23: 1 (January 1977), 32-40.

24. Don M. Gottfredson and Michael R. Gottfredson, "Data for Criminal Justice Evaluation: Some Resources and Pitfalls," in Malcolm W. Klein and Katherine S. Teilmann, *Handbook of Criminal Justice Evaluation*, (Beverly Hills, Calif.: Sage Publications 1980), p. 100.

25. Ibid., p. 101.

26. Joseph F. Sheley, *Understanding Crime: Concepts, Issues, Decisions* (New York: Wadsworth Publishing Co., Inc., 1979), pp. 28-29.

27. *Criminal Victimization in the United States January-June 1973* (Washington, D.C.: U.S. Department of Justice, Law Enforcement Assistance Administration, U.S. Government Printing Office, November 1974), Vol. 1, and *Criminal Victimization in the United States: 1973 Advance Report* (Washington, D.C.: U.S. Department of Justice, Law Enforcement Assistance Administration, U.S. Government Printing Office, May 1975), Vol. 1.

28. See, for example, A. D. Biderman, et al., *Report on a Pilot Study in the District of Columbia on Victimization and Attitudes Toward Law Enforcement*, Field Survey I (Washington, D.C.: President's Commission on Law Enforcement and Administration of Justice, U.S. Government Printing Office, 1967). Also see, *Criminal Victimization in the United States: 1973* (Washington, D.C.: U.S. Department of Justice, Law Enforcement Assistance Administration, U.S. Government Printing Office, December 1976), p. 68.

29. James P. Levine, "The Potential for Crime Overreporting in Criminal Victimization Surveys," *Criminology* (November 1976), 307-30.

30. See, for example, U.S. Department of Housing and Urban Development, Office of Policy Development and Research, *The 1978 HUD Survey on the Quality of Community Life* (Washington, D.C.: U.S. Department of Housing and Urban Development, 1978), pp. 194-99. Also see George H. Gallup, *The Gallup Index, Report No. 154* (Princeton, N.J.: The American Institute of Public Opinion, May 1978), p. 30.

31. Peter H. Rossi, et al., "The Seriousness of Crimes: Normative Structure and Individual Differences," *American Sociological Review*, 39 (April 1974), 224-37.

32. James P. Levine, et al., *Criminal Justice: A Public Policy Approach* (New York: Harcourt Brace Jovanovich, Inc., 1980), p. 516.

33. John Bramham, *Practical Manpower Planning*, 2nd ed. (London: Institute of Personnel Management, 1978), pp. 43-44.

34. See Wildhorn et al., op. cit. for a wide-ranging discussion of related issues. Also see, Harry O. Lawson and Barbara J. Gletne, *Workload Measures in the Court* (Williamsburg, Va.: National Center for State Courts, 1980).

35. John K. Hudzik, et al., *Criminal Justice Manpower Planning: An Overview* (Washington, D.C.: U.S. Law Enforcement Assistance Administration, U.S. Government Printing Office, 1981). Interviews with several corrections officials in the course of gathering data in this project indicated this directly.

36. Albert J. Reiss, Jr., *The Police and the Public* (New Haven, Conn.: Yale University Press, 1971).

37. See Frank Sistrunk, et al., *Methods for Human Resources in the Criminal Justice System: A Feasibility Study* (Tampa, FL.: Center for Evaluation Research, University of South Florida, 1980), Vol. 1.

38. Hudzik, et al., op. cit., see Chaps. 3 and 4.

39. Ibid.

40. Bassett, op. cit., pp. 107-26.

41. Gilbert Skinner, Training Division, School of Criminal Justice, Michigan State University and John Sullivan, Training Division, School of Labor and Industrial Relations, Michigan State University, from unpublished training packages.

42. Alfred Blumstein, "Planning Models for Analytical Evaluation," in Klein and Teilman, op. cit., p. 245.

43. National Advisory Commission on Criminal Justice Standards and Goals, Advisory Task Force on Information Systems and Statistics, *Criminal Justice System* (Washington, D.C.: U.S. Government Printing Office, January 1973), p. 34.

44. Ibid., pp. 100-101.

45. Michael J. Hindelang and Carl E. Pope, "Sources of Research Data in Criminal Justice," in Emilio Viano, ed., *Criminal Justice Research* (Lexington, Ma.: Lexington Books, 1975), p. 142.

46. Susan Katzenelson, "Analysis of the Criminal Justice System with Offender-Based Transaction Statistics (OBTS)" in Leonard Oberlander ed., *Quantitative Tools for Criminal Justice Planning* (Washington, D.C.: U.S. Department of Justice, Law Enforcement Assistance Administration, 1975), pp. 83-89.

• Chapter 12 •

METHODS OF DATA COLLECTION FOR CRIMINAL JUSTICE PLANNING

This chapter focuses on how data for planning purposes can be collected. Although the sources of criminal justice planning data are numerous, and although there are several alternative methods for collecting and analyzing data, certain principles of data collection and analysis prevail no matter what the data being collected or by what means.

This chapter examines basic research concepts and their importance in the collection and analysis of data. The central concepts discussed are research design, operationalization and measurement, validity and reliability, sampling, and basic alternative modes of data collection. These are complex and multifaceted concepts; our discussion will touch only briefly on some of their more central aspects, and will relate these basic research concepts to the collection and analysis of some of the kinds of data discussed in Chapter 11.

BASIC PRINCIPLES GUIDING DATA COLLECTION AND ANALYSIS

Chapter 11 distinguished between data and information, noting that information generally stands for data that has been given some meaning or interpretation. One of the examples used was unemployment-rate data, which could be used as a measure of economic potential (unused labor force), or as a measure of economic illness (recession or depression). The process by which data are given meaning, the rules involved in interpretation of data, fall within the principles and procedures of research. Without adherence to these rules and procedures, the process of turning data into useful information for planning purposes will be faulty and the ensuing interpretations may well prove to be incomplete and inaccurate.

Data without rules and contexts for interpretation have no meaning. Consider, for example, a simple and apparently trivial scowl on an employee's face when listening to a supervisor explain some new procedure. Taking any special note of this may seem nonsensical because although the scowl may have had sufficient impact for the supervisor to consider it noteworthy, its importance may end there. However, nonverbal cues can often be used as indicators of how people feel. The scowl, if it were of a particular kind, may indicate that the employee does not agree that the new procedure will be useful or practical: the scowl could perhaps be used as a sign that the employee may attempt to find ways of avoiding or subverting the new procedure. Training supervisors to notice and to record nonverbal as well as verbal data on employee reactions might be important for complete and accurate assessment of the acceptability of agency policy and procedures. For this reason, the collection of data on something as apparently trivial as facial expressions can have a purpose behind it: that purpose ultimately gives any data meaning and turns data into information.

Data are facts, or knowledge for the sake of knowledge. Information, on the other hand, is "knowledge for the sake of purposeful action."[1] Research design closely governs the determination of purpose or reason for the collection and analysis of data. Put another way, research design is a plan of action for collecting and interpreting data to answer questions deemed important.

Research Design

"The design of a [particular] piece of research must depend upon the particular purpose that the research is intended to serve."[2] Indeed, one of the usual features of a research design is justification of the research and identification of the objectives of the research.[3] Most, if not all, research begins with a question or problem deemed to require examination and perhaps resolution. Planning is similarly founded.

Not all problems brought to the attention of the planner require a full-scale planning or research effort: research involving extensive collection and analysis of data and information is not always required (see Chapter 8). But in those situations where immediately available information does not appear sufficient for planning purposes, new information must be secured. This moves the planner squarely into the role of researcher, a role governed by the basic principles of research and research design.

The concepts used in the research design, the nature of the data to be collected, the mode of its collection, and the directions governing analysis and interpretation of data are specified in the research design and depend on the topic chosen for analysis. For example, an agency head may note an uneasiness about the payoff in continuing a certain program—say, a domestic-dispute follow-up counseling program. The uneasiness may have originated in complaints from those who have been the recipients of follow-up counseling. These complaints may even have found their way into the papers. Agency decision-makers may request that planners examine the situation by documenting the problem and by proposing changes, if possible. Any subsequent collection of data is justified only if it addresses the question at hand.[4] The research design specified not only what data are relevant, but also, implicitly, what data are assumed to be irrelevant. Julian Simon offers the sound advice to "think at length, think in detail, think about everything *before* collecting data."[5] Too often, research is undertaken in ignorance of Simon's plea, with the result that much unnecessary data are collected and some necessary data are not collected. Even more damaging, a giant data-collecting vacuum cleaner may be turned loose to suck up every bit of data within reach. The resulting data pile, often unmanageable and collected at great expense, may never be much used. The indiscriminate collection of data is not only an expensive undertaking, but it can make planning itself seem a wasteful endeavor.

There are numerous ways of picturing the steps involved in the research-design process. Figure 12-1 shows the essential steps and is an amalgam of views expressed by numerous commentators. It relies heavily, however, on the formulations of Earl Babbie[6] and Robert Mayer and Ernest Greenwood.[7]

Figure 12-1 appears to characterize research design as largely a linear process. In truth, however, numerous reciprocal and feedback arrangements characterize research design (some of which are shown by directional arrows). For example, answers to the questions of Stage III may require profound alteration of the original purpose of the research determined at Stage I. Certain research methods, modes of operationalization, or data-analysis techniques may not be available, thereby limiting or altering the original research purposes. These same limitations may affect which variables can subsequently be measured—some may not be measurable because the requisite data cannot be secured. This influences conceptualization of the research topic. Thus, in actuality, the research design is a dynamic interplay and consideration of the various topics presented in Figure 12-1.

The research design process answers many more detailed questions than those listed in Figure 12-1. Entire books have been written just on the proper design of research.[8] The purpose here, however, is not to describe the design process in detail but to point out that data collection is driven by the answers to questions in Stages I and II of Figure 12-1; data collection should not drive the basic research or the planning process.

Among other things, Stage I of the design process helps to settle two crucial questions for the planner. The first question involves what decision-makers and policy-makers want—what their questions are. As Carol Weiss points out (see also Chapter 1), research conducted for agency decision-makers does not seek knowledge for the sake of knowledge, as may be the case

Figure 12-1. Steps in the Research Design Process Applied to Planning

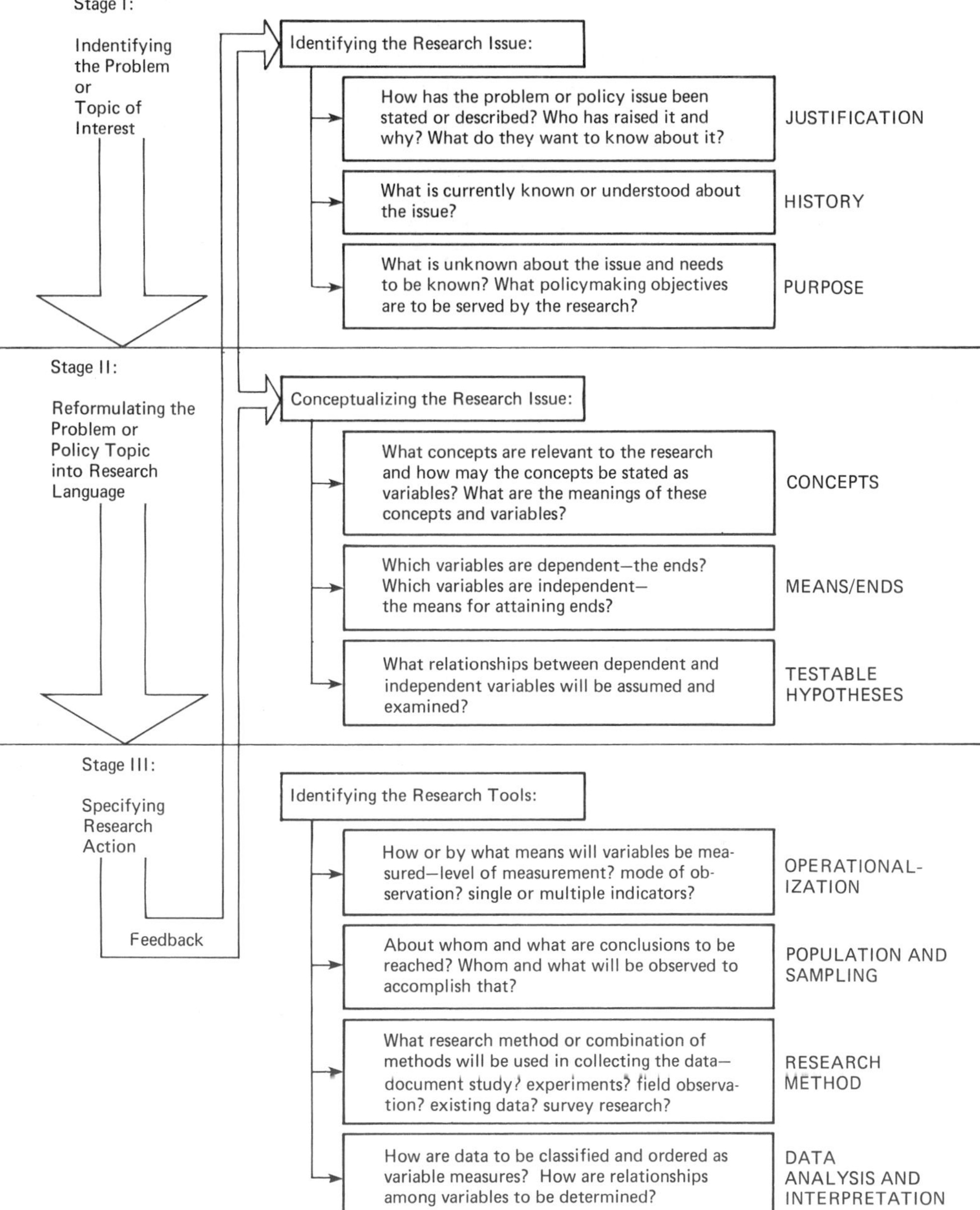

in basic research.[9] Rather, agency-based planning research (and evaluation research) necessarily focuses on the decision-maker's questions and not on those of the planner. Although there may be, and often is, considerable room for the planner to draw up his own research agenda, the central focus of planning is on the administrative and programmatic concerns of the decision-maker.

The second question in Stage I of the design process determines whether or not an extensive research undertaking is required. Deciding that some issue requires fresh research, or deciding that existing information is sufficient to answer the question, begins with an analysis of what is already known about the question raised by the decision-maker. This normally includes a search of existing information, reports, and knowledge. If existing information is sufficient to permit resolution of the issue or question, the need for a full research effort diminishes or disappears. Searching for existing knowledge (gaining an historical perspective) not only applies to agency-based planning research but is also something that almost any researcher does before choosing and defining a topic for research.[10]

If existing knowledge and information does not seem adequately to apply to the current question or issue, the planner needs to decide what is not known and what needs to be known. As gaps in information and knowledge are identified and judged in need of remedy, the planner begins to identify the need for and the purpose of the research.

Stage II of the design process is crucial in determining the specific kinds of data that will be required. Although Stage I provides a general perspective, Stage II requires more explicitness. Identifying the relevant abstract concepts and variables focuses attention on the basic points that must be examined in the research. One result of Stage II is that, when completed, it provides the conceptual framework for the proposed research: it specifies which concepts and variables are relevant (for example, productivity, employee performance, client attitudes, employee knowledge and skill); it specifies which relevant relationships between means and ends need to be tested (for example, that client attitudes toward agency services are partially dependent on agency productivity, which is dependent on employee performance, which is dependent on employee knowledge and skills). From this, the planner generates what are believed to be relevant testable hypotheses. With explicit and relevant concepts, variables, and hypotheses specified, the research can be clearly focused.[11] There is always the danger that, during conceptualization, mistakes will be made and some important concepts and variables excluded, while others included turn out not to be important. Nonetheless, if the planner is to avoid the pitfall of unfocused and thereby unmanageable research, he or she must make decisions about what is to be included and what is to be excluded. If mistakes in conceptualization are discovered during the course of research, supplementary research may be undertaken to correct the mistake.

Conceptualization provides a general plan to guide the intended research.[12] Without such a guide, research takes a "shotgun" aproach: the research is only generally aimed at the issue or question of interest in the hope of hitting on something. One frequent drawback of such research is that many unnecessary data are collected while necessary data are ignored or missed. "Shotgun" research, although perhaps useful for general exploratory purposes,[13] is of little use in dealing with specific concerns raised by decision-makers. Decision-makers prefer that planners not just go out and find something out about the problem area, but that they deal with policy concerns posed by the decision-maker. Conceptually focused research is oriented toward, and capable of doing, this.

Stage III of the design process translates a general and conceptual understanding of the intended research into concrete procedures to be followed and things to be done. This phase requires the planner/researcher to identify exactly how certain variables are to be measured, what the measurement tools will be, what the research or data-collection methods will be, and how analysis will be conducted. These are complex issues, and there are often many ways of resolving them. Yet, Stage III is crucial because it translates the research from the abstract to the concrete and the measurable. Three principal steps are used:

1. *Each concept and variable identified in Stage II is operationalized for purposes of measurement.* In this context, operationalization means specifying how an abstract concept or variable is to be measured in the real world.[14] The objective in doing this is to become more concrete about the specific kinds of data to be collected, and about how these specific data relate to the chosen concepts (e.g., specifying that intelligence will be measured with a certain standardized intelligence test).

2. *The sources of the various data are specified.* This is a two-step process, beginning with an identification of the class (e.g., all those who have received domestic-dispute follow-up counseling). The second step involves deciding whether data need to be directly gathered from all potential sources in this class, or from

only a sample (only some of the people who have received domestic-dispute follow-up counseling). If the decision is to sample, the assumption is that findings derived from a few of the people can be generalized to all in the population of interest.

3. *The method of collecting the data is chosen.* This is sometimes referred to as choosing the research method or the mode of observation.[15] There are several standard options to choose from, including document study, experiments, field observation, analysis of existing data, and survey research. Once one or more of these methods have been chosen, the planner-researcher must decide on specific procedures to be followed because each of the standardized research methods have several more detailed alternatives associated with them.

All these steps are interrelated. For example, how concepts are operationalized will help to determine appropriate sources of data. And, in turn, decisions about both operationalization and data sources greatly influence the choice of research method. Competent planners need to have more than a cursory understanding of the research process and should acquire general research skills, developed perhaps through course work and actual experience with conducting research (see Chapter 7 and some of the resources listed in the end-notes to this chapter).

Several issues in research design that have particular importance in the collection and analysis of planning related data will be briefly discussed.

Operationalization and Measurement

Use of the term *operationalization* in Figure 12-1 may give the impression that it is relevant at only one point in the design effort (namely, in determining how variables will be measured). In fact, the need to operationalize confronts the researcher constantly, and concerns more than the development of concrete measures for variables.

Fred Kerlinger distinguishes between *measured operational definitions* and *experimental operational definitions*.[16] A measured operational definition describes how a variable is to be measured, and this is the meaning of operationalization adopted thus far; an experimental operational definition, on the other hand, describes how a researcher will manipulate an independent variable in an experimental situation. Consider, for example, the question of whether giving positive feedback to employees is associated with increased productivity. The independent variable (feedback) may first be defined as "communication" from supervisors, and then experimentally manipulated among groups of employees, some of whom are praised and others never. Specifying how the independent variable will be manipulated is an experimental operational definition.

Mayer and Greenwood remark that operationalization also applies to defining the study population and the samples to be drawn from that population.[17] (This point will be discussed more fully under the heading, "Populations and Samples.")

Earl Babbie notes that "operationalization goes on and on" because of the constant need to re-examine the choice of how to measure variables as the research progresses. Babbie's point, well taken, is that "operationalization is a continuing process, not a blind commitment to a particular measure that may turn out to have been poorly chosen."[18] Perhaps, for example, a particular intelligence test chosen is either not available, or has not been designed to measure the particular aspect of intelligence that is of interest. Rethinking how to measure intelligence, and perhaps selecting a different intelligence test, would be part of the operationalization re-examination process.

The difficulties inherent in measuring intelligence illustrate another aspect of operationalization—that no operational definition can express all aspects of a concept.[19] Human intelligence is so complex and diverse a phenomenon that no manageable device could ever hope to measure all of its manifestations. Indeed, the operationalization of almost any concept or variable usually focuses only on some aspect of it. It is critically important, therefore, that the operational definition of the concept or variable be suitable to measuring the particular aspect of interest. Consider, for example, an attempt to define operationally the concept of violent crime. Does *violent crime* mean only crime that results in bodily harm, or does it include the destruction of property as well? Should it be defined as all index offenses, or as only some of the index offenses (e.g., homicide, rape, robbery, aggravated assault)? The Attorney General's

1981 Task Force on Violent Crime apparently found the task of operationalizing the concept of violent crime too difficult because there is no clear definition of it in their report.[20] Yet, without an unambiguous definition of the concept it is impossible to determine what to measure and what data to collect.

Given these inherent complexities in operationalization, it is rare that any concept is directly measured and tested in research. Rather, it is only the operational definition that is subsequently tested.[21] The implication of this is that there are two or more distinct operational definitions for most variables and concepts, and each definition may ultimately produce different research results. Consider, for example, a situation in which a planner is asked to devise a program that will affect violent crime. How the planner (or the policymaker) operationally defines the concept will profoundly affect not only the purpose of the planning exercise (the ends) but the means for achieving the ends, and for measuring achievements as well. If violent crime is defined as including only bodily harm, certain program implications result; if violent crime is defined as including the threat of bodily harm, other program implications may result. Thus, operationalization becomes an issue at the very beginning of the research design (Stage I in Figure 12-1), as well as in the later stages.

Often a single operational definition of a concept is insufficient and multiple operational definitions (to be simultaneously used) can be recommended.[22] Employee performance, for example, is a complex concept and there are numerous ways of measuring different aspects of it. One way would be to gather appraisal information from supervisors' evaluations of their employees. In this case, employee performance is operationally defined as measured by what the supervisor thinks about the employee. Another option might be to keep track of the number of "formal" complaints issued against the employee by supervisors, clients, or the general public. In this case, employee performance is operationally defined as measured by the number of negative complaints filed against the employee. The performances of many individual employees will be rated differently according to which of the two operational definitions is used. But one might wish to argue that both measures (and others) are tapping different but nonetheless important aspects of performance. The argument may continue that multiple measures should be used so as to tap as many of these important dimensions as is manageable and possible, or that some means should be devised of developing a composite measure of job performance from several operational measures. Developing composite measures involves the construction of indices and scales. Further discussion of these is beyond the scope of this chapter: constructing indices and scales involves some special problems and research requirements.[23]

Operationalization also concerns mode of observation and level of measurement. Mode of observation is the means by which data are to be collected. Level of measurement was partially addressed in Chapter 11, where the differences among nominal, ordinal, interval, and ratio data were noted. The level of measurement profoundly affects how much can be learned about a given concept and how relationships involving the concept can be analyzed. Certain statistical techniques are applicable only to certain levels of measurement. As was noted in Chapter 11, interval-level data are often more precise than ordinal data in measuring relative differences among subjects or situations. Choosing an operational definition for a concept sometimes allows for choices to be made among levels of measurement. Some measurement tools may yield only ordinal data while others yield interval data. Operationalization should therefore take into account the level of measurement of the data that will subsequently be produced and whether or not this will be sufficient to address the policy questions of the planning research.

Reliability and Validity

Reliability and validity are of central importance to the conduct of research and both are immensely complex concepts.[24] Only the more salient of their aspects will be discussed as a means of introducing their importance to all forms of research, including planning-related research.

Reliability refers to the stability and accuracy of measurements; *validity* refers to the degree of correspondence between the concept intended to be measured and what actually is measured.[25] Questions of validity are appropriately raised at every phase of a research endeavor.

The question of validity is particularly important in relation to the development of operational definitions. If data produced through the use of a chosen operational definition are not a valid measure of a concept, then the collection process may turn out to have been misdirected. For example, assume that the question involves the "productivity" of inmate industries in a state prison system. Assume also that only one product is made and sold on the open market for whatever price it can bring. Assume further that *productivity* is defined as growth or decline in the number of product units produced each year, but that the prison has no record of how many units are turned out annually. Information is available, however, on the amount of money brought in each year from the sale of this product. Now, if productivity is measured as *annual revenue generated through sales*, a certain correspondence between revenue and products produced might be assumed. Thus, revenue would be an indirect operational measure of productivity.

However, several problems threaten the *validity* of this operational measure of productivity in this prison industry. First, what was produced may be different from what was sold. To keep inmates busy, many products may have been turned out, but some of the products may have been warehoused because there was no market for them. Revenues do not reflect or "count" these unsold products. Moreover, the sale price of the product may have fluctuated wildly from year to year. Without a constant sale price, changes in revenue do not reflect changes in unit production.

Assume, however, that none of these threats to validity exist and that annual revenues do accurately reflect the number of units produced each year. The problem then is not validity, but it may be reliability.

Whereas validity concerns the correspondence between the concept and its operational definition, reliability concerns the relationship between the operational definition and the specific measurements that are made.[26] Suppose that the guards have been selling products on the sly, or that the prison keeps the money from sales in a cigar box, and that revenue records are sloppy. In this situation, although revenues are a valid indicator of production, the measurement of revenues is not *reliable*. The sales figures are not reliable, stable, and accurate reflections of reality.

Validity is a matter of the truth of an operational definition while reliability is a matter of the consistency of its measurement. Thus, even if operational definitions of concepts and variables are valid (true), the measurement devices may not be reliable (consistent) enough to permit accurate conclusions. And reliability is not simply a problem of having inaccurate data on which to base measurements: reliability can also be threatened by an imprecise operational definition that may lead to inconsistency in measurement.[27] If the operational definition leaves some doubt about what is really being measured and how, subsequent measurement may not be based on a uniform set of procedures and data. Thus, the data may measure slightly different things, perhaps even different aspects of some base concept. Such "mixed" data do not provide stable and accurate (reliable) reflections of the concept that was to be measured.

Collecting data for planning purposes is, therefore, not just a matter of answering the questions posed in Figure 12-1. Rather, these questions must be answered in such a way that the validity and reliability of the data subsequently collected are enhanced.

Population and Sample

Population and *sample* concern who and what will be studied or examined. A *population* is defined as all persons or things falling within the interest of the research design; a *sample* is some portion of or subgroup of this population. Sampling is used to control the amount of data by limiting it to a portion of the population of interest. When resources and time are insufficient to permit collecting data from or on the entire population, sampling, properly done, can provide the means for collecting data from only a portion of the population, which later can be used to make generalizations about the entire population. For example, if the question involves community attitudes toward the provision of police services, a properly drawn sample of citizens can provide the needed attitudinal information—information that would be similar to that provided by a survey of the entire population.

Assuring representativeness in samples is no easy matter. Some forms of sampling, however, are more conducive to representativeness than others.

The basic sampling options are simple random sampling, probabilistic sampling, and nonprobabilistic sampling.[28] In simple random sampling, the sample is drawn from the population randomly, so that every person or thing within the population has an equal chance of being selected. The objective is to screen out bias that would result from using an unrepresentative sample.

The attempt to screen out bias is the attempt to eliminate personal bias—that is, the natural proclivity to stack the deck in favor of what is subjectively preferred. For example, suppose that planners are asked to find out what employees think about a new plan for employee promotions. The planners, working with the personnel department, have devised this plan and think it makes a great deal of sense. In this kind of situation, there may be a natural tendency (a bias) to sample the opinions of certain kinds of employees and not of others—to sample those employees, perhaps, who are perceived to be "team players" and to ignore those employees who are not. But if bias creeps into the sampling process, opinions are not being collected from a representative sample of employees but from only those perceived to be team players. Bias can make for both invalid and unreliable collection and analysis of data. Simple random sampling, as described in any competent research-methods text, helps to screen out this kind of bias.

Probability sampling uses the principles of random sampling at one or more of the stages in the process of selecting a sample; nonprobabilistic sampling does not employ random sampling procedures and thus stands little chance, if any, of screening out bias. Systematic sampling, stratified sampling, and cluster sampling are the most commonly used forms of probabilistic sampling and, together with simple random sampling, are normally the most effective procedures in minimizing bias.[29]

Systematic sampling begins with a list of subjects or elements (say 500) from which a sample (say fifty) is drawn. The process begins with the random selection of the first case and then the selection of every *k*th case after that (called the sampling interval) until we have our fifty cases. In this example, after the random selection of the first case, every tenth ($k = 10$) case would be selected. *Stratified sampling* compensates for the population varying greatly on some set of important issues (for example, class standing among students or age among the population of interest). The population is, therefore, not homogeneous. To assure "adequate" representation of these subgroupings in the population, stratified sampling takes a predetermined proportion of the sample from each subgroup. *Cluster sampling*, very commonly used, is the successive random sampling of sets and subsets. For example, assume that the population of interest is the citizens of the state who live in incorporated cities. Drawing a random sample from this population would be tedious, if not impossible. To ease the process, a random sample of cities within the state might first be chosen, and then subjects from these cities randomly chosen.

Nonprobabilistic forms of sampling include quota sampling, purposive sampling, and accidental sampling.[30] Although these methods do not appreciably screen out researcher bias, they have some uses. For example, purposive sampling is often used when a clear definition of the population is not available or when a clear basis upon which to draw the sample is unknown. In these cases, judgment takes the place of random selection in the attempt to select what presumably will be a typical or representative sample.

The weakest form of nonprobabilistic sampling (or of any kind of sampling) is accidental sampling—a sample composed of whoever or whatever seems conveniently available. An example of accidental sampling, often used in student research projects, is to interview or survey students in a given class as if they were representative of all students. Or there is the procedure sometimes used by newspapers and television and radio stations: the man-in-the-street interview: a reporter stands on a street corner and interviews whoever comes along. The representativeness of findings from such surveys is extremely dubious. It is possible that only certain kinds of people, having certain kinds of opinions or viewpoints, will be passing a certain street corner (for example, stockbrokers predominate on Wall Street).

This overview of the several complex issues involved in determining a sample or a population makes clear that the collection of valid and reliable data requires accurate definition of the population of interest. Samples must accurately represent the total population. If these conditions are not met, both the validity and the reliability of subsequently collected data are open to question.

Alternative Data-Collection Methods

There are numerous alternatives available for the collection of research data for planning purposes. The two overarching alternatives in research design are *experimental* and *ex post facto*. Experimental research permits data to be collected under conditions in which the researcher can control the independent variable because the independent variable has not yet occurred and had its effect. For example, if the aim is to collect data on the effects of alcohol on driving, a controlled research project might be designed and implemented to measure the effects of differing levels of alcohol on driving ability. Ex post facto research designs do not allow us such a degree of control over the independent variable. The situations that the research investigates have already happened or happen as the research is being conducted; the researcher exercises no control over these events.

In an ex post facto design the researcher can still collect data about alcohol consumption and driving ability, but he has less control over what he actually collects and subsequently finds out. Suppose, for example, that instead of running a controlled experiment, the researcher merely rides along in a squad car on a Saturday night and "witnesses" cases of aberrant driving behavior. He or she might observe that a preponderance of such cases involve those who have been drinking. With such observation there is some basis for correlating drinking and dangerous driving, but the correlation is not certain because such factors as the amount of alcohol consumed, or the contributing psychological or physical condition of the driver, cannot be controlled. Data and conclusions depend upon who is on the road that particular Saturday night.

Experimental designs are considered to be the most powerful data-collection devices available because they are best suited to "proving" whether or not an independent variable has had an effect (and what effect) on a dependent variable. True experimental designs seek to establish proof of cause and effect by collecting data in such a way that other potential causes of an observed effect are eliminated as possibilities. Two of the most often used examples of "sound" experimental designs are the classical design and the Solomon four-group design. Figure 12-2 displays these two designs with some accompanying interpretation.

Unfortunately, true experimental designs are often too expensive or beyond our control to set up and make good use of. The Kansas City Preventive Patrol Experiment,[31] which had some flaws, some deviations from the classical model presented in Figure 12-2, encountered community resistance when it was discovered that manipulations of the independent variable (amount of patrolling) would mean significant reductions in patrolling certain of the city's neighborhoods. Not everyone was willing to take on the potential risks of the experiment.

The ethical dilemmas posed in experimental design are also a problem. Numerous researchers have proposed experimental designs as means of evaluating the effectiveness of criminal justice programs (for example, evaluating the effectiveness of juvenile diversion in a treatment program). Random assignment of cases or subjects to control and experimental groupings has often been resisted by decision-makers (police, judges, and corrections officials) who argue that substituting random assignment for their normal decision-making criteria gives rise to grave ethical and policy questions. Gilbert Geis has commented on correctional research:

> Few persons . . . would be apt to say that the cause of science is sufficient to support an experiment in which, without exception, persons convicted of first-degree murder during a given year are executed in order to determine whether capital punishment does in fact have a deterrent impact when categorically applied. Probably just as few persons would maintain that it is unjust to allow a convicted offender to choose between probation in the jurisdiction where he committed his offense and probation in one a thousand miles away, because an investigator wants to determine whether there is a deterrent factor in voluntary removal from the eliciting scene of criminal circumstances.[32]

When experimental situations are too costly or prohibited by political or value considerations, the alternative involves selection of a quasi-experimental research method[33] or an ex

Figure 12-2. Examples of True Experimental Designs

The Classical Experiment

[R]	Experimental Group	pretest → treatment → post-test
	Control Group	pretest → no treatment → post-test

Subjects are randomly ([R]) assigned to the two groups to avoid selection bias as a source of group differences (each group, after random assignment, is assumed to have an equivalent composition across any relevant variable). The two groups are similarly pretested on the dependent variable (e.g., driving ability) prior to any treatment (e.g., being given alcohol). Only one group is treated. Both groups are given a post-test. Post-test scores are compared and any difference (after noting or controlling for differences in group pretest scores) is assumed to be caused by the treatment. The objective of the classical design (as well as the Solomon design below) is to eliminate *all* but the treatment as a possible cause of any differences between the groups.

The Solomon Four-Group Design

[R]	Group 1	pretest → treatment → post-test
	Group 2	pretest → no treatment → post-test
	Group 3	treatment → post-test
	Group 4	no treatment → post-test

To eliminate the possibility that pretesting somehow contaminates the experimental findings, another "control" group is added and another "experimental" group, neither of which is pretested. Eliminating pretest interaction as a source of contamination in the findings helps to increase the generalizability of the findings.

post facto technique. Ex post facto techniques are most commonly used as means of collecting data in social and organizational research, because of the inherent limitations imposed on true experimental research.

There are several standard modes of observation available to researchers. Most of them, with the exception of the experiment, are of practical necessity used primarily in ex post facto forms of research. Figure 12-3 lists and briefly defines several of the more generally used alternatives to the experiment as a mode of data collection.

As will become clear in the second part of this chapter, there is some correspondence between the *kinds* of data to be collected and the *mode* of collecting them. For example, there is a natural tendency to employ survey-research methods when gathering data about community and political values. There is a natural tendency to employ "analysis of existing data" as the mode when collecting data about budgets. Some forms of data suggest the possibility and wisdom of using more than one method. As indicated in Chapter 11, for example, data about crime may be secured from existing records (UCR) or through survey techniques (victimization surveys), each providing slightly different but important pieces of information.

The choice of mode is often largely dependent on both the kind of data needed and the manner in which concepts and variables have been operationalized. For example, if the aim is to secure historical budget data, an analysis of existing records may provide the required information. On the other hand, if the aim is to determine people's attitudes and viewpoints about the history of the agency's budget, survey techniques may be the only means of collecting that data.

The mode of collection chosen is also greatly influenced by practical concerns such as time and money and by considerations of where the data are and how to get at them. Even within a particular mode, field research for example,

Figure 12-3. Primary Alternative Modes of Data Collection to the Experiment

Field Observation:

Field observation is the collection of data through techniques of direct observation by which the researcher observes subjects or conditions of interest. Case studies, participant observation, obtrusive and unobtrusive observation (the researcher as a researcher being noticeable or not noticeable to subjects) are alternative means of conducting field research. An example of field research would be a planner/researcher observing budget hearings as a means of gathering data to predict future agency budgets. Or a planner/researcher might "ride along" in patrol cars to observe current operating procedures. The danger in obtrusive field observation is that the researcher's presence may alter what would otherwise be the normal behavior or condition. The principal general advantage of field observation is that the researcher may be made aware of things that he would not otherwise have thought of when collecting data by other means.[34]

Analysis of Existing Data:

As noted in Chapter 11, many sources of data for planning purposes involve existing records. The analysis of these records is a useful and relatively inexpensive means of securing requisite data. The dangers of using existing data and records involve the ecological fallacy (as discussed in Chapter 11), yet the normal record-keeping functions of public agencies often provide a convenient gold mine of data for planning purposes.

Survey Research:

Survey research is composed of two related but slightly different alternative data collection activities: questionnaires and interviews. In both cases the researcher solicits answers from respondents to questions on topics of interest. Closed-ended answer formats (the respondent is given a set of answers from which to choose) and open-ended answer formats (the respondent may give any answer, in his or her own words) may be used. Interview surveying provides for direct question-answer contact between the researcher and the subject, and permits greater latitide in pursuing and following up on questions than does the questionnaire format. Both the questionnaire and the interview survey are adaptable to collecting a wide variety of kinds of data: descriptive, explanatory, exploratory, prescriptive, evaluative, etc. Survey research is particularly useful in collecting original data from a study population that is too large to observe directly through, say, field observation.

there are several alternatives: personal interviews, mail questionnaires, and telephone surveys, for example. The costs of these in money and in time, vary. They also vary in their suitability for dispersed subject populations. When the subject population is dispersed, mail questionnaires are usually the most efficient means for querying subjects; personal interviews and telephone surveys are less so.[35] Telephone surveys generally yield data more quickly; mail questionnaires and personal interviews take some time. Personal interviews are expensive; mail questionnaires and telephone surveys tend to be less. Practical considerations weigh heavily in the choice of a mode of data collection and although a research purist may consider them extraneous, the practical business of research-oriented planning precludes their being ignored.

COLLECTING DATA FOR CRIMINAL JUSTICE PLANNING

Chapter 11 listed three kinds of often useful planning data (environmental, organizational, and system) and these categories were subdivided into twelve subcategories. This chapter focuses on the collection of environmental and organizational data, because system data largely originate with these two.

The purposes of collecting environmental and organizational data and the validity and reliability of the data are prime concerns. Obviously, not all that could be said about collecting the basic forms of planning-related data would fit into one chapter, perhaps not even into one book. The purpose here will be only to highlight some of the more important issues encountered with regard to each type of data and also to comment on the more obvious alternative modes for collecting them. The research principles discussed earlier provide a means of thinking through and weighing the alternatives.

Crime Data

The importance of crime data for criminal justice planning efforts seems clear. Patterns and trends in criminal behavior determine the demands placed on the criminal justice system and its agencies. Although important aspects of the work done by criminal justice agencies may not strictly be crime-related (e.g., police provision of emergency services), crime is still a major determinant of the amount and kind of workload facing most criminal justice agencies. An understanding of current crime patterns, and the ability to project trends in them, is therefore critically important to the planning process.

Two major sources and types of crime data are UCR data and victimization-survey data. Each of these has its own peculiar drawbacks. It is important to examine the alternative ways in which they operationalize the collection of crime data and the validity and reliability with which they do so.

To the extent that UCR data are intended to produce an accurate summation of criminal events and allow comparison of the kinds and rates of criminal events from jurisdiction to jurisdiction, UCR data contain several threats to the validity and reliability of findings about crime. Not all law-enforcement agencies participate in UCR, and not all those that do provide all of the data requested. In any case, however, only reported crime is recorded, and even when a crime is reported, a police officer has some discretion in deciding how to label the reported crime, or even whether there is sufficient evidence to record it. That there is subjective manipulation involved in agency labelling of criminal events and, more important, that agencies use different criteria in undertaking these manipulations, pose grave questions about the consistency with which UCR data are collected, coded, interpreted.[36]

UCR data-collection procedures thus contain numerous threats to validity and reliability because they fail to operationalize the meaning of criminal events consistently, and because the recording and reporting of events is not done consistently. Also, if UCR data are assumed to be representative of the actual numbers and kinds of criminal events taking place, the problem remains that only reported crime is reflected and that some crimes are more consistently reported than others. For example, it is probably true that most homicides are reported although there may be a few mistakes made in labelling some deaths. Rape, on the other hand, is such a shocking and demeaning event for the victim that it has historically been underreported. Sheley, comparing 1975 Uniform Crime Reports with 1973 victimization-survey results, indicates, for example, that the actual incidence of rape may be nearly four times that officially reported.[37] But, even when rape is reported, the victim may be subjected to charges of "precipitation" (which questions whether the legal requirements for rape have been met).[38] Breaking and entering, if the dollar-value loss is slight, often goes unreported because of public belief that the police will do nothing about it—so why bother? On the other hand, breaking and entering that results in a large dollar-value loss is probably more regularly reported. Thus, not only are all crimes not reported but some *types* of crimes are more regularly reported than others. Any attempt, therefore, to argue that UCR data are representative of the "population" of crime is exceedingly risky.

Victimization surveys have attempted to overcome some of the more serious obstacles to validity and reliability by screening out problems associated with using only reported crime. They also seek to eliminate variance produced through police manipulation of the criminal events reported by victims. Although the survey method has problems of its own, it is a method by which the victim can record firsthand knowledge of criminal activity. If the survey sample is representative and the respondents are answering truthfully and ac-

Figure 12-4. Sample National Crime Survey Questionnaire

HOUSEHOLD SCREEN QUESTIONS

29. Now I'd like to ask some questions about crime. They refer only to the last 12 months– between_______1, 197__ and _____, 197___, During the last 12 months, did anyone break into or somehow illegally get into your (apartment home), garage, or another building on your property?
☐ Yes – How many times? _______
☐ No

30. (Other than the incident(s) just mentioned) Did you find a door jimmied, a lock forced, or any other signs of an ATTEMPTED break in?
☐ Yes – How many times? _______
☐ No

31. Was anything at all stolen that is kept outside your home, or happened to be left out, such as a bicycle, a garden hose, or lawn furniture? (other than any incidents already mentioned)
☐ Yes – How many times? _______
☐ No

32. Did anyone take something belonging to you or to any member of this household, from a place where you or they were temporarily staying, such as a friend's or relative's home, a hotel or motel, or a vacation home?
☐ Yes – How many times? _______
☐ No

33. What was the total number of motor vehicles (cars, trucks, etc.) owned by you or any other member of this household during the last 12 months?
(057)
0 ☐ None– SKIP to 36
1 ☐ 1
2 ☐ 2
3 ☐ 3
4 ☐ 4 or more

34. Did anyone steal, TRY to steal, or use (it/any of them) without permission?
☐ Yes – How many times? _______
☐ No

35. Did anyone steal or TRY to steal part of (it/any of them), such as a battery, hubcaps, tape-deck, etc.?
☐ Yes – How many times? _______
☐ No

INDIVIDUAL SCREEN QUESTIONS

36. The following questions refer only to things that happened to you during the last 12 months- between_____1, 197__ and _____, 197___ . Did you have your (pocket picked/purse snatched)?
☐ Yes – How many times? _______
☐ No

37. Did anyone take something (else) directly from you by using force, such as by a stickup, mugging or threat?
☐ Yes – How many times? _______
☐ No

38. Did anyone TRY to rob you by using force or threatening to harm you? (other than any incidents already mentioned)
☐ Yes – How many times? _______
☐ No

39. Did anyone beat you up, attack you or hit you with something, such as a rock or bottle? (other than any incidents already mentioned)
☐ Yes – How many _______
☐ No

40. Were you knifed, shot at, or attacked with some other weapon by anyone at all? (other than any incidents already mentioned).
☐ Yes – How many times? _______
☐ No

41. Did anyone THREATEN to beat you up or THREATEN you with a knife, gun, or some other weapon, NOT including telephone threats? (other than any incidents already mentioned)
☐ Yes – How many times? _______
☐ No

42. Did anyone TRY to attack you in some other way? (other than any incidents already mentioned)
☐ Yes – How many times? _______
☐ No

43. During the last 12 months, did anyone steal things that belonged to you from inside any car or truck, such as packages or clothing?
☐ Yes – How many times? _______
☐ No

44. Was anything stolen from you while you were away from home, for instance at work, in a theater or restaurant, or while traveling
☐ Yes – How many times? _______
☐ No

45. (Other than any incidents you've already mentioned) was anything (else) at all stolen from you during the last 12 months?
☐ Yes – How many times? _______
☐ No

46. Did you find any evidence that someone ATTEMPTED to steal something that belonged to you? (other than any incidents already mentioned)
☐ Yes – How many times? _______
☐ No

47. Did you call the police during the last 12 months to report something that happened to you which you thought was a crime? (do not count any calls made to the police concerning the incidents you have just told me about.)
☐ No – SKIP to 48
☐ Yes – What happened?
____
(058) ☐☐ ☐☐ ☐☐

CHECK ITEM C ➡ Look at 47. Was HH member 12 + attacked or threatened, or was something stolen or an attempt made to steal something that belonged to him?
☐ Yes – How many times? _______
☐ No

48. Did anything happen to you during the last 12 months which you thought was a crime, but did NOT report to the police? (other than any incidents already mentioned)
☐ No – SKIP to Check Item E
☐ Yes – What happened?
____
(059) ☐☐ ☐☐ ☐☐

CHECK ITEM D ➡ Look at 48. Was HH member 12 + attacked or threatened, or was something stolen or an attempt made to steal something that belonged to him?
☐ Yes – How many times? _______
☐ No

CHECK ITEM E ➡ Do any of the screen questions contain any entries for "How many times?"
☐ No – *Interview next HH member. End interview if last respondent, and fill item 13 on cover.*
☐ Yes – *Fill Crime Incident Reports.*

curately, many of the problems posed by UCR data are eliminated. Figure 12-4 is one page from such a victimization survey.[39]

Although victimization surveys may sidestep many problems of nonreporting, and although they permit direct recording of victim information, they do not avoid all possible threats to validity and reliability, and they also impose added costs on the data-collection operation. The data base for UCR statistics usually exists as part of police-agency records, but victimization surveys represent an added expense, it can be rather substantial. There are other problems with victimization surveys that may undermine the accuracy of the data collection and its interpretation by researchers. Among other things, the survey sample may not be representative of all victims; respondents may not understand or may misinterpret questions; respondents may deliberately be deceptive in filling out the questionnaire; and researchers may fail adequately to interpret the meaning of respondent answers (i.e., miscode the information provided).

Although deliberate deception is often hard to uncover in survey responses, careful checking of responses can sometimes uncover obvious attempts at deception. One researcher, for example, reported the findings from an attempt to check the addresses given by witnesses as part of a prosecutor's management-information system (PROMIS). In this particular study, conducted in the Washington, D.C. area, several witnesses listed their address as 1600 Pennsylvania Avenue.[40] Obviously, most attempts at deception can be expected to be more skillfully concealed, but a careful check of survey data will often uncover some of these deceptions or discrepancies.

Several years ago, Wesley Skogan summarized some of the important threats posed by victimization surveys and compared them with the kinds of threats posed by UCR data. Figure 12-5, designed by Skogan, summarizes the main points.[41]

There is, of course, much more that could be said about collecting crime data, but only two further points will be made here. The first is that it is impossible to eliminate all threats to validity and reliability when collecting crime data (or any data for that matter). No research design guarantees the complete elimination of threats, and so it falls to the researcher to be aware of what these threats are in each procedure and to take them into account when using and interpreting data.

The second point concerns the purposes for which the data are being collected and are to be used. What if, for example, the purpose behind collecting crime data is to gauge as accurately as possible the extent of criminal behavior in a given community? The planner might well want to use a victimization-survey approach because that has been shown to reflect actual community crime levels more accurately. On the other hand, if the purpose is to gauge the amount of crime-related workload being put on a police department (perhaps also to gauge trends in crime-related workloads), the use of existing UCR data and their associated data bases may be all that is necessary. Although victimization surveys ask respondents whether they reported the criminal event to the police and what action, if any, the police took, existing agency records may report the same information in approximate fashion, and without the added cost of a survey. And in this case, unreported crime may not be of interest as unreported crime can hardly be expected markedly to affect the workload of a police department.

The dictum to follow in any effort at collecting data (including collecting data on crime) is to consider what must be found and why, and then to choose the best means possible to secure the data (while balancing cost concerns against concerns for validity and reliability). Although UCR data has several problems associated with it, it may be the most appropriate source of information, given certain planning purposes. Alternatively, victimization-survey data may be the most appropriate source of information for other planning purposes. Thus, choice of a mode of data collection depends on the kind of data provided through its use and whether those data are suited to the questions of interest.

Collecting Other Environmental Data

Some environmental data are qualitative and subjectively grounded. Data about agency missions and goals and data about public and political values are particularly so grounded. Nonetheless, the planner confronted with securing data and information about missions, goals, and values has several alternative data-

Figure 12-5. Some Sources of Measurement Error

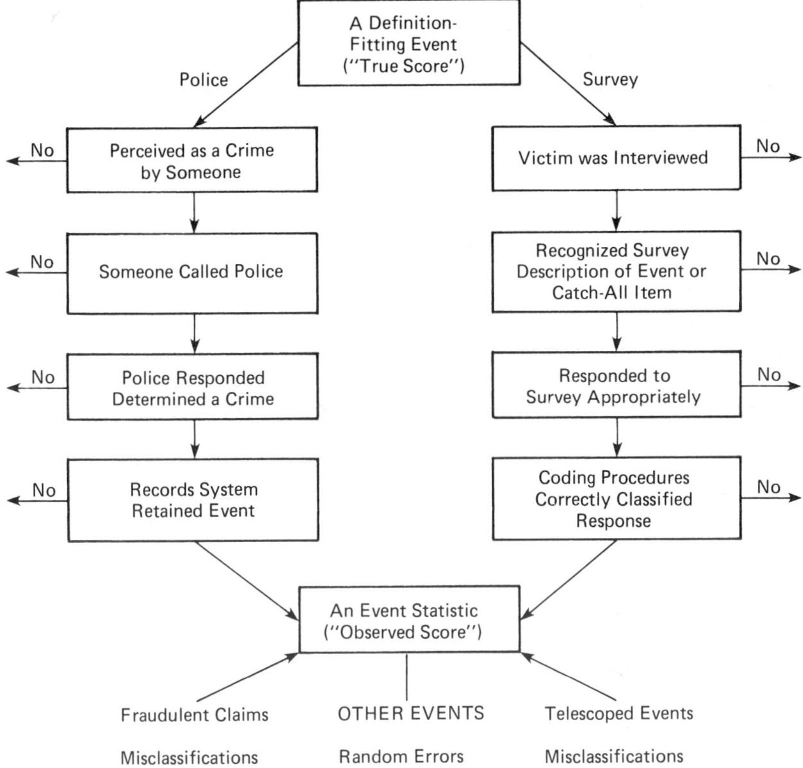

Reprinted with permission from the Journal of Criminal Justice, Volume 3, Wesley G. Skogan, "Measurement Problems in Official and Survey Crime Rates", © 1975, Pergamon Press.

collection approaches available. One option is to scan official agency and jurisdiction publications for statements about these points. If the agency has a formal statement of missions and goals, this can be analyzed as a starting point, though the planner must be careful to distinguish between ostensible and operative goals (see Chapter 6). In some agencies, statements of missions and goals may be included in employee policy manuals or in training materials. They might also be found attached to, or as integral parts of, agency budget proposals (see Chapter 13). Analyses of recent budget decisions made by budget authorities (especially written and verbal responses to agency budget requests) may provide insight into underlying public and political preferences for agency activity. And the recommendations of the agency itself to fund certain programs and to reprioritize budget allocations will be partially reflective of operative missions and goals. The planner may also wish to examine speeches made by agency managers or by local political leaders for additional commentary on missions and goals and on public and political values related to the work of the agency.

Besides (or instead of) analyzing existing documents, planners may survey or interview relevant agency personnel and outside officials to gather information on missions, goals, and public and political values. This is a particularly useful technique when existing documentation is insufficient or when existing documentation does not appear to be a valid and reliable indicator of actual (operative) missions and goals. A carefully constructed sequence of questionnaires and interviews of several such respondents not only may provide information about ostensible and operative goals, but may also allow the planner to measure the degree of goal and value consensus among respondents.

Besides surveys and document analysis, an inventive and resourceful planner/researcher may seek to devise an observational data-collection technique in order to observe the behavior of agency managers and employees and infer underlying or controlling goal preferences. Although such observational techniques are costly, and although they pose several potential threats to validity and reliability (can underlying goal preferences be validly inferred from observed behavior?), useful information concerning the difference between ostensible and operative goals may be secured by employing them.

Environmental data on the economy, the budget, the population, and the labor market are less qualitatively oriented and subjectively grounded than are data about missions and goals. Also, depending on the particular need for such data, existing documents of a wide variety are normally available from which the planner may glean the requisite information. For example, chambers of commerce, banks, the U.S. Department of Commerce and state commerce departments, and a host of other public and private organizations regularly publish statistics and commentary on economic conditions for localities, states, and the nation. These reports not only assess current economic situations but often include projections. Population data aggregated for the nation and broken down by state, standard metropolitan area, county, city, census tract, and city block, provide a wealth of information about the socioeconomic characteristics of the population.[42]

The U.S. Department of Labor and state departments of labor publish several kinds of statistics and commentary on labor-market conditions, including information about salary and wage levels, characteristics of the labor force, labor-force saturation, and data on unemployment and underemployment. All these existing sources of economic, population, and labor-market data usually provide a sufficient data base from which planners may glean characteristics of several agency-relevant environmental conditions. Figure 12-6 lists some of the kinds of statistical information currently available from the Federal government that might be useful to criminal justice planners. There are, of course, innumerable other kinds of statistics available.[43]

Existing data sources present, of course, some difficulties. The data may not be displayed and disaggregated in such fashion as to allow the planner readily to focus on the subject or geographical area of interest. Also, to get precisely the information needed, and all the information needed, the planner may have to consult several sources. Indeed, all existing data normally need manipulation to fit the particular needs of the planner, and unless the planner is careful in making these manipulations, his conclusions will be invalid.

Not all data needed about populations and budgets are readily available in existing documents or reports. For example, although jurisdictions and agencies normally keep detailed reports of revenues, expenditures, and current and previous budget requests and budget authorizations, some information about budgets is not to be found in existing documentation. Sometimes, for example, a planner is interested in knowing what kind of long-range budget thinking is going on and this may be found only in the heads of policy and decision-makers. Questionnaires and interviews may provide some of this information. Planners may also wish to gauge the views of agency decision-makers and policy-makers about the adequacy of agency budgets: this, too, will not normally be reflected in readily available documents. Again, questionnaires and interviewing may offer means for securing the information.

Survey techniques are often also useful to supplement existing information on jurisdiction populations. Perhaps existing census data on population characteristics are dated; perhaps they are not suitably disaggregated; or perhaps they are not available about a population variable of interest. Suppose for example that agency planners need up-to-date information about the percentage of the service population that does not speak English or that uses English only as a second language. This may be important to know in estimating the need for bilingual personnel. One option for estimating such parameters is to survey departmental personnel about the number of times (or rough percentage of times) that the individuals they come into contact with do not speak English. Perhaps, alternatively, departmental personnel can be directed to start reporting each instance and situation in which service clientele have trouble speaking English or cannot speak it at all.

A source of "population information" sometimes overlooked is that provided by surveys of citizens' or clients' attitudes. Citizen

Figure 12-6. Sample Statistics Available and Useful for Planning

- Census of Population
- Current Population Reports:
  series on population characteristics, special studies, population estimates and projections, federal-state cooperative program for population, special censuses, and consumer income.
- Social Indicators
- Monthly Labor Review
- Occupational Manpower and Training Needs
- Special Labor Force Reports
- Current Governments Reports:
  public employment, city employment, local government employment in selected metropolitan areas and large counties, county government employment
- Area Wage Surveys:
  metropolitan areas, United States and regional summaries
- Employee Compensation and Payroll Hours:
  selected manufacturing and nonmanufacturing industries
- Handbook of Methods for Surveys and Studies
- Area Trends in Employment and Unemployment
- Criminal Victimization in the U.S.
- Expenditure and Employment Data for the Criminal Justice System
- National Prisoner Statistics
- Juvenile Court Statistics
- Statistical Series:
  series of reports including juvenile court statistics
- Statistics on Public Institutions for Delinquent Children
- Handbook of Labor Statistics
- Census of Governments
- City Employment
- City Government Finances
- County Government Employment
- County Government Finances
- Governmental Finances:
  covers federal, state, and local governments
- Taxes and Intergovernmental Revenue of Counties, Muncipalities, and Townships

surveys take as their population of interest the entire population falling within the agency's area of jurisdiction or service. Clientele surveys are more focused and usually take as their population of interest only those who have come into contact with or have been provided service by the agency. Citizen and clientele surveys are often directed toward securing people's attitudes toward, and perceptions of, the agency and its provision of services. One such citizen survey was used as part of the Kansas City Preventive Patrol Experiment. Figure 12-7 lists the concepts and subconcepts that were used in this survey.[44]

In reviewing these brief comments about sources of data and modes of collecting the various kinds of data about the environment, it is useful to keep in mind several basic points about research design. First, always be clear about the research questions being asked. Second, carefully consider the types of operationally defined data necessary to deal with these questions. Third, consider the alternative modes available for collecting these data, and choose the mode that seems best to balance cost-effectiveness against losses of validity and reliability. Fourth, after choosing a mode of data collection, do not ignore the threats to validity and reliability that lurk within any of the data-collection alternatives.

There is a natural temptation to use existing documents and reports to secure requisite environmental data. In many, if not most, cases confronting the planner, this temptation wisely reflects the fact that existing data are the most cost-effective alternative. And besides, there may be no other alternative available for securing the data. For example, it would be impractical for police agencies to undertake relatively accurate appraisals of the general economy that would rival what commerce departments and banks already provide as part of their specifically designated tasks. Nonetheless, analysis of existing data is not the only alternative available for collecting environmental data, and in some cases, there will not normally be extant data about certain aspects of the environment. In these situations, planners may well need to devise survey or observational techniques that particularly lend themselves to securing attitudinal data from, and about, the environment.

Figure 12-7. Citizen Attitudes Toward Police: Concepts Included in Kansas City Preventive Patrol Experiment Survey of Citizens

1. Need for more neighborhood police officers
2. Need for more police officers in the entire city
3. Perception of time neighborhood officers spend on car patrol
4. Preference for amount of time police should patrol
5. Perceived amount of time police spend on aggressive patrol
6. Amount of time community prefers police spend on aggressive patrol
7. Perception of neighborhood police-community relations
8. Perception of neighborhood police officers reputation
9. Reputation of Kansas City police officers
10. Respect for neighborhood police
11. Effectiveness of neighborhood officers in fighting crime
12. Effectiveness of Kansas City police in fighting crime
13. Police treatment of whites
14. Police treatment of minorities
15. Harassment by neighborhood police officers
16. Harassment by Kansas City police officers
17. Change in neighborhood police officers
18. Satisfaction with police service
19. Neighbors' respect for neighborhood officers
20. Attitude of officer citizen spoke to most
21. Demeanor of officer citizen spoke to most
22. Characteristics of the encounter
23. Satisfaction with the encounter
24. Response time evaluation
25. Citizen general satisfaction with police

Organizational Data

Chapter 11 addressed at some length many of the issues associated with requisite organizational data for planning purposes (workloads, job data, employee data, performance data), and several concerns relevant to research design, validity, and reliability. This section, however, will focus attention almost entirely on the alternative modes of data collection that can be used to secure these types of organizationally focused data, and stress that threats to validity and reliability in collecting organizational data may be partially addressed through the use of multiple modes of data collection.[45]

Unlike environmental data, organizational data focuses on internal aspects of the agency. It may sound too obvious to mention, but this means that the source of most organizational data is within the agency itself, that the agency may be able to exercise greater control over what organizational data it collects than is the case with environmental data. Cost considerations and questions of validity and reliability still constrain how an agency planner elects to go about collecting the requisite organizational data, but within these kinds of constraints there is significant room for maneuver.

Consider, for example, the need to collect individual employee-performance data. Several alternatives present themselves. The planner may survey the employees' supervisors, asking them to rate several aspects of employees' job behavior. Alternatively, employees themselves may be surveyed through questionnaires and interviews about their performance. Existing data in the form of daily logs may be reviewed to determine how much of what kind of work individual employees engage in. Employees may be periodically observed obtrusively or unobtrusively by outsiders and rated on how well they are performing their duties.

For something as elusive as employee performance, multiple measures may be better than only one kind of measure. And multiple measures will often imply several modes of data collection. Ratings based on supervisory and employee surveys can be compared to ratings derived through observational techniques. Although an observer may catch the employee "having a bad day," this can be balanced against the longer-term basis on which supervisors rate employee performance. So, too, supervisory ratings of employees may reflect personal bias on the part of the supervisor; impartial observation by an outsider can be used to counterbalance this bias. By using multiple data-collection modes and sources, the planner can offset the obstacles to validity and reliability inherent in any one mode. Figure 12-8 indicates some of these alternative meanings and sources of performance data, and several alternative modes of collection.[46]

Workload data can be collected through several alternative modes. A document study of daily logs or similar records provide insight into

Figure 12.8. Sample Measures of Employee Performance and Data Sources

Grade in academy
Ever resigned from department
Supervisor ratings
Number of occasions of sick leave, each period
Total number of sick days, each period
Number of occasions when sick leave was adjacent to other types of leave, each period
Number of occasions of injury time, each period
Total number of injury days, each period
Number of occasions when injury time was adjacent to other types of leaves, each period
Number of occasions of suspension time, each period
Total number of occasions of suspension time, each period
Automobile accidents
Incidents of injury to prisoners
Number of arrests
Number of citations issued
Chargeable automobile accidents
Number of times weapon fired
Field training officer rating
Previous promotions, by date
Data of any demotion
Reason for demotion
Date of last internal transfer
Testing scores
Commendations, number and source
Complaints and disposition

the kinds of activities or work confronting the agency and its employees. Alternatively or additionally, the planner may wish to interview agency employees for information about the kinds of work they do. Both document study and interview techniques may focus on uncovering trends in workloads as well as determining how workloads vary by shift or season. Questionnaires, distributed to employees, gather some of the same kinds of information that might otherwise be gathered through the more time-consuming and costly method of interviewing.

Firsthand observation is an additional alternative for collecting workload data, but the cost involved in participant observation and the questions often raised about the representativeness of the data collected make reliance on this mode a problem. Nonetheless, observational studies provide useful supplemental information not normally collected, or not collected well, through logs and surveys. For example, police log sheets may record calls for service along with "time out" and "time in" data, but log data are not normally detailed or sensitive enough to reflect validly what actually happens in responding to calls for service. The actual meaning of workload is thereby lost. Moreover, official log entries and survey responses may be manipulated, deliberately or accidentally, much as UCR data bases are manipulated. Observation may provide a basis for uncovering some of these manipulations and correcting for them.[47]

Collecting job-focused data begins with an analysis of existing agency job descriptions. These job descriptions may contain information related both to the nature of duties and to the knowledge and skills necessary for successful performance. Another form of document study might be an analysis of existing data collected as a result of earlier job analyses conducted in the agency. If existing data in the form of reports, studies, or descriptions do not seem sufficiently detailed, up-to-date, or accurate, the planner may elect to undertake one or more of the several established job-analysis techniques (see Chapter 14). All these techniques make use of the standard data-collection modes. Employees may be surveyed through questionnaires or interviews (usually both) in an effort to determine what they do in their various jobs; these employees may also be asked to report the kinds of knowledge and skills they think essential to performing their jobs. Alternatively, trained observers, using standardized job-analysis criteria and rating scales, can be used to observe directly the nature of employee work in various jobs, and to categorize and describe that work. Trained observers can also be used to sort out what kinds of knowledge and skills seem crucial to doing the job.

Employee-focused data—data about employee characteristics—lie in personnel records. Descriptive data on the number of employees in various job classifications, their age, their sex, and other personal data can be obtained through official agency documents. Questionnaires can be used to supplement these sources, perhaps specifically directed toward gathering data on employee career preferences or job-related attitudes and opinions. Gathering data for an employee skills bank may involve questionnaires and interviews, document study (in the form of searching personnel files or analysis of performance evaluations), observation of employees on the job, and tests of employee skills and knowledge.

Constraints to Data Collection

A number of constraints impinge on the agency data-collection effort. Constraints to data collection can be defined as those events, conditions, or factors that limit the agency's ability to collect a particular kind of data, or to use the most effective means for doing so. Experiments, as a means of data collection, are rarely feasible. The inability to use experiments affects reliability and validity because the experiment is particularly conducive to diminishing such threats. Also, although multiple measures and multiple modes of data collection can provide checks on validity and reliability, even a single-method data collection is often expensive and time-consuming enough without multiplying the expense with overlapping methods.

The kinds of constraints facing agencies when collecting data are numerous but chiefly include money, in-house expertise and skills, time, manpower, accessibility of data, and standards of validity and reliability.

Money is often the most significant of any of the factors. Money does more than pay for sufficient *numbers* of people to collect data; the amount of money available clearly influences the degree to which the agency can afford to hire *trained* experts to collect data in a valid and reliable manner. How much money there is influences whether an agency is able to undertake multiple modes of data collection; even when only one mode can be afforded, financial constraints may mean picking a less expensive mode of data collection, even though that mode is not the most valid or reliable. The document search, for example, is often the least expensive mode of data collection; field studies are usually more expensive; observational studies are often the most expensive. In field studies, interviews tend to be the most expensive techniques, telephone interviews less expensive, and questionnaires least expensive. The relative expense associated with alternative modes of data collection does indeed enter into the decision about which mode of data collection to select.

The lack of sufficient in-house skill often precludes the selection of certain modes of data collection. For example, if the existing data in documents are clear, collecting and recording the necessary data through document search may be little more than a clerical chore. But to conduct field research and observational studies, data collectors generally need a fair amount of prior training in what to look for and how to record data in an unbiased fashion. Interviews particularly require training and experience, for it is easy for an interviewer to fall into directing, and therefore biasing, a respondent's answers.

Time frequently imposes severe constraints on data collection in criminal justice agencies. Especially in those agencies where crisis management is a way of life, planners are often directed to "find out something about this as soon as you can." Observational modes of data collection are very time-consuming, field research takes only slightly less time than observational studies. If extant data can be found, planners pressed for time will be forced to rely entirely on document search, even when the existing document data are flawed in validity and reliability.

These and other kinds of constraints affect validity and reliability. In the short term, there may not be much that the planner can do about these constraints, but there are some long-term efforts that planners and planning units can undertake that may ultimately mitigate some of the effects of these constraints. The first is for planners to consider the kinds of data currently collected and kept by the agency with a view to improving the validity and reliability of these existing and on-going efforts. Although these data may be collected in other agency units for purposes other than planning, the more the planners can increase the compatibility between those needs and those of planning, the more available requisite planning data becomes.

A second useful strategy is for planners to anticipate as best they can what upcoming data needs may be. This is often more easily said than done, but if planners can anticipate emerging issues, time constraints on collecting requisite data are diminished. For example, anticipating the need for field research to collect certain kinds of data will often provide the lead time necessary to design and conduct the necessary field-data collection.

SUMMARY

It ought to be obvious that valid and reliable data collection itself requires intensive planning—planning in depth. Anyone truly interested in becoming a competent planner should delve much more deeply into research methods and procedures. Several of the basic texts referred to in the end-notes will go some way toward providing a deeper understanding.

But what data to collect and how to collect it is not immediately obvious to planners or to anyone else. Answers to several important questions must first be obtained. These questions are naturally part and parcel of the research design and answering them meaningfully means determining what is needed and *why*, operationally defining these needs in such a way that the data collected are valid and reliable bases for generating information for planning purposes.

Anyone who has done research knows that design questions never stop. Indeed, research is a constant process of refining what one needs to know, what he or she wants to know, and how he or she finds it out. This chapter has described the kinds of basic questions that guide the initial design of research and the decisions about what data to collect and why. Figure 12-1 summarized some of the most central questions planners must answer before beginning the collection and analysis of data for planning purposes.

· *Chapter 12* ·
NOTES

1. Glenn A. Bassett and Harvard Y. Weatherbee, *Personnel Systems and Data Management*, The American Management Association, 1971, pp. 15–25.
2. Julian L. Simon, *Basic Research Methods in Social Sciences*, 2nd ed. (New York: Random House, Inc. 1978), p. 8.
3. Robert R. Mayer and Ernest Greenwood, *The Design of Social Policy Research* (Englewood Cliffs, N.J.: Prentice-Hall, Inc., 1980), p. 69.
4. See, for example, Russell L. Ackoff, *Scientific Method: Optimizing Applied Research Decisions* (New York: John Wiley & Sons, Inc., 1962).
5. Simon, op. cit., p. 109.
6. Earl R. Babbie, *The Practice of Social Research*, 2nd ed. (New York: Wadsworth Publishing Co., Inc., 1979), p. 107.
7. Mayer and Greenwood, op. cit., p. 74.
8. For example, see Dennis P. Forcese and Stephen Richer, eds., *Stages of Social Research: Contemporary Perspectives* (Englewood Cliffs, N.J.: Prentice-Hall, Inc., 1970); and Kenneth D. Bailey, *Methods of Social Research* (New York: The Free Press, 1978).
9. Carol H. Weiss, *Evaluation Research: Methods of Assessing Program Effectiveness*, (Englewood Cliffs, N.J.: Prentice-Hall, Inc., 1972), p. 6.
10. Bailey, op. cit., see Chap. 2.
11. Mayer and Greenwood, op. cit., p. 70.
12. Fred N. Kerlinger, *Foundations of Behavioral Research*, 2nd ed. (New York: Holt, Rinehart and Winston, 1973), p. 21.
13. Daniel Katz, "Field Studies," in Leon Festinger and Daniel Katz, *Research Methods in the Behavioral Sciences* (New York: The Dryden Press, 1953), pp. 56–97.
14. G. A. Lundberg, *Foundations of Sociology* (New York: Macmillan Publishing Co., Inc., 1939), see pp. 471–535 in particular.
15. Babbie, op. cit., see Part 3.
16. Kerlinger, op. cit., p. 31.
17. Mayer and Greenwood, op. cit., p. 211.
18. Babbie, op. cit., p. 154.
19. Kerlinger, op. cit., p. 32.
20. *Attorney General's Task Force on Violent Crime: Final Report* (Washington, D.C.: U.S. Department of Justice, August 17, 1981).
21. Hubert M. Blalock, Jr., *Social Statistics* (New York: McGraw-Hill Book Company, 1960), pp. 10–11.
22. Ibid.
23. See for example, Babbie, op. cit., Chap. 12, and Marvin E. Shaw and Jack M. Wright, *Scales for the Measurement of Attitudes* (New York: McGraw-Hill Book Company, 1967).
24. See Ernest R. House, *Evaluating with Validity* (Beverly Hills, Calif.: Sage Publications, 1980), for some interesting viewpoints on this issue.
25. Kerlinger, op. cit., pp. 443, 457.
26. Babbie, op. cit., p. 49.

27. Blalock, op. cit., p. 9.

28. Kerlinger, op. cit., see Chap. 8.

29. See Philip J. Runkel and Joseph E. McGrath, *Research on Human Behavior: A Systematic Guide to Method* (New York: Holt, Rinehart and Winston, 1972), Chap. 5, and Babbie, op. cit., Chap. 7, for a description of these.

30. Kerlinger, op. cit., p. 129.

31. George L. Kelling, et al., *The Kansas City Preventive Patrol Experiment: A summary Report* (Washington, D.C.: Police Foundation, 1974).

32. Gilbert Geis, "Ethical and Legal Issues in Experiments with Offender Populations," in Susette M. Talarico, ed., *Criminal Justice Research* (Anderson Publishing, 1980), p. 222.

33. See Donald T. Campbell and Julian C. Stanley, *Experimental and Quasi-Experimental Designs for Research* (Chicago: Rand McNally & Company, 1963). Also see Donald T. Campbell and H. Laurence Ross, "The Connecticut Crackdown on Speeding: Time-Series Data in Quasi-Experimental Analysis," in Talarico, op. cit., pp. 70–88.

34. Katz, op. cit.

35. David Nachmias and Chava Nachmias, *Research Methods in the Social Sciences*, 2nd ed. (New York: St. Martin's Press, Inc., 1980), p. 202.

36. For additional points see Federal Bureau of Investigation, "Uniform Crime Reporting: Uses for Criminal Justice Planning," in Leonard Oberlander, ed., *Quantitative Tools for Criminal Justice Planning* (Washington, D.C.: U.S. Department of Justice, U.S. Government Printing Office, 1975), pp. 30–31.

37. Joseph F. Sheley, *Understanding Crime: Concepts, Issues, Decisions*, (New York: Wadsworth Publishing Co., Inc., 1979), pp. 34–35.

38. See Lynn A. Curtis, "Victim Precipitation and Violent Crime," in Burt Galaway and Joe Hudson, eds., *Perspectives on Crime Victims* (St. Louis: The C.V. Mosby Company, 1981), pp. 168–71.

39. M. Joan McDermott, *Criminal Victimization in Urban Schools* (Washington, D.C.: U.S. Department of Justice, National Criminal Justice Information and Statistics Service, U.S. Government Printing Office, 1979), p. 47.

40. Frank Cannavale, Jr., quoted by Joyce Deroy, "Data Reliability and Data Purification," in Oberlander, op. cit., p. 124.

41. Wesley G. Skogan, "Measurement Problems in Official and Survey Crime Rates," *Journal of Criminal Justice*, 3:1 (Spring 1975), 21.

42. See Ronald E. Crellin, et al., "Data-Use Tools and Techniques Available to Criminal Justice Professionals," in Oberlander, op. cit. pp. 165–96.

43. Bureau of the Census, *Statistical Abstract of the United States: National Data Book and Guide to Sources*, 100th ed., (Washington, D.C.: U.S. Department of Commerce, U.S. Government Printing Office, 1979), see pp. 964–1011 for additional listings.

44. Kelling, et al., op. cit., pp. 32, 34, 35.

45. Marc G. Gertz and Susette M. Talarico, "Problems of Reliability and Validity in Criminal Justice Research," in Talarico, op. cit., p. 166.

46. George L. Kelling and Mary Ann Wycoff, *The Dallas Experience: Human Resources Development* (Washington, D.C.: Police Foundation, Vol. 2, 1978), p. 52; and John E. Boydstum and Michael E. Sherry, *San Diego Community Profile: Final Report* (Washington, D.C.: Police Foundation, 1975), p. 39.

47. Gary W. Cordner, "Police Patrol Workload Studies: A Review and Critique," *Police Studies*, 2 (Summer 1979), 50–60.

· *Part V* ·

CRIMINAL JUSTICE PLANNING APPLICATIONS

This part examines three specific kinds of planning: fiscal planning, manpower planning, and strategic planning. Although there are many other areas of application, these are particularly important to managing organizations and systems.

Chapter 13 examines the requirements of fiscal planning and presents several alternative formats for budget-planning purposes. It also discusses budget justification and accountability, from both internal and external perspectives. The environment is the source of funds and the place where agency resource requests are approved or denied. Political and fiscal constraints confront the budget planner and must be considered as part of the fiscal-planning process. The last section in Chapter 13 considers some of the factors involved in successfully advocating the budget plan.

Chapter 14 addresses manpower planning. It presents several alternative definitions and uses of manpower planning in organizations and distinguishes agency-based manpower planning from broader efforts at the state and national levels in manpower forecasting and manpower programming. It also examines several analytical techniques used in manpower planning, with special attention to forecasting and job-analysis techniques, and reviews recently collected data about the level of manpower-planning activity in criminal justice agencies.

Chapter 15 focuses attention on the overall guidance given through strategic-planning efforts. It delves into the meaning of strategic planning, distinguishes it from tactical planning, and discusses how strategic planning can become a major force for innovation. It also presents an example of strategic planning in a criminal justice agency, and discusses the need for—and some of the basic impediments to—system level strategic planning in criminal justice.

· Chapter 13 ·

FISCAL PLANNING

One of the hits of the musical *Cabaret* was a catchy tune with the refrain "Money makes the world go round." This line, although something less than the whole truth, reminds us—as if we needed reminding—that money is an essential fuel driving organizations and their programs, whether public or private. The planned management of money is one of the chief tools available to the manager in controlling, coordinating, and directing the organization. Fiscal planning may be seen as the science and art of deciding what can be bought when everything needed or wanted cannot be. Indeed, few organizations enjoy the luxury of truly boundless resources; the money making them "go round" is limited.

As no planner can expect for long to avoid the necessity of fiscal planning, and as money is so central to the functioning of any organization, this chapter focuses on the particular options available in fiscal planning.

A GENERAL PERSPECTIVE

One estimate puts 1958 criminal justice expenditures in the U. S. at some $2.86 billion,[1] and 1977 expenditures at $21.57 billion.[2] But the depreciation of the dollar owing to inflation, and the relative inaccuracy of data collection before 1969, make this growth less than it appears. There has, however, been growth, as Table 13-1 demonstrates. The figures for this table are taken from the 1971-77 reporting period, by which time data collection was relatively consistent from one year to the next.[3]

A total system expenditure increase of 105 per cent recorded for the 1971-77 period should, of course, be corrected for inflation, which ranged from about 5 per cent to 11 per cent per annum nationally during the period. And certainly movements such as police unionization and the resulting wage-and-fringe-package demands inflated costs even more. It is mostly guesswork how much of the 105 per cent growth was real, but if even a 9 per cent average annual inflation rate for the period is assumed, real growth would approximate $4 billion over the six years.

An alternative way of conceiving and documenting the real growth, given the labor-intensive nature of the field,[4] is to examine system-personnel growth during the same period. Table 13-2 indicates percentage growth in the field as a whole and for selected sectors in the field during the period 1971-77.[5]

These systemwide expenditures represent a substantial outlay of public funds. And the budgets of individual criminal justice agencies are themselves substantial. For example, New York and California have correction-agency budgets exceeding $300 million a year. The smallest states, however, still have correction-agency budgets that range from $10 million to $20 million annually, while most states' annual corrections budgets range from $40 million to $125 million.[6] In 1978, the largest city police departments had yearly budgets that averaged over $267 million. The budgets of the smaller city police departments (those serving a population of 10,000 to 25,000) were on the average well in excess of $602,000 per annum. And medium-size police departments (those serving a population of 100,000 to 250,000) had budgets that averaged nearly $7 million.[7]

The growth of criminal justice expenditures and the size of individual agency budgets illustrate how complex and expensive criminal justice programming is. It also points out that fiscal planning in almost any agency involves large sums, and that the resulting need for budget planning in any agency is no petty matter. But what is perhaps more important is that the size of the budgets may appear shocking to the general public and may lead some to question the necessity of such expenditures.

Table 13-1. Criminal Justice System Expenditures 1971-77

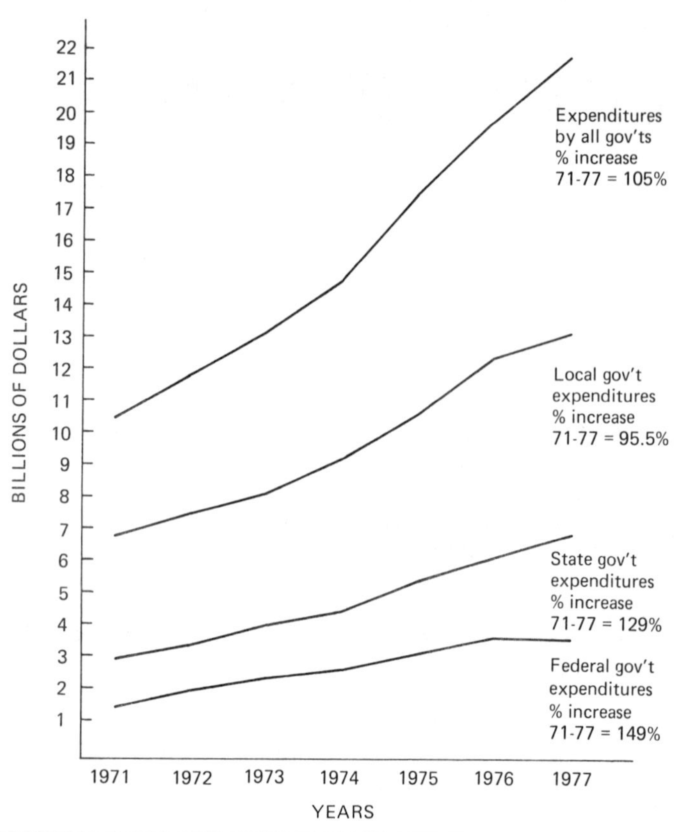

Table 13-2. Percentage Growth From 1971 to 1977 in Personnel Employed at All Government Levels

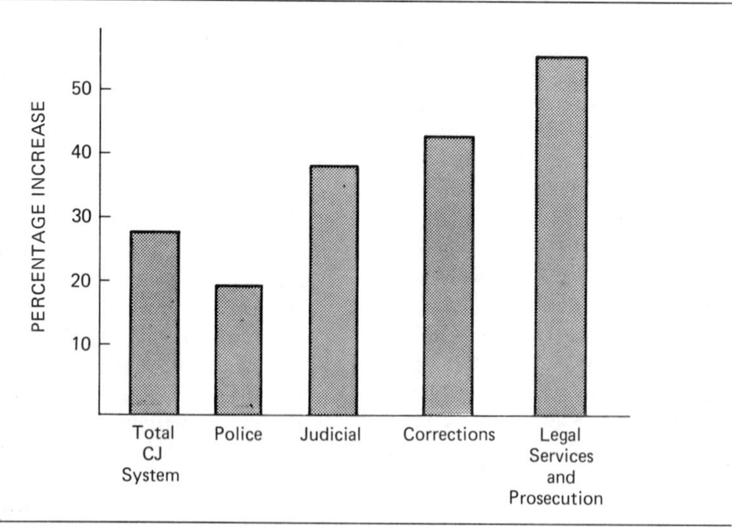

Public Questions

The general growth in public-sector resources[8] is partially attributable to the post-World War II philosophy that new problems could be solved with new money. Others have argued that the reasons for growth are more complicated (international commitments, poulation growth, higher living standards, and increased reliance on government to provide security).[9] But whatever went into making this philosophy, a general public faith in the benefits to be derived from government spending did seem to prevail after World War II.

By the mid 1970s, this philosophy had come under increasingly critical review, and two fundamentally conservative views emerged: that increased government funding leads to increased waste; that government is inherently incapable of efficiently and effectively performing many of the functions assigned it. For example, during Congressional hearings in 1978 in which the Federally financed cancer-research program was being reviewed, inquiry focused on why an infusion of over $2 billion in Federal money had not yet produced a cure for cancer. It may be argued that the taxpayers' revolt[10] that also began coming to a head during the same period reflected a general public awakening to the idea that new money does not necessarily lead to the discovery of solutions. Concommitantly, the advent of "sunset legislation" was a recognition that many government programs outlive their usefulness and, more important, that many government programs and agencies never do the job they were intended to do. ("Sunset legislation" stipulates a definite time limit for governmental programs. If they are not at the time specifically renewed by legislative action, they cease to exist.)

The demand for efficiency and effectiveness in government programs is ageless. The cries are louder during some periods than they are during others, and public organizations in general and criminal justice agencies in particular now face, after years of growing budgets, the need to demonstrate the efficiency and the effectiveness with which they spend resources and achieve objectives.

There is little comfort in the notion that the growth in public and private income in this country since World War II has had few parallels in world history. A return to normality and decreased growth and prosperity will require artful budget planning if programs and services are to be maintained. In the public sector, declining revenues confront rising costs—already the painful reality in many jurisdictions—and this requires decision-making and the setting of budget priorities. Those least able to plan and to defend their budgets may be most susceptible to budget cuts.

Managing Resources and Accomplishing Objectives

Fiscal planning (or budgeting) is not merely balancing the checkbook or the organizational ledger every year. Budgeting encompasses setting policy, determining optimal levels of work that can be undertaken with given resource levels, and maximizing the attainment of goals. Fiscal planning is also concerned with securing as many resources as possible or as are needed. Thus, fiscal planners are politicians, policymakers, planners, evaluators, and designers of work programs. In 1954, Frank P. Sherwood, writing for a United Nations publication, recognized the policy-making nature of budgeting, and he emphasized the advantages of undertaking what he called the management approach to budgeting:

> In contrast [to the fiscal approach,] the management approach is premised on an attempt to delve deeper into the budget process than its financial manifestations. From an organizational point of view, such an approach removes the budgeting function from the authority of the finance department and places it in a staff relationship to the chief executive. Perhaps the key to management budgeting is the idea of planning. Planning demands, above all, the collection of facts relevant to the problem. It suggests the presence of alternatives, each of which has been assessed before decisions have been taken. . . . Only with a comprehension of these facts is it possible to mold budget estimates into a plan. . . . It is questioned whether the fiscal approach makes full use of the budget preparation and execution phases as devices of executive control. By making a comprehensive, continuous audit of program goals, achievements, and needs the coordinating capacity of the top administrator is said to be enhanced.[11]

Sherwood's orientation to fiscal adminstration is radically different from the rather commonplace notion that budget personnel are really only green-visored, crisp-suited accountants, who have a constant supply of sharp pencils and an adding machine, and who use both prodigiously. The wider policy-making view of budget planning is implicitly recognized in several more recent definitions of budgeting:

> Public budgeting involves the selection of ends and the selection of means to reach those ends. Public budgeting systems are systems for making choices about ends and means.[12]
>
> A budget is a document, containing words and figures, which proposes expenditures for certain items and purposes. . . . The budget thus becomes a link between financial resources and human behavior to accomplish policy objectives.[13]
>
> A budget [is] a plan of financial operation embodying an estimate of proposed expenditures for a given period and the proposed means of financing them.[14]
>
> [Public] budgeting is primarily a process by which determinations are made as to the amount of manpower, materiel, and money to be used by a government or other entity and the allocation thereof among competing claims or demands.[15]

There are two general purposes behind effective money management and planning. The first general purpose is to run an organization in a way that is satisfactory to management. The second is to be able to justify to those who allocate money that requested funds are necessary and that funds received are well spent. Each of these purposes stands on its own and even in the face of stingy or defiant money appropriators, the wise administrator will seek to allocate funds internally in ways that maximize the efficiency and effectiveness of each expenditure. Thus, the improvement of resource-planning skills (budgeting) can serve internal and external agency needs, separately or together.

The general public's suspicion of, and ire over, government spending is not simply a dislike of high taxes. More fundamentally, people are confused over what the spending is accomplishing, or disagree with the purpose of that spending, or both. Tax revolts, which have a substantial history in this country, usually signal such confusion or disagreement. What in many cases causes public ire and decreased appropriations is the failure of agency management to publicize the concrete benefits.

Fiscal Planning: Public Agencies Compared to Private Agencies

There are important similarities between private and public fiscal planning. First, budgeting for both is the mechanism by which scarce resources are assigned. The economic concept of scarcity is a pervasive concern not only for General Motors, but for the district court as well, because the decision to buy certain goods and services precludes the buying of other goods and services. Second, in both sectors the decision to assign resources to certain areas instead of to others is tantamount to determining priorities, to setting goals and objectives. Third, in both sectors, the assignment of fiscal resources and the accounting and auditing of resource use is a means of controlling and coordinating the diverse activities of often complex organizations.

But beyond these basic similarities, there are important differences between the private and the public sectors. Perhaps the most important of these differences is that private organizations use profit as the measure for evaluating management performance, but public agencies do not expend resources with the purpose of generating income and subsequent profits.[16] A police department does not fund patrol units as a means of generating profit for the departmental coffers. The encyclopedia salesman can add up his income or his profit and have a measure of his success.

There are, or course, exceptions. For example, some police departments may measure the value of their traffic-patrol sections by comparing costs to income generated through issuance of traffic citations; some prison work programs are deliberately conceived to turn a profit that will be used to defray other expenses; and fire-inspection licensing-fee structures may be set to provide revenue for other functions of the fire department.

In general, however, the absence of profit as a measure of effectiveness in public budgeting not only complicates the comparison of dollar return to dollar investment for a single program; but also complicates the problem of comparing the relative merits of expending resources on one program (e.g., the police) to expending resources on another program (e.g., education or corrections). Consider the view of Robert Lee and Ronald Johnson:

Public budgetary decisions, for example, frequently involve allocation of resources among competing programs that are not readily susceptible to measurement in terms of dollar costs and dollar returns. There is no ready means of comparing the net value of a life saved through cancer research and one enemy death on the battlefield; these units simply cannot be equated. The absence of clear-cut measures of profit and loss may be a partial explanation of why government and not business provides these services.[17]

Many, perhaps most, public-service programs cannot be easily compared for the purpose of deciding how budget allocations are to be made among them, and many public-service programs are intentionally economic "losers." Few private firms will provide a service at a loss. Yet, society has determined that certain services must be provided to all citizens through public agencies, in part because a free economy will not produce the service or will offer the service at a rate that only the wealthy can afford.

The Problem of Budget Accountability

The provision of such services as law enforcement, adjudication, and correctional programming outside the free-market pricing mechanism leads to several problems. It becomes difficult, for example, to determine whether the cost and amount of services rendered meets with public approval. Initially, budgetary accountability meant legal compliance–whether or not public funds were being spent for authorized items. Requisition and order forms, personnel-position authorizations, quarterly and annual account reports, and audits were all developed to prove that funds were spent properly. But those control procedures limited accountability to the input side of public-agency transactions–to the objects or resources allocated to an agency. Measurement and control of inputs hardly accounts for outputs or explain whether the expenditures resulted in a *beneficial* delivery of goods and services. For example, although the purchase of twenty new squald cars or a fire truck may be authorized and appropriate that is no guarantee that they will be used efficiently and effectively in the provision of police or fire services.

The requirement that a relationship be drawn between inputs and outputs lies at the heart of making public agencies accountable, and the public sector has responded in two ways. First, public agencies have relied heavily on formal rules to guide their personnel,[18] and this may be especially true in police and correctional agencies. Second, agencies have undertaken *cost/benefit analysis.*

Cost/benefit analysis involves the construction of ratios comparing the value of inputs to the value of outputs or outcomes. Fiscal decision-making that collects and analyzes only input data stands no chance of undertaking cost/benefit analysis or of determing the effectiveness and efficiency of resource utilization. Unfortunately, most fiscal administrators in criminal justice today still consider only input data. Some managers think, "Rational justification of my budget request doesn't mean a thing: I'll get whatever I am going to get, no matter what I do." It is a dangerous way of thinking, especially in an era of increased competition for scarce resources. It is a way of thinking better suited to periods of budgetary stability or growth, not to periods of scarcity and increasing public scrutiny.

To the experienced manager effective budgeting in a political environment cannot be learned from a textbook, life is the best teacher. There are, however, basic principles, ideas, and concepts that will serve to guide the inexperienced and perhaps even offer the battle-scarred administrator some new approaches to the perennial budget wars. Political savvy and political clout will continue to have an impact on budgetary decision-making, and the ultimate issue of agency survival will no doubt depend on such political awareness. But survival at *what level of prosperity*? That is another question. Especially in an era of decreasing resources, managers with sound budgetary procedures and the ability to publicize the benefits accruing from expenditures will have an edge over the rest.

OPTIONS FOR BUDGET-PLANNING AND ACCOUNTABILITY

Recent developments in public budgeting have been primarily directed toward finding a substitute for profit as a measure of performance and accountability. These efforts have yielded three major options: control, or line-item, budgeting; management, or performance, budgeting; and planning, programming, and budgeting (PPB). The most recent variant of PPB is zero-base budgeting (ZBB).

Bertram Gross,[19] Allen Schick,[20] and Nicholas Henry[21] have all characterized the development of public budgeting in roughly similar fashion, emphasing a three-stage development that gradually shifted analysis from its focus on inputs toward a focus on the relationship between inputs and outputs. The views presented here are similar to theirs.

The line-item, management, and PPB options bring substantially different kinds of information into the budget-planning process, and they address very different questions of accountability. As will be seen, early budgeting theories provided only a very simplistic approach to planning and accountability; the more recently developed options provide for greater sophistication and complexity.

Criminal justice agencies today vary in which of the three major budgeting options they use: although most criminal justice agencies currently use line-item budgeting, several employ a management or performance orientation to budgeting, and a few are using a PPB or a ZBB approach. There is, however, a trend to be seen, and it is away from the line-item option and toward the other options.

Lump-Sum Budgeting

Before 1900, the predominant form of "budgeting," if it can be called that, was *lump-sum budgeting*. It is still practiced in some jurisdictions and seems particularly common in judicial budgets. Under lump-sum budgeting, as the term implies, an agency is given a lump sum to cover all costs during the coming year. Accountability is simply defined under this system: "Don't spend more than the lump." Except for certain legal strictures, there are few controls on how the money is spent. Budget plannning under this approach is usually very simplistic: for example, a judge may sit down once a year to determine what the court will need to keep going for another year. The budget-planning process ends with the judge writing a letter asking for so many dollars for the coming year. The letter usually provides little detailed justification for the amount requested.

Line-Item Budgeting

The first real changes in public budgeting evolved roughly between 1900 and 1921 and were a response to public pressure to control officials and their use of funds.[22] The budgeting format that developed under these pressures was limited to collecting and analyzing resource (input) data. The legislative branch appropriated specified amounts of money for the purchase of only certain goods and services, and agencies were subsequently audited to determine whether their purchases had been in accord with legislative action.

This early form of budgeting Allen Schick has labeled *control budgeting;*[23] it is more familiarly known as *line-item budgeting*. Under this system, specific amounts of money are appropriated for certain items only. The item categories may be general (personnel, equipment, supplies, and so on) or more detailed (secretarial, professional, pencils, bullets, and so on). The more detailed the specifications, the more control is being exercised, but control and accountability are measured only in terms of resource expenditure. Such a system leads to little formal consideration of whether or not work is being done and whether or not objectives are being attained.

Figures 13-1 and 13-2 are hypothetical examples of line-item budgets for a policy agency. Both tables employ a typical line-item format, in which certain dollar amounts are specified for certain kinds of expenditures (or certain numbers of dollars for certain "line items"). The difference between the two tables is the amount of detail in the various lines. Figure 13-1 has only general-expenditure categories, while Figure 13-2 breaks down these general categories.

The nature of control and accountability in line-item budgeting is (within certain tolerances) simply expressed: "Don't spend more for, say, travel than the sum you have requested and that has been approved." And, in an attempt to make sure that there are not too many surprises in the form of overexpenditures, purchasing controls are imposed (e.g., purchasing forms, personnel-authorization forms, travel-authorization forms, and the like).

Figure 13-1. Summary Line-Item Budget (in Thousands)

Past Year		Current Year		Appropriation Category		Budget Plan	
Budget	Actual	Budget	Experience Update	Code #	Account Name	Agency Request	Review Recommendations
1	2	3	4	5	6	7	8
15,602	15,001	17,518	17,300	100	Salaries and Wages	20,687*	
4,213	4,050	4,730	4,671	200	Fringe Benefits	5,585	
468	480	526	583	300	Supplies and Materials	621	
936	954	1,051	1,166	400	Equipment	1,241	
780	885	879	970	500	Contractual Services	1,034	
21,999	21,370	24,704	24,690	Totals – All Codes		29,168	

*This figure coincides with the Wages and Salary Total In Figure 13-2

Management Budgeting

The next development in public budgeting was probably initiated as a result of Roosevelt's New Deal and the concomitant expansion in the size of government budgets and in the number and kinds of government programs and services. The heyday of laissez-faire economics and politics ended with the coming of the New Deal, and the philosophy of active government stewardship gained popularity. And certainly, as Roosevelt's New Deal programs encountered the shrunken tax bases produced by the Great Depression, significant new resources could be found only through more efficient use of resources already available. It no longer seemed sufficient merely to control what resources bought; instead, resources had to be managed,

Figure 13-2. Personnel Salaries and Wages: Detail Line Item (Uniform Classifications Only)

Personnel Classifications		Number of Positions				Wage & Salary Totals (in thousands)	
		Past Year-Authorized	Current Year		Budget Request	Current Budget	Budget Request*
Code	Title		Authorized	Filled			
110	Chief of Police	1	1	1	1	46	50
111	Deputy Chief	2	3	3	3	117	126
112	Patrol Commander	1	1	1	1	35	38
113	Captain	6	7	7	7	220	238
114	Lieutenant	33	33	32	33	917	990
115	Sergeant (Incl. Det.)	125	130	120	135	3,120	3,510
116	Officer IV (Incl. Det.)	200	215	204	215	4,579	4,945
117	Officer III (Incl. Det.)	100	108	108	120	2,086	2,520
118	Officer II	100	155	139	160	2,712	3,040
119	Officer I	155	100	95	125	1,570	2,125
130	All Non-Sworn Titles	98	120	110	135	2,116	3,105
100	Totals/All Titles	821	873	820	935	17,518	20,687

*Includes an approximate average 8% pay raise
Estimate for all personnel classes.

and this meant making agencies accountable not only for their expenditures, but for the amount of work or activity they generated as well.

Management- or performance-budget planning became the successor to control budgeting. The emphasis of this new budgeting form was on the efficiency with which resources were spent and managed, and this meant comparing dollars spent to work performed. Budget data were collected not only on resources but on work as well. Efficiency comparisons were based on analyses of activity-unit costs and budget officers became concerned with such matters as reducing the costs of carrying out specific activities. For example, during budget hearings, a police department might be asked the average cost of patrolling a mile of city streets, and why the cost was what it was. Or a fire department might be asked to compute the average cost of making a fire call.

The development of the management or performance orientation to budgeting brought new forms and new data to the budget-planning process. The line-item control forms remained, but added to them were activity/work-unit forms that spelled out both the quantity of work to be performed by the agency and the unit cost of that activity. Figure 13-3 is an example of one such form.

Column 1 of Figure 13-3 requests that the various kinds of work or activity of an agency be divided into general categories. Columns 2-4 request information on the quantity of work activity in each of these general categories during the past, current, and upcoming year. This information allows for comparison and analysis of trends. Columns 5-7 request cost information for each category of work activity for each of the three years. Such cost estimates represent those portions of all budget-line items (e.g., personnel, supplies, and equipment) considered to be devoted to the particular work category. Columns 8-10 calculate ***unit cost*** for each of the three years by dividing dollar costs by the total number of work units proposed in each category. Column 11 indicates the unit-cost standard for each category. The standard may be based on last year's performance, legislative requirement, or a proposal by an advisory group or professional association. Accountability tends to be measured by comparing Column 11 with Columns 8-10 to determine whether the agency is performing its work efficiently. Indeed, efficiency is defined somewhat arbitrarily in terms of whether the figures in Columns 8-10 match or exceed the figures in Column 11.

Although bringing performance and workload data into the budget-planning process raises the level of sophistication with which issues of accountability can be addressed, it also makes the budget-planning process more complicated. Agency budget planners need to estimate work levels and need also to estimate how the total budget for the agency is to be divided among work categories. Either of these tasks is difficult.

Because agencies must think through and fill out forms like that shown in Figure 13-3, performance or management budgeting forces a substantial change in how public agencies are to be held accountable. Proper expenditure is not the only criterion of accountability; also important is the question of whether expenditures result in an appropriate (efficient) level of work activity and in appropriate activity costs. But a problem remains: even if resources

Figure 13-3. Workload Performance Summary Form (work-units and dollars in thousands)

Work Unit Name		Number of Work-Units			Applicable Dollar Costs			Work-Unit Average Cost			
		Past Year	Current Year	Budget Plan	Past Year	Current Year	Budget Plan	Past Year	Current Year	Budget Plan	Unit Co Standa
	1	2	3	4	5	6	7	8	9	10	11
A	Part I Crime Investigation										
B	Calls for Service (Crime)										
C	Calls for Service (Non-Crime)										
D	All Others										

are expended as authorized, and even if a great deal of work is efficiently undertaken, there is no guarantee that the work accomplishes anything of value.

Planning, Programming and Budgeting

This problem of value led to a third development in public budgeting: PPB, or planning, programming, and budgeting.[24] PPB represents the first structured effort in public fiscal planning to include data on the attainment of objectives. The effect of linking resources and activities to goals and objectives in budget planning was revolutionary. For example, a prison budget would no longer be defended in such terms as, "That is what our budget has always been" nor, "we need that much money in order to hire 160 custodial officers." Under PPB, justification would have to be provided: "We need the proposed budget level to hire 160 custodial officers to help us to achieve our objective of around-the-clock maintenance of the safety and security of inmates through control and prevention of suicide, prison crime, and prison disorder."

The "programming" portion of PPB refers to the process by which resources, activities, and goals are brought together in a structure such as a welfare program or a public-safety program. Program structures are typically pyramidal, with the most general goal at the top and with each successive layer less general and more detailed in its subgoals, outputs, activities, and subactivities. Lower layers are understood to "lead to" higher layers. Figure 1-3 (see Chapter 1)[25] and Figure 13-4 are simplified examples of program structures.

Once a program structure has been laid out, it is linked to the budget forms that ask for detail concerning work or activity programs, work-program costs, and line-item appropriations. Exactly how this is done varies, but usually a workload-performance form (as in Figure 13-3) and a line-item budget form (as in Figures 13-1 and 13-2) are attached. The resulting budget package, representing the budget plan, so to speak, contains the following kinds of information in something like the following order:

1. *A program structure* that links general objectives to specific work or activities.
2. *A workload or performance plan* that details the amount of work and the dollar cost of work in a number of areas.
3. *A line-item budget* that details the categories (line items) for which funds will be expended.

Clearly, of the various budgeting procedures—line-item, management, and PPB—only PPB makes explicit use of all the key elements of planning (i.e., resources, activities, and objectives). But the linking of program and financial decision-making under PPB raises serious problems for the budgetary process: it increases the complications, costs, and time involved in planning. Presumably, under PPB, resources are allocated with the supposition that their use *will cause* some objective to be achieved. Yet, causality is difficult to predict, or even to establish after the fact. For example, suppose $1 million is appropriated to a Part I crime-prevention program and later Part I crime decreases. Is there a causal connection? Perhaps. But what if unemployment also decreases during that period? Is the million dollars, or the drop in the

Figure 13-4. Sample Program Structure

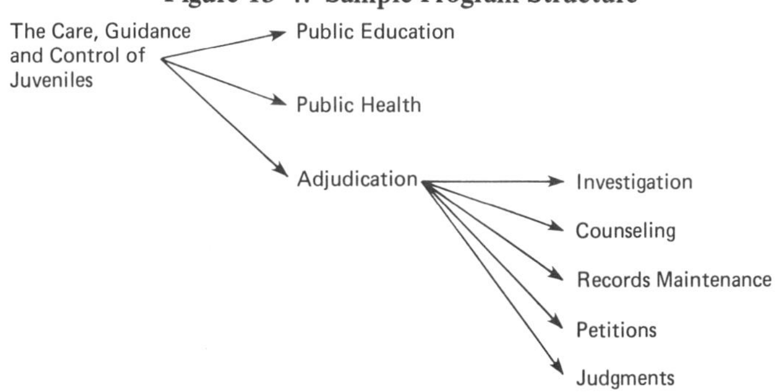

unemployment rate, the "cause" of the decrease in crime?

Under PPB there also tends to be a tremendous problem of data overload. PPB requires that alternative means, their respective costs and benefits, and their respective linkages to goals be considered as a part of the budgetary process. Because of the time and costs associated with considering alternatives, many budgetary scholars have questioned the practicality of PPB. Aaron Wildavsky, in *The Politics of the Budgetary Process,* advises: "If you are interested more in being, than in appearing, rational, don't do it!"[26]

Zero-Base Budgeting

The basic principles of PPB have been retained in the "latest" development in the public fiscal-administration sector. There have, however, been numerous attempts at fine-tuning these principles since the early 1970s. One of the more interesting results of these attempts is zero-base budgeting (ZBB). Peter A. Pyhrr, while a member of the research division of Texas Instruments, developed the methodology for ZBB, which was first put into operation in 1970 at Texas Instruments. It was claimed that as a fiscal-management tool for the private sector, the new budgeting procedure would improve profitability, redirect effort, and reduce budgets.[27] The potential use of this approach in public-sector fiscal decision-making was not long ignored. By 1973, ZBB had been introduced by then-Governor Jimmy Carter as a means of preparing executive budget recommendations for the state of Georgia.

The Presidental campaign of 1976 found Carter championing ZBB as an appropriate and needed tool at the Federal level. The response of the general public to ZBB was, almost without exception, positive—who would openly resist the adoption of a new fiscal planning procedure that promised to cut budgets, to reestablish governmental priorities, and to increase efficiency and effectiveness? At the same time, however, public understanding of ZBB was very limited. And in large measure it can be argued that the public did not care to know how, why, or even whether, ZBB really worked. The primary interest was directed toward its promised results: budget cuts, new priorities, greater efficiency and effectiveness.

Although ZBB is a variant of PPB, it has several distinctive features. First, ZBB assumes that each agency and each organizational subunit starts the budget planning process from a *zero base* (hence the term). This starting point contrasts with the more traditional *base-budget approach,* in which each year's new fiscal planning effort is based on the present year's authorized budget. Under the ZBB approach current programs and activities must be satisfactorily *re*justified, and the request for new or expanded programs justified separately. In theory, this is the ultimate form of "sunset" legislation, because the annual fiscal review of budget proposals could conceivably determine that no agency programs continue to be justified, and the agency's budget might therefore be eliminated.

The second distinctive feature of ZBB is the requirement to construct *decision packages.* "A decision package identifies a descrete activity, function, or operation [of an organization] in a definitive manner for management evaluation and comparison with other activities."[28] All the activities, functions, or operations of the organization that can be defined in a discrete fashion must be addressed by individualized decision packages. Thus, the unit of analysis for fiscal administrative purposes becomes the activity. For a fire department, for example, each fire run, inspection, granting of a permit, or prevention of a fire is an activity unit, or could be. Each class of these activities would become a separate decision package, and each decision package would require that a number of questions be answered.

The information that must be provided in each decision package has in practice varied among jurisdictions but tends to include the following:

1. A description of the activity being proposed
2. An explanation of how the activity relates to goals and objectives
3. A description of what the consequences will be of not undertaking the activity
4. A statement of how performance will be measured
5. An analysis of the alternative ways in which the activity can be undertaken and the relative costs and benefits of each, and the selection of one of the alternatives

6. A review of the differing levels of activity that can be undertaken and their associated costs
7. A budget of required resources for the chosen alternative

Figure 13-5 is a hypothetical decision package for one activity or work area of a probate court. It deals only with that portion of the probate court budget and program involving prejudgment custody-award investigations in divorce proceedings. A quick review of Figure 13-5 shows that several kinds of "accountability" questions are addressed: Sections 1-3 state objectives and relate objectives to proposed activities; Section 4 is a summary of proposed workload and performance data; Section 5 attempts to alert budget reviewers to the potential negative consequences of not providing the requested funds for this activity area; Sections 6-7 consider alternative ways and levels of performing this activity; Section 8 is a line-item summary of the requested budget amount for this activity area. Note that the activity was not funded in Fiscal Year 1980, but that it was funded during the "current" fiscal year (1981), and continuation is being requested for Fiscal Year 1982.

The third distinctive feature of ZBB is the requirement that decision packages and their associated costs be ranked according to their relative importance. To fulfill this requirement, agencies must estimate how important each activity package is in relation to all the other activity packages proposed. If the total that the agency requests cannot be funded, cuts are usually made by lopping off the lowest-ranked package or packages. The elimination procedures assume that the central budget agency and the executive authority agree with the rankings given by the agency, and that each package constructed by the agency provides the required information and has sufficient justification.

Figure 13-6 gives the "prejudgment custody-award investigation decision package" a rank relative to some other hypothetical activities probate courts undertake. Each of the other activities would have had decision packages developed for them. In a sense, the decision-packages ranking provides a quick summary of all probate court activities and costs in the order of their presumed relative importance.

So much for the theory of ZBB. What happens in practice? The limited experience of the few agencies that have adopted ZBB does not yet indicate that the process leads to budget-cutting or that it necessarily increases the efficiency and effectiveness with which the agency performs its assigned functions. There is no known instance of an agency having been eliminated, or its budget drastically reduced, simply becauuse it adopted a ZBB process.

Eliminations and reductions tend to remain political decisions, regardless of the information provided or the budget format. Insofar as political pressures develop to eliminate, to reduce, or to alter functions, tasks, and activities, or simply to require additional justification for current expenditures levels, the adoption of a ZBB format tends to force agencies to conduct structured annual self-examinations. But an agency with a strong bias against change, in the absence of external pressure to force change, will alter little if anything under a ZBB format, or indeed under any format. Thus, it is a mistake to view ZBB as the cure-all for governmental waste, ineffectiveness, and high taxes. But if retrenchment becomes necessary, ZBB becomes a potentially useful tool for assembling and organizing the pertinent range of information necessary to making the required fiscal and managerial adjustments.

Which Option Is Best?

One can argue that ZBB (and other PPB variants) is better than line-item or management budgeting because it requires explicit consideration of objectives, activities, and resources. This would also appear to be a matter of common sense, given the kinds of information being presented and considered as a part of the PBB/ZBB budget planning process. The most information is considered under a PPB/ZBB format (e.g., Figure 13-5) and the least under a lump-sum and a line-item format (e.g., Figure 13-1).

There seem to be several distinct contributions the ZBB approach can make to the budget-planning process.

1. It forces an agency to think of justifying its budget requests in terms of (first) proposed activites and (second and more important) in terms of the relationship of those activites to objectives.
2. If the budgeting process is annual (as it usu-

Figure 13-5. ZBB Decision Package[29]

PACKAGE NAME	FACILITY/UNIT	RANK
Prejudgment Custody Award Investigation 1 of 3	54th Probate Court	3

PURPOSE (Section 1)

Prejudgment Investigation of the past and likely environments offered by each parent. Findings to enable court to determine likely environments offered by each parent, essential information for the court in reaching custody decisions, optimizing care of the child.

DESCRIPTION OF ACTIVITY (Section 2)

1 Investigator I, 1 Investigator II, 1 Steno II. Investigation of a maximum of 500 individuals per year (250 divorce proceedings per year involving juvenile custody issues). Interviews to be of each party to the divorce proceeding. Work unit is individual interviewed.

ACHIEVEMENTS FROM ACTIVITIES (Section 3)

Allowing the systematic interviewing under oath of the parties to determine the nature of their community ties, employment, income, health, criminal record, and custody justification.

QUANTITATIVE MEASURES (Section 4)	fy 80 actual	fy 81 budget	fy 82 request	Percent fy 82/fy 81
NUMBER OF WORK UNITS PERFORMED	–	500	500	100%
COST PER WORK UNIT	–	$128	$134	105%
WORK UNITS PER MAN-HOUR 5760 MH available 48 weeks	–	.1 rounded	.1 rounded	100%
NUMBER OF PERSONNEL	–	3 FTE	3 FTE	100%

CONSEQUENCES OF NOT APPROVING PACKAGE (Section 5)

1) Court delays in having to secure information through court testimony.
2) Professional interviewers not being available to gather and to analyze information.
3) Information gathered will not be systematic but dependent on the whims of courtroom proceedings.

ALTERNATIVES (DIFFERENT LEVELS OF ACTIVITY) AND COST (Section 6)

2 of 3 Extending interviewing to offspring to gather pertinent information, including their desires for custody and reasons therefore: 18K—addition of one Juvenile Caseworker II to interview 350 offspring annually.

3 of 3 Extending interviewing to interested and knowledgeable other parties for the purpose of information corroboration: 16K—add one Interviewer I to conduct 300 additional interviews.

ALTERNATIVES (DIFFERENT WAYS OF PERFORMING THE SAME ACTIVITY) (Section 7)

1) Contracting with County Department of Social Services at a per unit cost of $100. Budget: $50,000. Rejected because court would not receive top priority for interviewing, and serious delays would thereby be caused.

2) Contracting with A. G. Smith firm. Per unit cost: $170. Rejected because of expense and because of difficulties in court maintaining control.

COST ESTIMATES (Section 8)

OBJECT CODE	fy 81	fy 82
PERSONNEL	44K	48K
FRINGE	9K	10K
CONTRACTUAL	–	–
TRAVEL	1K	1K
SUPPLIES	4K	4K
EQUIPMENT	3K	1K
CONSTRUCTION	–	–
TELECOM.	3K	3K
OTHER	–	–
TOTAL	64K	67K
% OF TOTAL FROM GRANTS	10%	0

Figure 13-6. Decision Package Ranking (Dollars in Thousands)

RANK	PACKAGE NAME	FY 81 BUDGET			FY 82 REQUEST				CUMULATIVE FY 82 REQUEST	
		Total $	State $	# Pers.	Total $	State $	# Pers.	State $ as a % of FY 81 State Budget	Cumulative State	Cumulative % of FY 81 State Budget
		1	2	3	4	5	6	7	8	9
1	Judgments	100	100	3	110	110	3	38	110	38
2	Court Proceedings: transcription	100	100	6	108	108	6	37	218	75
3	Pre-judgment custody investigation 1 of 3	64	57.6	3	67	67	3	23	285	98
4	Post-judgment custody investigation 1 of 3	35	35	1.5	39	39	1.5	13	324	111
5	Pre-judgment custody investigation 2 of 3	–	–	–	18	10	1	3	334	114
6	Pre-judgment custody investigation 3 of 3	–	–	–	16	16	1	5	350	119
	TOTALS	299	292.6	13.5	358	350	16.5			

ally is) it forces the agency to review both its expenditures and programs in some fashion on a yearly basis.

3. It requires agencies to think of alternatives: alternative ways of performing a given activity; and alternative amounts of the activity.

4. Opportunity is given to be clear about the consequences of not funding a given level of activity. This may be particularly crucial when considering the politics of budget planning.

5. Accountability is broadly based (namely, control-, management-, and objectives-oriented); the justification of budgets is potentially broadly based.

There are, however, several problems and costs associated with the more advanced or complete forms of budget planning. Obviously, more kinds and amounts of information are needed, and this in itself puts a burden on the planning process. Also, the more advanced budgeting formats require more explicit kinds of justification and accountability. If agency budgets, apparently justified under the less complex budgeting formats such as line-item, cannot now be justified under the more advanced formats (e.g., ZBB), someone may decide that the agency's budget is "wasteful" and ought to be eliminated. There is no question that such problems in the use of the more advanced budgeting formats are stressful to managers and planners alike. Finally, rational approaches to agency accountability, as implied by a ZBB approach to budget planning, for example, may not square with political notions of accountability—or, at least, they may not appear to square very well.

POLITICAL REALITIES AND BUDGET-PLAN ADVOCACY

One of the most disturbing aspects of budget planning is that politics often appear to overrule rationally or objectively determined plans. Indeed, criminal justice agencies often see their budget requests as "regularly butchered by the politicians." The distinction between political and rational decision-making is not easily made: one man's rationality may be another man's politics, everyone tends to view his own decisions as rational and to view those who disagree as "irrational." "uninformed," or "politically motivated."

The final control over a criminal justice agency budget resides outside the agency in elected bodies. Because these bodies do in fact exercise significant power, there is a great temptation to view them as overwhelming forces, not impressed by factual argument or influenced by agency pleas. The question, of course, is whether this view is correct.

In 1979, 250 of the nation's largest police departments and the fifty state departments of corrections, surveyed by the School of Criminal Justice at Michigan State University, were asked to rate their ability to influence budgetary allocation.[30] A majority of respondents felt that the most important factor in securing additional revenues during affluent periods was the quality of the budget presentation. Although a majority of respondents thought that objective appraisal of agency need had far less impact during periods of economic decline, over 40 percent of the respondents indicated that rational planning and quality budget presentation had at least a moderate influence on curtailing the size of budget cuts made during hard times. Thus, politics was seen to affect budget decision-making variously, but the respondents did not seem to view politics as an overwhelming force, or at least not as one not susceptible to conscious agency manipulation.

Underlying Conditions

There are many factors that help create a political environment receptive to rational budget planning, and one of the most important is the reputation of the top management of the agency. Reputations for efficiency and effectiveness in using authorized funds, and the style of managerial advocacy, are particularly important.

1. Efficiency Reputation

If top management is perceived by outsiders, and especially by the general public, as running an efficient operation, the agency can expect more positive than negative budget treatment. Reputations for efficiency do not guarantee protection from budget slashes, but certainly agencies that are perceived as badly managed may be the first ones reviewed for cuts by budget analysts and elected officials.

Unfortunately, facts about agency efficiency do not necessarily speak for themselves. It is the obligation of top management to establish the agency's reputation for efficiency by actively presenting its interpretations of the facts.[31] For example, the head of a probation department may point out that average costs per case have been declining over a three-year period, reflecting greater efficiencies. An adversary of the probation department may use the same facts, however, to demonstrate inefficiencies—noting that the average case cost far exceeds the national average. The probation director might counter that special problems or circumstances in the state fully explain the higher-than-average costs, that they therefore are not a product of inefficiencies but a consequence of the peculiarities of the state or locality.

2. Effectiveness Reputation

Measures and interpretations of efficiency are only one set of criteria on which the reputation of an agency's management stands. Another is the agency's effectiveness, its ability to achieve objectives. Unfortunately, many criminal justice agencies have a problem in this respect: crime rates and recidivism rates among parolees either show no improvement or increase, and court case backlogs continue. One response to such a situation is for management to argue that the department is unable, given insufficient funding levels, to cope with the environment of crime. But such an arguement is usually nonproductive, because heads of all sorts of agencies make similar arguments when they are trying to get more money.

The important issue is the importance the missions of an agency are deemed to have in relation to the missions of other agencies. An excellent case in point was the experience of criminal justice agencies in California immediately after the passage of Proposition 13. There, criminal justice agencies made service-level arguments in an attempt to hold the line against impending massive budgetary decreases. Police budgets generally suffered little, if any, decrease; probation and parole agencies suffered heavy budget cuts. It is widely held among California criminal justice practitioners that probation's relative deprivation followed from views about the uncertain importance of probation missions as compared with police missions.[32] The public, and hence political decision-makers, could imagine comparatively safe streets without probation caseworkers, but they could not imagine safety without police.

Attempts to establish agency effectiveness require the collection of data and may involve controversial issues. For example, Eli Noam argues that the overcrowding of court dockets has led to sentence reductions through plea-bargaining.[33] Because of overcrowding, judges and prosecutors perceive plea-bargaining as a time-efficient means of disposing of cases although it bypasses, in a sense, the judicial process. Issues of "justice" aside, any attempt to secure additional court resources on the grounds that plea-bargaining results in sentence reduction ought to have supporting documentation. The objective of such data collection would be to demonstrate that more resources are required to achieve the goals of certainty of conviction, swiftness of conviction, *and* appropriateness of the sentence. Plea-bargaining, an accomodation to overcrowding and inadequate funding, could be shown to affect these three judicial goals negatively.

3. Reputation for Requesting Funds and for Using Funds

In addition to reputations for efficiency and effectiveness, the agency's past budget experience–whether the agency has consistently underspent or overspent budgets, whether it is perceived as padding budget requests–is an important strategic factor.

Underspending. Popular wisdom has it that unspent funds at the end of one year will lead to budget cuts in subsequent years. There is more than a grain of truth to this adage, and it is supported by numerous case histories. It is so widely accepted as truth, however, that as the fiscal year draws to a close there are often mad scrambles to spend the unspent funds. Increasingly limitations are being imposed on such behavior, such as strict line-item accounting and refusal by budget authorities to authorize the use of reversionary funds in other account categories. But the practice continues.

End-of-the-year buying sprees, where permitted, carry potentially negative consequences, for agencies risk establishing reputations for frivolous expenditure. Significant amounts of unspent monies toward the end of the fiscal year can signal poor budget planning, and whether the agency turns back the funds or scrambles to spend them, the result can be the same: a questionable budget-planning reputation. The agency appears to be, if it is not in fact, a suitable target for economizing measures.

Overspending. A conscious strategy of "planning to overspend," coupled with requests for supplemental midyear appropriations is deliberately used by some agency managers to augment meager budgets. Their assumption seems to be that city, county, or state budget officials always have contingency funds (called slush funds until the Watergate era) on which to draw for emergencies. There are legal questions surrounding contingency funds, but the common assumption is that they exist. Indeed, as one highly placed budget official of a large city remarked in 1978, "There isn't a city manager worth his salt who doesn't have at least 5 percent of his budget hidden away some place for emergencies."[34]

There is little doubt that contingency funds exist, but there is also little doubt that most states and localities today face far greater constraints than they did just a few years ago. Indeed, the manager who consciously counts on supplemental appropriations today is running a high risk of incurring the substantial ire of superiors and of being left holding the bag.

When budget authorizations do not seem to permit adequate funding of mandated services, the manager has an uneasy choice–honoring the legal mandate or staying within the authorized budget. There is no simple resolution of this dilemma. Some managers have chosen to stay within their budgets, risking legal challenge for failure to provide mandated services. This can be a dangerous game, but the manager, in doing so, retains his reputation as a "team player," and he may be able to rely on external forces to keep alive the issue of insufficient funding.

Many administrators and planners are insulted by the suggestion that they be team players. But managers need to be realistic: budget planning is a game of negotiated trade-offs, each side giving up a little and getting a little. Budget plans that ignore constraints imposed by tight or shrinking revenues will appear unrealistic; they may well be treated as plans drawn up by fools "who ought to know better," and they invite indiscriminate red-lining by budget analysts. The idea of compromise may seem to conflict with a grander notion that the professional, armed with the facts, knows what needs to be done. But this is rarely the case in the public sector. As Victor Thompson concludes:

> The solution of a social problem is properly described with such words as *compromise, con-*

sensus, majority, negotiation, bargaining, coercion, etc. If the "solution" cannot be described in such terms, then it is not the solution of a social problem.[35]

Michael White notes that Thompson's view may be trivial[36] but Thompson does point out that one person's facts are too often challenged by another's and that advocacy is the means most often employed to achieve a compromise between different positions arising from different facts or from different interpretations of the same facts.

Views differ on the appropriate methods of advocacy. At one extreme is the view that he who shouts loudest gets most. At the other extreme is the view that he who shouts loudest most alienates superiors and decision-makers. Management is expected at least to inform superiors of needs; the failure to do so is not excused by the desire not to make waves. Outside decision-makers are quick to blame agency top management when significant problems suddenly emerge without warning. If management has been able to anticipate a budget problem but has failed to inform external budgetary authorities, management is properly to blame. And the opportunity to inform decision-makers about long- as well as short-range needs should not be lost, if for no other reason than that many budgetary problems require significant lead-time for resolution. Management must take an active hand in establishing need, as suggested by an agency manager quoted by Rufus Browning:

> We don't hesitate to lay our problems on the line. I would not refrain from reflecting a need.
>
> The budget is supposed to reflect the judgment of the administrator. There is no point in playing it cozy in trying to second-guess everybody along the line. The budget should reflect only felt needs, nothing more, or less.[37]

Basic Steps and Elements in Affecting Political Decision-Making

There are several basic factors involved in making any particular budget plan seem reasonable and justified. Neither separately nor together are these factors sufficient to guarantee favorable treatment, but they make the budget plan appear to have been carefully conceived and realistic in relation to current conditions. These factors are listed in Figure 13-7.

1. Distinguishing Short-Range from Long-Range Needs

Methods for distinguishing short-term from long-term needs seem traditionally to rely on a form of decision-by-default: those needs that stand little chance of funding this year are considered long-range goals while those for which funding may be possible are short-term goals. There is, of course, an inescapable logic implied in this approach, but its simplicity ignores the fact that the decisional process at least *ought* to give explicit consideration to a variety of factors before such determinations are made. Figure 13-8 summarizes these factors.

2. The Issue of Budget Padding

Agencies rarely admit to padding budget plans, yet popular wisdom has it that requests must be padded if the agency is finally to be granted what it "really" needs. This view is based on the empirical observation that budget requests are in fact cut by political decision-makers. It also seems consonant with the view that it doesn't hurt to ask.

The term *padding* cannot be objectively defined because one person's definition of what is necessary will differ from another's. Few agencies actually request resources that do not in one way or another relate to their basic missions or goals, and almost all requests can be

Figure 13-7. Key Factors in Making a Budget Appear Reasonable

1. The budget proposal appears to have adequately distinguished short-range from long-range needs.
2. The budget does not appear to have been padded.
3. The proposed budget is consonant with politically acceptable priorities—priorities that are supported by the general public.
4. Justification arguments are supported by facts (data on workloads, performance goals, and costs/benefits).

Figure 13-8. Budget-Planning Time Perspectives

Short–Range: Usually, the coming year.	1. Immediate need is established. 2. There is basic political and/or public consensus over the goals implied by the funding. 3. Agency has capability of implementing the work program to be funded (the technology exists and can be implemented). 4. Detailed work programs and action steps can be enumerated. 5. Funding may be for continuing existing programs, or for new programs meeting the above criteria.
Mid–Range: Usually, 2 to 5 years	1. Based on projections (of the not too distant future) of changes reasonably certain in the agency or its environment—changes which have budgeting implications (e.g., replacing a physical plant, trends in legislation that alter agency missions or agency mode of operation, changing population, demographic, or social characteristics altering nature of clientele served). 2. Immediate need is not critical but is projected to become important in the 2-to-5 year period. 3. Budget commitment may entail funds for needs assessment, analysis of alternative responses or the gradual development of an agency response through a 2-to-5-year plan to shift existing resources or to secure additional funding. 4. May involve significant shifting of agency priorities or goals for which political acceptance needs to be secured.
Long–Range: Usually, 5 years or more.	1. Projections of agency and environmental changes, which by virture of the length of the projection period have only a weak degree of certainty. 2. Work or action programs are not proposed in any specific sense; rather, the long-range projections represent a perspective that carries only generalized implications for the design of current programs and budgets.

judged relevant to some degree. In reality, determining whether a budget is padded depends on two factors: the agency's range of need, and the agency's range of expectations.

The Range of Need. The range of need may be seen as to fall between two extreme levels of funding, one of which may be defined as *rock bottom*, and the other as *design specifications.* Rock-bottom levels are those below which mandated functions or services (for example, court mandates that *all* inmates receive specified physical and psychological examinations at the point of reception; or state requirements that police departments file written reports of all traffic accidents involving a certain dollar value or personal injury) would not be provided at minimally required levels.

Rock bottom may also contain expenditures for service levels that, although not mandated, are in the view of top management absolutely critical to minimally effective performance of primary agency missions (for example, minimally required staffing for homicide investigation or investigations of Part I crimes in general.) Beyond rock-bottom levels, defined as funding essential to mandated services, definitions of minimum needs are determined by subjective judgment.

Appeals to judgement can be supplemented by conventional wisdom or standards promulgated by such professional organizations as the

American Bar Association, the International Association of Chiefs of Police, or the American Correctional Association. But conventional wisdom may simply be a collection of questionable past practices, and promulgated standards may be hard to defend. For example, many jurisdictions, when pressed by budget analysts, have discarded as indefensible on any objective criteria the old standards, involving number of police required per thousand population served.

A more usual way of establishing rock-bottom levels is to appeal to established community standards. These standards are based on the service levels the particular community has come to expect (or wants to continue). One police department, for example, recently faced an approximate 20 per cent cut in authorized positions. It elected to keep the patrol force at full strength, while drastically cutting other units, because of perceived community priorities. Other examples include appeals by law-enforcement agencies to maintain established calls for service or response times, appeals by courts not to increase case backlogs, and appeals by correctional establishments to continue preparole psychological-assessment programs that have been shown to screen out significant numbers of premature or potentially dangerous releases.

Although definitions of *rock bottom* can be loose, looser still are definitions of *design specifications.* Generally, the idea of upper level of need rests on proposed expenditures that appeal to professional standards, design specifications, and/or commonly accepted work-program goals. What is suggested is a level of proposed funding based on the query, "If money were less a problem, what could we profitably use to achieve our missions better?"

Some political jurisdictions have recognized the importance of this kind of upper-range budget planning and require that agencies annually submit two budget documents: one based on continuation of current effort and one called an *improvement budget*. The improvement budget allows agencies to rank expenditures for new or expanded program areas in the event that additional revenues are made available. But even under these procedures, agencies are still left with the question of how much they might realistically request in the form of new or expanded program funds.

Upper ranges of need must be realistically grounded in the possible. This may sound contradictory to the position taken earlier that needs should be expressed regardless of possibilities. This procedure is safe for agency determinations of rock-bottom needs, but much less so for top-of-the-range needs. An agency's rock-bottom needs should not be conditioned by what it can expect to get; however, what an agency would like to request—what "design" it would like to specify"—must be conditioned by what it can expect.

The Range of Expectation. A range of expectation is established partly by guesswork and partly by objective appraisal. Forecasts of general economic conditions for the jurisdiction in question are one important piece of information available from city, county, state, or Federal budget bureaus. Projections by private organizations, such as banks and chambers of commerce, are useful, too. Besides, the jurisdiction chief executive's annual budget letter usually contains information about economic forecasts and revenue projections.

The availability of revenue is only partially determined by general conditions. Other factors are changes in requirements mandated among all agencies in the jurisdiction—requirements that may alter traditional divisions of the available funds. Changes in political perceptions of the importance of an agency's mission vis-à-vis missions of other agencies, and changes in tax-generated revenues owing to rate changes (e.g., millage votes) are also important.

As general revenue forecasting is at best an imprecise science, and as forecasting the revenues likely to be made available to any given agency is even less precise, it is generally not wise to settle on a single figure of projected revenue. Establishing a *range* of expected revenues (with the bottom and top of the range set as the lowest and highest amounts likely to be awarded) is more realistic.

Wildavsky is largely correct that changes in budgets from one year to the next tend to be adjustments built around the previous budget.[38] Indeed, budget cuts and increases are usually expressed as percentage deviations from the prior year's budget. Even under zero-based budgeting formats, in which the last year's budget is not assumed as the starting point, the cumulative rank ordering of decision packages is expressed in terms of costs compared to last year's budget (see Column 9 of Figure 13-6.)

And even those city and county jurisdictions currently using zero-based formats ultimately express final budget policy in such terms as *the 95 per cent budget* or *the 105 per cent budget.*

Need Compared to Expectation. Establishing a range of expectations is a form of contingency planning, and when the range of need is compared to the range of expectation, agencies are able to plan their expenditure priorities on the basis of a number of funding contingencies. In the recent past, public agencies were more likely than not to confront a set of need and expectations ranges that, overlaid, allowed for the meeting of rock-bottom needs and probably more. Figure 13-9 shows that the lowest likely revenues to be received are sufficient to cover rock-bottom needs and other needs as well, it also shows that revenues likely to be available are normally not enough to cover all needs.

Lately, however, the public sector has witnessed the shift of the need range to the right (greater need for funds), owing to inflation and continuing demands of the public for improved service levels, while the expectation range has remained stationary or shifted to the left (fewer available funds), owing to growing public ire over tax levels and rates. As a result of these shifts, there is the distinct possibility in many jurisdictions that even rock-bottom needs will not be properly financed. Thus, many agencies now confront a situation graphically depicted in Figure 13-10.

Padding. Real budget padding involves requesting funds for items or programs that cannot be justified on reasonable grounds. In other words, padding is a request for expenditures even beyond "design specifications." Agencies that consciously pad their requests in this fashion court negative reputations and the strong likelihood of retribution.

The important question is, given a range of needs and a range of expectations, how much should an agency request? The answer is neither simple nor straightforward, but the following principles seem reasonable to apply:

1. *Never ask for less than rock-bottom needs.* Doing so is an abrogation of management responsibility. If budget authorities nonetheless require the submission of a total budget less than rock bottom, management must be explicit about the dire consequences that will ensue.
2. *Rarely request more than what the highest level of revenues likely to be obtainable will allow.* To do otherwise casts management and the agency in the role of fools who ought to know what the facts are.
3. *Never ask for more than design specifications* (as that term has been defined), as it places the organization in the position of having to defend requests by their very nature only weakly supportable (and perhaps seen to constitute obvious attempts to pad).

The application of these principles usually leaves a range within which an agency must set the final request. If the jurisdiction's budget procedures allow, it is often useful to request alternative levels of funding, beginning with rock bottom and moving through successive increases that may end with design specifications.

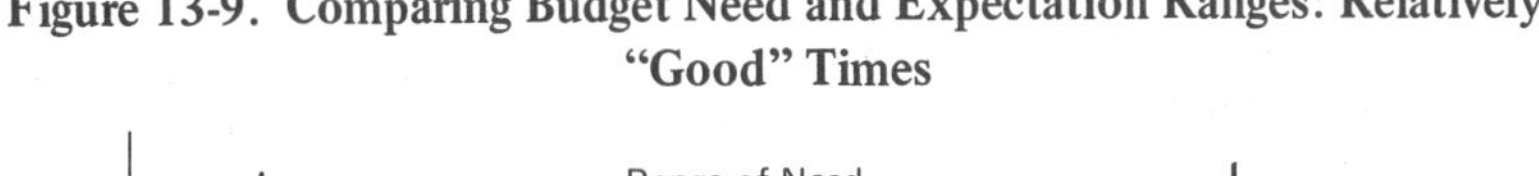

Figure 13-9. Comparing Budget Need and Expectation Ranges: Relatively "Good" Times

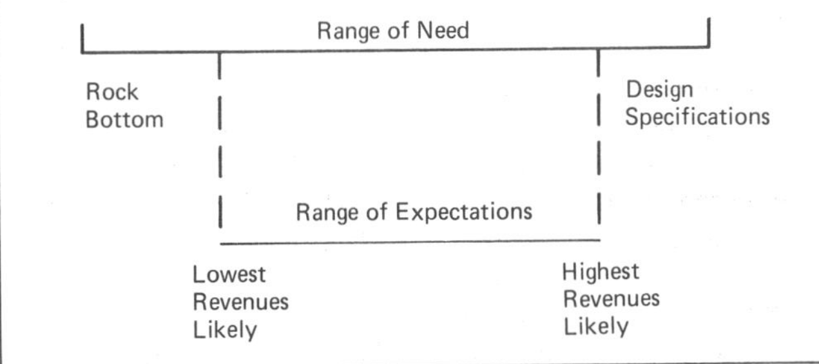

Figure 13-10. Comparing Budget Need and Expectation Ranges: Relatively "Tight" Times

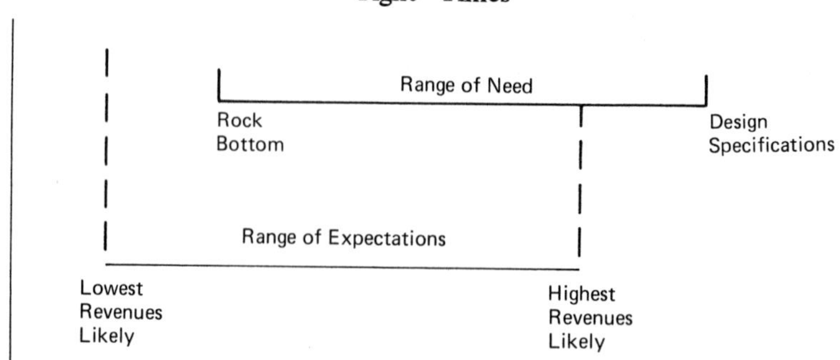

Each layer of addition should be carefully explained in terms of the benefits expected from the expenditure *and* the consequences expected from not funding. If a single request level must be submitted, need and expectation must be balanced according to the principles suggested and according to the best judgment of management about what will appear realistic and be defensible.

3. The Relevant Facts

The organization and presentation of the budget plan to decision-makers and to the public takes art. Too many facts will confuse issues, too few will make an argument seem weak; irrelevant information raises needless problems; inaccurate information calls into question the technical capabilities of management, the failure to interpret or to organize information adequately opens the door to erroneous conclusions on the part of decision-makers.

Because the justification of budgets may lead to reviews of nearly every aspect of organizational life, managers are often tempted to assume that the more information presented, the better. This assumption, followed to the extreme, leads to the creation of mammoth budget documents that go largely unread while critical or essential arguments get lost. An alternative way of viewing the need for supporting information is to decide that each separately identifiable budget request needs two kinds of justification: work programs and objectives to be pursued through the expenditures must be made clear, and the consequences of *not* funding must be made clear too. Such a budget presentation focuses reviewers' attention on the two most relevant issues in the approval of budget plans. Indeed, the pressures of politics are such that expenditures are approved not only on the promise of what will be accomplished if the budget plan is funded, but also on the threat of what may happen if the budget plan is not funded.

Although this approach provides a focus for assembling the facts relevant to budget justification, it does not indicate which facts or how many are necessary. There are no hard rules about this because budget authorities differ widely from jurisdiction to jurisdiction in what they require. Some jurisdictions require very little documentation (as under a line-item format); others, a great deal (as under a PPB/ZBB format). The current trend, however, is toward the requirement of more supporting documentation and information.[39]

Regardless of the amount of information required or permitted, there are standard issues or questions that agencies should attempt to address concisely as a part of their budget plans:

1. Will the resource request yield specific and identifiable units of work activity?
2. Is the proposed expenditure clearly related to a proposed set of objectives related, in turn, to primary agency missions?
3. Can the objectives and work programs be achieved by less costly means?
4. What is the likelihood that proposed work programs and objectives will be accomplished?
5. What will be the consequences of funding only part of the request? of not funding any of it?

The reality of budget planning and budget

forms in most jurisdictions is that the information provided in answers to these questions is not specifically requested or required. This is especially true of line-item budgeting, but less true of PPB and ZBB procedures. The important point, however, is not whether such information is requested, but that such information, concisely presented, supports the request and the overall budget plan.

SUMMARY

Fiscal planning has been singled out for special treatment because of the importance of resources to organizations. Also, as most budget-planning processes are annual, fiscal planning is often the single most regularly occurring form of planning within organizations.

Several differences exist between private and public organizations, and some of these differences make fiscal planning in the public sector much more difficult. The lack of profit measures in public agencies, the great difficulties inherent in measuring the benefits of public service, make budget justification in the public sector exceedingly difficult. Budget justification and budget accountability are key activities associated with fiscal planning; failure to adequately perform them has often left organizations with grossly insufficient resources with which to do their work and attain their objectives.

Budget justification and accountability are greatly influenced by the kinds of information brought into the budget process. Lump-sum, line-item, performance or management, and PPB/ZBB budgeting formats are the chief alternative models available for guiding fiscal planning. Each brings different information to the process; some bring more of the needed information than others. PPB/ZBB formats, although costlier in time and required expertise, offer the best available means for maximizing the relevant kinds of information necessary for effective budget justification and accountability: information about resources, activities, and objectives. Ultimate forms of justification and accountability rest on the ability to link resource needs to required work and activities and these to goals and objectives. A line-item format emphasizes resources; a management format emphasizes resources and activities, a PPB/ZZB format considers resources, activities, and objectives.

This chapter has also focused on the relationships between the agency's resource needs and the agency's environment, where resource requests are approved or denied. Outside decision-makers must be informed of resource needs, but they confront political and fiscal constraints when reviewing budget requests. An agency's reputation for efficiency and effectiveness, and its history of overspending or underspending, are central to developing a favorable budget-review climate. The ability of the agency to distinguish short-range, middle-range, and long-range needs is also crucial. Finally, the budget request is a blending of art and science, and also a consideration of agency needs balanced against realistic expectations about funding.

A budget-planning process that considers resources, activities, and objectives in an interrelated fashion is most consistent with the basic planning models presented in Chapter 3. Also, the blending of economic cost/benefit analysis with political realities and constraints makes fiscal planning consistent with a bounded rational-model for planning.

· *Chapter 13* · NOTES

1. *Historical Statistics of the United States: Colonial Times to 1970*, Bicentennial Edition, Part I, (Washington, D.C.: U.S. Bureau of the Census, 1975), p. 416.

2. Timothy J. Flanagan, et al., eds., *Sourcebook of Criminal Justice Statistics–1979* (Washington, D.C.: U.S. Law Enforcement Assistance Administration, National Criminal Justice Information and Statistics Service, U.S. Government Printing Office, 1980), p. 5.

3. Ibid., p. 7.

4. Michael R. Gottfredson, et al., *Sourcebook of Criminal Justice Statistics–1977* (*Washington, D.C.*: U.S. Department of Justice,

Law Enforcement Assistance Administration, National Criminal Justice, Information and Statistics Service, U.S. Government Printing Office, February 1978), pp. 44, 64, 1975 total system expenditures of approximately $17.25 billion can be compared to 1975 total system employee payrolls of approximately $13.91 billion. Thus about 81 per cent of system expenditures are for personnel payroll.

5. Flanagan, et al., op. cit., p. 25.

6. Ibid., pp. 12–21.

7. Ibid., p. 40.

8. James A. Maxwell and J. Richard Aronson, *Financing State and Local Governments,* 3rd ed., (Washington, D.C.: The Brookings Institute, 1977), pp. 244–45.

9. Marshall A. Robinson, et al., "Why Have the Activities of Government Grown?" in James W. Davis, Jr., *Politics, Programs and Budgets: A Reader in Government Budgeting* (Englewood Cliffs, N.J.: Prentice-Hall, Inc., 1969), pp. 5–8.

10. This refers broadly to the several initiatives in several states either to reduce taxes or to put constitutionally mandated ceilings on taxation. California's Proposition 13 is probably the best-known example.

11. Frank P. Sherwood, *The Management Approach to Budgeting* (Brussels: International Institute of Administrative Sciences, 1954), p. 10.

12. Robert D. Lee, Jr. and Ronald W. Johnson, *Public Budgeting Systems,* (Baltimore: University Park Press, 1973), p. 1.

13. Aaron Wildavsky, *The Politics of the Budgetary Process,* 2nd ed., (Boston: Little Brown and Company, 1974), p. 1.

14. Lennox L. Moak and Kathryn W. Killian, *Operating Budget Manual* (Chicago: Municipal Finance Officers Association, 1963), p. 3. The authors quote the early 1960s draft definition of budgeting of the National Committee on Governmental Accounting.

15. Ibid., p. 3.

16. For a discussion of this and related concepts, see Alice M. Rivlin, *Systematic Thinking for Social Action* (Washington, D.C.: The Brookings Institution, 1971), see Chap. 3 in particular.

17. Lee and Johnson, op. cit., p. 3.

18. Anthony Downs, *Inside Bureaucracy* (Boston: Little, Brown and Company, 1967), p. 59.

19. Bertram M. Gross, "The New Systems Budgeting," *Public Administration Review,* 29 (March–April 1969), 113–37.

20. Allen Schick, "The Road to PPB: The Stages of Budget Reform," in Fremont J. Lyden and Ernest G. Miller, eds., *Planning, Programming, Budgeting: A System approach to Management* (Chicago: Markham, 1972), pp. 15–40.

21. Nicholas Henry, *Public Administration and Public Affairs* (Englewood Cliffs, N.J.: Prentice-Hall, Inc., 1975), pp. 158–83.

22. Jesse Burkhead, *Government Budgeting* (New York: John Wiley & Sons Inc., 1956), pp. 1–29.

23. Schick, op. cit.

24. There are actually numerous labels applied to the PPB system. All of them, however, generally contain the notion of adding a program orientation to the budgeting process.

25. Robert J. Mowitz, *The Design and Implementation of Pennsylvania's Planning, Programming, and Budgeting System* (University Park, Pa.: Pennsylvania State University, Institute of Public Administration, n.d.), p. 52.

26. Wildavsky, op. cit., p. 208.

27. Peter A. Pyhrr, *Zero-Base Budgeting: A Practical Management Tool for Evaluating Expenses* (New York: John Wiley & Sons, Inc., 1973), from the dustcover of the hardbound edition.

28. Ibid., p. 6.

29. *Zero-Base Budgeting,* Department of Corrections, Illinois (undated pamphlet). Forms adapted from this document.

30. John K. Hudzik, et al., *Summary Information from the Manpower Planning Project Interviews: Confidential Report,* School of Criminal Justice, Michigan State University, East Lansing, Mich., 1980.

31. For a discussion of problems and processes associated with interpreting "facts," see James Cutt, *A Planning, Programming, and Budgeting Manual: Resource Allocation in Public Sector Economics* (New York: Praeger Publishers, Inc., 1974). Also see Walter Williams and John W. Evans, *The Politics of Evaluation: The Case of Head Start* (mimeographed, 1969). Williams and Evans make the point that "the milieu for meaningful program evaluation involves an interaction of methodology, bureaucracy, and politics; it will therefore often be the case that attacks against evaluations will be made which are methodological in form but ideological in concern."

32. Hudzik, et al., op. cit.

33. Eli M. Noam, "The Criminal Justice System: An Economic Model," in Stuart S. Nagel, ed., *Modeling the Criminal Justice System* (Beverly Hills: Sage Publications, 1977), p. 42.

34. Hudzik, et al., op. cit.

35. Victor Thompson, quoted by Michael J. White, "The Impact of Management Science on

Political Decision Making," in Fremont J. Lyden and Ernest G. Miller, *Public Budgeting: Program Planning and Evaluation,* 3rd ed. (Chicago: Rand McNally & Company, 1978). p. 405.

36. Ibid.

37. Thomas J. Anton, "Roles and Symbols in the Determination of State Expenditures," in James W. Davis, Jr., *Politics, Programs and Budgets: A Reader in Governmental Budgeting* (Englewood Cliffs, N.J.: Prentice-Hall, Inc., 1969), p. 121.

38. Wildavsky, op. cit.

39. This is a finding of the Michigan State University Manpower Planning Development Project. John K. Hudzik, et al., *Criminal Justice Manpower Planning: An Overview* (Washington, D.C.: U.S. Law Enforcement Assistance Administration, Government Printing Office, 1981).

·Chapter 14·

MANPOWER PLANNING

This chapter explores alternative definitions, purposes, and applications of manpower planning, takes a more detailed look at some of the analytical undertakings associated with manpower planning, and reviews the current level and nature of criminal justice manpower planning.

Criminal justice manpower planning is a comparatively new field of analytical activity. Although the focus of manpower planning is obviously on manpower, its boundaries and its purpose are somewhat vague, partly because manpower planning itself is still an emerging and experimental field, but also because many variables influence the availability of human resources for criminal justice agencies, and these variables introduce substantial complexity into efforts to plan, to acquire, to develop, and to use criminal justice manpower.

The importance of manpower planning in criminal justice seems clear enough. Estimates vary, but over 80 per cent of expenditures in criminal justice are for personnel. The criminal justice system is labor-intensive and the functioning of the system is vitally dependent on the efficient and effective use and deployment of personnel. At a very minimum this means that criminal justice agencies must seek cost-efficient and effective means of acquiring, developing, and utilizing these human resources. This is no easy matter. Numerous factors constrain agency attempts to implement policy based on rational analysis of manpower requirements.

DEFINITIONS, PURPOSES, APPLICATIONS OF MANPOWER PLANNING

There is no simple definition of *manpower planning*. There are, however, several definitions that begin to suggest the purposes behind manpower planning. Tom Lupton believes that agency managers expect clear prescriptions:

> Please give us, in a language we can understand, some practical tips on what we (the managers) have to do now, if in the immediate future (e.g., tomorrow) and in (say) five years' time, we are to ensure that the essential jobs in the organization are occupied by persons with skills, competences, and other relevant personal attributes (e.g., age, sex, temperament) appropriate for the efficient performance of those jobs.[1]

Lupton's plea indicates that one of the principal jobs of manpower planning is forecasting (accurate quantitative and qualitative predictions of future manpower needs), and also the generation and testing of alternatives because Lupton's manager would like to have foolproof, cause-and-effect prescriptions for how to meet personnel needs. Neither forecasting nor generating and testing alternatives is easy, especially when they must be done with assurance and certainty.

The greater difficulty, and perhaps the real difficulty, resides in the scope of manpower planning—a scope that has been seen to be so great that it needs to be fully integrated with all of the other management processes.[2] Knowing what is required in numbers and kinds of people and knowing what needs to be done to secure them can involve nearly every aspect of organizational life and organizational management: agency goals and missions, job and task requirements, workloads, recruitment processes, selection, training, assignment, and so on, and the internal and external factors that influence not only the need for human resources, but the ability to acquire them as well.

The Scope of Manpower Planning

D. J. Bartholomew has identified three themes in manpower-planning undertakings.[3] The first theme is statistically oriented—matching the workforce supply to the job-defined demand for people. The second theme is people's motivations, aspirations, and expectations, on which the supply of workers for any occupation is vitally dependent. The third theme is the balance between supply and demand—planning for the effective acquisition, development, and utilization of workers.

Implicit in Bartholomew's themes is the idea that manpower planning can focus on several different units of analysis. One level deals with whole occupational groupings: bricklayers, doctors, police officers. An example of this is the U.S. Department of Labor's attempts to project manpower requirements in the years ahead for various occupational groupings nationally, regionally, and so forth.[4] At another level, manpower planning can focus on the individual agency and its manpower needs. At the lowest level, the unit of analysis is the individual, and the concerns of analysis are the number and kinds of occupational alternatives presented to individuals.

The U.S. Civil Service Commission's Bureau of Policies and Standards has addressed this issue of scope more directly by identifying three forms of manpower-planning activity:[5] (1) manpower-planning analysis, (2) manpower-planning programs, and (3) organizational manpower planning. The first two categories associate the term *manpower planning* with labor-market forecasting (determining how many workers are needed and how many are available in whole occupational groupings) and with the development of governmental-sponsored programs affecting manpower levels. The third category is particularly important for this discussion because it focuses on the manpower-planning undertakings within the individual agency.

Manpower-planning analysis includes labor-force analysis that results primarily in descriptive statistics showing dimensions and components of various labor forces and how these dimensions and components have changed over time. Other aspects of labor-force analysis include analytical and projective studies that, along with related factors, forecast upcoming features of the labor force. This kind of analysis is typified by Volume I of *The National Manpower Survey of the Criminal Justice System*, in which a particular projective model was employed to determine the number of criminal justice personnel that will be needed in various occupational groupings five and ten years in the future.[6]

Manpower-planning program activity is "oriented toward the development, administration and evaluation of manpower *programs*."[7] Such manpower programs include efforts to improve the employment status of particular groups included under Affirmative Action/Equal Employment Opportunity Commission programs. Other manpower programs may be concerned with such issues as gaps in the supply and demand of manpower, and may include special government-sponsored programs of training, retraining, and professional education to help close these gaps. The LEEP program is an example of a manpower-planning program instituted within and for the criminal justice system. The forty-seven state police officer standards and training councils' programs may be viewed, in intention at least, to be manpower programs as well.

Organizational manpower planning has different purposes, and two distinct yet related aspects. The U.S. Civil Service Commission Bureau of Policies and Standards dubs the first "workforce planning"—analysis of the numbers and kinds of people that are and will be needed to perform the organization's work. The second aspect, staffing-needs planning, includes determining the kinds of "future personnel management actions" that will be needed if the organization is to secure the numbers and kinds of people it needs. The methodologies involved in these related but different functions include the following:

> We would point out that the methodology of workforce planning, in its most typical form, is to start with (a) estimates of expected workload, to which are applied, (b) measures or assumptions of output per unit of labor time, and by this means to derive estimates of (c) the numbers and types of workers needed to produce the expected workload. Workforce planning methodology, that is, uses workload and work measurement data and derives "required workforce" plans.
>
> The methodology of staffing-needs planning, on the other hand, is to start with (a) the manager's "required workforce" plan, estimate (b) the personnel losses and shifts likely to take place during the planning period, and then to determine (c) what future personnel management actions will be needed to provide the required workforce. Thus, staffing-needs planning uses mostly personnel data and produces either suggested changes in management's workforce

plan or summary estimates of what must be done to provide the required workforce.[8]

Thomas Patten puts the alternative objectives and scopes of manpower planning rather succinctly by drawing a distinction between manpower planning done at the level of the economy and that done at the level of the organization.[9] In Patten's view, manpower planning at the level of the economy is concerned with planning the preparation and employment of the labor force for the jobs needed by society, and involves implementation of policies designed to increase the job opportunities available, to improve training, and to enhance the use of manpower. Patten views manpower planning at the level of the organization as being focused instead on the needs of individual organizations, "the process by which a firm insures that it has the right number of people, and the right kind of people, in the right places, at the right time, doing things for which they are economically most useful."[10] For an organization to accomplish this, all aspects of the agency's personnel administration and the agency's environment (particularly the labor market, the general economy, and the agency's budget) must be brought under consideration. Organizational manpower planning also requires an understanding of the agency's goals and missions, the jobs necessary to meet goals, and the personnel necessary to fill the jobs. Because of these broad requirements, organizational manpower planning has to be fully integrated with all the other managerial functions.

Elements of Organizational Manpower Planning

What seems especially clear is that organizational manpower planning must be vitally concerned with obtaining and analyzing information related to the present and future supplies of, and needs for, human resources. This includes information not only about the number of people needed, but about the kinds of people needed as well. Obtaining this information requires answering seven key questions:

1. What are (will be) the goals and objectives of the organization?
2. What are (will be) the organization and work-tasks necessary to achieve the goals and missions?
3. Who are (will be) needed to accomplish the work-tasks?
    a. What knowledge and skills should they have?
    b. How many with each kind of skill are needed?
4. What is (will be) the inventory of human resources available?
    a. Developed inventory: People who are appropriately trained and skilled and are employed by the organization.
    b. Undeveloped inventory: People employed in the organization but not sufficiently trained or skilled.
5. What is (will be) the gap between the numbers and kinds of people needed and those trained and available within the organization?
6. How available are (will be) developed, developable, and undevelopable workers in the labor market? (This is a measure of the supply of "raw materials" not at present possessed by the agency.)
7. What are the alternative means available to bridge the gaps between supply and demand, gaps existing either now or in the future?

Organizational manpower planning, properly conceived, however, is not simply a matter of collecting and analyzing information related to these seven key questions. Beyond collecting information, providing forecasts, and determining gaps between supply and demand, organizational manpower planning involves the implementation of policies and programs that will focus on closing the projected gaps between supply and demand. This is the action component of manpower planning, and in the words of B. R. Morris, manpower planning thus includes *manpower management*.[11]

Manpower management is a broad concept that includes the development of policies governing the acquisition, development, and utilization of manpower, and the implementation of specific personnel-administration processes to put those policies into force. Planning per se is closely associated with both of these features of manpower management because planning-oriented analysis provides the information essential for the design and implementation of personnel-administration policies and procedures. A. R. Smith suggests that manpower planning plays a kind of systems-engineering role by developing and exploiting information for manpower-management purposes.[12]

This view of organizational manpower planning has been characterized by other researchers and scholars. Cascio, for example, quoting Cresap, McCormick, and Paget,[13] says that manpower planning leads to the construction of staffing plans that in turn lead to staffing and development, the measurement of organizational performance, and the production of results. In Figure 14-1, manpower planning and personnel administration are not subsets of one another; instead, they are conceptually related processes linked under manpower management. Manpower policy-making is based on planning information, and it sets forth broad-gauged recommendations and requirements that form the general plan of action to secure, to develop, and to utilize human resources. Personnel administration also makes use of planning-derived information to guide development of the specific decisions that put personnel policy into action.

There are those who draw a distinction between manpower planning and human-resources planning, owing to the historical origins and initially limited sphere of manpower planning. Originally, manpower planning was limited to quantitative forecasts of the labor market and of job opportunities. Some hold that manpower planning is concerned only with those issues, and that forecasting efforts, qualitative forecasts, and personnel-administration practices should be defined as human-resources planning.[14] Patten, Morris, Smith, Bartholomew, Cascio, and others clearly do not view manpower planning in such a limited way.

Applications of Organizational Manpower Planning

Planning's numerous applications or uses for various aspects of manpower management fall largely within several general categories, characterized in terms of some of the undertakings that commonly fall within them.

1. ***Forecasting Human Resources.*** Forecasts may focus on one or more of the following kinds of issues: the availability of numbers and kinds of personnel from the labor market; the availability of numbers and kinds of personnel from within the organization; changes in the composition of the agency workforce and the outside labor pool (e.g., aging, educational levels, and so on); changes in workloads and resulting changes in needs for manpower within the organization; projections of employee-turnover rates; and projections of employee-learning curves dependent on time and experience in the job. These forecasts may be short-range (say, a year) or for longer-range, (say, five or ten years).

2. ***Forecasting Relevant Environmental Variables.*** Crime trends, budget forecasts, economic trends, population trends, and the like will not only greatly affect the need for manpower in

Figure 14-1. The Manpower-Management Process

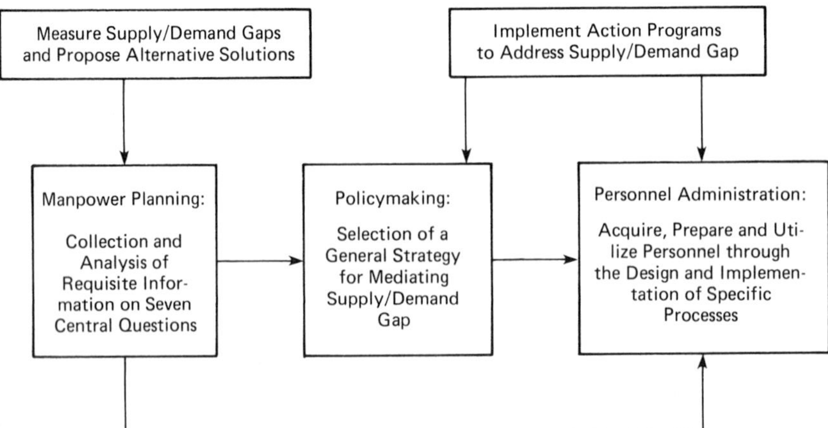

criminal justice agencies, but will also determine the availability of manpower and the conditions under which manpower will be available to the agency now and in the future. Forecasts of impending change in these variables is vital to planning personnel policy in organizations.

3. ***Projecting Effects of Personnel Practices.*** Established or existing practices in recruitment, selection, training and development, assignment and reassignment, compensation, and motivation of personnel produce current results that may not be the same in future periods. As conditions change, so do the effects of the practices. Thus, one contribution of planning is in forecasting the likely effect of existing personnel procedures under future conditions. Also, however, planning techniques can indicate the likely effects of alternative practices. It has often been noted, for example, that when communities enjoy a substantial economic boom, the labor market tightens and there are fewer qualified applicants for jobs in some types of criminal justice agencies (e.g., institutional corrections). Such a situation would have implications for where and how agencies recruit and for how they train and develop the recruits they do attract.

4. ***Predicting and Projecting Human-Resource Problems.*** A human-resource problem arises when the gap between the supply of personnel and the need for personnel is sufficient to "endanger" the organization's ability to perform its mission in an acceptable fashion. *Endanger* and *acceptable fashion* are relative terms; they are defined by the standards of the community and those of agency decision-makers. However, planning has several distinct roles to play in dealing with such human-resources problems. First, planning techniques can assist in predicting such problems (e.g., high turnover rates resulting from retirements). Second, planning can assist in identifying and weighing alternative remedies to these problems; for example, by forecasting the effects of personnel practices on the gap between personnel supply and demand (e.g., the effects of adopting early and staggered retirement plans, or the effect of early recruitment of key replacement personnel), planning may help at least to identify the likely consequences of altering personnel practices.

5. ***Planning the Resolution of Extant Human-Resource Problems.*** The four categories just described all include the words *forecasting* or *projecting* and imply that manpower planning looks toward the future and identifies its implications for the organization. However, manpower or human-resource planning also examines alternatives and their consequences for dealing with existing organizational problems—problems that need not be anticipated because they are already here. None of the planning literature has dealt with this idea very much, but it is a principal concern of manpower planning in many organizations.

The Realities of Organizational Manpower Planning

As A. R. Smith notes, manpower-forecasting techniques are largely based on past trends and regularities and the projection of these into the future. "Forecasting must make due allowance also for foreseeable changes in policy, organization, and technology which may break the established trends and relationships."[15] These changes often cannot be properly anticipated and, thus, the forecasts are flawed. There is also substantial evidence to suggest that the interest of criminal justice agencies in forecasting is limited, and that agency managers are more interested in planning the resolution of existing problems than they are in forecasting either for their own sake or to anticipate agency manpower problems.[16] Indeed, as crisis environments appear typically to confront criminal justice agencies, managerial efforts normally concentrate on the disposal of immediate problems, especially in a timely fashion. *Timely fashion* can often mean a rush to judgment, especially if a framework for data and for analytical experitise is not already in place to allow a rational and reasoned approach to understanding the problem and to finding either optimal or satisfactory solutions to it.

Actually, the reasons for the low-level development and use of the more complex manpower-planning techniques, such as forecasting, are more involved. Different criminal justice agencies have different needs for manpower-planning analyses. Some of the factors influencing the needs of a particular agency include the size of the agency, the present and future stability of the agency and its community, and the degree of decisional flexibility given agency managers in making policy based on manpower-planning analyses. Even though the use of, and perhaps the need for, analytical manpower-planning techniques vary from agency to agency, most criminal justice agencies, if not all, need to undertake some form of manpower planning. Principally, this means organizing manpower-planning activities around key issues or frequently occurring difficulties associated with the costs and with the productivity of personnel. These difficulties might include expanded mission-and-service expectations, inadequate performance and productivity on the part of employees, cost inefficiencies, duplication of services and manpower, or turnover. The function of organizational manpower planning is to formulate an understanding of these difficulties, and to resolve them within the planning contexts discussed in Chapter 3.

Figure 3-1 presented four alternative planning contexts: rational, research, problem-solving, and disjointed incrementalism. Two of the four contexts are relevant here for finding a practical starting point for agency-based manpower-planning activities: research, in which goals are clear but alternative relationships between means and ends are not; problem-solving, in which goals are unclear but alternative relationships between means and ends are known. These two situations are frequently encountered by such public organizations as criminal justice agencies, and it is within the confines of these alternative situations that agency-based manpower planning can reasonably develop.

When goals are clearly understood but the means of achieving those goals is not, planning focuses on research or discovery. That is, manpower-planning efforts concentrate on finding the alternative means for achieving the desired goals and on collecting and analyzing data to determine the likely consequences of each alternative.

Consider a situation in which a city police department has to provide services to a large, newly annexed area. The general goals are fairly clear, although the new areas to be served may differ from established areas in demographics, socioeconomic characteristics, and type of business activity. These differences may require a different mix of programs and services. This, together with the obligation to provide services to more people over a larger area, will have obvious implications for manpower planning. The objective of manpower planning in such a situation is to "research" the means of meeting the new requirements for mission and service.

In this example, the first phase of manpower "research" is workforce planning, to use the terminology of the U.S. Civil Service Commission. Among other things, this phase may involve collecting and analyzing information about mission, need and demand, organization design, and jobs, roles, and tasks. This will yield basic information on personnel needs. The second phase is *staffing-needs planning* (concerning the kinds of personnel-management action that will have to be taken to provide the required workforce). This involves consideration of the recruitment, selection, development, and assignment practices that will help in acquiring, developing, and utilizing manpower. Research-oriented planning must be conducted with an awareness of the political and technical constraints imposed on the agency. For example, although new areas may have been annexed, the police agency may not be free to hire new and "needed" personnel. Research-oriented staffing-needs planning must therefore devise alternative assignment schedules and organization structures to "cover" the new areas with existing manpower resources.

Manpower planning that addresses a specific and identifiable organizational problem is related to research-oriented planning. Problem-focused planning concentrates on discovering what the problem is and how the problem can be addressed, much in the way that research-oriented planning concentrates on discovering the means to achieve a known goal. The difference is, however, that problem-focused planning begins with an organizational problem to be solved rather than an organizational goal to be achieved. For example, the problem may be that the agency is not able to attract qualified job applicants in sufficient numbers, or that current selection and promotion procedures do not meet affirmative-action requirements, or that the agency confronts high turnover rates that seriously threaten agency performance. The objective of manpower planning in any of these circumstances is to discover means by which these problems can be addressed. Problem-focused manpower planning seeks to identify those personnel-management actions that will resolve the problem.

Baum has noted that "the work of planners is described more accurately as problem formulation than as problem-solving."[17] It is rare that a given manpower problem can be described and understood in a single way. Most problems have multiple meanings and multiple causes, and can be understood from alternative vantage points. The manpower planner must pose alternative responses to alternative views of the problem.

Both research-focused and problem-focused planning have a common purpose: the prime role of each is to provide decision-makers with information on alternative ways of either achieving goals or solving problems. Both are concerned with generating information, and both are committed to finding the relationships between means and ends that permit goals to be achieved and problems to be solved.

A SAMPLING OF MANPOWER-PLANNING ANALYTICAL ACTIVITIES

Chapters 11 and 12 discussed various kinds of research designs and methods of collecting and measuring data for criminal justice planning. Most of those designs and methods are applicable in one form or another to the collection of data for manpower planning. In this chapter, however, attention is focused on some of the analytical techniques more closely associated with manpower planning. Two are especially important: job analysis and manpower forecasting. There are of course numerous other projects and techniques associated with manpower planning. These include, but are not limited to, job description, job classification, job evaluation, job restructuring, selection validation, personnel specification, performance appraisal, manpower simulation, and manpower inventory.[18] These will be briefly discussed (except manpower simulation and manpower inventory, which are discussed within a more detailed treatment of forecasting).

Job-Focused Analyses

Job-focused data are important for manpower-planning purposes. Knowledge of the roles and tasks that comprise an agency's jobs now, and what they will be in the future, is central to determining the numbers and kinds of people needed to do the agency's work. *Job analysis* is a group of related techniques for collecting and analyzing data about what the jobs of the agency are or will be. According to the U.S. Employment Service, job analysis is a process for determining the nature of specific jobs, and for determining the tasks that comprise the job, and the skills, knowledge, abilities, and responsibilities required of the employee for successful performance of the job.[19] Some of the specific and more regularly used job-analysis techniques include the position-analysis questionnaire, the critical-incident technique, the job-element method, the ability-requirement scale, and the functional job analysis (see Figure 14-2).[20] Each of these techniques makes use of one or more of the commonly recognized data-collection methods: interviewing, survey questionnaires, observation, the collection of expert opinion, or the construction of written narratives. Job-analysis data provide task-oriented information (what is the job about) and attribute-oriented information (what employee skills and knowledge are required in the job), both of which are needed by the agency to construct job descriptions.

Job description identifies the relevant duties, accountabilities, and employment standards for various jobs in the agency.[21] These job descriptions are subsequently important for understanding how jobs should be classified and arranged. *Job classification* and *job evaluation* arrange and rank jobs by their importance for achieving organizational goals, or by the technical level of the job and task and the level of skills and knowledge required of personnel.[22] This is crucial for subsequent efforts to determine which jobs are related, to permit transfer of employees from one job to another, and to set priorities for acquiring various kinds of employees.

Job restructuring is the rearrangement of specific tasks and roles for various kinds of jobs. It determines the kinds of roles and tasks best grouped with one another under a particular job heading—those that comprise the most efficient and effective combination of activities for individuals assigned to those jobs. These analyses are important to more effective and efficient use of agency personnel, and they affect how many and what kinds of personnel are needed by an agency. *Personnel*

Figure 14-2. A Sample of Alternative Approaches to Job Analysis

The Position-Analysis Questionnaire is a structured job-analysis instrument containing 187 worker-oriented job elements, categorized into six major general aspects of work in given jobs (information input, mental processes, work output, relations with other persons, the work environment, and miscellaneous characteristics). These categories and the 187 criteria are used to rate jobs and to compare them with one another.

The Critical-Incident Technique, applied to job analysis, records critical or outstanding incidents associated with job behavior. Through observation, or through the recounting of several critical incidents in the form of stories and anecdotes, a composite picture of the essential elements and behaviors necessary to performing a job can be inferred.

The Job-Element Method focuses analysis on human or worker attributes, especially those considered essential for superior performance on the job. A small group of experts is assembled. Key knowledge, skills, abilities and other personal characteristics are identified and ranked according to their importance for each job.

Ability-Requirement Scales focus on general abilities rather than on specific skills as the categories and variables by which job attributes are measured. Thirty-seven abilities are grouped into four major categories (mental ability, physical ability, ability to process incoming sensory material, and ability to take action based on incoming sensory material). Jobs are analyzed, compared, and ranked according to how much each of these abilities is involved.

Functional Job Analysis, one of the more commonly recognized work-oriented job-analysis techniques, focuses on what the worker does—on the machines, tools, equipment, or services used, and on how the job's tasks require the worker to relate to data, people, and things. The essential feature of all work-oriented job-analysis methods (such as functional job analysis) is to isolate and to describe the essential tasks that go into making up a job.

specification determines the kinds of people needed to fill organizational jobs, and *selection validation* ensures that the criteria and the application of criteria for selecting employees from among job applicants are related to essential job features.

Personnel requirements may refer to minimum qualifications as well as to desirable qualifications.[23] Selection criteria refer to the valid means of measuring these qualifications in job applicants (e.g., tests and interviews). Both are important in the subsequent effort to define the kinds of people needed by the agency. The organization has no valid means for determining the kinds of people it needs unless it has first analyzed the task and attribute requirements of its jobs.

The utilization of job analysis in criminal justice, especially by law-enforcement agencies, has been substantial.[24] By and large, this activity has been spurred by suits, threats of suits, or fear of suits alleging that requirements, selection criteria, and promotional practices in agencies were not validly related to job content. Numerous court rulings primarily (although not exclusively) related to issues of EEOC/Affirmative Action, have made clear that the only legitimate basis for establishing qualifications, selection criteria, and promotional standards is a valid relationship to performance of the work, tasks, and roles of the job.

There are, of course, other reasons for using job analysis and related techniques. State-level commissions on police-officer standards and training have increasingly undertaken statewide job analyses of police work as a basis for setting minimum training standards and for planning training programs.[25] Job-analysis information is particularly useful for determining the substantive content of training-program requirements. Anchored in job-analysis data, these training programs have more relevance for, and greater utility in, developing personnel who perform better on the job.

Job-analysis data provide the principal mechanism for evaluating the validity of personnel practices and procedures, including recruitment, selection, training, performance evaluation, and the assignment and reassignment of personnel. Criteria for evaluation of employees' performance, for example, are best derived from an understanding of the actual jobs and the expectations management has about employees' performance in fulfilling the duties associated with those jobs.

Job-analysis data are also important in planning for personnel needs and for planning the acquisition of personnel. Without job data, for example, decisions about the procedures and policies to govern future recruitment and selection of personnel are anchored only in loose perceptions about the work of the agency and about the kinds of people best suited to perform that work.

One difficulty with the present use of job-analysis techniques in criminal justice is a tendency to concentrate analysis efforts almost exclusively on describing the present nature of jobs, ignoring the question of how these jobs may change, or may need to be changed, in the future. For example, the job analyses by comissions on police-officer standards and training have been undertaken to describe current jobs in order to set minimum entry and training standards. Many of these analyses ignore the fact that jobs change. As role expectations of criminal justice agencies change, the tasks associated with particular jobs, and the concomitant attributes desirable or required in employees will also change. This affects the agency's search for qualified job applicants, its choice of procedures for selection, training, assignment, and evaluation. Clearly, job analysis should be oriented toward the future as well as toward the present.

Manpower Forecasting

Chapter 9 discussed the forecasting stage of planning. Manpower forecasting is specifically concerned with determining the future needs for manpower and with future supplies of manpower. These forecasts enable a manager to design policies and procedures that will ensure that the agency has enough workers in the future, doing enough of the right kind of work, and doing it well. They supply decision-makers with the information essential to choosing policies that will result in neither too many nor too few of the right kinds of workers in the future.

As can be imagined, forecasting undertaken for these purposes is a complicated business and subject to all of the constraints and difficulties discussed in Chapter 9. Within these constraints, however, manpower forecasts provide information about likely changes in relevant environmental variables and about probable resultant changes in the missions and roles of criminal justice agencies. Project STAR (System Training and Analysis of Requirements) is one notable example of an attempt to determine such matters for the criminal justice system.[26] The STAR volume, *The Impact of Social Trends on Crime and Criminal Justice,* analyzes several social and crime trends to determine their implications for the nature of the missions and roles of criminal justice agencies.[27] On the basis of these projections, STAR turned toward *role analysis* and task-construction techniques to determine the kinds of roles, tasks, and activities that would be required of criminal justice agencies to operationalize present and future missions and objectives. This had obvious implications not only for the present but also for the future content of criminal justice jobs and for qualitative projections of need.

Forecasting probable changes in the missions, roles, and tasks of the agency is the first step in what is referred to as *manpower forecasting.* Forecasting the demand for labor has two aspects: the first concerns quantitative demand (the number of people needed in the future to fill required agency jobs); the second concerns qualitative demand (the *kinds* of people required).

There is another aspect of manpower forecasting that is equally important to questions of demand: *supply forecasting*, which concerns projections of the probable number and kinds of people likely to be available to staff the future jobs of an agency. Thus, the principal role of manpower forecasting is to predict both the future supply of labor and the demand for labor,[28] to identify gaps between the two, and to determine policy alternatives designed to close any gaps.

Manpower-Demand Forecasting. One of the principal difficulties associated with demand forecasting is that it attempts to predict future manpower needs on the basis of an analysis of factors external to the organization that influence the amount and kinds of services expected of the agency. These external factors include social, economic, demographic, and other environmental variables, along with public preferences about kinds and amounts of services. Public preferences are often vague or conflicting, and often shift; attempts to determine what they are, let alone what they will be, are exceedingly difficult. Nonetheless, to the extent that an agency is able to isolate relevant variables and to gather information on these variables, demand forecasting can proceed.

Wikstrom has identified six steps that, in his view, form part of all demand-forecasting models and techniques:[29]

1. Identifying the essential business or production factor (missions, roles, tasks)
2. Analyzing the historical and current behavior of that factor with regard to the employment of manpower
3. Calculating productivity ratios
4. Projecting a trend in employment from productivity
5. Making necessary adjustments where appropriate
6. Projecting required manpower for the target time period

These steps are neither simple nor easy. In Step 1, criminal justice agencies often must consider multiple missions, roles, and objectives that have multiple consequences for the several kinds of people the agency will need. In institutional corrections for example, production factors may relate to the number of inmates, their security classification, the kinds of services that need to be provided inmates, and so forth. These multiple production factors require that the agency secure not only the right number and right kind of employees, but the right *mix* of employees as well. Thus, there are multiple manpower demands that must be projected and met.

Wikstrom's Steps 2 and 3 depend on an agency's ability to collect and to analyze historical data on the amount of production (services) provided, and to consider also the number and kinds of personnel that were available to provide these services. For example, such data might establish that Prison X has had 800-1,000 inmates per year over the last five years, a custodial staff of 325-375, and a treatment staff of 60-75, with the treatment staff annually providing a certain average amount and range of services to inmates. Step 4 uses the historical information on productivity ratios per employee, changes and trends in productivity, and changes and trends in the level of employment compared to the level of production to determine what the historical trends have been. Step 5 analyzes productivity and productivity trends to determine whether there are any identifiable anomalies in the trends. For example, part of the historical data may have reflected a brief, one-year experience when inmate good time (early release for good behavior) was done away with, resulting in a significant increase in inmate man days during that year. If "good time" has subsequently been restored, the prison's productivity trends should be adjusted to account for the temporary effects of the experiment.

After these five steps have been completed, Step 6 requires using all the collected and analyzed data and information to project trends for service levels and numbers of employees needed. The projections naturally assume either that productivity-ratio trends will hold constant or that they will increase or decrease for one reason or another. For example, an increase in productivity ratios might be predicted owing to technological breakthroughs in mechanical security devices that reduce the need for custodial staff. Or a decline in productivity ratios might be predicted owing to recent court orders that require larger numbers of staff for the present number of inmates.

This six-step procedure for forecasting manpower demand obviously relies heavily on accurate predictions of the demands for service that will be made of the organization in some foreseeable future. It also depends heavily on assumptions about productivity rates—whether these will remain essentially the same, extend historical trends, or run counter to those trends.

The methods for forecasting manpower demand are essentially the same forecasting techniques discussed in Chapter 9. Opinion-based forecasting is one obvious alternative: through the use of administrative surveys or the Delphi technique, opinions about what will happen in the future can be collected. But as Armstrong notes, such opinion-based data may either be opinions about what people expect to happen in the future, or they may be what people tell us they intend to *do* in the future—the latter being intentions forecasting.[30] In the case of intentions forecasting, agency management may be asked about its plans or intentions to alter agency missions and roles and what the implications of those alterations will be for manpower demand.

Rule-of-thumb demand forecasting is another alternative. For example, a police agency may project its future quantitative manpower needs on population projections and on the application of a rule of thumb that there "ought" to be *x* officers per thousand population. A corrections agency may do the same thing by projecting inmate populations and, on that basis, establishing staffing ratios. Unfortunately, although rules of thumb are often convenient and simple to use, they tend to reflect the status quo, and the results to which they lead are often questionable.

The more powerful and more complicated techniques for demand forecasting involve the use of statistical models (see Chapter 9).[31] Statistical-model forecasting most frequently employs one or more of the following: extrapolation, simple regression analysis, and econometric modelling. In extrapolation, Markov-chain analysis and moving-averages methods are often used.

Demand forecasting in criminal justice has largely been limited to judgmental techniques. Two notable exceptions, however, are the forecasting efforts of the National Manpower Survey[32] and the forecasting potential of JUSSIM.[33]

The National Manpower Survey forecast demand by using a theoretical model that related criminal justice manpower needs to changes in such demographic characteristics as age, per capita income, degree of urbanization, and unemployment. Changes in these and other environmental variables were assumed to have an effect on crime levels, which were assumed to have a subsequent effect on criminal justice workload and employment. The model required the collection and statistical analysis of many forms of data related to these variables—data that established historical perspectives and trends in productivity and productivity ratios. The statistical computations provided the basis for estimates of the number of new employees that would be required throughout the criminal justice system five and ten years hence.[34]

JUSSIM, the interactive computer-simulation model, can project manpower demand. JUSSIM is based on historical data for a particular jurisdiction, including data on crime, system transactions such as decisional-branching ratios, manpower, and costs. Assumptions about crime levels and decisional-branching ratios are manipulated in order to estimate demand for manpower, and changes in that demand, among the various components of the criminal justice system within that jurisdiction.

Supply Forecasting. As noted by the U.S. Department of Employment and Productivity, "forecasts of future labor demand alone will be of limited value unless the manager is able to relate them to the current and future supply condition."[35] Manpower-supply forecasting is concerned with projecting the availability of manpower for the agency. Future availability is dependent both on available internal supplies (employees within the organization) and available external supplies (suitable workers from the labor market). When assessing manpower supply, agencies begin by taking account of manpower within the organization and comparing it to the manpower that may be demanded in the future. The difference (if there is any) becomes the measure of the number of people who must be recruited from the outside labor market.

The particularly important aspect of measuring external supply is not what the agency will need from the labor market, but what the agency can hope to *get* from the labor market. Supply-forecasting techniques are often the same as those used to forecast demand (judgmental and statistical techniques in particular). Fortunately, there are usually some data and forecasts available for criminal justice agencies to use in making supply projections. Reports from state agencies (e.g., employment commissions), the U.S. Bureau of the Census, the U.S. Department of Labor, and the U.S. Department of Education provide useful information about the nature and size of the future labor force. This information can be analyzed to determine changes in labor-market trends that may affect the availability of manpower. Forecasts of an expanding economy and a tight labor market, for example, will have obvious implications for the availability of manpower for employment in criminal justice.

Measuring the internal supply of manpower is the starting point for supply forecasting. An analysis of that workforce provides information about the numbers and kinds of personnel at present working in the agency. This can be compared to determinations of the projected changes in manpower demand that will arise with changes in missions and jobs. Meeting these new demands, by finding the right future supply of manpower, will normally mean undertaking a combination of adjustments to the current workforce (retraining) and attracting additions to that workforce through the recruitment, selection, and development of new personnel.

Manpower inventories (sometimes referred to as *skills inventories*) are the most commonly used means for recording data and information about the current qualitative makeup of the internal labor supply. In supply forecasting, manpower inventories can be used as a basis for comparing the present inventory to that needed in the future. Differences between the two inventories suggest the need to recruit new skills from among current employees and/or to recruit new kinds of employees suitably skilled for the future jobs of the agency.

The labor force of an agency is not static; it will assuredly change over time. Thus, another essential technique in supply forecasting is change-in-labor-force analysis that attempts to project changes in the agency's current labor force. For example, it can be assumed that the current labor force will age, change in knowledge and skill levels, and so on. Change-in-labor-force analysis permits projections of these predictable changes, upon which can be based estimates of their effect on the present internal supply of manpower.

Analyses of turnover and absenteeism have proven to be particularly crucial for subsequent projections about internally available manpower. Turnover data are such things as natural wastage (owing to death or illness), discharges (firings or dismissals), and voluntary wastage (quitting). All these factors very much affect the availability of manpower for agency jobs. The higher the turnover rate, the higher the necessary-replacement rate—if the number of agency employees required in the future stays at least at current levels.

Turnover analysis should distinguish between the loss of individuals the agency would rather *not* lose and the loss of individuals (e.g., by death) the agency either cannot prevent losing or does not choose to prevent losing (e.g., an individual who seems unlikely ever to perform at minimal levels). Although all forms of turnover affect future supplies of manpower, the agency may wish to take action to prevent appropriately skilled and performing manpower from quitting. To the extent that the agency is able to prevent avoidable forms of turnover, present turnover rates and trends may decline in the future (thus raising projected estimates of how much of the present internal supply of manpower will be carried into the future).

Although the kinds of data and information required for manpower planning are quite extensive, and although many of the associated analytical activities are complex and costly, this does not necessarily preclude manpower planning from criminal justice.

MANPOWER PLANNING IN CRIMINAL JUSTICE

Manpower planning in the criminal justice system may best be characterized as new and untested. It is just beginning to emerge as a recognized focus of managerial concern in criminal justice agencies. The basis for this assessment, and for much of the material presented in this section, is the 1980 study of criminal justice manpower planning conducted by the School of Criminal Justice at Michigan State University.[36] Much of our understanding of the current state of criminal justice manpower-planning activity is derived from the findings of that study.

Interviews in depth were conducted in over 100 agencies, and lengthy questionnaires were sent to 250 law-enforcement agencies, the fifty state planning agencies, the forty-seven commissions on police-officer training and standards, the fifty state departments of adult corrections, and 125 local probation agencies and juvenile authorities. Return rates averaged over 70 per cent.

Perceptions of Manpower Planning and its Utility

General findings from the Michigan State University (MSU) study support the notion that criminal justice manpower planning is largely an emergent phenomenon lacking uniform meaning or purpose. Among other things, the term *manpower planning* was not found to be uniformly defined or clearly understood by respondents. When defining manpower planning in operational terms, respondents tended to limit their definitions to the context of their agency's prime mission or to cast it in terms of a particularly pressing problem facing them at that time. For example, some police and corrections respondents saw manpower planning primarily as manpower deployment (patrol or beat design, computer-assisted scheduling and dispatch, and corrections poststudies). Others viewed manpower planning as concerned with issues of recruitment, selection, and training. Very few respondents saw or defined manpower planning as incorporating notions of forecasting in any of the senses discussed in this chapter.

Although many or most of the elements of manpower planning could be found in various agencies throughout the system, few agencies had adopted a comprehensive understanding of the term. Instead, personnel-administration processes such as recruitment, selection, training, and assignment were viewed as distinct activities rather than as a set of interrelated processes affecting the present and future condition of agency manpower. Indeed, certain kinds of undertakings associated with manpower planning (forecasting, job analysis, selection validation, and so on) were undertaken in the agencies surveyed, but not with any explicit goals or orientation to the future. Such activity focused on the resolution of existing problems within the narrower confines of a personnel-administration framework rather than within those of a manpower-planning framework.

The reasons for this are complex but include the lack of technical expertise necessary to adopt more comprehensive manpower-planning frameworks, the lack of sufficient money and time to devote to planning-related analytical activities, and political exigency. Most respondents saw "politics" as circumscribing–variously, but usually severely–the influence of planning-derived rational plans and policies. One respondent from a state department of corrections indicated, for example, that the department had developed rather sophisticated workload and manpower projection models and had presented these year after year to justify increased personnel-allocation levels. These apparently effected no decision to award additional funds for manpower–that is, until the corrections system experienced severe inmate disturbances. As a result of these disturbances and the attention they received in the press, new funds for increased manpower and new prisons were awarded–not on the grounds of rational manpower-needs analysis, but in response to the recent crisis.

Respondents generally drew a distinction between the effects of rational manpower planning during good economic times and its effects in bad economic times. During good times, rational planning and the information it produced seemed to be accorded greater attention by outside decision-makers; during bad times, rational analyses of need tended to be lost in the rush to reduce overall governmental expenditures. Naturally, many of these views may be based on the selective perceptions by respondents: requests for additional personnel, based on rational analysis or not, have a better chance of being funded during times of general economic expansion than during times of contraction. Nonetheless, respondents consistently reported only a bounded environment within which rational, need-based manpower analysis could have influence. Most respondents viewed the budget process and its allocation of personnel positions as essentially political in nature and only marginally influenced by rational considerations arising from manpower-needs analysis. Other rather severe constraints were often reported by respondents–constraints imposed by civil-service comissions, EEOC, unions, and state or local personnel offices. These outside agencies had an impact on the criminal justice agency's ability to hire the kind of personnel needed, to assign and promote employees, and to allocate its human resources.[37]

In view of these conditions, some respondents conveyed an uneasiness about further developing their agency's manpower-planning capability. Many respondents were often unclear and unconvinced about what the more sophisticated forms of analysis would accomplish beyond what they already knew or needed. For example, one respondent from a department of state police indicated that the department had developed and implemented a rather sophisticated system for projecting workloads and resulting manpower requirements.[38] After some experience with the model it was discarded and the department returned to a simpler and less costly projection model. The reason given was that the simpler projection model appeared to provide as much useful and accurate information as the more complicated and costly model.

Although this department did abandon more complex forecasting models, and apparently for reasonable cause it did not abandon planning as an activity.

It seems clear that the ability and desire of agencies to undertake manpower planning varies with the situation and depends on a number of factors. One factor is the attitude of the jurisdiction's chief executive toward the agency's adoption of more analytically based assessments of manpower needs. If the chief executive encourages such analytical efforts, especially to support budget requests, agency manpower-planning activity increases in amount and in sophistication. Another factor, as could be expected, is the size of the agency. The larger agencies, with more complicated personnel-management situations, are more likely than smaller agencies to adopt various analytical techniques such as forecasting, job analysis, and the like, and to find value in them. A third and important factor involves the degree to which the agency feels itself constrained by external agencies, such as civil service departments, EEOC, budget offices, and the like. The MSU study found, for example, that when working relationships between the criminal justice agency and these other agencies were perceived as cooperative, interest in implementing more sophisticated manpower planning increased; when the relationship was strained or control over agency personnel matters was a matter of dispute, interest remained low.

Although these responses appear to present severe constraints on the practicality and utility of manpower planning in criminal justice, the MSU report notes several other developments likely to lead to increased use of analytical techniques in the years ahead. One of these developments, the responses indicated, is that there is increasing pressure from local and state budget and personnel offices and from jurisdiction chief executives to support budget requests and personnel actions with more analytical and empirical information. In part, this reflects an increase in managerial and administrative expertise among the city managers and the county executives who now enter government service.

Another set of factors involves union activities, court suits, EEOC/Affirmative Action procedures and requirements, and increasing sophistication in the budget process itself, all of which have put pressure on agencies to supplement intuition and guesswork in their personnel requests and personnel practices with empirically-oriented analyses of needs, policies, and procedures. A third development reported by respondents involves recent trends displacing decision-making power about personnel to forces outside the agency (courts, civil service, regulatory agencies). This apparently has speeded up recognition by agency planners and managers that many factors affect the ability of the agency to secure and to allocate manpower and has led to a growing appreciation of the need to become more sophisticated in the treatment and analysis of these factors.

In sum, criminal-justice manpower planning may be characterized as developing but certainly not fully developed. What also seems clear from the general findings of the MSU study is that the meanings, purposes, and elements of manpower planning as applied to criminal justice agencies will continue slowly to evolve.

The Availability of Manpower-Planning-Related Data

The MSU Manpower Planning study also focused on the availability of manpower-planning data and the use of various planning-related analytical techniques in the criminal justice system.

Two hundred and fifty of the nation's largest police departments were surveyed to determine whether or not they collected thirteen basic types of information.[39] The response rate was 66 per cent. All fifty state departments of corrections were similarly surveyed, and their response rate was 76 per cent.[40] Respondents were asked to indicate whether or not they had such information, whether they collected it regularly or occasionally, whether they received it from another agency. Respondents were also asked to rate the importance of each type of information for management and planning efforts. A brief summary of general findings from each of the police and corrections surveys is presented in Table 14-1. (Note that only the 250 largest police departments were surveyed: although these represent only about 1.5 per cent of the law-enforcement agencies in the country, they account for about half of police employment nationwide.)

Police Respondents. The responses indicate that almost 90 percent of the police departments surveyed regularly collect workload and employee-training data, and that a very large majority also regularly collect evaluations of employee performance, and information on personnel-turnover rates, and about the education of employees. In addition, over half the agencies at least occasionally collect data on employee assignment preferences, changing requirements of agency jobs, characteristics of applicants, job satisfaction, and social and economic trends. Another kind of information (characteristics of the area labor market) is available to a majority of the respondents' departments, often from another agency. Only two of the varieties of manpower-planning information listed were not available at least to a majority of the police agencies: rewards offered by competing employers, and career orientations of the labor market.

As for the perceived importance of the information for their agencies, respondents rated workload data as most valuable, followed by data on employee training, employee performance, and turnover rate. These were also, as would be expected, the kinds of information most agencies reportedly collected regularly. At the other end of the scale, the kinds of information rated as least important were also those collected least often: characteristics of the area labor market, rewards offered by competing employers, and career orientations of the labor market. The one type of information for which present practice and rated importance differ substantially was about the job satisfaction of employees: although 40 per cent of the police agencies do not collect or receive information about job satisfaction, and only 13.5 per cent regularly collect it, the respondents rate such data as fairly important (see Table 14-1).

Corrections Respondents. The figures in Table 14-1 reveal a pattern of responses recorded for police respondents roughly similar to that of corrections respondents. One finding not made clear in the table is that corrections respondents generally reported less ***regular*** collection of these data than did police departments; a greater percentage of corrections agency respondents indicated proportionately greater incidence of "occasional" data collection in all categories.

In general, the kinds of manpower information reported by police and corrections respondents as being most frequently and regularly collected are those oriented toward

Table 14-1. Police and Corrections Agency Responses on Types of Information Collected and Importance of the Information

TYPE OF INFORMATION	POLICE RESPONDENTS (N=164)		CORRECTIONS RESPONDENTS (N=38)	
	Percentages responding that the information is either collected by the agency or has been secured from another agency	$\bar{X}$ importance rating assigned by respondents on a scale of 0 = no importance to 5 = strong importance	Percentages responding that the information is either collected by the agency or has been secured from another agency	$\bar{X}$ importance rating assigned by respondents on a scale of 0 = no importance to 5 = strong importance
Work loads performed by the agency	99%	4.6	94%	4.2
Personnel-turnover rate	97%	3.8	97%	4.2
Training undergone by employees	99%	4.0	100%	4.2
Employee educational attainment	95%	3.2	84%	3.2
Employee assignment preferences	90%	3.1	57%	2.9
Employee performance evaluations	95%	4.0	100%	4.3
Employee job satisfaction	59%	3.0	64%	3.5
Characteristics of applicants	76%	3.1	57%	3.2
Characteristics of area labor market	60%	1.9	62%	2.5
Career orientations of labor market	38%	1.5	32%	1.9
Rewards offered by competing employers	50%	1.9	53%	2.1
Changing requirements of agency jobs	78%	3.0	84%	3.4
Social and economic trends that may affect the agency (e.g., population trends, racial composition, economic status, etc.)	84%	2.9	84%	2.7

internal management of the agency and resource allocation (workloads, training, performance evaluations). The kinds of information least often collected or received by police and corrections agencies are those focused on the labor market (career orientations, rewards offered by competing employees, and labor-market characteristics).

Respondents were not asked to make qualitative evaluations about the data they did collect and keep. Thus, for example, although the vast majority of agencies reported collecting turnover data, there was probably great variation in the quality and utility of these data from agency to agency. The findings shown in Table 14-1 suggest that the indicated percentages of respondents collected the various data in some form, but probably smaller than indicated proportions did so in any detailed and sophisticated way.

Manpower-Planning Analytical Undertakings

The MSU study also examined planning-related undertakings within the police and corrections agencies surveyed. A list of ten different kinds of activities were presented to respondents, and they were asked to report whether the activity was undertaken, and if undertaken, whether it was undertaken by the agency itself or by an outside contractor or by another government unit (such as a state personnel department or a department of civil service). The results are summarized in Table 14-2.

Police Respondents. The responses indicate that a majority of the police departments undertook four kinds of projects themselves: performance evaluation, training-needs assessment, manpower inventory, and personnel-information systems. In addition, when activities undertaken on behalf of the police agencies by contractors or by other government units are counted, the responses indicate that the majority also undertook job analysis, selection validation, and job redesign. Less than half of the agencies indicated that they had undertaken, or had had undertaken for them, labor-market analysis, career-path analysis, or manpower simulation. The vast majority of the respondents who reported that the tasks had not been undertaken by, or for, their agencies also reported that the results of

Table 14-2. Police and Corrections Agency Responses on Types of Manpower-Planning-Related Activities Undertaken

	POLICE RESPONDENTS (N=164)		CORRECTIONS RESPONDENTS (N=38)	
	Percentage responding activity is done by the agency	Percentage responding activity is done for the agency by a contractor or by another governmental unit	Percentage responding activity is done by the agency	Percentage responding activity is done for the agency by a contractor or by another governmental unit
Job analysis	42%	12%	43%	8%
Selection validation	23%	13%	14%	11%
Manpower inventory	81%	1%	51%	5%
Performance evaluation	88%	*	86%	6%
Personnel information system	69%	*	39%	11%
Labor market analysis	7%	*	3%	3%
Career path analysis	21%	4%	14%	6%
Manpower simulation (e.g., personnel processing and career path models)	12%	*	11%	3%
Job redesign	33%	2.5%	42%	6%
Training needs assessment	83%	*	71%	20%

* Less than 1%

such pursuits would be useful if available. In particular, the responses clearly indicate that, in the opinion of the respondents, police departments would benefit from career-path analysis and manpower simulation. A third of the respondents also indicated that labor-market analysis, though not undertaken, would be useful, but 20 per cent reported that such analysis was not likely to be useful.

Most frequently undertaken for police agencies by contractors or by other government units were selection validation, labor-market analysis, and job analysis. Selection validation and job analysis were primarily undertaken by jurisdictional civil service or jurisdiction personnel units or contractors; labor-market analysis was usually undertaken by a government labor department, a manpower-administration agency, or an economic-development agency. To a lesser extent, police agencies were also helped with personnal-information systems and job redesign, usually by a jurisdictional civil service personnel unit.

Corrections Respondents. Roughly similar response patterns emerge from police and correctional agency respondents (see Table 14-2). One noteworthy difference, however, is in the relative frequency with which outside contractors and other governmental agencies are used to undertake these tasks. Police respondents report a slightly higher use of outsiders in conducting job analyses. Corrections-agency respondents report higher use of outsiders in all but one of the remaining categories (selection validation). In part, this is owing to the fact that correctional respondents were from state departments of corrections and had more professional services available to them from their state personnel departments than did police respondents, most of whom were from city and county police departments.

Both police and correctional respondents indicate that, as was true of the collection of manpower-planning information, the most frequent undertakings by police agencies were those closely related to internal management (performance evaluation, training-needs assessment, manpower inventory). The least frequent undertakings were externally focused (labor-market analysis), or else required special technical capabilities (manpower simulation, career-path analysis, job redesign).

An important qualifier to these findings is that the categories of undertakings used in the surveys were not described in any detail in the survey instrument. As a result, survey respondents had only the category labels for direction, and the meanings of these may not have been uniformly interpreted. For example, *job analysis* has numerous specific and alternative techniques associated with it. Respondents may have answered according to their agency's experience with one or more of these, or respondents may have answered on the basis of only a general understanding of work-analysis techniques.

SUMMARY

This chapter surveyed some of the more central and important aspects of manpower planning, with specific attention to criminal justice organizational manpower planning. It should be evident that manpower planning is concerned with issues and processes that parallel those of general planning. The focus of manpower planning, as a subset of general planning, is, however, on the human element within the organization. Criminal justice is a labor-intensive field, and although over 80 per cent of the system's monies are spent for human resources, criminal justice manpower planning is probably only now beginning to emerge with any clarity or consistency. Nonetheless, pressures are building for agencies to become more sophisticated and analytical in managing their human resources. Continued development of the criminal justice agency's ability to conduct manpower planning therefore seems to be required.

The use of job-analysis techniques and the use of supply-forecasting and demand-forecasting methods are central to organizational manpower-planning efforts. It is clear that there are several ways of approaching job analysis and forecasting. It is also clear that any summary discussion of these techniques, as was undertaken in this chapter, masks some of the complexity involved in manpower planning. Agencies vary in their need for, and their ability to conduct, manpower-planning analysis. The choice among alternative ways of approaching job analysis, forecasting, and the like depend on the agency's situation and environment.

· *Chapter 14* ·
NOTES

1. Angela M. Bowey, *A Guide to Manpower Planning* (London: Macmillan & Company, Ltd., 1974), taken from the foreword by Tom Lupton, p. ix.

2. See John Bramham, *Practical Manpower Planning* (London: Institute of Personnel Management, 1978); David J. Bell, "Manpower in Corporate Planning," *Long-Range Planning*, 9 (April 1976), 31-37; Norbert F. Elbert and William J. Kehoe, "How to Bridge Fact and Theory in Manpower Planning," *Personnel* (November-December 1976), 31-39; and Keith Ray, "Managerial Manpower Planning: A Systematic Approach," *Long-Range Planning*, 10 (April 1977), 21-30.

3. D. J. Bartholomew, ed., *Manpower Planning* (Middlesex, England: Penquin Books, 1976), pp. 7-10.

4. See, for example, Bureau of Labor Statistics, *Occupational Outlook Handbook* (Washington, D.C.: U.S. Department of Labor, U.S. Government Printing Office). A revised edition of the handbook is published every two years.

5. *Planning Your Staffing Needs: A Handbook for Personnel Workers* (Washington, D.C.: U.S. Civil Service Commission, Bureau of Policies and Standards, 1977).

6. *The National Manpower Survey of the Criminal Justice System*, Volume One, *Summary Report* (Washington, D.C.: National Institute of Law Enforcement and Criminal Justice, Law Enforcement Assistance Administration, U.S. Government Printing Office, 1978), Chap. 4.

7. *Planning Your Staffing Needs*, op. cit., p. 4.

8. *Planning Your Staffing Needs*, op. cit., p. 6.

9. Thomas H. Patten, Jr., *Manpower Planning and the Development of Human Resources* (New York: Wiley-Interscience, 1971), p. 14.

10. Ibid., p. 14.

11. B. R. Morris, "An Appreciation of Manpower Planning," in Bartholomew, op. cit., p. 29.

12. A. R. Smith, "The Philosophy of Manpower Planning," in Bartholomew, op. cit., pp. 20-21.

13. Wayne F. Cascio, *Applied Psychology in Personnel Management* (Reston, Va.: Reston Publishing, 1978), p. 157.

14. Frank Sistrunk, et al., *Methods for Human Resources in the Criminal Justice System: A Feasibility Study* (Tampa, Fla.: Center for Evaluation Research, Human Resources Institute, University of South Florida, 1980).

15. Smith, op. cit., p. 22.

16. John K. Hudzik, et al., *Criminal Justice Manpower Planning: An Overview* (Washington, D.C.: U.S. Law Enforcement Assistance Administration, Government Printing Office, 1981), p. 9.

17. Howell S. Baum, "Analysts and Planners Must Think Organizationally," *Policy Analysis* (Fall 1980), 479-94.

18. See, for example, William F. Glueck, *Personnel: A Diagnostic Approach* (Dallas, Tex.: Business Publications, Inc., 1978).

19. U.S. Employment Service, Occupational Analysis and Industrial Services Division, *Training and Reference Manual for Job Analysis* (Washington, D.C..: U.S. Government Printing Office, June 1944), p. 1.

20. Sistrunk, Vol. I, op. cit.

21. R. I. Henderson, *Job Descriptions: Critical Documents, Versatile Tools* (New York: AMACOM, 1975), and Frank Sistrunk, et al., *Critiques of Job Analysis Methods* (Tampa, Fla.: Center for Evaluation Research, Human Resources Institute, University of South Florida, 1980), Vol. 2, p. 10.

22. Sistrunk, Vol. 2, op. cit., p. 11.

23. Ibid., p. 12.

24. National Criminal Justice Reference Service, *Police Job-Task Analysis: An Overview* (Washington, D.C.: Office of Criminal Education and Training, National Institute of Law Enforcement and Criminal Justice, Law Enforcement Assistance Administration, U.S. Department of Justice, November 1978).

25. Law Enforcement Assistance Administration, *Proceedings of the National Symposium of Job-Task Analysis in Criminal Justice* (Washington, D.C.: U.S. Department of Justice, 1978).

26. Charles P. Smith, et al., *Role Performance and the Criminal Justice System*, Vol. I, *Summary*, Vol. 2, *Detailed Performance Objectives*, Vol. 3, *Expectations of Operational Personnel* (Cincinnati: Anderson Publishing Company, 1976).

27. Project STAR National Advisory Council, *The Impact of Social Trends on Crime and Criminal Justice* (Cincinnati: Anderson Publishing Company, 1976).

28. Cascio, op. cit., p. 164.

29. W. S. Wikstrom, in Cascio, op. cit., pp. 171-173.

30. J. Scott Armstrong, *Long Range Forecasting: From Crystal Ball to Computer* (New York: John Wiley & Sons, Inc., 1978), p. 75.

31. Glueck, op. cit., Chap. 4.

32. *The National Manpower Survey of the Criminal Justice System*, Vol. 6: *Criminal Justice Manpower Planning* (Washington, D.C.: National Institute of Law Enforcement and Criminal Justice, Law Enforcement Assistance Administration, U.S. Government Printing Office, 1978).

33. Alfred Blumstein, "A Model to Aid in Planning for the Total Criminal Justice System," in Leonard Oberlander, ed., *Quantitative Tools for Criminal Justice Planning* (Washington, D.C.: U.S. Department of Justice, Law Enforcement Assistance Administration, 1975), pp. 129–45, esp. pp. 141–44.

34. *The National Manpower Survey of the Criminal Justice System*, Vol. 6:, *Manpower Planning* (Washington, D.C.: National Institute of Law Enforcement and Criminal Justice, Law Enforcement Assistance Administration, U.S. Government Printing Office, 1976).

35. Department of Employment and Productivity, *Manpower Forecasting*, 1968, p. 14.

36. Hudzik, et al., op. cit.

37. John K. Hudzik, et al., *Summary Information from the Manpower Planning Project Interviews* (East Lansing, Mich.: School of Criminal Justice, Michigan State University, 1980). Confidential report.

38. Ibid.

39. Gary W. Cordner, *Survey of Law Enforcement Agencies* (East Lansing, Mich.: Manpower Planning Development Project, School of Criminal Justice, Michigan State University, 1980).

40. Tim Bynum, *Survey of Correctional Agencies* (East Lansing, Mich.: Manpower Planning Development Project, School of Criminal Justice, Michigan State University, 1980).

•Chapter 15•

STRATEGIC POLICY PLANNING

The concept of strategic planning has been touched on at several points in this book. In Chapters 1 and 2, strategic planning was associated with efforts to discover basic missions and with long-range planning. Chapter 8 linked strategic planning to the setting of basic agency purposes, and tactical planning to the setting of short-range objectives. In Chapters 1 and 13, the term *suboptimization* was discussed, and a distinction drawn between outputs and outcomes; outcome planning was viewed as strategically oriented; output planning, as tactically oriented.

The purpose of this chapter is to pull together these and other viewpoints to address strategic policy-planning concerns in criminal justice. It will delve into the conceptual aspects of strategic planning, focusing on the central role of strategic planning in making and implementing policy. It will also consider an example of strategic-planning applications in a criminal justice organization, and some of the basic impediments to strategic planning at the system level of criminal justice.

Strategic planning can be viewed as the keystone to effective planning at both the agency and the system levels. Without strategic planning, the planning effort risks being directionless, suboptimizing, noncomprehensive, and uncoordinated. These negative consequences may serve as powerful inducements for planners to consider strategic issues carefully; yet strategic planning is difficult. Difficult or not, evasion of strategic-level questions and policy issues seriously threatens the utility of the overall planning effort.

STRATEGIC PLANNING, POLICY-MAKING, AND POLICY IMPLEMENTATION

Strategic planning and policy are intimately related. Policies are the means by which organizations guide the actions and decisions of people within the agency. Policies are anticipatory because they seek to guide future action and decisions. For example, an organizational policy governing the recruitment and selection of new employees is meant to guide the future efforts of the agency to attract and to select the best people for work within the agency. Policies may be generally and strategically oriented or they may be operationally and tactically oriented. Thus, recruitment and selection policies may be said to guide these processes generally, perhaps specifying the kind of employee generally sought by the agency (e.g., college graduates) and also specifying the general strategies that will be used to attract and to select new employees (e.g., national advertisement). At a lower level there can be much more specific and operational oriented policies governing how recruitment and selection will be carried out step by step (e.g., advertisement in college newspapers followed by on-site visits of recruiting teams). Thus, there can be strategic policies designed as guides to action and behavior for the strategic portions of plans, and there may be tactical policies designed as guides for the tactical portions of plans.[1] Strategic policies provide guidance for the formation of tactical policies;

tactical policies help to implement strategic policies and to make them concrete.

Planning ought to be oriented to action; unless some action is recommended and implemented through planning, the planning process may come to be little more than empty intellectualizing. Policies are the principal link between the ideas expressed in plans and the actions undertaken by the organization. A good plan either implicitly or explicitly specifies the policies that will govern future actions and behavior. The essential relationship between policies and plans in manpower planning was indicated in Chapter 14 (Figure 14-1); its principles apply to planning in general.

Chapters 1 and 2 discussed the planner's widening choices and the decision-maker's narrowing choices. What is really meant is that planners present alternative policies to decision-makers while decision-makers select which of these policies are to be implemented. The important strategic decisions of management, therefore, involve selection from among alternative guides for action and behavior.

Approaches to Strategic Planning

George Steiner draws a distinction between intuitive-anticipatory and formal approaches to strategic planning.[2] Intuition has been the mainstay of most organizational strategic-planning efforts and, until recently, was the only means by which organizations could anticipate long-range developments and design strategic policies to meet the future. Characteristically, the intuitive approach to strategic planning is supported and guided by one principal organizational actor, often the agency head. Alfred Sloan, commenting on Will Durant's efforts to forge General Motors into one of the most massive organizations in history[3] notes that Durant's vision was guided by flashes of inspiration rather than by the formal process of gathering and analyzing data and using formal forecasting techniques. The historian Sidney Hook, commenting on "heroes in history," notes that the major agents of change in geopolitical history have been those who were at the right place at the right time and who also were inspired with an intuitive vision of the future.[4] Abraham Kaplan notes the importance of intuition to any form of inquiry and suggests that sometimes there is no substitute for it in reaching understanding.[5]

The major alternative to intuition, formal and institutionalized strategic planning within the organization, has developed over the past few decades. Characteristically, a formal approach to strategic planning carries several consequences—among them, the fact that the intuitive insights of one individual will no longer be relied on to forecast future events or to manipulate that future. Strategic planning may well come to involve several top managers in an on-going fashion (perhaps through the formation of a long-range planning committee, as discussed in Chapter 7). The collection and analysis of data become routinized and directed toward securing the kinds of information that will permit the forecasting of trends and their manipulation; the environment of the agency is regularly monitored for clues about changes in major demands and supports; analysis is routinely undertaken to determine the kinds of short-range, middle-range and long-range changes in agency structure and functioning that must be made to meet or to shape the future.

One of the most widely recognized innovators of formal strategic-planning approaches was Robert McNamara who, first at Ford Motor Company and later at the Defense Department, attempted to create a formal and on-going structure within these organizations to institutionalize the process of considering the future and developing strategic plans to confront it. For McNamara, strategic planning was synonymous with long-range planning, and *effective* strategic planning was an on-going formal process within the organization.

Unfortunately, distinctions drawn between intuitive and formal approaches to strategic planning convey the impression that the two are mutually exclusive. But as Steiner ably points out, the two approaches are often immeshed within organizations to the betterment of the strategic-planning effort.[6] Formal strategic-planning efforts tend to be empirically based, requiring concrete data and interpreting those data. The intuitive approach relies more heavily on feelings and insights. When data are insufficient and knowledge is incomplete, feelings and insights may help. Steiner summarizes the blending of the two approaches:

> In a fundamental sense, formal strategic planning is an effort to duplicate what goes on in the mind of a brilliant intuitive planner. But

formal planning cannot be really effective unless managers at all levels inject their judgments and intuition into the planning process. Nor, on the other hand, will formal planning be effective if top managers reject it in favor of their own intuition.[7]

Strategic Planning: What It Is and Is Not

The Literature of planning is filled with such terms as *comprehensive planning*, *systematic planning*, *long-range planning*, *total planning*, and *overall planning*. These terms tend to be roughly synonymous with *strategic planning*. Although strategic planning does often result in the development of a general plan (or blueprint) for the future, strategic planning is better understood as a process: a process by which basic organizational missions, goals, and objectives—the basic means for achieving them—receive constant scrutiny. It is the element of continuous updating that characterizes strategic planning.

Richard Vancil finds that strategy has three aspects: an understanding of the overall long-range purposes and objectives to be pursued by the agency; an understanding of the constraints that currently keep the organization from meeting its long-term objectives; a framework within which the agency's current short-range and middle-range policies and plans can be more comprehensively understood.[8] Vancil's points are well taken, but a fourth characteristic should be added: consideration of the need for change and innovation.

Strategic planning is a major force for innovation and change within organizations not only because it focuses on the future and on the changes the agency will confront, but also because it is concerned with the most fundamental aspects of organizational purpose and programmatic commitment. One of the principal roles of strategic planning is not only to focus on the fundamental aspects of organizational life, but also to consider the need for change in these fundamentals.[9] The prime missions and goals of agencies, the basic program mixes, and the overarching policies that guide the day-to-day activities of personnel in the agency are the focus of strategic planning. For Robert Anthony, strategic planning begins with a search for the "best *main* topics" that govern the fundamental conditions of organizational life.[10]

There are times when strategic-planning efforts run counter to more traditional managerial concerns over control. Managerial control, and its allied concept of operational control, focus on keeping the accepted procedures and work of the agency running smoothly. The objective of managerial and operational control is not change but rather efficient and effective operation within the status quo dictated by missions and programs as currently understood.[11] When strategic planners offer suggestions for fundamental change, the status quo is threatened and managerial and operational control confronts a "disordered" organizational climate.

Thus, one natural reason for reluctance to undertake strategic planning is that it may well disturb a situation that seems relatively comfortable and familiar. Even more threatening is the perception of strategic-planning efforts as focused on futuristic, pie-in-the-sky objectives and policies that carry impractical and unrealistic prescriptions for change. This potential of strategic planning for overreaching the need for, and possibility of, effective change has led several commentators to warn that strategic-planning efforts must balance creativity with practicality, finding the middle ground between reaching for the future and being realistic about constraints posed by the present.[12]

Most of the resistance to strategic planning results from fear that strategic planning may recommend dramatic changes that discard the status quo and by uncertainty about what the changes accomplish. For example, adopting a major change in correctional strategy, such as deinstitutionalization, challenges the more traditional modes of correctional programming, and there may be also great uncertainties about the effects of the change on institutional programming, budgets, and the safety and well-being of society as well. Securing an organizational commitment to change is never easy, but it can be made easier if the strategic-planning process does incorporate development of a consensus as one of its concerns.[13] When strategic analysis and decision-making encourage open dialogue at several organizational levels, and when strategic planning is perceived as a continuous process of adjusting plans in the light of new information, the process itself can seem less threatening.

Developing a consensus does not mean so compromising a strategic plan to accommodate everyone's interests that is loses its punch or direction. Rather, a relatively open strategic-planning process can help alleviate some of the fears occasioned by the rumors (often unfounded) that follow hints of major changes in organization strategy.

Strategic planning also involves developing a repertoire of potential responses to major contingencies that may confront the agency.[14] For example, one function of strategic planning is to consider major mission and programmatic priorities as these are contingent on budget appropriations. A contingency involving significant budget reductions may well involve strategic decisions about the missions and programs that are to receive favored treatment or any treatment at all. Preparing for such major kinds of contingencies is a function of strategic planning.

There are several things that strategic planning is not. As George Steiner summarizes it, strategic planning is not cutting-and-pasting existing plans into one big volume. Strategic planning does not necessarily result in the production of massive and highly detailed plans of action, policies, and operational procedures.[15] Strategic planning normally does not concern itself with day-to-day operational concerns such as seasonally altering police-beat configurations, or maintaining the daily schedule for inmates. Indeed, such details of organizational functioning become relevant to strategic-planning efforts only when an overall assessment of the agency's missions and programs is underway (e.g., reconsideration of the kinds of police services delivered; or of the basic modes by which they are delivered; reconsideration of the basic mission of a correctional facility).

Peter Drucker suggests what strategic planning is not. "It is not forecasting . . . [it] does not deal with future decisions . . . and [it] is not an attempt to eliminate risk."[16] For Drucker, forecasting is so imprecise a science that we often do not even know how to set probabilities about what the future will look like. Strategic planning is therefore of less value in predicting the future than in attempting to shape the future.

Strategic planning is not a passive acceptance of probable futures; it is an active future-shaping endeavor. In the private sector, an example of active strategic planning is a new product-marketing strategy that attempts to create a demand that would not otherwise be there. In the public sector, efforts by an organization to innovate, to adopt new missions and programs when there is no public or political pressure to do so, represent efforts strategically to shape the future of services rendered by public agencies. Presumably, such efforts represent agency decision-makers' expert judgments about what is needed rather than simply what is demanded. Creating the supports for major and needed changes is the major contribution of entrepreneurial management.

Strategic planning is a matter of formulating present decisions that will move an agency into the future. It does not put decisions off until tomorrow but seeks to make today those decisions that are required to achieve a desired future.

Finally, as Drucker notes, "It is futile to try to eliminate risk, and questionable to try to minimize it. . . ."[17] Strategic planning does not eliminate risk because it is inherently a risk-taking activity.

Strategic planning is related to issues of efficiency and effectiveness and to outputs and outcomes. Efficiency is relationship of unit costs to the performance of work, and the achievement of objectives; effectiveness is the degree to which objectives are achieved; output is measured in terms of the amount of work performed; outcome is measured in terms of the achievement of basic objectives. Strategic planning is more centrally concerned with effectiveness and outcomes than with efficiency and output. For example, strategic planning of juvenile-delinquency programs focuses on such matters as the effects of various program options on, say, juvenile recidivism. Increasing the efficiency of a particular program option or determining how to increase the amount of work performed is less a concern of strategic planning and more a concern of tactical or operational planning. Thus, in examining basic objectives and missions, the role of strategic planning is directed toward outcomes; tactical planning may seek to manipulate matters so as to maximize efficiency and output.

Strategic and Other Forms of Organizational Planning

Strategic planning provides the foundation on which tactical and operational planning proceeds. It offers guidance to these lower-level, more concretely focused planning efforts by

Figure 15-1. Strategic and Other Forms of Organizational Planning (Adapted from George A. Steiner, *Strategic Planning* [New York: The Free Press, a Division of Macmillan Publishing Co., Inc., © 1979]).

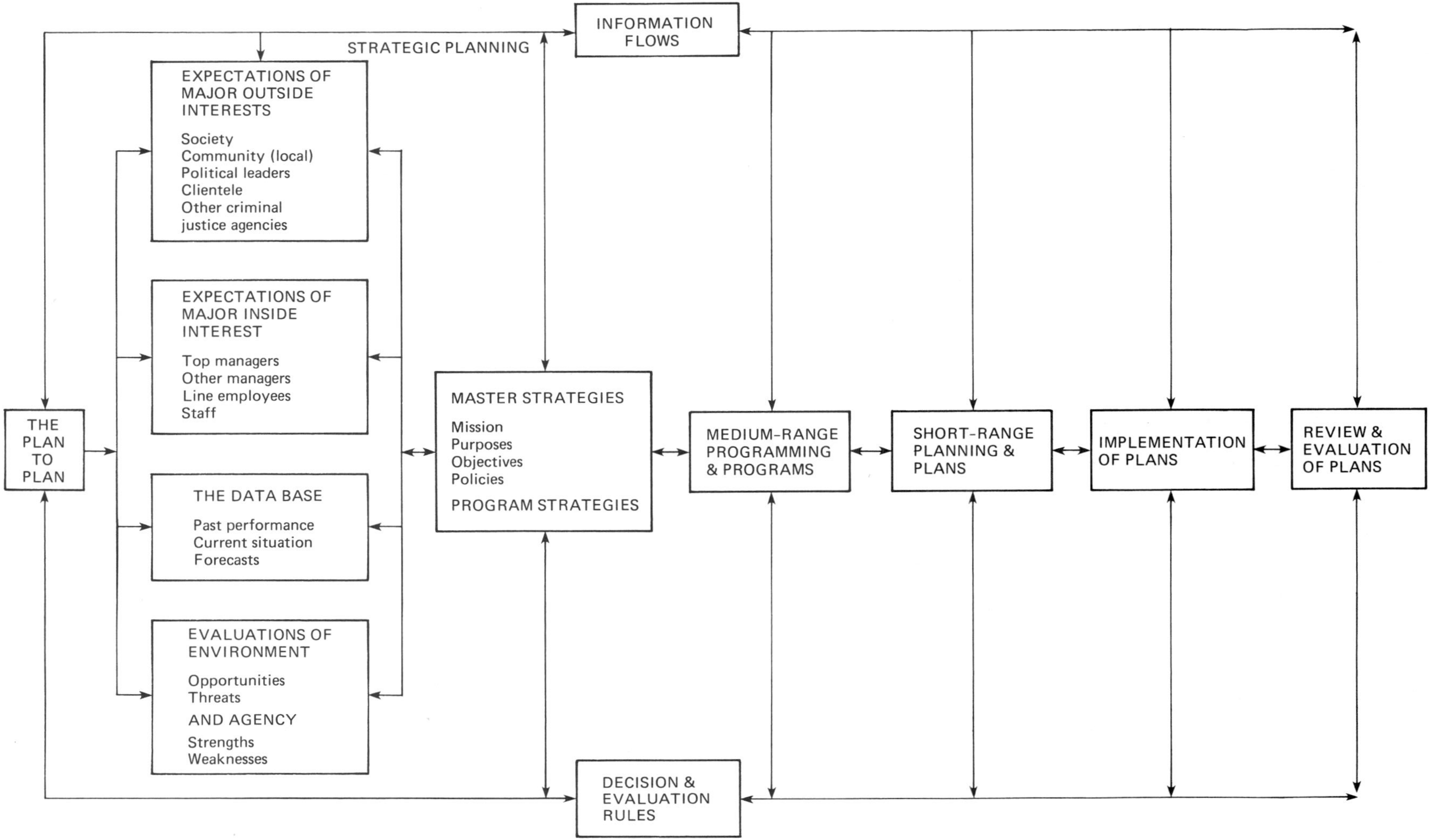

providing an understanding of the basic long-range objectives and program options to be pursued by the agency. Strategic planning provides the comprehensive overview of agency purpose by answering fundamental questions about organizational life: What are the agency's basic missions and objectives, and are changes required in them? What are the major program options to be followed by the agency, and how are these related to long-range objectives? What are the major alternative expectations for the future, and what are the contingencies for dealing with these alternatives?

The interaction of strategic planning with other forms of planning is complex. George Steiner has attempted to display some of these interactions for companywide planning in the private sector;[18] Figure 15-1 is an adaptation of Steiner's basic scheme to the public sector.

STRATEGIC PLANNING IN A CRIMINAL JUSTICE ORGANIZATION

Police organizations provide a good illustration of the kinds of problems that can result from failure to undertake strategic planning, and of the benefits that can be reaped when an organization does plan strategically. The discussion that follows could just as easily apply to the courts, to corrections, or to any other type of criminal justice agency.

The Traditional Approach

Police agencies, and all organizations, are faced with decisions about how to use their resources. They make these decisions with or without planning. One of the most significant choices made in police departments pertains to use of patrol resources. Police agencies typically devote 70-100 per cent of their personnel and total resources to the patrol function; the agency is responsible for responding to citizen calls for service and for patrolling when not handling calls.

One of the basic decisions that police departments face with respect to the use of patrol officers has to do with temporal allocation. The police agency is expected to answer calls and to patrol twenty-four hours a day, seven days a week. No single individual actually works all those hours, so the police department has to decide how many people should be working at different times. At least one half of all police agencies in the United States solve this problem by equal-shift staffing, which results in having the same number of patrol officers working at all times.[19] This solution reflects, of course, a lack of planning. These police agencies have not determined that equal-shift staffing is the most efficient or effective way to use resources, but have instead abdicated their responsibilities and fallen back to the most conventional and convenient practice available.

A more analytical, professional approach to the use of patrol resources is employed by many police departments, especially the larger ones. These agencies invest time and energy in analyzing the problem before deciding how to allocate their resources. The actual distribution of patrol workload is determined, and it is commonly discovered that there is substantial variation in the volume of calls for service at different times of the day and on different days of the week. The allocation of patrol resources is then matched to the workload, so that what is termed *proportional coverage* is achieved. In addition to just being more logical, this approach offers some specific benefits. For example, it is less likely that during busy times the workload will exceed the resources available, because during typically busy periods more personnel will be working. Consequently, there will be fewer occasions when a call cannot be answered because all units are tied up, and overall the police response time will be optimized (i.e., kept as short as possible). Also, the workload of officers on different shifts is equalized, thus reducing the boredom of some and the overtaxing of others. This practice also then equalizes patrol time on all shifts, instead of some shifts overabundant in patrol time while other shifts have little or none.

This analytical approach to the utilization of patrol resources, although clearly an improvement over the equal-shift staffing approach, does *not* amount to strategic planning. It is focused on outputs and efficiency (reducing response time, more equitable distribution of workload) rather than on outcomes and effectiveness. It avoids or ignores any serious consideration of basic goals and missions, directing attention instead at efficient resource utilization. It also fails to incorporate any forecasting or any serious attempt to generate and test alternatives. It is really an example of limited tactical or operational planning rather than of strategic planning.

A Strategic Approach

The best way to begin strategic planning is to go back to basics. What are the goals of police patrol? Because patrol is such a major component of the police mission, its goals are presumably very much like those of the entire organization. In the broadest sense, the police are expected to contribute to the attainment of the criminal justice goals: crime control, public tranquillity, justice, due process, efficiency, and accountability. The police are probably particularly expected to provide crime control and public tranquillity, and to use the other four goals as guidelines.[20] An elaboration of police goals, consistent with this view, has been offered by Herman Goldstein:

1. To prevent and control conduct widely recognized as threatening to life and property (serious crime).
2. To aid individuals who are in danger of physical harm, such as the victim of a criminal attack.
3. To protect constitutional guarantees, such as the right of free speech and assembly.
4. To facilitate the movement of people and vehicles.
5. To assist those who cannot care for themselves: the intoxicated, the addicted, the mentally ill, the physically disabled, the old, and the young.
6. To resolve conflict, whether it be between individuals, groups of individuals, or individuals and their government.
7. To identify problems that have the potential for becoming more serious problems for the individual citizen, for the police, or for government.
8. To create and maintain a feeling of security in the community.[21]

All these goals are applicable to the patrol function. In certain agencies some of the goals might be specifically the province of another specialized unit (a traffic division, for example, facilitates the movement of people and vehicles) but patrol is an all-purpose function that encompasses all the goals. In practice, however, resource demands and possibilities inevitably conflict, so that it will be helpful to know which of the goals take precedence.

This is the point at which the planner could be best served by public and political input to the planning process. The eight goals are general enough to apply to any community, but the problem of which ones to emphasize over others might vary from place to place, or from time to time. Through the kinds of methods discussed at the end of Chapter 8, the planner should seek citizen guidance about priorities. Assume that such guidance has been obtained, and that two goals have been given priority over the others: preventing and controlling serious crime; aiding individuals in danger of physical harm. This does not mean that the other goals can be ignored, but only that, all other things being equal, patrol should give the greatest attention to serious crime and potential physical harm.

These are problem-oriented goals, and the planner would next want to learn something about the problems of serious crime and physical harm in the community. This would basically entail problem analysis of the sort that characterized the resource-utilization approach discussed in the preceding section. The difference is that now problem analysis is undertaken within the context of the strategic-planning process, and is guided by some explicit goals that help to provide direction to the kinds of information to collect and analyze. For example, the goal of controlling and preventing serious crime would naturally lead to an examination of the extent of such crime, the different types of serious crime, the times and locations of such crimes, and the characteristics of their perpetrators. Instead of focusing only on when these crimes are reported to the police (when the calls for assistance come in), the planner would be led to inquire about when they are *committed*, because the goal is to control and prevent crimes, *not* to just equalize workload or minimize police response time.

Before attention is turned to alternative ways of pursuing the goals of the patrol function, some thought must be given to the future. Are there any reasons to believe that the characteristics of the problems will change? Given the recent cutbacks in Federal funding for various kinds of social services, will not the police be called upon more and more to assist those who cannot care for themselves? On the other hand, if petroleum prices and scarcity lead to fewer miles driven each year by the public, less police attention to facilitating the movement of people and vehicles may be justified. The increased use of mass transit might result in different kinds of police problems, though.

These are general considerations related to the future. Any particular community and its police department might want to take notice of more specific local changes. Is the size of the community growing or shrinking? Is the age composition of its population changing? Are new highways, schools, shopping malls, or industries planned? These and other kinds of local changes, as well as more general trends in society, might have important implications for the police and for the patrol function.

It would also be necessary to forecast the availability of resources for the police and the patrol function. Little would be served by the development of grandiose and expensive plans in a community with a shrinking tax base and scarce public resources to allocate. By contrast, growing communities may be expected to make more and more resources available to their police (as well as more and more problems, of course), and the planner would want to take this into account.

At this point, with goals in mind, the planner knows something about the problems and about the future. It is time to generate alternatives. First he or she would review current practices, as these represent one way of carrying out the patrol function. He or she might find that the current approach includes proportional coverage as the guide to allocation, with calls for service handled as they are received by patrol units assigned to beats. When not handling calls, the units patrol their beats, which primarily involves riding around the area in marked police cars.

The review might reveal that from time to time the police department has used saturation patrol in response to "crime waves," assigning several marked police units to small areas that were experiencing large numbers of street crimes, and has sometimes also fielded unmarked patrol units when regular and saturation patrol seemed unable to reduce the incidence of street crimes. As alternative approaches, then, the review has identified regular patrol, saturation patrol, and unmarked patrol.

Extending the search reveals that much of the thinking up to this point has been inadequate. Although goals were carefully identified, some unexamined assumptions constricted analysis of the problem and review of alternatives. One assumption was that all calls for service had to be handled right away, and that handling them required that a patrol unit be dispatched to the scene. Another assumption was that the more quickly the patrol unit got to the scene, the better. In general, traditional conceptions of patrol were guiding the planning, instead of the question, "What do we need to know in order to figure out how best to attain our goals?"

Search activity leads to these realizations because it reveals that some police departments have been doing some unusual things—and apparently not out of caprice but with considerable justification. For example, some agencies are not responding immediately to every call for service, because it has been found that many crimes have happened long before the police are called.[22] Some agencies are also experimenting with different ways of utilizing free patrol time, because it has been found that traditional, routine, random, preventive patrol has little effect on crime or on citizens' feelings of safety.[23] Other agencies are increasing the extent to which patrol officers investigate crimes, because it has been found that detective follow-up investigation is rarely productive, whereas the information collected by the patrol officer at the scene from witnesses and victims is an important factor in case solution.[24]

Again, it is best to go back to basics. The focus is identifying alternative ways of using patrol resources in order to attain certain goals, especially those of preventing and controlliing serious crime and aiding individuals in danger of physical harm.

Reviewing and searching could lead to the identification of quite a few alternative ways of using patrol resources. Some of these are complete alternatives, while others are really components that might be combined into alternatives, perhaps by using morphological forced connections (discussed in Chapter 10).

Allocation and Deployment
Equal-shift staffing
Proportional Coverage by time and day of call
Proportional coverage by time and day of occurrence

Locus of Call Handling
Over the telephone

Mail-out
Come to station house
At the scene
Call-Handling Alternatives
Conflict management
Arrest diversion
Summons in lieu of arrest
Referral to other agency
Modes and Tactics of Patrolling
Marked patrol v. unmarked patrol
One-officer v. two-officer units
Car patrol v. foot patrol v. stationary patrol
Random preventive patrol
Directed deterrent patrol
Directed apprehension patrol
Community-oriented patrol
Decoy operations
Surveillance
Follow-up investigations
Who Handles Calls
Communications personnel
Nonsworn personnel
Referral to other agency
Patrol unit
Immediacy of Call Handling
Immediately
Calls prioritized and stacked
Later by appointment
Later as possible
Multiple Feature Methods
Split-force patrol
Crime-control teams
Team policing

The effects of each alternative and component would have to be estimated, especially in their relation to the primary goals (preventing and controlling serious crime and aiding those in danger). The task would probably begin with a look at previous research on the effects of these alternatives. Quite a lot of research has been done on the effects of all kinds of police tactics and programs,[25] and some of it would be very helpful for evaluating these alternatives. The research has not provided a tremendous amount of certain knowledge, however, and most of it focuses on what does not seem to work.

Because there is not much certain knowledge on which to base either estimations or models, judgment would have to be exercised in narrowing down the set of alternatives. Then the most promising ones could be tested through limited implementation. It would be very important to carefully evaluate each implemented alternative, to learn its effects. Careful evaluation would be particularly necessary if the alternatives tested were combinations of several components, for the effects of each component should be sorted out, if possible.

Limited implemention (in one part of the jurisdiction) might be undertaken of the following alternatives: proportional coverage by time and day of occurrence; delayed response to nonemergency calls for service and to crimes not in progress; handling of as many calls as possible without dispatching a patrol unit (over the telephone, mail-out, and come-to-the-stationhouse reporting); and directed deterrent patrol. If control groups and randomization have been appropriately used, and if a decrease in reported serious crime in this area resulted, it might be valid to infer that the decrease was caused by the alternative implemented. Even if that inference were valid, the relative contribution of the several components of the alternative would not be clear, unless the evaluation had been quite sophisticated. But that information is important. Did crimes "decrease" because people got fed up with the delayed responses and refrained from reporting some crimes? Did crimes decrease because the greater availability of patrol units led to very rapid response to true emergencies and crimes in progress? Or did crimes decrease because of the directed deterrent patrol tactic, which was designed to prevent crimes by having marked units concentrate their patrolling in high-crime areas?

If several of the most promising patrol alternatives were implemented on a limited scale, and each carefully evaluated, it should be possible to determine which promises to be most effective in achieving the goal. But when the alternatives are being compared and one or more about to be chosen, it must be remembered that the two priority goals were not the only considerations. For example, a very aggressive patrolling strategy that involved stopping and frisking numerous people on the street might promise the greatest potential reduction in serious crime, but it would also endanger constitutional guarantees and detract from feelings of security in the community. Also, the various alternatives aimed at freeing patrol time for anticrime activities would strain police ability to resolve conflicts, to facilitate the movement of traffic, and to assist those who cannot care for themselves. This stage of the planning process, then, just prior to decision-making, might be another at which public input would be very helpful.

The Value of Planning

As the application of strategic planning to the police patrol function clearly shows, planning will not magically lead to obviously "best" solutions to problems. But it does seem to point in the right directions, and it encourages careful consideration of a much wider range of alternatives. The tendency in any organization is to look at problems narrowly and to restrict the range of ideas that are considered. Habitual responses may not be the best, but they are hard to shake off. Painstaking attention to the planning process, and to the goals, the future, and the alternatives, can greatly widen vision and counteract conventions.

Strategic-planning techniques, applied to the problem of allocation of police patrol resources, resulted in some innovative ideas that would probably increase the possibility of achieving the desired goals. They encouraged a focus on outcomes and effectiveness, rather than one on inputs, outputs, and efficiency. Actually, though, the situation is still more narrowly conceived than it might be. The focus should have been on how best to utilize *police* resources in order to attain the goals of the police. Analysis and planning may have resulted in retaining the traditional distinctions between patrol and detectives, but there was no reason why that convention had to be blindly accepted right from the start.[26] Clearly, it is crucial to focus on goals and their attainment, and to avoid taking for granted the ways in which things have always been done in the past.

SYSTEMWIDE STRATEGIC-POLICY PLANNING

Ideally, systemwide strategic planning provides overall system direction, promoting long-range coordination and minimizing dysfunction and duplication. The fragmented quality of the American justice-delivery system makes this ideal exceedingly difficult to achieve. Complex and disjointed authority structures have particularly negative consequences because strategic planning ultimately relies on someone or some group having sufficient authority, control, and influence to forge goal consensus and to bring the operations of numerous agencies into conformity with a strategic system policy.

Consider, for example, how problems of police-role definition are heightened when state police, sheriffs, and city police duplicate and compete with one another in providing services. As these three types of agencies usually are parts of different and independent political and budgetary jurisdictions, strategic-level decisions to minimize duplication normally requires voluntary cooperation. The problem is that minimization of duplication affects the basic missions of the agencies involved. Sheriffs may not be willing to relinquish law-enforcement activities within the city jurisdiction, and city police may not be willing to assign expressway patrol functions to the state police—even for reasons of efficiency and effectiveness. Such reluctance is often bred of the fear that surrendering missions and prime functions may lead to formal diminishment of the agency's legitimate missions (and, hence, of its budgets and manpower). Some put it more directly: "No $12,000-a-year planner is going to tell a big-city police chief what to do."[27]

Problems of Strategic Goal Dissensus

Some argue that many of the negative consequences of fragmentation can be mitigated through the creation of unified administrative structures in criminal justice (e.g., Skoler's concept of a state-level super-justice agency).[28] Yet, a formally centralized authority hardly guarantees cooperation, the elimination of dysfunction, or the coordinated pursuit of common goals and strategies. Even in the private corporation, where formal authority is firmly centralized in a chief executive officer and a board of directors, it is of overriding importance to secure the line managers' *acceptance* of the goals, policies, and programs that emanate from the strategic plan.[29] No strategic plan can be fully implemented unless some level of goal consensus has been first established throughout the organization. This principle applies to the individual corporation or agency, and to the criminal-justice system as a whole.

System-level strategic planning and decision-making often carry implications for fundamental change. Consider, for example, the strategic decision to adopt a career-criminal program. Although the prosecutorial function is most directly affected by such a decision, there is an assumption that coordinated emphasis will be put on the problem of habitual offenders throughout the system: special efforts at apprehension, prosecution, adjudication, and punishment or rehabilitation. Few people disagree with the premise that the vast majority of serious criminal activity comes from habitual offenders, and few may disagree with the idea that something "special" ought to be done about them. Agencies may differ, however, on what a career criminal is, and whether priorities should be set about certain types of criminal behavior and habitual offenders. These disagreements emanate not just from the lack of an overall administrative-control structure in the system; more important, they emanate from the different perspectives brought to bear on crime by the different people in the system. For example, the duty of judges is to adjudicate justly; the duty of police is to apprehend swiftly. The consequence is that the judge and the police officer approach the criminal event from different perspectives: police may perceive their efforts to apprehend the career criminal as hampered by judicial limitations on search and seizure, wiretapping, and other forms of electronic eavesdropping; judges may feel frustrated by the apparent indifference of the police to "working within the rules."

So, too, judges themselves are often distressed to find disparities among sentencing practices, and research has shown a substantial lack of consensus among judges about what are fitting sentences for particular types of offenses and offenders.[30] One solution to the problem of sentencing disparity is adoption of sentencing guidelines–which would represent a major change in the traditional view that sentencing is essentially a decision to be reached by the trial judge. And strict guidelines would challenge the traditional principle that the trial judge should be given flexibility within the law to impose the sentence that seems most appropriate to the case at hand.

Not even legislation of a new grand strategy would guarantee adherence to the new strategy. Mandatory "add-on" sentences for felonies committed with the possession of a firearm, for example, were part of a strategy designed to deter the use of firearms through stiffer penalties. The new laws are subverted in interesting ways: prosecutors use the law and its penalties as threats during plea-bargaining; judges may avoid the dictates of the law by decreasing the sentence on the "parent" felony to make room for the added sentence imposed by the firearms violation. Of course, not all–nor even a majority of–judges and prosecutors may act in such ways, but enough may to threaten the intent of the strategy involved.

Problems of Resource Allocation

Want of money has been a prime hindrance to the implementation of strategic system-level plans. Malcolm Feeley and Austin Sarat report a general feeling among LEAA and SPA administrators that there was never enough money available during the life of LEAA to permit comprehensive strategic innovation in the system. Indeed, many SPA administrators eschew the idea that they and their agencies could be responsible for coordinating the day-to-day activities of line agencies; rather, they see their role as using the limited resources made available to them to fund and to promote "only a few good ideas."[31]

It can of course be argued that the SPAs and LEAA were created only to generate and to test the strategic ideas that could reorient the delivery of criminal justice services, and that line agencies would necessarily have to carry out the operational dictates of these new strategic innovations. However, in the absence of sufficient new funds, a major strategic reorientation of the system and its agencies (to concentrate, for example, on the career criminal or to undertake a "crime-specific" campaign) would necessarily mean reassigning resources from more traditional agency activities. Securing the cooperation of disparate line agencies in reassigning scarce resources has always been a problem. Typically, agencies resisted adopting a strategic change when it meant that an established activity would have to be reduced or dropped in order to fund new activities suggested by the strategic innovation.

Strategic change is frequently viewed by organizations as "adding on" programs rather than as changing the configuration of existing programs. In part, this is because organizations are traditionally reluctant to tamper with the status quo. Yet, in the private sector, strategic decisions often result in the dropping of an established product line in favor of a new product line–sometimes even in the shifting of existing resources to a fundamentally different set of company outputs. Established programs in the public sector tend to be highly resistant to change and to major alteration. Evaluation efforts in almost all public agencies tend to be focused on new programs while old and established programs are evaluated far less frequently, if at all. When the effect of a system-level strategic plan is to propose alterations in the traditional ways in which many semi-independent agencies go about their business, coordinated innovation becomes even more difficult.

Subrosa Systemic Accommodations

Although coordinated innovation and change resulting from the conscious design and implementation of strategic plans do not characterize criminal justice policy and decision-making at the system level, one can find examples of subrosa and sometimes unconscious attempts among system components to adopt strategies of mutual adjustment. For example, police often adjust their law-enforcement and arrest procedures to actions by prosecutors and judges. If prosecutors and judges in a jurisdiction treat the possession of a small amount of marijuana as low-priority offense and take a lenient attitude toward it, police will tend to enforce possession statutes less rigorously. An overcrowded county jail and prison system will often lead judges to consider dispositions other than incarceration for certain kinds of offenses. Such an adjustment in sentencing proclivities may well be occasioned by the realities of jail and prison overcrowding and not by any fundamental change in the judge's attitude toward incarceration as a legitimate and useful sentence for these offenses.

What is important to understand about these subrosa mutual accommodations is that although they represent a form of coordination and cooperation among system components, it would be hard to argue that a conscious and formal effort at strategic planning and policy-making has preceded the mutual adjustment. Of course, the police may consciously plan to give marijuana possession a low priority for enforcement in the future, and the judge may consciously plan to alter his sentencing practices until the jails and prisons are less crowded. But neither action resulted from strategic-planning efforts: they represent changes in tactics rather than any conscious re-examination of basic strategic policies.

The first part of this chapter underscored the importance of strategic planning as the primary means by which organizations and systems direct and coordinate their programs and activities. Criminal justice strategic planning at the system level is underdeveloped and deserving of greater attention. It may sound useless to champion further development of system strategic planning, given the severe constraints on any form of system-level planning in criminal justice, but strategic planning at the systems level is the principal means by which system coordination can be attained.

The more useful structures for strategic-planning purposes coming out of the LEAA experience were the advisory bodies to state and regional criminal justice planning agencies. These advisory bodies were intended to be broadly representative of all significant criminal justice agencies within a jurisdiction, and more recently they generally have been. The frequent and regular meetings of representatives from such agencies to discuss overall system goals and crossagency policies is the principal means available by which to begin forging conscious strategic system policies. It is, of course, helpful if the advisory bodies have some authority to negotiate forms of coordination among system components, acting, for example, through the budget review process. But what has seemed most crucial and helpful in the recent past is the discussion that takes place within these advisory bodies: agency representatives exchange information about the goals, problems, policies, and programs pursued by the various agencies within the jurisdiction. Though the authority to enforce certain forms of coordination and accommodation is absent, some forms of coordination and cooperation have been forged out of the information-exchange process itself.

SUMMARY

This chapter has examined several features of strategic planning, and applied them to the individual criminal justice agency and to the system as a whole. Strategic planning focuses on the overall direction and purpose of organizations and systems. It focuses on basic goals and missions and on the achievement of effectiveness and outcomes. Strategic planning is action-oriented: its prime intent is to shape the future rather then merely to forecast or to predict it.

Strategic planning is inherently a risk-taking activity and one that often threatens the status quo of organizations and systems. This can make strategic planning threatening to those in management who are primarily concerned with managerial and operational control. Strategic planning tends, therefore, to be viewed with suspicion by those who prefer not to examine established assumptions and procedures. But strategic planning can be the major force for innovation and change within organizations–innovation and change that includes a conscious examination of traditional assumptions and practices. It is often painful to examine a long-standing practice or assumption and find it wanting and in need of revision. But basic assumptions must be constantly re-evaluated in light of prime goals and missions.

Strategic planning in organizations and systems can be a product of one person's intuition and insight, or the product of a formal, ongoing strategic-planning process. Or, strategic planning may be, and often profitably is, a product of both intuition and formally institutionalized procedures. Whether by intuition or through formal structures, however, reviews of basic organization and system features, and recommendations for fundamental change and innovation, are the principal products of strategic-planning efforts.

The criminal justice system, with its complex authority arrangements and multitude of actors and roles, makes system-level strategic planning a difficult chore. Nonetheless, the need to examine basic assumptions, the need for coordination and cooperation, and the need to minimize dysfunction confront the system even as they confront individual agencies. The regular meeting of agency heads or representatives to exchange information, to examine basic assumptions and policies, and to reach accommodations is a useful first step in promoting system-level strategic planning. Achieving strategic-level consensus in the criminal justice system is, and will continue to be, exceedingly difficult because of the conflicting goals among the various agencies of the system. Yet, strategic planning can give the system and its agencies overall guidance and direction and do much to further productive innovation and change in the delivery of justice services.

· *Chapter 15* ·
NOTES

1. See, for example, Dalton E. McFarland, *Management: Principles and Practices* (New York: Macmillan Publishing Co., Inc., 1970), Chap. 9.
2. George Steiner, *Strategic Planning* (New York: The Free Press, 1979), pp. 8–10.
3. Alfred E. Sloan, Jr., *Adventures of the White Collar Man* (New York: Doubleday & Company, Inc., 1941), p. 104.
4. Sidney Hook, *The Hero in History: A Study in Limitation and Possibility* (New York: John Day Co., Publishers, 1943).
5. Abraham Kaplan, *The Conduct of Inquiry* (San Francisco: Chandler Publishing Company, 1964), pp. 14–15.
6. Steiner, op. cit., p. 10.
7. Ibid.
8. Richard F. Vancil, "Strategy Formulation in Complex Organizations," in Peter Lorange and Richard F. Vancil, *Strategic Planning Systems* (Englewood Cliffs, N.J.: Prentice-Hall, Inc., 1977), p. 4. Originally appeared in *Sloan Management Review* (Winter 1976).
9. Robert N. Anthony, *Planning and Control Systems: A Framework for Analysis* (Boston: Graduate School of Business Administration, Harvard University, 1965), see Chap. 2.
10. Ibid., pp. 10–23.
11. Ibid., p. 67.
12. John K. Shank, et al., "Balancing 'Creativity' and 'Practicality' in Formal Planning," in Lorange and Vancil, op. cit., p. 159. Originally appeared in the *Harvard Business Review* (January–February 1973).

13. Xavier Gilbert and Peter Lorange, "Five Pillars for Your Planning" in Lorange and Vancil, op. cit., p. 38. Originally appeared in *European Business* (Autumn 1974).

14. Charles M. Mottley, "Strategic Planning," in Fremont J. Lyden and Ernest G. Miller, *Public Budgeting: Program Planning and Evaluation* (Chicago: Rand McNally & Company, 1978), pp. 125–42.

15. Steiner, op. cit., pp. 15-16.

16. Peter F. Drucker, "Long-Range Planning Means Risk-Taking," in David W. Ewing, *Long-Range Planning for Management* (New York: Harper & Row, Publishers, 1964), pp. 7-10. Originally appeared in *Management Science* (April 1959).

17. Ibid., p. 9.

18. Steiner, op. cit., p. 17.

19. William G. Gay, Theodore H. Schell, and Stephen Schack, *Improving Patrol Productivity*, Vol. 1: *Routine Patrol* (Washington, D.C.: U.S. Government Printing Office, 1977), pp. 23–25.

20. Herbert A. Simon, "On the Concept of Organizational Goal," *Administrative Science Quarterly*, 9 (1964), 1-22, discusses the manner in which goals commonly serve as constraints as well as targets.

21. Herman Goldstein, *Policing a Free Society* (Cambridge, Ma.: Ballinger, 1977), p. 35.

22. Tony Pate, et al., *Police Response Time: Its Determinants and Effects* (Washington, D.C.: 1976), and Kansas City Police Department, *Executive Summary: Response Time Analysis* (Washington, D.C.: U.S. Government Printing Office, 1978).

23. George L. Kelling, et al., *The Kansas City Preventive Patrol Experiment: A Summary Report* (Washington, D.C.: Police Foundation, 1974).

24. Peter W. Greenwood and Joan Petersilia, *The Criminal Investigation Process* (Santa Monica, Calif.: Rand Corporation, 1975).

25. For reviews of this research, see George L. Kelling, "Police Field Services and Crime: The Presumed Effects of a Capacity," *Crime & Delinquency* (April 1978), 173–84; Gary W. Cordner, "Police Patrol Research and Its Utilization," *Police Studies*, 2 (Winter 1980), 12–21; and David J. Farmer, "Thinking About Research: The Contribution of Social Science Research to Contemporary Policing," *Police Studies*, 3 (Winter 1981), 22–40.

26. For some guidance in planning for the utilization of police resources, see Donald Cawley and H. Jerome Miron, *Managing Patrol Operations: Manual* (Washington, D.C.: U.S. Government Printing Office, 1977); Donald F. Cawley, et al., *Managing Criminal Investigations: Manual* (Washington, D.C.: U.S. Government Printing Office, 1977); and Richard G. Grassie and Timothy D. Crowe, *Integrated Criminal Apprehension Program: Program Implementation Guide* (Washington, D.C.: Law Enforcement Assistance Administration, 1978).

27. Malcolm M. Feeley, and Austin D. Sarat, *The Policy Dilemma: Federal Crime Policy and the Law Enforcement Assistance Administration, 1968–1978* (Minneapolis: University of Minnesota Press, 1980), p. 75.

28. Daniel L. Skoler, *Organizing the Nonsystem* (Lexington, Ma.: Lexington Books, 1977), pp. 266–72.

29. Gilbert and Lorange, op. cit., pp. 43–44.

30. Marvin Zalman, et al., *Sentencing in Michigan: Report of the Michigan Felony Sentencing Project* (Lansing, Mich.: State Court Administrative Office, 1979), see Chap. 4.

31. Feeley and Sarat, op. cit., p. 72.

• INDEX •